A Documentary History of Yonkers, New York

Volume Two, Part One: The Unsettled Years

1853–1860

Joseph P. Madden

HERITAGE BOOKS
2015

HERITAGE BOOKS
AN IMPRINT OF HERITAGE BOOKS, INC.

Books, CDs, and more—Worldwide

For our listing of thousands of titles see our website at
www.HeritageBooks.com

Published 2015 by
HERITAGE BOOKS, INC.
Publishing Division
5810 Ruatan Street
Berwyn Heights, Md. 20740

Copyright © 1994 Joseph P. Madden

Heritage Books by the author:

*A Documentary History of Yonkers, New York,
Volume One: The Formative Years, 1820–1852*

*A Documentary History of Yonkers, New York,
Volume Two, Part One: The Unsettled Years, 1853–1860*

*A Documentary History of Yonkers, New York:
The Dutch, the English and an Incorporated American Village, 1609–1860*

All rights reserved. No part of this book may be reproduced or transmitted in any form or by any means, electronic or mechanical, including photocopying, recording or by any information storage and retrieval system without written permission from the author, except for the inclusion of brief quotations in a review.

International Standard Book Numbers
Paperbound: 978-1-55613-930-7
Clothbound: 978-0-7884-6107-1

Table of Contents

Introduction v

List of Associated Documents ix

Chapter One
      Demographics and Economics 1

Chapter Two
      Life in Yonkers 17

Chapter Three
      The Village Charter 41

Chapter Four
      Yonkers Politics 63

Chapter Five
      More Real Pillars of Yonkers and Some Others 77

Chapter Six
      Yonkers 1853 - 1860 262

1858 Map of Yonkers by Thomas C. Cornell 300

References 327

Index 329

Introduction

The period 1853 through 1860 was a spectacular period of growth in Yonkers history. The town, and especially the village, grew rapidly in population and industry. While New York City increased its population by 58% between 1850 and 1860, the population of Yonkers grew by 187%. (New York Times-8/5/1865 p.4, c.4) The principal cause for this rapid population growth was immigration that came mostly from Ireland. Large numbers of immigrants came from other European countries also, but by far the largest numbers came from Ireland. The Irish exodus began in the 1840s due to a potato famine, and the exodus continued throughout the 1850s. While starvation was a potential reality in Ireland, jobs and a better way of life were available in America. In Yonkers the 1850s also saw businessmen with discretionary money investing in the construction of large homes and buildings purposely designed to be used as stores with tenements above them. What developed was a vicious cycle of economic and population growth. As the wealthy built large homes and commercial property was developed, an available population of immigrants and investors came to Yonkers eager to work and make their fortunes. The industries which grew the most were the service industries, light manufacturing, and construction. However, throughout the 1850s farming in Yonkers continued to decline.

Meanwhile, the mercantile industry was one of the tertiary industries that grew at an enormous rate. The number of merchants and their growing wealth became a part of national history when this group was immortalized by the internationally famous Broadway play, *The Merchant of Yonkers*, or as most of us came to know it, *Hello Dolly*. This critical period in the history of Yonkers also saw the adoption of gas lighting for homes, and street lamps were being discussed. The Yonkers Gas Light Company was formed, and it produced gas from coal. It also dug up village streets to lay pipes, but it eventually led to an overall better night life. This was also a period of time when the railroad was giving serious competition to steamboats and sailing vessels. In comparison to the period 1820 to 1852, these short eight years produced a hundredfold more dramatic economic, social, and political changes.

The period also showed a dramatic increase in real estate values and personal wealth. However, a similar socio-economic distribution of that wealth existed in 1860 as it did in 1850. The period was one of continued economic growth except for the Panic of 1857. However, in Yonkers the Panic seemed only to moderate growth for a short period of time. The 1857 Panic did not bring the rapid growth to a halt. It is true though that many individuals were affected by the Panic. For instance, the hat industry in Yonkers was forced to close its factories for a short period of time causing temporary unemployment, there was a rapid turnover in speculative properties, and some individuals went bankrupt. However, the national depression of 1857, and probably the first international depression of consequence, only slowed growth in Yonkers, and as already noted the slowed growth rate was only for a short period of time.

The years 1853 through 1860 saw dramatic changes in local government and government services. In 1855 the village of Yonkers was incorporated. In doing so a local fire department, police department, and a public health department were created. Except for the fire department the remaining two did use the word department to describe themselves, but as they evolved they took on all the aspects of true governmental departments.

Nationally these years were a period of time when political alliances were shifting rapidly. The old Whig Party saw its demise and so did the American Party and the Know Nothings. Then as if to fill a political void the Republican Party was born partly out of the ashes of the Whig Party, partly out of the ashes of the American Party, partly out of the ashes of the Know Nothings, and partly out of a realignment in the Democratic Party. As national political power was shifting, so was the political power in the town of Yonkers. In 1860 the shifting political sands helped elect Abraham Lincoln President of the United States, thereby sealing the destiny of the next 20 years in the North, and the next 100 years in the South. No community was left untouched by the election of Lincoln, and Yonkers was no exception.

Originally, this volume was intended to cover the period 1853 to 1872. However, the amount of material available proved to be staggering, and it would have been far too large a manuscript. One of the reasons for the increased information was the availability of the *Yonkers Examiner*, the *Yonkers Herald*, and the *Yonkers Gazette* on microfilm. Having these newspapers available meant that important additional information on period life styles, economics, and politics could be documented.

Also, the Town Record Book for this period of time has quite a bit more information in it than the earlier Town Record Book. As the years went by the pages in the record book for each year increased dramatically. With the additional information in the record book and in the newspapers, the size of the chapter dealing with the microbiographies of some Yonkers residents also increased dramatically. Then there are the Associated Documents. In the first volume there are thirty-one of them. For the years 1853 to 1872 there are over one hundred documents. When all of these aspects were taken into consideration, it became apparent that a narrower time period had to be chosen.

The format for this volume is similar to the format in the first volume. Chapters One through Four deal with developmental and interpretive historiographies. Chapter Five deals with the microbiographies of some Yonkers residents. The reader should be careful in this chapter because some information was gleaned from the 1860 census which has some inaccuracies. The remaining chapters are transcriptions of the Town Record Book and Associated Documents. Where credit is given for information E is used to denote the *Yonkers Examiner* followed by a date, page number(s) and column, USC is used to denote the 1860 United States Census, and in the case of a book the author's last name followed by a page number is used.

Associated Documents

1. 1855 Resolution to Prohibit Bathing
2. 1855 Ordinance on Bathing
3. 1855 Corporation Ordinance
4. 1855 Resolution Prohibiting Picnics
5. 1855 Resolution Prohibiting Steamboat, etc., Landings
6. 1855 Resolution Authorizing Prosecution of Steamboat Captains
7. 1855 Resolution Authorizing Prosecution of Steamboat Captains
8. 1855 Resolution Calling for a Meeting of the Taxable Residents to Determine if Street Lamps Should be Placed on a Section of Broadway
9. 1856 Report on the Charter Amendments
10. 1856 Locust Hill Avenue Boundaries
11. 1857 List of Taxable People
12. 1857 Resolution to Pay Poundmasters for Killing Stray Dogs
13. 1857 Resolution to Forward Amended Charter to Albany
14. 1857 Petition of F.S. Gant Concerning Milk Cows
15. 1857 Resolution to Amend Ordinances
16. 1857 Ordinance to Regulate Picnic Landings
17. 1857 Ordinance on Picnics
18. 1857 Petition of J.C. Derby in Reference to Bathing in the Hudson River
19. 1857 Resolution Concerning the Smoke Coming From George Russell's Factory
20. 1857 Order to Pay Hugh Curran
21. 1857 Resolution to Procure Handcuffs
22. 1857 Order to Pay Hugh Curran
23. 1857 Order to Pay Hugh Curran
24. 1858 Resolution to Appoint a Special Committee Concerning the Poor
25. 1858 Order to Pay the Street Commissioners
26. 1858 Order to Pay M.F. Rowe
27. 1858 Order to Pay Thomas C. Cornell
28. 1858 Order to Pay William H. Post
29. 1858 Order to Pay Frederick A. Coe
30. 1858 Order to Pay Thomas C. Cornell
31. 1858 Order to Pay M.F. Rowe
32. 1858 Resolution Concerning Elections
33. 1858 Order to Pay Hugh Curran
34. 1858 Resolution Referring Charter Amendments to a Committee
35. 1858 Report of Committee Concerning Amendments to the Charter
36. 1858 Minority Report on Amending the Charter

37. 1858 Resolution to Sign the Preamble to the Charter Amendments
38. 1858 Preamble and Resolutions to Amend the Charter
39. 1858 Resolution Authorizing a Warrant to Collect Taxes
40. 1858 Appointment of Bailey Hobbs as President Pro Tem
41. 1858 Ordinance on Bathing
42. 1858 Appointment of a Committee to Amend the Village Charter
43. 1858 Village Map
44. 1859 Appointment of Bailey Hobbs as President Pro Tem
45. 1859 Resolution Appointing a Committee to Engross the Charter Amendments
46. 1859 Resolution Authorizing a Committee to Send Charter Amendments to Albany
47. 1859 Resolution Concerning Elections
48. 1859 Appointment of A.C. Mott as Clerk Pro Tem
49. 1859 Resolution Thanking W.W. Woodworth
50. 1859 Resolution Thanking Bailey Hobbs
51. 1859 Resolution Concerning the Legality of an Election
52. 1859 Report of a Special Committee on Charter Amendments
53. 1859 Appointment of A.W. Gates as President Pro Tem
54. 1860 Report of Special Committee on Laying Gas Pipes
55. 1860 Letter from Thomas C. Cornell Concerning the Gas Company
56. 1860 Resolution to Have Nuisances Abated
57. 1860 Resolution to Procure Handbills
58. 1860 Resolution Fixing Property Taxes
59. 1860 Resolution Ordering Police to Arrest People Firing Guns
60. 1860 Petition of John Loud
61. 1860 Letter of Cyrus Cleveland

Chapter 1

Demographics and Economics

If the increase in population between 1820 and 1850 was large, the increase between 1850 and 1860 was downright dramatic. The town of Yonkers grew during those ten years by 7,734 people for a 187.2% growth rate. The following tables show what age categories had the most growth for white males and females.

Age	MALES 1850	1860	Diff.	FEMALES 1850	1860	Diff.
00-09	471	1494	1023	419	1511	1092
10-19	360	1050	690	434	1145	711
20-29	452	1088	636	457	1459	1002
30-39	344	999	655	295	986	691
40-49	205	608	403	145	515	370
50-59	101	248	147	107	228	121
60-69	60	124	64	65	131	66
70-79	25	42	17	27	61	34
80-89	11	9	(2)	20	11	(9)
90-100	2	0	(2)	1	1	0

One age category, 20-29, for both males and females is skewed, with the female skew being quite dramatic. The reason for the skew is that during the 1850s large numbers of Irish females immigrated to the United States and eventually to Yonkers where a significant amount of them took jobs as servants. A large portion of the overall population growth came from Irish immigrants, but there were also immigrants from Scotland, Germany, England, and other countries, as well as people who moved to Yonkers from other states and other parts of New York. The following table, which assumes no deaths in any age category between 1850 and 1860, demonstrates that when anticipated population is compared with the actual population the skew in the 20-29 age group is even larger than is represented in the preceding table.

	MALES			FEMALES		
Age	Antic.	Act.	Diff.	Antic.	Act.	Diff.
10-19	471	1050	579	419	1145	726
20-29	360	1088	728	434	1459	1025
30-39	452	999	547	457	986	529
40-49	344	608	264	295	515	220
50-59	205	248	43	145	228	83
60-69	101	124	23	107	131	24
70-79	60	42	(18)	65	61	(4)
80-89	25	9	(16)	27	11	(16)
90-100	11	0	(11)	20	1	(19)
100+	2	0	(2)	1	0	(1)

The above table also shows that while the male and female age groups 30-39 do not appear to be skewed, they in reality are. If the age groups 20-29 were normal then the age groups 30-39 would show an obvious skew. Interestingly, Yonkers gained 366 more females than males in their 20s when anticipated totals are compared. This was a result of the high rate of female servants who came to Yonkers. By 1860 the total white female population had grown by 207% to 6,048, while the white male population grew by 178.8% to 5,662. Females out numbered males by 386. Of these females, 371 can be found in the 20-29 age group. In 1850 the difference in males and females in that age group was only 5 in favor of females. In the total population in 1850 males outnumbered females by 60. By 1860 females outnumbered males by 386. Consequently, the female population outgrew the male population by 447.

Meanwhile, the black population continued to decline as a percentage of the total population. In 1850 the black population was 3.17% of the entire population. By 1860 it stood at only 1.3%. This decline as a percent of the total population was in the face of a numeric increase in the black population. In 1850 there were 131 blacks living in Yonkers. By 1860 the number increased to 155 for a 15.5% increase.

Coming back to the white population, the 1850s showed a dramatic increase in the number of young children. The increase dropped the average male's age from 24.97 in 1850 to 23.2 in 1860. The average female age also dropped from 24.9 in 1850 to 22.92 in 1860. Consequently, quite a few of the newcomers to Yonkers were married couples who had young children. The increase in the number of children was almost as great as the skews in the male and female populations in the age category 20 to 29. However, the overall increase in population during the 1850s occurred in all age categories below 70, and that increase in population was phenomenal.

During the 1820s the population of Yonkers increased by 11.0%. Then during the 1830s the population skyrocketed by 68.6%, followed by another, though more modest increase, of 39.2% during the 1840s. The growth rate of the 1850s, though, was unbelievable. It stood at a fantastic 187.2%. The following graph will illustrate the enormously high population growth rate.

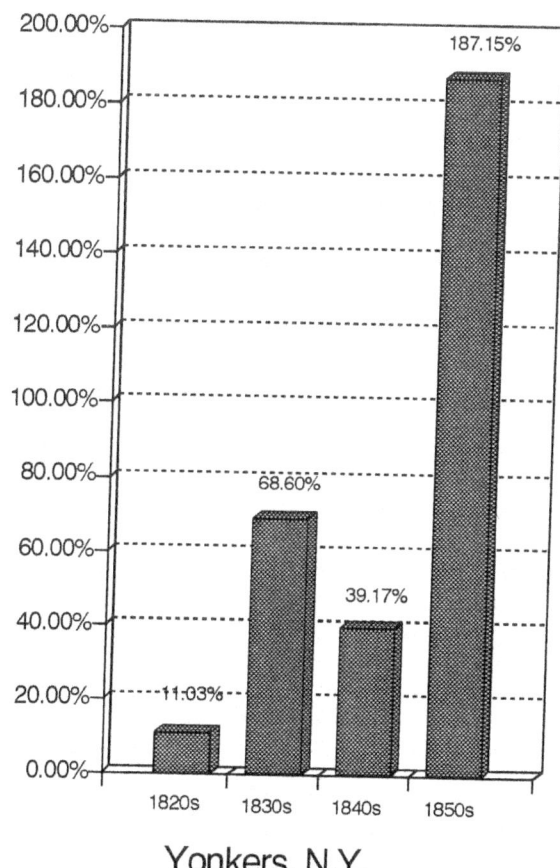

Population Growth 1820 - 1860

With the numerical increase in the population came an increase in the number of occupations. In 1850 there were at least 100 different occupations. In 1860 there were at least 177 different occupations. They included 2 accountants, 1 boat agent, 3 insurance agents, 3 real estate agents, 3 agents, 3 architects, 3 artists, 19 attorneys, 1 auctioneer, 15 bakers, 1 band box maker, 1 cashier, 3 bank tellers, 2 bank presidents, 3 bankers, 4 barbers, 8 bartenders, 1 bell hanger, 39 blacksmiths, 1 master blacksmith, 6 boarding house owners, 2 boat makers, 13 boatmen, 6 bookkeepers, 4 brewers, 1 brick maker, 22 brokers, 5 builders, 11 master builders, 34 butchers, 4 cabinet makers, 4 carmen, 160 carpenters, 2 carpenters apprentices, 1 carpet manufacturer, 1 carpet weaver, 15 carriage makers, 2 chemists, 12 cigar makers, 1 city weigher, 19 clergymen, 102 clerks, 2 post office clerks, 1 coach painter, 65 coachmen, 1 collector, 1 commission dealer, 2 confectioners, 6 contractors, 94 cooks, 6 coopers, 1 coroner, 1 corset maker, 1 crockeryware maker, 1 custom house employee, 2 dentists, 1 deputy sheriff, 4 medical doctors, 1 draftsman, 2 draw bridge tenders, 25 dress makers, 1 driver, 1 drum maker, 12 dyers, 5 editors, 1 engineer, 3 engravers, 1 secretary of the Erie Railroad, 6 express transportation employees, 139 farmers, 2 fishermen, 6 foundry workers, 1 foundry owner, 118 gardeners, 1 gas company owner or employee, 4 gas fitters, 2 gas works employees, 61 gentlemen, 1 glass blower, 1 glass manufacturer, 1 glazier, 3 hack drivers, 3 harness makers, 5 hat manufacturers, 1 hat trimmer, 245 hatters, 1 hide and fat employee, 2 hotel owners, 1 India rubber employee, 1 inspector of pork, 1 instrument maker, 1 insurance company employee, 1 iron worker, 11 jewelers, 651 laborers, 84 farm laborers, 11 landlords, 9 laundresses, 1 leather dealer, 1 leather dresser, 1 locksmith, 35 machinists, 2 mahogany workers, 1 market man, 84 masons, 2 master masons, 1 matron, 4 mechanics, 245 merchants, 5 milkmen, 9 millers, 6 milliners, 1 millwright, 4 morocco dressers, 1 morocco factory owner, 114 molders, 122 none reported, 45 nurses, 2 oystermen, 1 packer, 67 painters, 3 peddlers, 1 plasterer, 10 plumbers, 3 porters, 2 postmasters (one in the village of Yonkers and the other at Mosholu), 4 printers, 2 publishers, 1 quarryman, 12 railroad workers, 1 rigger, 1 rubber factory owner, 2 saddlers, 2 sailors, 8 sash and blind makers, 16 sawyers, 4 seamen, 20 seamstresses, 562 servants, 2 ship builders, 2 ship captains, 1 shipper, 2 shipwrights, 2 shoe binders, 52 shoemakers, 6 silk factory workers, 2 silk manufacturers, 8 skin dressers, 5 sloop captains, 1 soda factory owner, 1 steamship company owner, 1 steward, 14 stone cutters, 1 stone mason, 1 stone polisher, 4 surgeons, 2 surveyors, 1 tobacconist, 25 tailors, 1 tanner, 85 teachers, 40 teamsters, 2 tinsmiths, 12 tinners, 1 undertaker, 2 in the United States Navy, 1 varnisher, 1 vinegar maker, 15 waiters, 4 watchmen, 2 water works employees, 2 weavers, 6 wheelwrights, 1 wine maker, and 10 people whose occupation could not be read.

The increase in some occupations in the ten years between 1850 and 1860 was very dramatic. The hat industry added 148 employees for a 152.6% increase. Coachmen increased by 48 for a 282.2% increase. Butchers increased by a modest 28, but that was a 466.7% increase. Merchants increased by 206 for a 528.2% increase, while the number of clerks increased by 92 for an incredible 766.7%. Some occupations had relatively smaller percent gains, but had a large population increase. Laborers increased by 266 or 69.1%, and carpenters increased by 68 or 73.9%. On the other hand the decline of farmers continued. In 1860 the census reported 139 farmers. That was a loss of 71 farmers for a 33.8% decline, and they only constituted 3.6% of the work force. If farm laborers are added to the farm work force, then the percent of workers involved in agriculture rises only to 5.7% of the total work force. Yonkers by 1860 was definitively not an agricultural society. Rather, the town's economy had become primarily a mercantile, construction and manufacturing economy.

The above 1860 increases in occupations and the number in previously identified 1850 occupations sheds light on what economic industries helped to populate Yonkers in 1860. The construction industry contributed 1,135 persons which was 585 additional people over 1850. Service industries contributed 1,713 people which was an additional 1,388 people. Light industry contributed at least 551 people which was an additional 315. Professionals added another 53 persons which was an increase of 43. The most significant increase though was in the number of children which rose by at least 2,768. A large portion of this increase can be explained by the fact that an increasing number of families had moved to Yonkers. These five categories account for about 65.9% of the total population increase. A large portion of the remaining increase can be attributed to married non-working women who came to Yonkers with their husbands.

The above statistics explain what happened in Yonkers between 1850 and 1860, but they do not explain why it happened. It's a historical fact that large numbers of immigrants came to the United States and Yonkers during this period of time, and they came for a variety of reasons. Immigrants from Ireland, Scotland, England, Germany, and other countries came to the United States to find work, wealth, and freedom. It was also a period of our history when Americans were migrating across the country, and many came to Yonkers. For most people who came to Yonkers there was a commonality that existed amongst them; they needed employment, and jobs were available in Yonkers. The question then must be asked, why did Yonkers offer so many jobs in so many different occupations?

By 1860 a rather large number of men with discretionary money had moved to Yonkers. These men sparked increases in the service industry, in manufacturing, in light industry, and construction as well as influencing an increase in the number of professionals. In the service industry servants, cooks, gardeners, nurses, and coachmen were hired by most people who had a gross estate in excess of $500. Frequently, they hired several servants, gardeners and nurses. In manufacturing the hat industry went through a growth period fueled by an increase in monetary investments that led to more jobs. Alexander Smith had not yet opened his carpet shop in Yonkers, but Otis had begun his elevator business. Men with money also invested in building large homes, tenement buildings, and stores with apartments above them. Men like Getty, Radford, Ferris, Wheeler, and Farrington all built buildings that were several stories high. During the height of the Panic of 1857 Radford was constructing two buildings near the Broadway bridge. The buildings were four stories high and their estimated cost was $10,000. During the same period of time other men were also putting up buildings, doing renovations and moving other buildings to make way for bigger and better ones.

The Ferris building was going up on the corner of Palisade Avenue and Locust Hill Avenue and it was three stories high. Baldwin was renovating a building he had just recently bought from Getty. The building was on Broadway and Dock Street and a new glass front was being added to it. Devoe had just finished a building near the river on Dock Street. It was going to be rented out as a steam sawmill. At the same time he was moving another building from the east side of Broadway to the site of the sawmill. Several buildings on Broadway and Main Street were either being taken down or moved. Meanwhile MacFarlane was renovating a three story brick building on the corner of Main and Mill Streets. (E-7/2/57 p.2, c.5) Even the village government got into the act by putting up a three story village hall that had a 25-foot frontage and was 58 feet deep on Palisade Avenue. The village also built a firehouse that cost $2,800 on the corner of Palisade Avenue and Engine Place.

Because men with some discretionary wealth were willing to invest money in construction, jobs in the construction industry were created. As servants, carpenters, masons, and laborers came to Yonkers they in turn spawned the development of rather low income housing which in turn needed more people in construction to build those houses.

All of these people needed services such as butchers, grocers, barbers, and clothing stores. Consequently, people came to Yonkers to take advantage of a growing consumer economy. They opened shops and stores all over the town. Grocers advertised that they would deliver groceries any place in the village and most of the township, and they were good to their word.

While secondary and tertiary industries were growing rapidly, farmers were dwindling in number. However, the remaining farmers were growing quite wealthy. The increasing consumer market was large and nearby, thereby giving the farmer a larger market while reducing transportation costs. The average gross estate of a farmer in Yonkers stood at $18,507.19, while the average gross estate of a doctor was $13,375.00. The average wealth of farmers was even higher than the average wealth of merchants whose average wealth stood at $15,261.89.

It is quite apparent that men with discretionary investment wealth were the catalysts for the increase in the population and wealth. They literally created work that was filled by immigrants and Americans alike. They created other opportunities for other men with investment money to come to Yonkers and take advantage of the rapidly growing consumer sector. In the past most historians thought the railroad was the major catalyst for the rapid growth of Yonkers. Brown said that the railroad "immediately altered the entire aspect of practically everything." (p. 91) Walton intimates that the growth of the village as well as the old "Aquehung community" on the Bronx River grew because of the railroad. (pp. 153-54) However, a comparison between the village of Yonkers and the Aquehung community is not a legitimate comparison. When the railroad came to the east boundary of the town of Yonkers in the early 1840s no dramatic growth patterns developed. When the railroad came to the west side of the town of Yonkers in the late 1840s it was only one more factor in the growth pattern of the area. While the railroad was a growth factor it was not the major factor in the growth of Yonkers. That old concept was and is too simplistic. To be sure it did make Yonkers more accessible, but it was not the catalyst for growth. People would have come to Yonkers without the railroad as long as there were jobs to be had, and those jobs were there. Consequently, the most important catalyst for growth was the willingness of men with discretionary incomes to invest their money. More specifically, it was the money that was invested in the building of homes, stores, and tenements that initiated and continued the rapid economic development of Yonkers. Manufacturing during the 1850s added little growth and was only a minor factor. For instance, the hat industry added only 148 new employees, while there were 206 new merchants added to the population of Yonkers. The men with discretionary money to invest created the jobs that caused the rapid population growth, and they helped drive the gross valuation of Yonkers land in 1857 to $3,929,103, or $282 per acre. This was the highest town valuation in Westchester County. (E-1/7/58 p.2, c.2) By 1860 the census shows that the gross estate of Yonkers residents grew to $13,045,135 with an average estate of $3,356.09.

However, while Yonkers was growing wealthy, a similar socioeconomic disparity that existed in 1850 also existed in 1860. In 1860 only 27 men, representing a mere 0.7% of the work force, controlled $4,836,500, or about 37.1% of the total wealth. The occupations of these 27 men were 8 farmers, 7 merchants, 6 gentlemen, a broker, an artist, a manufacturer, a banker, a railroad secretary, and a pork inspector. Each of these 27 men controlled $100,000 or more. A larger disparity existed between those above and below the average gross estate. 453 people in the work force (11.7%) were above the average gross estate and they controlled $12,320,100 or 94.4% of the wealth. The economic disparity of 1850, as noted in Volume I, became much wider by 1860.

While wealth was increasing and most people who wanted work had jobs, all did not go smoothly between 1850 and 1860. The Panic of 1857 was a serious disruption in an almost unbroken and unprecedented economic growth pattern in both the United States and in Yonkers.

In the United States the period 1850 to 1856 was a time of financial prosperity. Europe was investing in railroads, California gold was paying the national debt, railroad building led to an increase in the production of pig iron and coal, cotton exports were up, and wheat and corn were being exported to Europe.

However, in 1857 things dramatically changed. The Crimean War came to an end and Europe reported record crop yields. In July, open gang warfare broke out in New York City amongst rival gangs, and didn't end until August. The Metropolitan Police force and the militia were unable to stop the fighting, and the fighting only ended in August because of boredom. One of the New York City newspapers, the *Herald*, used the gang warfare to issue gloom and doom predictions. The paper saw the gang warfare as a reflection of the general decay in American society, which was especially strong in business circles. The paper began attacking Wall Street brokers, wealthy railroad companies that were supposedly undercapitalized, poorly capitalized banks, and it claimed a panic was on the way. However, all the muckraking of the *Herald* had no effect on the stock market. In spite of all the published doom and gloom the market actually rose slightly.

However, on August 11, the oldest flour and grain company in New York City, N. H. Wolfe & Co., failed. After the failure of this company the business environment steadily worsened until finally Wall Street succumbed and collapsed. "The Wall Street collapse had been caused in part by weakness, speculation, and over expansion, but a lack of a strong force in the district was also to blame." (Sobel, p. 102)

After the collapse of the stock market, pressure began to mount on the banking system, and in early September banks began to fail and runs on New York City banks became frequent. Bank runs and the feeling of insecurity toward banks led to gold hording. Gold in circulation began to drop, and with a strong anxiety toward paper currency, trusted specie was taken out of circulation. The severe contraction led to problems in the railroad system, and they began to fail.

The banking situation stabilized quickly as news of a large gold shipment from California reached New York. However, the steamer *Central America*, with $1.6 million in gold, sank off Cape Hatteras on September 12 during a hurricane, and all the gold was lost. When the news of the sinking reached New York City, a new wave of panic commenced and business failures became more frequent. As news of the American panic swept into Europe, they called it the Western Blizzard. Panic also began to spread across the old continent causing the first international depression of modern times.

It took until mid October to stabilize the banking system in New York City, but loans and money in circulation remained depressed. The stock exchange also stabilized in October, but it didn't show any real positive strength. The United States was at the bottom of a depression that was flattening out. Recovery was off in the distance and the bottom of the depression lasted until late 1858 when recovery began. However, it wasn't until early 1859 when a strong recovery finally began to develop.

Although all cities and communities were affected by the depression, New York City was affected the worst. The crime rate shot up (especially murders), riots were commonplace, mobs broke into coal yards to steal fuel, and they even broke into stores to steal Christmas gifts. (Sobel, pp. 77-110)

In Yonkers the 1857 to 1859 depression also took its toll. Thieves broke into homes and stables and took anything of value. The incidents were so frequent that both public and private night watches were put on. However, that did not stop the robberies even though they did seem to reduce their frequency. Robberies were just a symptom of the depression, and at its lowest point all aspects of Yonkers' society were impacted by the depression.

Early in the Panic the hat factories in Yonkers, and the iron works in Spuyten Duyvil, closed forcing hundreds of breadwinners out of work. The situation in the hat industry was further exacerbated by production in the state prison. Inmates in the state prison made hats that were sold on the open market and thus they were in direct and unfair competition with private manufactures. Other signs of growing desperation were seen in street and road construction, and an apparent need for cash by large landowners. Road construction had grown into, particularly in the village of Yonkers, an important economic industry and employer. During 1857 expenditures on streets and roads were down by one sixth over 1856, and much of this drop in construction came in the second half of the year. The need for cash to supplement a declining cash flow resulted in a land-selling panic. The advertising pages of the village newspapers were littered with hundreds of lots up for sale. (E-10/1/57 p.2, c.1, E-10/22/57 p.2, c.2, E-12/31/57 p.2, c.4)

As bad as things were, the leaders of Yonkers were not insensitive to the problems of the unemployed. The situation was significant enough to be noted during the Village Board of Trustees meeting on August 23, 1858 where Getty mentioned that employment was scarce and Underhill rejoined him by saying unemployment was very high. Both men agreed that if Spring Street were opened at least some men would be put to work. The *Yonkers Examiner* observed sarcastically, that while unemployment was high and there was widespread poverty in Yonkers, the bars were doing well.

The Panic of 1857 left many Yonkers men unemployed resulting in widespread poverty. Josiah Rich, and other men of some means, were being approached daily by beggars in the streets. Rich, in a letter dated January 8, 1858 sent to Bailey Hobbs and the village Board of Trustees, indicated he had helped as much as he could, but people were literally starving. He urged that the Board do something and he advocated a meeting of all the residents of the village be called. The Board responded by appointing a committee of three to receive contributions, and after some debate appropriated $25 for the relief of the poor. While $25 went a long way in those days, it was not nearly enough money. Also, while governments, which included the village, town, and county, were active in assisting the poor, a depression of this magnitude, in a village comprised of large numbers of unemployed working men, found the various governments totally unprepared to handle the situation.

Other Yonkers leaders took matters into their own hands by calling for a mass meeting of the town's residents which was held on Saturday evening, January 16, 1858. Numerous members of the village were at the meeting. Judge Baldwin was elected chairman and J. H. Stedwell was appointed secretary.

The purpose of the meeting was to discuss the current condition of unemployment, the large number of people in a state of poverty, and how to go about giving aid to all of the town's poor. Opinions and suggestions came from Rockwell, Baldwin, Drake, Rich, MacFarlane, Lawrence, Smith, Cozzens, Gourlie, Underwood, Hibbard, Radford, Getty, Baxter, Mason, Cleveland, and Woodworth. As a result of the discussion Josiah Rich offered a motion to divide the town and the village into districts and to appoint visitors to go about the town and identify the poor. New York City had by this time already organized the New York Society for Ameliorating the Condition of the Poor, and it was the intent of the Yonkers meeting to model their organization after that of the city.

During the meeting an executive committee was appointed to oversee the activities of the organization. The committee originally consisted of Anson Baldwin, Thomas O. Farrington, Josiah Rich, H. A. Underwood, D. MacFarlane, R. L. Bucklin, F. S. Cozzens, T. R. Hibbard, H. N. Bashford, S. D. Rockwell, and Thomas C. Cornell. Before the meeting adjourned, Robert P. Getty, Lawrence Post Jr., J. M. Mason, J. H. Stedwell, A. T. Gourlie, and S. B. Cowdrey were added. These were men not only of good intentions, but they were amongst the wealthiest and respected men in Yonkers.

The Yonkers attack on poverty had phases and several approaches. First was the necessity to identify who was in need of their help. This was done by men and women who went throughout the town physically identifying the poor, and the adoption of a subscription book where the needy could sign up for relief. Once the needy were identified they could receive money and food. In the first approach Thomas O. Farrington was appointed treasurer of the association and all monies donated to the association were looked after by him. Anyone who made a donation became a member of the association.

The first monies donated came from Edward Weston, $25, W. T. Coleman, $25, H. A. Underwood, $25, John Garrison, $5, Nelson Ackert, $5, C. M. Odell, $20, S. D. Rockwell, $5, Waring, Baldwin and Company, $50, A. T. Gourlie, $25, Jeremiah Robbins, $10, H. W. Bashford, $25, R. L. Bucklin, $10, D. MacFarlane, $10, Thomas C. Cornell, $10, J. A. Welles, $10, and Thompson and Brevoort, $10. The initial amount collected was $270.

The rules of the association were to regard each applicant for aid as being entitled until proved otherwise, give aid only after personally visiting each home, to give only what was immediately necessary, to give what was least embarrassing, to give less in quality than what might be procured through working, except for sick people, to give aid at the right moment and not prolong it except as was needed, to give no aid to those who could not work except in extreme conditions and only for a couple of days until the case could be given to the Poor Master or the county Almshouse, and to discontinue aid to anyone who will not work. The executive committee made arrangements with local grocers and order forms were given to visitors, and each visitor had to keep an accurate accounting system and report to the executive committee the first of each month.

The committee even went so far as to divide the healthy from the sick and what each could receive. The healthy received bread, Indian meal, rice, potatoes, beans, peas, salt pork, dried fish, and molasses. The sick received the same but also tea, sugar, milk, and fresh meat. Fuel was also distributed to those in need.

The town and the village were divided separately into districts small enough not to inconvenience men and women who were appointed visitors. The visitors for the town district were in district A, which was north of the village line, between the Saw Mill and Hudson Rivers, and the visitors were Mr. and Mrs. E. F. Shonnard. District B was north of Hunt's Bridge Road from the Saw Mill River to the Bronx River, and the visitor was Samuel B. Cowdrey. District C was south of Hunt's Bridge Road from Tibbet's Brook to the Bronx River, and the visitors were Mr. and Mrs. G. J. Mankin. District D was south of the village line between Tibbet's Brook and the Hudson River, and the visitors were Dr. and Mrs. E. N. Bibby.

There were ten districts within the village. District number one was north of Ashburton Avenue from Broadway to the Saw Mill River, and the visitors were Mr. and Mrs. David Stewart who lived on the corner of Broadway and Ashburton Avenue. District number two was north of Wells Avenue to the village line and west of Broadway, and the visitors were Mr. and Mrs. H. O. Weed who lived on North Broadway. District number three was south of Ashburton Avenue to Pond Street and the Saw Mill River, and the visitors were Mr. and Mrs. Duncan Ralston who lived on Ashburton Avenue. District number four was south of Wells Avenue to Prospect Street between Broadway and the Hudson River, and the visitors were Mr. and Mrs. J. M. Drake who lived on Buena Vista Avenue. District number five was south of Pond Street from Broadway to the Saw Mill River, and the visitors were Mr. and Mrs. Archibald Baxter who lived on Locust Hill Avenue. District number six was south of Prospect Street to the village line and west of Riverdale Avenue, and the visitors were Mr. and Mrs. Joseph Agate who lived on Buena Vista Avenue. District number seven was north of Elm Street to Hunt's Bridge Road from the Saw Mill River to Tibbet's Brook, and the visitors were Mr. and Mrs. William Montgomery who lived on Walnut Hills. District number eight was south of Prospect Street to the village line from Broadway to Riverdale Avenue, and the visitors were Mr. and Mrs. D. MacFarlane who lived on Broadway. District number nine was between Broadway and Guion Street south of Elm Street and the Saw Mill River, and the visitors were Mr. and Mrs. T. R. Hibbard who lived on Guion Street. Finally, district number ten was south of Elm Street to the Village line and east from Broadway and Guion Street to Tibbet's Brook, and the visitors were Mr. and Mrs. Lawrence Post who lived on Mechanic Street.

The job of each visitor was to receive names of needy people, identify other needy persons and families, personally visit the homes of the needy in order to ascertain their need, and to distribute the aid. (E-1/21/58 p.2, c.1,2,3,5)

Another approach to distribute relief to the poor was an appeal to farmers in the town to make donations of farm products. Lawrence Post, Jr. set aside a part of his house on Mechanic Street to accept donated produce from farmers. The *Examiner* of January 21, 1858 published a very sensitive appeal to farmers by stating "When coming to the village, a bushel of potatoes or a bag of meal will not encumber their wagons or impoverish their substance. However trifling the gift, it will do some suffering family a benefit for which they will be grateful."

Another idea being bandied about was a sort of make work program. It was hoped that the committee could make arrangements for the able-bodied unemployed to work at reduced wages.

By the end of January, 1858 the association had collected almost eight hundred dollars, and farmers were beginning to help. However, the problem seemed to be worse than what was first thought. The visitors were bringing "to light many cases of silent suffering" and "instances of heart rending destitution are reported to us frequently." The following people made donations to the association before the end of January, 1858; James Purdy, $3, J. B. Kinslow, $5, George Gilroy, $5, Richard Lawrence, $25, L. R. Condon, $5, Lawrence Post, $1, Robert P. Getty, $25, James Bashford, $5, Rev. R. Baird, $10, Rev. E. Lynch, $10, Ebenezer Lyon, $1, James M. Drake, $25, William H. Anderson, $1, A. W. Greenleaf, $25, Vail and Elting, $10, J. F. Jenkins, $10, Hoyt and Brother, $5, Joseph Agate, $25, J. C. Luce, $20, H. L. Atherton, $25, H. F. Spaulding, $25, W. D. Cromwell, $25, S. D. Babcock, $25, C. H. P. Babcock, $10, J. S. Hawkins, $3, Frederick S. Cozzens, $50, Archibald Baxter, $25, William W. Scrugham, $10, Edward Underhill, $15, William Bell, $25, Ackerman and Deyo, $25, and H. A. Suau, $10. In addition to the above there were six anonymous donations amounting to $22. (E-1/28/57 p.2, c.1,2)

Eventually some of the monies collected by the association went to hiring unemployed men. These men were hired at four shillings per day to break stone and the stone was to be sold at or below cost during the spring. A large quantity of stone was expected and the stone's quality was good enough to make macadam for roads.

However, by February, 1858 the depression seemed to be easing in Yonkers. Workers in the hat factory were back to work, and the *Examiner* chided the workers by noting "the hatters generally ought to have been the last to feel the evils of a few weeks of want of work, for their wages for a long time have been high and work has been abundant for several years."

At the Village Board of Trustees meeting of February 8, 1858 Van Pelt moved that the $25 donation to the association approved at a previous meeting be rescinded. His reason for making the motion was that the poor were being well kept. The Board then voted in favor of the motion, but President Woodworth vetoed the motion. However, a second vote, which was unanimous, overrode the veto. (E-2/4/58 p.2, c.4, c.6 and 2/11/58 p.2, c.6)

By early March, 1858 conditions in Yonkers had not really improved that much, and the Association was in trouble. They reported that they had collected $1,115, including two new $5 donations from Frederick A. Beck and David Stewart, and for the most part judiciously gave out $1,055 leaving a balance of only $60. In giving out that money they reported they had aided about 150 families for a total of nearly 1,000 people. The men working at breaking stone were heads of families that would have received direct aid anyhow and by the beginning of March there was quite a bit of stone ready to be sold for road making. However, the season for selling the stone was still some time off and these as well as other families still needed aid. Also, some people had pledged a donation which had not been turned in. The Association urged them to do so, and asked other citizens of Yonkers to donate money. (E-3/4/58 p.3, c.3 and p.2, c.7)

In reading the minutes of the Village Board of Trustees in the *Yonkers Examiner* it is clear that the new Village Hall was used to give temporary housing to the homeless during the depression. Whether these were residents of Yonkers or drifters is not clear, but the keeper of the hall reported on March 1, 1858 that 283 persons were given lodging.

The plea for additional help did not go unnoticed. By April 1 an additional $435.83 was collected. Donations came from James C. Bell, $20, Isaac H. Knox, $10, William Montgomery, $25, J. B. Smith, $10, George B. Skinner, $10, Doctor Amos W. Gates, $10, Josiah Rich, $25, William Duke, $1, Treasurer of Association 1856, $11.83, Mr. Gourlie, $45, Elisha G. Otis, $5, John Copcutt, $5, Gotlieb Glasser, $4, William Radford, $25, E. Clapp, $20, William T. Coleman $50, J. Robins, $10, Charles Baird, $5, Edward Underhill, $5, William C. Waring, $10, J. H. Knox, $10, S. Mayo, $5, S. D. Rockwell, $2, Ralph Shipman, $5, John H. Williams, $10, A. Baldwin and Son, $25, C. M. Odell, $10, Thomas W. Ludlow, Sr., $20, Rev. W. W. Rand, $5, S. Quick, $5, John Hobbs, $5, F. W. Birdsall, $20, and Henry W. Bashford, $10.

Over the winter the depression was so deep that many people became homeless. The Village and Town of Yonkers agreed to allow the homeless to stay in the jail at the Village Hall and to pay for their accommodations. However, by April, 1858 the situation of the homeless was such that the Town of Yonkers refused to pay the Village of Yonkers to keep the homeless at the Village Hall, but in a very generous spirit the Village Board of Trustees authorized the keeper to continue to allow the homeless to stay there.

The depression also cut into the resources of the Bank of Yonkers. In its quarterly report of July 16, 1857 the bank had resources of $332,602.80 with loans and discounts of $190,185.16 and demand deposits of $66,910.66. By April 15, 1858 their resources had dropped $73,187.50 to $259,415.30 which was a 22% loss. Loans and discounts dropped to $130,831.82 for a 31.8% loss, and demand accounts fell to $55,475.27 for a 17.1% loss.

The May 6, 1858 issue (p.2, c.6) of the *Yonkers Examiner* noted that the marble quarrymen had been laid off and hurt severely by the depression. However, the paper saw the depression coming to an end and noted that the owners of the quarry were about ready to resume operations.

On Monday evening July 12, 1858 the Village Board of Trustees learned that the depression was beginning to take its toll on the Fire Department. Until this time the members of the Lady Washington Hose Company Number 2 were able to take care of their equipment themselves. However, "because of the hard times," in a letter to the

Board they requested the village to help maintain the fire truck. (E-7/15/58 p.2, c.3)

The depression hit property owners and manufacturers equally. Even wealthy property owners like Rich and Woodworth had several properties foreclosed. S. Coates had his gas heaters auctioned off and Captain Edward Underhill had his machinery auctioned. In the latter case Underhill was able, in a very short period of time, to open the Yonkers Ale Brewery on Chicken Island.

In preparation for the winter the ladies of the Goodwill Society of Glenwood and Yonkers sponsored a series of lectures designed to raise money for the poor. The first lecture was on money by R. J. De Cordova, known as the Deacon of Glenwood, the second by William W. Howe, the Chief Justice of Glenwood, on a Turrish Point of View, and the third by Robert Sewell on The Pioneer. Tickets were 50 cents. (E-9/23/58 p.4, c.6,7)

During the summer of 1858 the panic seemed to ease somewhat in Yonkers. However, with the onset of winter the Ladies of the Goodwill Society continued their efforts to raise money. Winter was a difficult enough time, but for the subsistence level worker it brought added burdens. Many workers in construction were laid off because of the cold weather, and the cold brought with it more expenses for fuel. In preparing for the season the Goodwill Society scheduled a meeting at the home of Mrs. H. O. Weed on Thursday, November 25th at 3 o'clock. The meeting was advertised and part of the advertisement read "In view of the necessity for early action in reference to the relief of our poor, it is earnestly hoped that all the ladies of this village who are interested in its objects will attend and give their aid to the Society." This plea may have been more of a reaction to a seasonal plight, when construction workers were not able to work as many days during the winter, rather than to a ongoing depression. (E-11/25/58 p.2, c.4,7)

However, nationally the depression did continue through January, 1859. The New York City *Inquirer* of January 10 noted that more than 6,600 poor people came to the Alms House Rotunda in the city during the last two or three days demanding relief. The paper suggested that over 50,000 people in the city were destitute. (E-1/27/59 p.2, c.4) The editor of the *Examiner* was quick to point out that the lowering of the tariff was the main culprit for unemployed people and what was needed was a high tariff to protect home industries. Meanwhile in North Castle a man named Tucker along with his wife and two children froze to death in a barn on Tuesday, January 18, 1859. They were homeless people who used the barn to avoid inclement weather. During the night the temperature must have plunged causing their deaths. (E-1/20/59 p.2, c.6) However, the same paper on January 27 noted that real estate in Mount Vernon was rising in value and many sales were being made. The editor was "gratified to be able to state" that Mount Vernon "exhibits unmistakable evidence of renewed vitality and progress."

The bottom of the depression in Yonkers lasted only a couple of weeks when the hatters were laid off. By the middle of February, 1858 they were back at work and it seems that most of them were able to make contributions to grocers in return for food. It is not entirely clear who was hurt most by the depression, but the drop in road construction indicates that laborers were probably hurt the most. Also, the drop in demand deposits probably restricted loans that slowed the construction industry during a period of time when weather was a natural restrictive for the industry.

Despite the Panic of 1857, Yonkers economically entered the 1860s with an excellent economic and work force base. Despite the bluster over slavery the economic outlook for Yonkers was very good and everyone expected the progress of the 1850s to continue through the 1860s.

Chapter 2

Life in Yonkers During the 1850s

Everyday life in Yonkers during the 1850s was fascinating. The political boundaries of the town were different, manufacturing was being established, Getty Square abounded with merchants, a variety of daily activities were available, medicine was an adventure, shopping offered a variety of choices, and rapid growth caused environmental problems and an increase in crime.

When current residents, and past residents, think about Yonkers they usually think of Yonkers as it is today with its current boundaries as they were established in 1872. Also, when we think of Yonkers in the days of old we think of the Getty Square area surrounded to the north, south, and east by farms. However, the town of Yonkers in the 1850s was a lot different. The town stretched from its current northerly boundary south to the Harlem River and then east to the Bronx River. It included not only the rapidly growing village of Yonkers, but also Mount St. Vincent, Mosholu, Riverdale, Kingsbridge, and Spuyten Duyvil which were areas that were also growing at a rapid pace. Moving easterly the town of Yonkers also included what is now Van Cortlandt Park, Kingsbridge Heights including the Jerome Reservoir, the lands occupied by Hunter College, the Bronx High School of Science, and DeWitt Clinton High School, the community of Woodlawn including Woodlawn Cemetery, the community of Norwood, a section of Bedford Park, and the northerly section of the Bronx Park including a good portion, if not all, of the New York Botanical Gardens.

During this period of history, the total area of Yonkers was comparable in land size to the entire area of New York City. The city had expanded by this time to include all of Manhattan Island, and residents of the city had developed a political and geographical identity with the city. It should be noted that political boundaries are often boundaries of an individual's geographical identity where loyalties and a sense of sentiment are developed. New York City had a good sense of geo-demographic cohesion bound by a strong, even though sometimes chaotic, political entity. A similar identity had developed in the town of Yonkers, but growth was beginning to tear it down. The development of the communities of Mosholu, Riverdale, Kingsbridge, and Spuyten Duyvil in South Yonkers along with the estrangement of the large property owner Augustus VanCortlandt over amending the village charter caused these communities not to be geographically or economically related to the village which, however, had become the dominant political entity in the town. Each community, including the village of Yonkers, was developing its own identity. In the case of the village, political boundaries were established which helped give the residents a sense of geographical identity. In the case of the communities to the south their only political and geographical identity was with the town of Yonkers. Their geographical proximity to New York City, their growth without a geopolitical identity of their own, along with stronger social and economic ties with the city than with the village, and a growing sense of political anomie in the town because of the increasing political dominance of the village naturally led to talk about a different political arrangement.

This was the period of time when, for a section of Yonkers, the seeds of secession and annexation to New York City were planted. They did not germinate and grow until a decade later because of the Civil War which sapped political strength and halted economic development. However, they were there in the ground just waiting. For instance, Andrew Haswell Green was an important political figure in New York City and "By 1860, he was arguing that New York City's boundaries had to be expanded." (Cohn, p.10) There is no evidence that the southern communities of the town of Yonkers were actually discussing secession from the town and joining New York, but the economic and political development of the village by 1860, and the economic development of thriving communities in the southern part of the town were the seeds waiting to be germinated.

Another aspect of Yonkers that we think about in historical terms is what used to be its great industrial base of elevators, carpets, and hats. However, the elevator industry during the 1850s was just beginning to grow, and Alexander Smith had not yet started his operations in Yonkers. On the other hand, the hat industry was well established during the 1850s.

Also, the 1860 census suggests there were several manufacturing industries in the town of Yonkers that have not been previously associated with the town. For instance, there was a foundry in the township and another one was to begin operations in the village. The foundry in the town was located in Spuyten Duyvil. Also, the census indicates that the town of Yonkers had a flourishing shoe manufacturing industry, a baking industry, a butcher industry, a soap factory, and a soda manufacturing industry. As noted above many of the manufacturing industries Yonkers was to become closely associated with in the future were still rather small in 1860. In 1860 there were only two weavers listed on the census that could be indirectly associated with the carpet manufacturing industry. However, Jeremiah Clarke manufactured carpets on the corner of Mechanic and Guion

Streets, James Mitchell manufactured carpets, and A. R. Van Houten had a carpet shop on Palisade Avenue. He may have also manufactured carpets until his shop burned down and he turned to construction. There was a palm-oil soap factory on Guion Street near Mechanic Street in Grant's Building, and the snuff factory on Mill Street was for rent. During 1859 a new hat factory was prepared to begin operations at the corner of Dock and Nepperhan Streets, and it was estimated that it would employ 300 to 400 people. On May 1, 1860 the Union Hat Factory, which made wool hats, was organized by William C. Waring, Anson Baldwin, and Hall F. Baldwin. During the same year the Eagle Hat Factory was in operation on Palisade Avenue near the Nepperhan River and Elm Street. During 1859 a new flour mill was opened in Devoe's Building at Nepperhan and Dock Streets. It produced 200 to 250 barrels of flour in a 24 hour period.

The village of Yonkers in and around Getty Square offered a variety of activities. Grocers, butchers, bakeries, ice cream parlors, barber shops, dentists, bookstores, doctors, drug stores, shoe stores, clothing stores, and hardware stores all crowded into the same area competing for space with manufacturing industries and housing. In the same area people could quench their thirst at Underhill's brewery on Chicken Island, or go to the reading room of the Yonkers Library Association to help quench a different kind of thirst. At night residents had a variety of activities. They could go to the circus, play billiards, listen to intellectual lectures, engage in debates, listen to opera, singing groups, or string quartet music, attend the Yonkers Evening School, or they could even go to the gymnasium to work out. On a lazy summer Sunday they could take a ride into New York City and enjoy the wonders of the then new Central Park. Before taking that drive they could attend church at one of the seven new churches which were in addition to the four old churches. The new churches were the Baptist Church established in 1852, the First Presbyterian Church established in 1853, the Westminster Presbyterian Church established in 1857, the Unitarian Church established in 1858, St. Paul's Episcopal Church also established in 1858, the Congregational Methodist Church also established in 1858, and the Congregational Wesleyan Methodist Church established in 1859. These churches joined St. John's Episcopal Church founded in 1752, the First Methodist Church established in 1828, the Reformed Dutch Church established in 1844, and St. Mary's Roman Catholic Church established in 1848. (E-3/31/59 p.2, c.2) Life was not too bad for those who could take advantage of the activities.

By 1854 the village even had its first bank. The Bank of Yonkers was opened August 10, 1854 with deposits of $11,926. Its first board of directors consisted of Dr. Amos Gates, Ethan Flagg, Robert P. Getty, Henry F. Devoe, Lemuel W. Wells, William H. Arthur, William G. Ackerman, Fielding S. Grant, William C. Waring, James L. Valentine, John Stillwell, and Henry W. Bashford. John Olmsted was the bank's first president. (Souvenir History, p.28)

During 1859 there was considerable talk about building a new railroad from New York City to Yonkers over an inland route. It was argued that Yonkers had become a regular suburb of New York City and it would help relieve the overcrowded conditions in Manhattan. New York residents would be able to move to an area that had lower rents, and they would still have access to the city for work. Yonkers residents, it was argued, would also benefit since the Hudson River Railroad did not run trains after 6:30 p.m. If the new railroad was built residents of Yonkers would be able to enjoy the night life of the city. However, Mayor Tieman of New York City vetoed the measure because he thought it was illegally hurried through their board. (New York Times. D21, 4:3 1859)

Gas lighting was becoming more commonplace by 1860. The Yonkers Gas Light Company had 300 consumers of their gas making evenings at home more enjoyable and somewhat less dangerous. However, modernity was slow in its arrival, and in medicine the residents of Yonkers had a wide variety of archaic and sometimes novel ways to remedy their ailments. Even though a somewhat successful vaccine for smallpox had been developed and other advances in medicine had occurred, the practice of medicine during the 1850s was still a mixture of science, guessing, alchemy, prayer, and hope. There was a glimmer of understanding of how some diseases came about, but the drugstore of the 1850s still carried leeches to suck out the bad blood that was thought to be at the root of most maladies. Leeches, however, were and are slimy creatures who adhere to the skin like vampires. They caused pain, and after being used, if they weren't removed very carefully they could, if allowed to explode, let loose a torrent of a patient's blood they just finished gorging themselves on. They left blotches on the skin that frequently took weeks to heal, and the wounds could become infected. Even to many of the people living in the 1850s, the use of leeches was an inconvenient, messy misery that might be avoided if they used the

> "Family dandelion compound called Cathartic Bitters for the cure of liver complaints and debility arising from an impure state of the blood. These bitters have the same kind of action on the human body, that the storms and hurricanes have on the air, or that the tides have upon the ocean. They purify what is judicious by copying nature who, we see, when she wishes to become purified, puts herself in commotion, which has the purifying effect. And so we, to induce purity in our bodies, bring about a natural commotion by artificial means, and experience has taught those who have adopted this course, and who for this purpose have used these bitters, they were in the right, because the result has been sound health, or in other words, every organ has been restored to a state of purity consistent with its functions.

> These Bitters act beneficially on the Liver, stimulating the secretionary organs and causing a healthy flow of the secretionary fluids, and should be continued until their effects are uniformally felt, for they are an effectual assistant of nature.
>
> These Bitters in our opinion will be found the safest and most effectual medicine ever offered to the public in the early stages of the following complaints: DYSENTERY, DIARRHOEA, CHOLERA, MORBUS, SCROFULA, URINARY DISEASES, LIVER COMPLAINTS AND DEBILITY, ARISING FROM A TORPID AND IMPURE STATE OF THE BLOOD.
>
> The bitters can be used with impunity and with extraordinary success in all diseases incident to females.
>
> They act promptly and efficiently on the secretionary and digestive organs and remove all tendency to dyspepsia; they give strength to the nervous and muscular systems, enliven the spirits and render life a blessing."

Some of the more prolific advertisements were those of Dr. Devines. He had five different advertisements that addressed almost every human misery, and he knew how to play on sentiments.

> "TO MOTHERS! Dr. Devines' Worm Lozenges. A safe and pleasant remedy for removing and destroying worms.
>
> There is no disease to which the human system is liable, that is more entitled to the attention of Mothers than those consequent on the irritation produced by worms in the stomach and bowels of children. These ills are not wholly confined to children, as we find even among adults the health impaired by stomach worms producing loss of appetite, night sweats, and a general prostration of the whole system. This Lozenge we know to be a reliable and effectual remedy for destroying worms, and one trial will convince you of its superiority over every other preparation now in use. This Lozenge is purely vegetable, and unlike all other worm remedies, it has to the child a pleasant and agreeable taste. In its use it is perfectly harmless and cannot injure the most delicate child; for infants the Lozenge can be dissolved in warm water."

Living in the late 1850s was a lot different than living today. Mankind was subject to hard work and walking. There was very little effort made to control insects and eating meat must have been an adventure. Men and women were subjected to all sorts of aches and pains and problems caused by insects; but, Dr. Devines had the answer in

> "THE HOOSIER LINIMENT. This liniment was used as a sovereign remedy among the early settlers of Indiana, as the pioneers were subject to bruises, cuts, sprains, and bites of poisonous insects, for which they found the Hoosier Liniment a certain cure. Recent experi-

ence has taught us that the Liniment possesses a soothing and healing power, in our opinion not possessed by any other Liniment in use, and is warranted on application, according to directions, to cure Salt Rheum, Scalds, Ringworms, Cuts, Sore Throat, Chilblains, Boils, Fever, Sores, Rheumatic Affections, Inflamed Eyes, Earache, Sore Breasts, Chafes, Catarrh, Ague in the Face, and Bleeding at the Nose without possibility of failure."

Viruses and bacteria have probably been around since the beginning of the universe. During the 1850s, just as today, people were subjected to the attacks of these infectious microbes. Today we take aspirins or stronger drugs to relieve symptoms. However, back in the 1850s when your throat was sore, your temperature was high, and you were coughing your head off you could take

"Dr. Devines' Influenza Lozenge. This Lozenge is pronounced by vocalists and others the best remedy ever discovered, in allaying inflammation of throat and clearing the voice. The influenza is hoarseness; when the disease is fully developed, is known by symptoms of fever and an increased quantity of phlegm in the throat, nose and windpipe. The Lozenge is the best remedy ever discovered to subdue hoarseness and allay inflammation of the throat, gums and tonsils.

Also, Madame Searing's COUGH COMPOUND CANDY. Of Horehound, Boneset and Wild Cherry, for Coughs, Colds, Croup, Whooping Cough, Consumption and Asthma."

The routine day activities of a long working day, an active night life, and the constant struggle to pay bills or increase wealth led many in the 1850s to minor and sometimes severe psychological problems. If you happened to be one of those persons back in the 1850s you could take

"Dr. Devines' Nervine and Invigorating Lozenge. Especially adapted to the relief and permanent cure of nervous diseases. Good for the following diseases: Physical Debility and Mental Prostration, Weakness of the General Organs, Hysterics, Bronchia, Hypochondriasis, Sick Headache, Tic Douloureux, Hemicrania, Local Paralysis, Spinal Weakness, &c.

There are those ever ready to cry humbug. Use my Lozenge for any of the above diseases, and you will be one of the Lozenges warmest advocates."

Work for both men and women, and even children, was usually quite strenuous in the 1850s, and led in some cases to serious muscle pains and back problems. Tuberculosis, or consumption, was also a serious and misunderstood disease. However, if you had any of these problems you could use

"Dr. Devines' STRINGENT PLASTER for pains in the back, side, or breast, and in cases of consumption should be used in connection with my Lozenge, as drafts on the feet, and as strengthening plaster. Spread thinly on sheep skin."

It has been said that competition and diversity made America. During the 1850s there was stiff competition in the drug business and it led to a diversity of drugs claiming similar cures. If you were unsure about using the liniment allegedly discovered by Indiana pioneers, and were not sure that Dr. Devines was all that divine you could use

"Dr. Sweet's Infallible Liniment. The great external remedy for rheumatism, gout, neuralgia, lumbago, stiff neck and joints, sprains, bruises, cuts and wounds, piles, headache, and all rheumatic and nervous disorders.
Dr. Stephen Sweet of Connecticut. The great natural bone setter.
Dr. Stephen Sweet of Connecticut, is know all over the United States.
Dr. Stephen Sweet of Connecticut, is the author of *Dr. Sweet's Infallible Liniments*.
Dr. Sweets' Infallible Liniment cures rheumatism and never fails.
Dr. Sweet's Infallible Liniment is a certain remedy for neuralgia.
Dr. Sweet's Infallible Liniment cures burns and scalds immediately.
Dr. Sweet's Infallible Liniment is the best known remedy for sprains and bruises.
Dr. Sweet's Infallible Liniment cures headache immediately and was never known to fail.
Dr. Sweet's Infallible Liniment affords immediate relief for piles and seldom fails to cure.
Dr. Sweet's Infallible Liniment cures toothaches in one minute.
Dr. Sweet's Infallible Liniment cures cuts and wounds immediately and leaves no scars.
Dr. Sweet's Infallible Liniment is the best remedy for sores in the known world.
Dr. Sweet's Infallible Liniment has been used by more than a million people, and all praise it.
Dr. Sweet's Infallible Liniment is truly a "friend in need," and every family should have it at hand.
Dr. Sweet's Infallible Liniment is for sale by all Druggists. Price 25 cents."

If none of these were to your liking you could take Dr. Herrick's pills and Kid Strengthening Plaster, or you could use the sure-fire Indian cure,

"OLD SACHEM BITTERS and WIGWAM TONIC. These delicious and far famed bitters are recommended by the first physicians of the country, on account of their purity and great medicinal virtue.

They are pleasant as nectar to the taste, and are pronounced the best tonic and stimulant ever offered to the public.

Their curative powers in cases of general debility, loss of appetite, constipation, etc., are unparalleled, and as a guarantee that we feel warranted in claiming what we do, we beg leave to state that our assertations are endorsed by Prof. Silliman of Yale College, Prof. Hayes of Massachusetts, and hundreds of others.

For sale by grocers, wine merchants, and druggists generally."

While some might question endorsements and the curative powers of the above drugs, nobody could out do Professor Holloway who produced his cures at 80 Maiden Lane in New York City. His advertisements were prolific, specific, and cured everything except a lover's broken heart. If in the 1850s you were looking for a panacea you had to

"MARK THESE FACTS! The testimony of the whole world.
Holloway's Ointment.
Bad Legs. Bad Breasts. Sores and Ulcers.

All description of sores are remedied by the proper and diligent use of this inestimable preparation. To attempt to cure bad legs by plastering the edges of the wound together is a folly; for should the skin unite, a boggy diseased condition remains underneath to break out with ten fold fury in a few days. The only rational and successful treatment, as indicated by nature, is to reduce the inflammation in and about the wound and to soothe the neighboring parts by rubbing in plenty of the Ointment as salt is forced into meat.
Diphtheria, Ulcerated Sore Throat, and Scarlet and other Fevers.

Any of the above diseases may be cured by well rubbing the Ointment three times a day into the chest, throat and neck of the patient; it will soon penetrate and give immediate relief. Medicine taken by the mouth must operate upon the whole system ere its influence can be felt in any local part, whereas the Ointment will do its work at once. Whoever tries the unguent in the above manner for the diseases named, or any similar disorders affecting the chest and throat, will find themselves relieved as by a charm.
Piles, Fistulas, Strictures

The above class of complaints will be removed by nightly fomenting the parts with warm water, and then by most effectually rubbing in the Ointment. Persons suffering from these direful complaints should lose not a moment in arresting their progress. It should be understood that it is not sufficient merely to smear the Ointment on the affected parts, but it must be well rubbed in for some considerable time two or three times a day, that it may be taken into the system whence it will remove any hidden sore or wound as effectually as though palpable to the eye. There again bread and water poultices, after the rubbing in of the Ointment, will do great service. This is the only sure treatment for females, cases of cancer in the stomach, or where there may be a general bearing down.

Indiscretions of Youth; Sores and Ulcers

Blotches, as also swellings, can, with certainty, be radically cured if the Ointment be used freely, and the Pills be taken night and morning as recommended in the printed instructions. When treated in any other way they only dry up in one place to break out in another; whereas this Ointment will remove the humor from the system, and leave the patient a vigorous and healthy being. It will require time with the use of the Pills to ensure a lasting cure.

Dropsical Swellings, Paralysis and Stiff Joints

Although the above complaints differ widely in their origin and nature, yet they all require local treatment. Many of the worst cases, of such diseases, will yield in a comparatively short space of time when this Ointment is diligently rubbed into the parts affected, even after other means have failed. In all serious maladies the Pills should be taken according to the printed directions accompanying each box.

Both the Ointment and Pills should be used in the following cases: Bad Legs, Bad Breasts, Sore throats, Chapped Hands, Bunions, Sore heads, Piles, Pneumatism, Tumors, Yaws, Elephantiasis, Chigoe foot, Chilblains, Skin Diseases, Glandular Swellings, Corns (soft), Bite of Mosquitoes and Sand Flies, Ulcers, Scalds, Sore Nipples, Fistulas, Gout, Burns, Scurvy, Lumbago, Cancers, Contracted and Wounds, and Coco bay."

Over-the-counter cure-alls of the 1850s weren't all that bad if you can remember cod liver oil. However, for real fun being a property owner on Main Street was where it really was at. The battle was led by John Copcutt who thought he was unfairly assessed for improvements made to Main Street. The battle over Main Street even reached into the boardroom of the Village Trustees. A war of words between John Copcutt and Josiah Rich had been fought earlier in the newspapers, and by 1858 Copcutt decided there might be an easier way in which to remedy apparent injustices done to him.

On Saturday, February 27, 1858 John Copcutt was nominated at a caucus of the village voters to run for the Board of Village Trustees. Nomination at the caucus was tantamount to election, and apparently there was little opposition to his nomination. On Tuesday, March 2, 1858 Copcutt was easily elected to the board even though he received ten less votes than Leonard M. Clark and Bailey Hobbs who were also elected. After the election the publisher of the *Yonkers Examiner* seemed to be very satisfied with the results. He was very complimentary of Copcutt's business shrewdness, but in the end he sounded a warning of things to come when he said "We are confident that he (Copcutt) will cooperate cordially and effectually with his fellow members in the promotion of the public welfare." (E-3/4/58 p.2, c.1,3)

The *Examiner* did not have long to wait for the Main Street battle to break out in the Trustee's board room. At a meeting of the board on Monday, April 26, 1858, Copcutt read a lengthy speech attacking the Town Board of Assessors and fellow board member Robert P. Getty. He accused Getty of pushing through the alterations to Main Street so his business at the Getty House would benefit. In a scorching attack he accused Getty of "...working to get money into his own pocket away from himself and other people on the line of Main Street." Getty rejoined Copcutt with facts of his own and concluded that "He thought the Board and all who listened to his (Copcutt's) long, disconnected and childish tirade would agree in thinking he might be suspected of insanity."

In the following issue of the *Yonkers Examiner* the paper called the fight in the boardroom "a discreditable exhibition of private ill feeling." The paper went on to say that Copcutt's attack on Getty was "not only disproved" but that Copcutt and the *Yonkers Herald* needed "to look up his proofs and make sure of his facts." (E-4/29/58 p.2, c.2,3,4)

During 1858 there were three people who refused to pay their entire assessment for Main Street. They were John Copcutt, J. Taylor, and none other than the president of the Village Board of Trustees, William W. Woodworth. Copcutt's total assessment was $2,476.00 on five lots. The lots and their assessments were located at 23 Main Street that was assessed $660.00, the Dock Right on Main Street that was assessed $700.50 (both of these lots were on the north side of Main Street), 26 Main Street that was assessed $531.50, 52 Main Street that was assessed $577.50 (both of these lots were on the south side of Main Street), and 69 Main Street that was assessed $6.50. The last lot was on the corner of Main Street and Market Place. By May 13, 1858 Copcutt had paid $1,375.70 of his total assessment. J. Taylor's lot was 15 and 17 Main Street on the north side of Main Street. His assessment was $188.00 and the full amount was due. Like Copcutt, Woodworth had five lots for which he still owed an assessment. The lots and their assessments were located at 9 Depot Street that was assessed $37.50 (this lot was on the west side of Depot Street on the corner of Main Street), the Steamboat Dock that was assessed $93.75, 40 Main Street that was assessed $161.44, the dock right at Market Place was assessed $25.31, and 10 and 12 Nepperhan Street on the south side that was assessed $37.50. His total assessment was $355.55 of which he had paid $94.05.

Notice was given in the local papers that a lien had been put on each lot and that all the lots were going to be auctioned off Saturday, June 19, 1858 if the assessments were not paid by June 18th. (E-

5/13/58 p.3, c.1,2,3 and E-6/3/58 p.3, c.3,4,5) The very next week Jeremiah Burns was added to the list. He owned a lot at 1, 3, and 5 on the north side of Nepperhan Street. He owed $75.00. By May 27, 1858 J. Taylor paid his debt, but the others had not. (E-5/27/58 p.3, c.3,4,5)

The foreclosure sale was put off by order of the Board of Trustees until Saturday, July 10, 1858. The sale of the properties as reported by the *Yonkers Examiner* of July 15 was again put off until July 19, and the next week the same newspaper reported that the sale was once again postponed until August 3.

The postponements were caused by a lawsuit brought by Copcutt which resulted in an injunction against the sale. However on Monday, August 2, 1858 Judge Emott removed the injunction and on the next day all the properties were auctioned. Ex-Board of Trustee member Rueben Van Pelt was Copcutt's attorney and on the day of the auction he gave notice that the sale would be contested.

The auction day finally arrived and the first lot sold, which had a snuff mill on it, was located at 26 Main Street. It was estimated that the property was worth $20,000. Robert P. Getty bought the property for one thousand years for $435.84. His was the only bid.

The second lot sold consisted of the dock right which was about 350 feet in length. Again Getty was able to obtain it for $465.64. The third parcel was lot 26 which was 246 feet on Main Street and from ten to fifty feet in depth. There were no bids on the lot and its sale was postponed for six weeks until Tuesday September 14. The fourth lot was 52 Main Street and it was 200 feet in length and went back to Hudson Street. Getty was able to obtain this lot for $386.30. F. A. Coe was able to obtain 65 Main Street, a small lot of 6 feet by 18 feet on the corner of Market Place for $18.02.

Coe also bought Woodworth's lot at 9 Depot Street that had 116 feet on Main Street and 140 on Depot Street for $57.37. Another lot owned by Woodworth on Market Place between Nepperhan and Main Streets containing a dock right was also bought by Coe for $43.21. (E-8/5/58 p.2, c.4 and p.3, c.3,4,5)

Getty and Coe were obviously the big winners. However, the former owners had one year in which to reverse the sale if they paid their assessments and the expenses of the auction. Finally, on September 14, 1858 the last lot of John Copcutt's was sold to William Wilson. (E-9/16/58 p.2, c.2)

The battle over Main Street tax assessments continued through March, 1859. Sniping by Copcutt at the previous Board of Trustees finally gave way to a lengthy speech at the board meeting on March 7 by Getty, that at first defended Copcutt, but then went into a long history of the argument. The following is a transcription of what Getty said as reported by the *Yonkers Examiner* March 10, 1859:

"It was with great regret that he found himself compelled to make any exception, but the truth and proper self-respect required, in closing his existing relations with the Board, now that its work was all finished, and no public interest could suffer from the time he might occupy, that he should briefly set right certain untrue allegations which had been made, and unjust imputations which had been thrown upon his own conduct and character. The duty to do this was much more urgent, from the fact that these allegations and imputations were now constantly receiving currency in the community, and had been made use of to his disadvantage, in recent events.

In April last, only about a month after Mr. Copcutt had taken his seat as a member of the Board, he made a carefully prepared speech, which was afterwards, at least with his acquiescence, published in the village, and this speech he must characterize as one of the most extraordinary in its indiscriminate attacks upon unoffending citizens that he had ever heard. It was more injurious if possible from its insidious suggestions and implications, than from its open assertions, both insinuations and assertions being utterly untrue. It introduced an unjust attack upon Mr. S. D. Rockwell, a private citizen, whose name had been suggested as Assessor, and whom Mr. Copcutt characterized as having been active in the opening of Main Street, and hence unworthy of public confidence. This was followed by an insinuation that the Town Assessor had been guilty of omitting the names of relatives or others, and had unjustly favored certain parties in the preparation of the Assessment Roll. Mr. Getty said that as long as he had lived in Yonkers, this was the first time he had ever heard a word breathed against the integrity of Col. Denslow, and it was well known that the imputation was untrue.

In the matter of opening and grading of Main Street, Mr. Copcutt had involved in his accusations the whole Board. And it was remarkable that whatever may have been the character of those proceedings, Mr. Copcutt should have been blamed for them, not the actual individuals who instituted and almost perfected them, for these he ranks among his friends, but only the present Board which had simply nothing to do in the premises but to carry forward proceedings instituted before they came into power, and which they were unable to arrest or discontinue. Mr. Getty did not wish to be understood as himself throwing any blame on the actions of the previous Board; he only wanted to show that they were alone responsible for what was done in opening and grading Main Street. While Mr. Radford was President, and Mr. Van Pelt, Mr. Farrington, Mr. Hobbs, and Mr. Merchant were Trustees, the whole character of the proceedings was fixed. The petition for opening Main

Street, was presented and referred to the Committee on Streets, on March 31, 1856. On May 5th, Mr. Van Pelt moved a resolution to inquire if one third of the property owners had petitioned, and recommended that the assessments be confined to the property fronting on the street, which was accordingly done, and the pendency of the question was advertised. On July 5th, the time advertised for the decision of the question, no opposition being made before the Board, the prayer of the petition was granted, and the street ordered to be opened, and application directed to be made to the Court for the appointment of Commissioners. On September first, it was officially announced to the Board that the Commissioners had been appointed, and they proceeded to discharge their duties by laying the assessment for the opening of the street, and it was not until the first of October that a remonstrance against the proceedings was received from Mr. Copcutt. But it was now too late to recede. The Trustees had now no power to undo what had been done, even if they wished to. The street was legally laid out, other parties had interests in it, and to this effect the Committee on Streets, to whom the remonstration was referred, made their report on the 10th of November, and on the same day the assessment roll was received from the Commissioners, accepted by the Board, and ordered to be sent to the Court for confirmation, and on the 24th of the same month, it was confirmed. Measures were immediately taken to proceed with the grading. On the first of December, notice was ordered to be given to parties to remove their buildings in the way of the street, and on the 16th of December, the Committee recommended a grade, which was adopted by the Board. On the same day a remonstrance, again too late to be of any service, was presented by Mr. Copcutt, and referred to the Committee on Streets, and on the 15th of January, 1857, a resolution offered by Mr. Radford, was passed, instructing the Committee on Streets to report plans and specifications for the grading. On the 18th of February, a resolution offered by Mr. Van Pelt, was passed, to compel the removal of all buildings within the street, before the first of May following. This was the last action taken by the Board as then constituted. When the new Board, consisting of Judge Woodworth, President, and Messrs. Van Pelt, Merchant, Hobbs, who held over, and Messrs. Getty, Flagg, and Devoe, new members, came into power in March, the street was already a fixed fact, the grade was established, the plans and specifications for the work had been ordered, and it only remained for them to fix the limits of the assessment district and have the work done. The assessment district was fixed by the new Board to include a large territory, and after due advertisement, the work was awarded on the 25th of May, to Jacob Read, at $5,991. The filling was to be made to a high grade, fixed by the previous Board, and which this Board had no power to alter, except on petition. On June 15th, another petition was received from Mr. Copcutt, and Mr. Getty, then in the Board, offered a resolution which was passed, directing the President to notify property owners interested, to meet with the Trustees, and from this ultimately resulted in the movement which led to a change in the grade, by which Mr. Copcutt's interests were greatly promoted, and a saving of more than $1,300 effected in the cost of the work.

Certainly the simple narrative of the facts must show that if Mr. Copcutt had any cause to complain of any one, it was not of the last Board of Trustees, as compared with the former one. And yet he alleges that some of us, said Mr. Getty, have been engaged in this matter in endeavoring to put money into our own pockets. He complains of the assessment for opening Main Street, that it was unjust to him, oppressive and iniquitous. Mr. Getty said he was not called upon to defend the actions of those commissioners, nor of the Board by which they were appointed for he had no control over either. But the assessments and awards would bear examination. There were two principal items which went to make up the Commissioners' report, one was the awards for land taken, the other was the assessments necessary to raise the sum to pay them. Now in making the award for land taken, commissioners must regulate their award by the actual value of that land, and the injury done to it, or to the buildings on it. If a road should be laid out through Mr. Copcutt's house, and so up the Saw Mill River valley, it would be necessary and just to allow a very much higher rate of compensation for the amount of land taken where it passes through the house and destroys it, than for another piece of land laying more remote, and with no buildings on it. The commissioners must estimate the fair value of land, and the injury done to what remains. Mr. Getty said that the lot of which one half was taken from him, on the corner of Broadway and Main Street, cost him in the open market $7,250, nor was it dear at the money, and the opening of the street destroyed a building, which could not have been built for less than $3,000. For the destruction of this building, and taking half of the lot which had cost him $7,250, and leaving a strip ten feet wide, and a hundred feet long, the commissioners allowed him only $3,500, and no man could truly say that they allowed him too much. For the land which was taken in the lower part of the street, they allowed what they thought under the circumstances it was really worth. For the land taken from Mr. Flagg adjoining that of Mr. Copcutt, they allowed at the rate of $750 per lot, for that taken from Mr. Copcutt, they also allowed the same rate of $750 per lot, and as they took near a lot and three fourths, awarded him $1,100, while for the adjoining land of Messrs. Rich, Scrymser, and Woodworth, they allowed $450 per lot. Mr. Getty thought Mr. Copcutt could make no complaint of the rate of his award as compared with that of his neighbors. He then proceeded to speak of the assessments. It was the land, he said, which was assessed, and not the man, and if any person owned a good deal of land, he must pay a large assessment. It appears that the assessment was laid at a certain rate per foot on the frontage of each portion. Taking the south side of the street from Broadway, it will be found that along the fronts of Mr. Getty, of Mr. Rockwell, or Mr. MacFarlane, and of Mr. Flagg, and down to Mr. Copcutt's land, the rate was uniformly four dollars per foot of front. But immediately on reaching Mr. Copcutt's land the rate falls to $2 per foot, this abatement was perhaps owing to the shallow depth of a portion of this land, but at any rate that was the fact, and immediately after passing Mr. Copcutt, the land of Rich & Co. is assessed at the rate of $3 per foot, while the next lot of Mr. Copcutt is again reduced to $2.75 per foot, while his opposite front on the dock is rated at a dollar and a half per foot, and the land of Rich & Co. beyond, is assessed at one dollar per foot. It can not, therefore, be alleged that Mr. Copcutt pays at a higher rate than his neighbors, and if his assessments are large it is because he has a large frontage, and having a very long frontage on which to pay assessments, and but a small portion of land taken for which he can receive an award, it must follow that the balance of assessment for him to pay is large. And yet he now not only refuses to pay his assessment, but indulges in the most unjust imputations, and unfounded and calumnious accusations against his neighbors.

Mr. Getty then went on to speak of the accusations which had been made against him by Mr. Copcutt, in reference to the first opening of Main Street by private agreement, previously to the incorporation of the village.

Mr. Copcutt said much of what he had himself contributed towards this first opening of the street, claiming that he had given the land for the whole width of the road for five hundred feet in length, besides giving $400 in money, and that in this he had been more liberal than his neighbors. Mr. Getty quoted the documents before him to show that while the whole length of the road through Mr. Copcutt's land was 480 feet, about 120 feet of it was already used as a road to the mill, so that he in reality only contributed 360 feet, and although he actually did give his note for $400, which, after having been once at his request renewed, he had paid, yet he had required us special concessions to himself, that Messrs. Rich, Scrymser, and Woodworth should relinquish to him their dock right to a front of 128 feet, and should open a road over their ground 1,045 feet in length, and that the parties should unite in relinquishing to him the exclusive use of a strip of land 10 feet in width along the side of the road built at the general expense. Mr. Getty thought therefore that whatever Mr. Copcutt may have contributed, whether in land or money, had been returned to him at the rate of more than two dollars for one.

Mr. Getty then proceeded to say that Mr. Copcutt had also charged that he had failed to carry out his agreements in the matter, and had specifically asserted that Mr. Getty had agreed that the wall along the creek on the north side of Main Street, should be built as low as the wall on the opposite side by the crane, and should be eight feet high. Mr. Getty denied this, and in proof he produced the original proposition in Mr. Copcutt's own handwriting, and signed by him, in which there was no allusion or reference made to the wall on the opposite side of the crane, or to making the wall eight feet high. Mr. Copcutt here asked to see the paper, which Mr. Getty handed to him, and Mr. Copcutt recognized his own signature. Mr. Getty went on to say that it was not true that he had ever agreed to do what Mr. Copcutt said that he had agreed to, and that consequently he could not, as Mr. Copcutt had alleged, have pledged his honor that the wall should be made to suit Mr. Copcutt's subsequently expressed wishes, but that waiving the question, whether the wall was as low as the specifications required, he had told Mr. Copcutt that if he would undertake to excavate the bed of the curb, and make the dock available he was quite willing to pay his portion of the expense of underpinning that small part of the wall which Mr. Copcutt alleged was not low enough, and Mr. Getty did not think the whole cost of it would be twenty five dollars. He could say for himself that he had only paid the money for the work on the certificate of Mr. Cornell, that it had been done in accordance with the specifications, and that if Mr. Copcutt disputed the fact let him produce some other surveyor, and let him examine the specifications and the work, and see if there was any discrepancy, and point out where it was, if it existed. But Mr. Copcutt had no right to set up his word unsupported by any evidence in opposition to everyone else, and Mr. Getty hoped that he would here after pay more regard to the reputation and character of his neighbors. He did not say that Mr. Copcutt was a bad man, or that he was willfully and knowingly doing a grievous wrong, but the fact remained indisputable that he had unjustly accused innocent men of crimes if which committed should banish them from society, and as Mr. Copcutt was in the habit of quoting Scripture, he would close by endeavoring to press upon him the observance of the precept, "'Thou shall not bear false witness against they neighbor.'"

> Mr. Copcutt replied, saying that he was taken unawares by these charges, and that it seemed to him - he would not say that it was so - but it seemed that a trap had been sprung upon him. But he said he would defend himself as well as he could, and he proceeded to reassert that his assessments had been very great, and that he did not think that he ought to pay them, but that if Providence meant that he should pay them, he should have to do so, but he should at least resist them as long as he could. He said that the amount of his assessments on Main Street, were about $2,200. He said that if the specification did not say that the wall should be as low as the wall at the crane, it said that it should be as low as low water, and the wall at the crane was down to low water, and the part of the new wall that was built as he wished it was eight feet high.
>
> He did not intend to impute any intention to do wrong to the Commissioners, but David, and Solomon, and Samson, three of the best men that ever lived, had committed sin, and the Commissioners might have done so too. He thought Mr. Bell had sinned through ignorance, and he was always ready to make allowance for the sin of ignorance."

The unrelenting Copcutt was not a man to let things sit. He hired Reuben W. Van Pelt as an attorney. Van Pelt filed a writ of Certiorari with the State Supreme Court, which was holding a special session in Brooklyn. The writ was addressed to the village President and Board of Trustees. He was trying to get a reversal on Main Street, Market Place, and parts of Nepperhan and Depot Streets based on irregularities. On hearing the arguments of Van Pelt and the village lawyers Coe and Wallis, the Supreme Court denied the writ. (E-7/7/59 p.2, c.3)

Thus after several years of quarreling and name-calling Copcutt lost his battle in the state's highest court in what was later to become a war over Main Street. What remained though must have been bitterness especially on the part of Copcutt.

Opening and working the village and town streets and roads was an important undertaking. During 1859 the contract for grading and opening Grassy Sprain Road was given to a Mr. Elliot of Eastchester at a cost of $2,970. (E-4/28/59 p.2, c.5) In 1860 the first street in Yonkers that was proposed to be macadamized was the Albany Post Road from Kingsbridge to Yonkers. The bill authorizing its construction passed the state legislature, and it authorized the town to raise money through borrowing to pay for its construction. However, the project was left on hold because, by mistake, the grading specifications of the road was left out of the engrossed copy. (E-4/19/60 p.2, c.3)

Sometime during 1859 a path was carved out of the steep almost cliff-like west end of Baldwin Place and steps were added near the bottom leading to North Broadway and the Baptist Church. Woodworth Avenue from Wells Avenue to Locust Street was first laid out in 1853. It was originally named Woodworth Street, but Judge Woodworth did not want the street named after him. Consequently, it was called Woodbine Street after his partner in their liquor business. During 1858 a new street was proposed that was to run continuously from Wells Avenue to Glenwood Avenue parallel and west of Warburton Avenue. The new street was to join Woodbine to Jones Place which extended from Ashburton Avenue to Lamartine Avenue, and Willow Street which extended from Gold Street to Point Street. Then it was proposed to extend the street to Glenwood Avenue which was originally named Railroad Avenue. The reason why there were breaks in what was to become the entire length of Woodworth Avenue was that the properties constituting the breaks were undeveloped. (E-4/21/59 p.2, c.5 and E-1/7/58 p.2, c.5)

Riverdale Avenue was opened in 1853 by Judge Woodworth, Atherton, and Babcock. This important thoroughfare originally ran from about St. Mary's Street to Adams Street. In reality Adams Street was a narrow continuation of Riverdale Avenue, but like Hudson and Prospect Streets it was a private street. However, the *Yonkers Examiner* considered it an important street that should be made 50 feet wide and extended to join Warburton Avenue "thus joining North and South Yonkers, and it will be the best route for our first line of omnibuses." (E-3/5/57 p.2, c.1 and E-5/16/57 p.2, c.1)

Some streets and sections that existed during the 1850s have had their names changed, do not exist, or have been substantially changed since 1860. Oak Hill Avenue ran north from Ashburton Avenue. According to Allison the street started at 139 Ashburton Avenue and ran north to High Street. Allison's map on page 170 shows Oak Hill Avenue as being St. Joseph Avenue. (E-7/26/60 p.2, c.4 and Allison, p.172) Kellinger Street, named after Dr. Kellinger, was on the south end of School Street and ran easterly. If Allison was correct Kellinger Street was the western end of Park Hill Avenue from about Waverly Street to South Broadway. (E-9/20/60 p.3, c.2 and Allison, pp.170,172) Walnut Hills was around the middle of Elm Street, and Vueville was just west of Fleming Park, which didn't exist then, near the top section of Oliver Avenue. (E-2/9/60 p.2, c.2 and E-11/3/59 p.3, c.7) Atherton Street started on the south side of Locust Street and ran south, somewhat parallel, with River Street to Dock Street. (VD, 1858 map.) During 1858 there was an attempt to change the name of Hunts Bridge to the West Mount Vernon Bridge because it was a more descriptive name for railroad passengers. (E-8/25/59 p.2, c.5) Hunt's Bridge Road was one of the main west to east roads for residents of the village. It began on the east side of the Saw Mill River where Walnut Street becomes Saw Mill River Road. It then followed the current Ashburton Avenue to Yonkers Avenue where it then went eastward to Mount Vernon. The current Yonkers Avenue generally follows the old line of Hunts Bridge Road. One exception to this is that the old Hunts Bridge Road crossed over the Bronx River and into Mount Vernon slightly north of the current Yonkers Avenue bridge. Also of interest was the attempt during 1857 to make a spring on Palisade Avenue above the bridge into a fountain like the fountain cared for by Copcutt below the snuff mill on Main Street. (E-5/7/57 p.2, c.1)

Life in Yonkers was an adventure. On good weather days, steep hills required physical effort to climb, and when they were covered with ice and snow they became dangerous. Medicine was enough to make one go into politics where the physical dangers were a little less. However, people were scurrying over the hills going to work, earning a living, or trying to increase their wealth, and they were highly involved in politics. While they were scurrying about, people in Yonkers, like people all over the world, had to take time out to eat.

Grocery stores were numerous and they offered a variety of products. A typical woman living in Yonkers during 1859 had many grocery stores to choose from. If she chose Thompson and Brevoort's "Family Groceries" store in the Radford Building she would find a variety of products. They carried teas, groceries of all kinds, wine, liquor, and general provisions. Some of the specific items they carried were oolong, which is a dark partly fermented tea, young hyson, which is a green tea from China, English breakfast and imperial teas, government java, Maricabo and Laguayra (which is a port city in northern Venezuela) coffees that came powdered, granulated, or crushed, refined and brown sugars, New Orleans, Puerto Rico and English islands molasses, hams and shoulders, extra No. 1 mackerel in barrels, halves, quarters, eighths, or sixteenths, fresh butter daily during the summer, imported wines and liquors, Havana cigars, crockery, glass, stoneware, and woodenware.

They delivered to Yonkers, Glenwood, Hastings, Spuyten Duyvil, Kingsbridge, and Fordham. Their wagons called for orders twice each day and then they delivered the orders. (E-3/10/59 p.3, c.4)

For the male who wanted to do some painting or fix up work he could go to the "Yonkers Paint Store" operated by J. Stevens on Dock Street near Warburton Avenue. There he could find white lead, linseed oil, boiled oil, Neat's Foot Oil, turpentine, varnish, putty, glass, japan, which is a glossy black lacquer, whiting, Paris white, Paris green, chrome green, imperial green, zinc paint, Croton mineral, Ohio mineral, chrome yellow, vermillion, Venetian red, lamp black, litharge, which is a yellowish monoxide of lead used in making glass, glue, yellow ochre used as a pigment, umbers also used as pigments, Prussian blue, Sienna Bt. & R., rottenstone, pumice stone, brushes of all kinds, burning fluid, camphene, alcohol, paper and paper hangings, window shades, cords, tassels, fixtures, fancy window paper, fireboard prints and borders, lettering, graining, marbling, gilding, glazing, and roof paint.

The hardware enthusiast could go to Chadeayne & Brothers hardware store on North Broadway in Radford's building in Getty Square. There he could find builders' and housekeepers' hardware of every variety including table and pocket cutlery, bathing tubs and showers, refrigerators, meat safes, Masser's patent ice cream freezers, Lady Devon sewing chairs, hinged carpet and folding camp chairs, Butler's voider and stand, lanterns, children's hobby horses, ranges, stoves, heaters, Boynton's furnace, cataract washing machines, wood, tin, and willow ware, plumbing equipment 15 cents below New York City prices, beer, wine bottling and key faucets, and tin, copper and sheet iron for roofing. They sold almost everything imaginable, but apparently no dishwashers.

The women who couldn't find what they wanted in Yonkers clothing stores could go to New York City and shop at Lord and Taylor who had three stores. One store was on Broadway, one was on Grand Street, and another one was on Catherine Street. There they could find foreign and domestic silks, dress goods, embroideries, hosiery, linens, cloths, cashmeres, gloves, laces, ribbons, mantillas, dusters, stella shawls, broche shawls, grenadine shawls, carpeting, oil cloths, rugs, matting, stair carpeting, curtain materials, cornices, upholstery goods, lace curtains, and window shades.

When they returned home from the big city, a glass of sarsaparilla made at the Sarsaparilla and Soda Water factory located at the head of Mechanic Street could clear their throats of the dust from the streets. The factory was owned by R. W. Nisbett who manufactured sarsaparilla and lemon sodas as well as mineral waters of all kinds. Wagons were sent to homes so people could order and receive deliveries everyday in the village, and twice a week in the country. (E-6/7/60 p.4, c.1,2,7)

Meanwhile a sale might be going on at Vail and Elting's in the Radford Building where a shopper could purchase a common cloak for $1.00, small sized handsome circular cloaks for $2.00 with larger ones costing from $2.50 to $5.00, raglans from $4.50 to $5.00, and heavy and warm blanket shawls from $3.50 to $4.50. They also had on sale crib and bed blankets, superb cashmeres and satinets with handsome French and Scotch embroidery, plain and figured velvet ribbons and dress trimmings, bleached and brown sheetings and shirtings, Irish linens, table damasks, scotch diapers, towelings, Russia crash, De Laines, Merinos, alpacas, bombazines, prints, and ginghams.

Yonkers was an interesting town and village during the 1850s. There were many activities. The sport of choice was cricket, but baseball was making headway. On July 4, 1859 the Mount Vernon regulars played the Mount Vernon Independents, who were from the suburbs, a nine inning game that began at 9:00 in the morning and ended around noon. The regulars beat the Independents 64-26. Yonkers had its first baseball team formed during September, 1859. There were 15 members who practiced on the Glenwood Green. They used the rules of the National Baseball Association. (E-7/14/59 p.2, c.5 and E-9/29/59 p.3, c.1)

Several years before Yonkers had its first baseball team the village trustees were playing a game of their own. The game was change the names of streets and see how the people can get angry. On May 25, 1857 Main Street, Mechanic Street and Guion Street from Mechanic Street to Ashburton Avenue all became Nepperhan Avenue. The resolution was introduced at the board of trustees meeting by Rueben Van Pelt. The vote affirming the measure was a three to two vote with Getty, Devoe, and Van Pelt voting in favor of it. Flagg and Hobbs voted against it. The *Yonkers Examiner* explained to its readers that the board was "in a facetious mood" and that it was a "joke" when it adopted the resolution. The paper continued to agitate for the resolution to be rescinded since "it was first opened as a lane to lead to the mills now occupied by the Nepperhan Dye mills, but which were built by a gentleman bearing the name Guion," and the paper was "in favor of retaining the old landmarks when possible." At the very next meeting Devoe moved that the measure be reconsidered since so many people were against it. The motion to reconsider was adopted and laid on the table. Eventually the resolution was rescinded. However, that part of Guion Street from Mechanic Street to Ashburton Avenue, and northward, remained Nepperhan Avenue. (E-5/28/57 p.2, c.4 & 6/4/57 p.2, c.5)

Not only did people who lived in Yonkers enjoy the activities, but also outsiders joined in extolling the virtues of Yonkers. In the April 16, 1857 edition of the *Yonkers Examiner* in a copied article from *Life Illustrated* entitled "Thirty Miles Around New York" the village of Yonkers was described as a "noble village, about seventeen miles out of New York, inhabited, like the villages of the New Haven road, in a great measure by New Yorkers. Here is style, and wealth, and expensive living; but they have good air, a first rate society, and all the fascination and fashion of the metropolis." Another article published May 14, 1857 which was taken from the *Missouri Republican* stated that "If you wish to live in a truly civilized and Christian manner, you will go to Yonkers, get a room that looks out on the Hudson, and swear eternal fealty to Nature. The town is famous for fine views, fresh air, matutinal (morning) cocktails, tea parties, bad puns, country gossip, city fashions, and pretty girls. The last commodity is so abundant as to be monotonous. An ugly woman would, by way of variety, be a positive relief." The swallows that skimmed along the Nepperhan River, where boys threw rocks at them, added even more beauty to Yonkers. (E-5/21/57 p.2, c.3)

However, growth, beauty and a national panic brought with them problems. Growth brought with it environmental problems that threatened many of the beautiful trees. Protests were being made that oak, chestnut and elm trees were being taken down unnecessarily to widen and straighten Warburton Avenue and Broadway. By July 6, 1857 the protest reached the village Board of Trustees where a protest letter was referred to the Committee on Streets. However, it wasn't until September 5, 1859 when a shade tree planting resolution came before the Board. To the chagrin of many the resolution was tabled on October 24, 1859. Trees were also endangered by people who hitched their horses to them. The horses ate the leaves, and bent over and broke the smaller trees.

Factories added there own special problems. On September 10, 1857 the village board of trustees passed a resolution ordering George Russell to either raise the smoke stack on his factory or adopt "some effectual method of carrying off the smoke."

Another problem caused by growth involved the increasing number of low-paid working people who came to Yonkers and who couldn't afford housing with baths in them. They became a public nuisance when they took baths naked in the Hudson River during daylight hours. Several resolutions were passed by the Board of Trustees regulating this activity.

The beauty and relative openness of Yonkers brought picnickers from New York City who enjoyed Fairy Grove, the clean air and the natural beauty of the area. However, they were frequently drunken brawling groups who entered the homes of Yonkers residents destroying and stealing what they could. Several attempts by the Board of Trustees to regulate the problem were adopted, but the problem persisted through the summer of 1859.

The Panic of 1857 caused the crime rate to soar. On Tuesday night September 21, 1858 at least seven homes were broken into. This series of burglaries led to the establishment of a night watch which was voted down by the village residents on Thursday, October 28, 1858 because they considered it too expensive. The village was also plagued by arsonists. The situation was so severe that on June 11, 1859 a $1,000 reward was authorized by the village board of trustees.

One of the most pervasive problems that confronted Yonkers residents was the ongoing problem of cattle, sheep, hogs, and geese wandering the streets untended. The animals entered yards, ate grass lawns, and destroyed plants and shrubs. They also left messy droppings that were smelly, unsightly and unhealthy. The problem was not an easy one to solve because the cattlemen, sheep herders, and hog owners were a rather powerful special interest group. These men drove their animals from barns through the streets of Yonkers to pastures and back again on a daily basis. Frequently, animals would break away from the drive and wreak havoc on property. Nevertheless, it was useful to have the animals in the streets because they ate the grass on the streets thereby keeping the grass under control. Also, in the case of milk cows, the grass in the streets was an additional food source for them. As was recognized by some of the members of the Village Board of Trustees this was an important source of milk for the children. Both the town and village governments wrestled with the problem for years. It was also a problem recognized by the state legislature which finally banned animals from the streets of Westchester county.

Growth also brought with it pressures for organized municipal services. With industry, merchants, and a large number of people living in a relatively small amount of space, health hazards, and the hazards of fires became serious concerns. Once the village government was established in 1855 a vehicle was developed that allowed for a more immediate response to alleviate some of the concerns.

In the area of health the charter allowed the board of trustees to organize themselves into a village board of health. The first documented meeting of the board of health was held on the evening of May 25, 1857 when the board divided the village into three health districts. Henry F. Devoe and Charles Merchant were assigned the north district which started on the northerly side of Ashburton Avenue and then went north to the village line. Reuben Van Pelt and Ethan Flagg were assigned the middle district which started on the southerly side of Ashburton Avenue and then went south to the north side of Main Street and then along Main Street to the north side of Mechanic Street and then east to the village line. The southern district was assigned to Robert P. Getty and Bailey Hobbs which started on the south side of Main Street and then along Main Street to the south side of Mechanic Street east to the village line and south to the village line.

Despite the glowing accounts of *Life Illustrated* and the *Missouri Republican*, there was another side to the village of Yonkers. With so many people crammed into a relatively small area, problems with garbage and other nuisances had to be addressed. Without proper means for the removal of garbage people all too frequently just threw bad meat, fish entrails, oysters and clam shells, and decaying vegetables into the streets and waters of the village. Other problems included dung from animals in the streets and dead animals left in the streets and sometimes in the waters of the village. Unregulated slaughterhouses frequently handled and disposed of fat and bad meat in dangerously unsanitary ways. The village board of health reacted to these problems with ordinances and regulations. On September 28, 1857 Bailey Hobbs reported that he had sent a letter to the owner of the hide and fat factory instructing him to move the factory from the village. In 1858 it became against the law to throw garbage or leave dung in the streets and slaughterhouses were regulated.

As serious as sanitation was to the health of the village, fire prevention and fires were just as serious. During the 1850s most light designed to hide the darkness of the night was either by candle or oil burning lanterns. Heat came from fire places, hearths, wood or coal burning stoves and ovens, and boilers. These heating devices posed a potentially serious problem to life and property in the village if they were not built or maintained properly. The new charter gave power to the board of trustees to inspect all fireplaces, chimneys and stoves, and if they were found unsafe they had the power to have them removed if not repaired.

The unsafe use of candles and oil burning lanterns were just as pernicious as a poorly built or maintained chimney. Fires caused by heating and lighting devices were an all too commonplace occurrence. Hence the village charter provided for a government run and regulated fire department. Prior to the establishment of the village fire department, and by 1853, businessmen such as Getty and Gant privately bought fire engines to protect their own businesses. A little later businessmen got together and bought a fire engine with stock investments in it. During October, 1855, under the new village charter, a vote was taken to fund $3,000 for the establishment of a fire department. The vote was rather close with 46 voting in favor and 30 against. Then in 1856 fire limits were designated. (Allison, pp. 165-6) However, the minutes of the village board of trustees indicate that the first attempt by the village to buy a fire engine wasn't until February 2, 1857. The village charter mandated a fire department, but it was an all volunteer department. To help man the new fire department the charter developed some plums for volunteers. The volunteers were exempt from serving jury duty and serving in the state militia except "in case of war, invasion or insurrection," and if a volunteer served for five years he was exempt forever from such services except under the same circumstances previously noted. Thus by 1857 a well-organized volunteer fire department had been established.

However, there were still serious problems. If a fire broke out further than hose lines could reach from the Nepperhan, water to extinguish the fire was hard to come by. Eventually, an attempt was made to strategically locate cisterns to alleviate this problem. Another problem was that fire trucks were hauled to a fire by the firemen, and all too frequently there wasn't enough men to pull them, or as was the case with one truck it was too heavy.

Even with these problems, the positive aspects of Yonkers were overwhelming. Town and village leaders saw only more growth and prosperity as they looked into the future. New industries were about to move into Yonkers, and older industries stood on the verge of rapid expansion. The people of Yonkers had many of the advantages of city life, but they also had all the advantages of a more quaint way of life. However, that quaint way of life was being eroded away as Yonkers began to move through the last full decade of not being a city in its own right.

Chapter 3

The Village Charter

Securing the first village charter was one political battle after another. Contrary to popular opinion the original village charter passed the state legislature on July 21, 1853. On Tuesday, August 2, 1853 the first village charter election was scheduled by the state legislature. However, the charter stipulated that a yes/no popular vote on the charter had to be held in order for the charter to be officially declared enforced, and that the notice of the election must be published and posted three weeks in advance. Consequently, the earliest possible date for a yes/no vote on the charter was Friday, August 11, 1853. More than likely the vote on the charter occurred on a Tuesday and it probably was held on August 16, 1853. If the charter of incorporation is taken literally, that meant there was an election for village officers prior to the incorporation vote. At this point in time there is no evidence that such an election was held.

The following is a transcription of the original village charter taken from the *Laws of New York*, Seventy-sixth Session pages 1178 to 1201.

Chapter 621.

AN ACT to incorporate the village of Yonkers.
Passed July 21, 1853, three-fifths being present.

The People of the State of New York, represented by the Senate and Assembly, do enact as follows:

1. Boundaries: All that part of the township of Yonkers, in the county of Westchester, contained within the following limits, to wit: Beginning at the Hudson River at the low water mark, at the southwesterly corner of the farm of Edward F. Shonnard, and running thence along the southerly line of said Shonnard's land, south sixty-three degrees east, five thousand one hundred feet, to the easterly margin of the Nepperhan River; thence southerly along the easterly margin of said Nepperhan River, five thousand one hundred feet, to the line between lands of Rev. R. Hubbard and lands of L. W. Wells, Ethan Flagg and W. W. Scrugham; thence along said line between lands of Rev. R. Hubbard and land of Wells, Flagg and Scrugham,

south fifty-three degrees and thirty minutes east, three hundred feet, to the easterly side of Walnut Street; thence following the easterly side of Walnut Street, and a continuation thereof, in the same direction, south thirty-two degrees west, five thousand two hundred feet, to the line between lands of Robert P. Getty and lands of Thomas W. Ludlow; thence following said line, between Getty's and Ludlow's land, through lands now or late of S. T. Williams, north seventy-six degrees and fifteen minutes west, to the westerly line of the old Albany Post Road, now called Broadway; thence through land of Thomas W. Ludlow, north seventy-six degrees fifteen minutes west, three thousand one hundred and fifty feet, to the Hudson River, at low water mark; thence northerly along the Hudson River, at low water mark, to the place of beginning, shall be hereafter known and distinguished as "The village of Yonkers," and the inhabitants residing within the bounds aforesaid shall hereafter be a body corporate and politic by the [type] and style of "The president and trustees of the village of Yonkers," by which name they and their successors may sue and be sued, complain and defend, answer and be answered unto in all courts and places whatsoever, and all manner of actions, causes and complaints whatsoever; adopt and use a common seal, and alter it at future; and take, hold, purchase, sell, assign and convey any personal or real estate, as the purposes of the corporation may require.

TITLE II
OF OFFICERS AND ELECTIONS

1. The officers of said village shall consist of a president and five trustees, one clerk, and treasurer, one collector, one street commissioner, and such other officers are hereinafter authorized to be appointed, all of whom shall be inhabitants of said corporate limits, and qualified to vote under this act.

2. An election shall be held in said village on the first Tuesday in August, 1853, for the election of the aforesaid officers, at such place and time of day as the inspectors hereinafter named shall designate, and of which such inspectors shall give at least six days notice by posting written or printed notices of the same in ten different public places in said village, or by publishing the same in the village newspaper, or both.

3. Robert P. Getty, William W. Woodworth and Thomas C. Cornell shall be the inspectors of the first election to be held under this act, on the first Tuesday in August, 1853. Such election shall be held and conducted, and the votes given thereat canvassed by the said inspectors, and the result declared in the manner prescribed in this act for other elections, as far as the same is practicable. In case any of the above named persons shall be unable or refuse to serve as

such inspector, then the remaining persons so named are hereby empowered and required to fill the vacancy occasioned by such inability or refusal to serve at such election.

4. Every person who shall have been a resident of said village for thirty days next preceding any election under this act, possessing the qualifications prescribed by the constitution to authorize him to vote for elective officers, may vote at any election held in pursuance of this act; but no person shall vote upon any proposition to raise a tax, or appropriate the same, at any meeting of election, unless he shall, at the time, be liable to be assessed for such tax.

5. An election shall be held on the first Tuesday in March, 1854, and on the same day in each and every year thereafter, for the election of the elective officers named in the first section of this title; and the trustees of said village, or any three of them, for the time being, shall be the inspectors of said elections, and shall give notice thereof, in the manner prescribed in section two of this title for the first election under this act. They shall declare the persons receiving the greatest number of votes duly elected to the respective offices to which they were chosen, and give a certificate of such result, signed by them, to the clerk of the corporation, who shall file said certificate, and record the same in the book containing the proceedings of the board of trustees, which record shall be sufficient evidence of such result.

6. The term of office of the officers to be elected, in pursuance of the last aforesaid section, shall expire in one year from the Tuesday next succeeding their election.

7. All laws relating to general elections for state officers, as far as the same shall be applicable, shall be deemed to apply to all elections authorized by this act; and the inspectors of all elections, under this act, shall have the same power and authority in all respects, as [far] as may be, as inspectors of elections in towns possess.

8. The treasurer, street commissioner, police constable and collector shall, severally, before they enter into the duties of their respective offices, execute a bond to the president and trustees of the village of Yonkers, their successors and assigns, in such sums, and with such sureties, as the board of trustees shall approve, conditioned that they shall faithfully execute the duties of their respective offices, and account for and pay all monies received by them respectively; which bond, with the approval of the board of trustees thereon certified by the clerk, shall be filed with the clerk of the village.

9. Every person who shall have been duly elected to any office in said village, in pursuance of this act, shall accept such office (in writing, to be filed with said clerk) within five days after personal notice in writing from the clerk of his election shall have been served upon him.

10. If any person, having been an officer in said village, shall not, within ten days after notification and request, deliver to his successor in office of all the books, papers, property, and effects of every kind in his possession belonging to said village, or appertaining to his office, he shall forfeit and pay, for the use of said village, [fifty] dollars, beside all damages caused by his neglect or refusal so to deliver.

11. The president shall be the executive officer of the village, and shall have power to call special meetings of the trustees when he shall think proper, or when requested so to do by any two of the trustees; shall preside at all meetings of said trustees; to give a casting vote on any question which the votes of the trustees are equally divided; to sign, as such president, all bylaws, rules, regulations, ordinances, orders, licenses, [?????], appointments, deeds, covenants and contracts made by the trustees in behalf of the said corporation, in all cases where, in his judgment, such instruments are not inconsistent with the provisions of this act; to see that all by-laws, rules, orders, regulations and ordinances, lawfully made by the trustees, are carried into effect and duly executed; to give the proper notice of every annual or special meeting of the inhabitants of said village held under the authority and for the objects specified in this act; to preside at all such meetings when convened; to collect all fines, penalties and forfeitures incurred under this act, or any by-law, rule, order, regulation or decision made in pursuance thereof; to commence and prosecute all such suits, in the name of the corporation, as shall be ordered or directed by the trustees; to pay all monies which shall come into his hands for the use of the corporation to the treasurer thereof, and take his receipt therefor; to sign and direct the payment of all accounts and demands against the said corporation that have been audited and allowed by the trustees, and all other legal drafts and demands upon the treasury of the said village; and to do all other such acts and things as may appertain or belong to the duties of such presiding officer, or which the said trustees may legally require him to do.

12. The clerk shall attend and act as clerk at all meetings and elections of the inhabitants and trustees and record their proceedings; keep all books and papers, and the seal of the corporation, and deliver the same to his successor on demand; and copies of all papers duly kept in his office, and transcripts from the records of the proceedings of the board of trustees, certified by him with the corporate seal, shall be evidence in all courts in all manner as if the original were produced; and for certifying the same he shall be entitled to receive six [????] folio from the person requiring the same.

The books and papers under his custody and control shall always be produced for inspection to any person who may be interested; he shall attend to the publication of all by-laws, ordinances, and notices which the trustees shall direct; notify all persons of their election or appointment to office under this act; and perform faithfully, such other duties as the trustees may, from time to time, lawfully direct or ordain. And the said trustees may allow to him such sum for his services as they deem proper; but the president and trustees shall receive no salary or compensation for their services under this act.

13. The clerk shall keep a poll list of the names of all persons voting at any election of officers of said corporation; and in case of his absence from any meeting of the inhabitants, such person shall be chosen or appointed therefor, by the trustees, shall, on such occasions, perform the duties appertaining to such clerk.

14. The treasurer shall receive all monies directed to be paid into the treasury of said corporation, and pay out the same, and shall render an account of the state of the finances to the trustees, whenever ordered by them, and shall deliver all monies, books, papers and property of the corporation, in his hands, to his successor in office, on demand. No money shall be paid by the treasurer for any purpose, unless directed and appropriated by a unanimous vote of the trustees, with a check of the clerk, countersigned by the president of the said village for the [???] being; and the treasurer in his settlement with the trustees shall be allowed for no monies, except such as to be paid out as above; and shall receive for his compensation one percent on all monies paid out by him to his successor in office, which compensation shall be ordered paid by said trustees, on inspection of his accounts, if the same is found correct.

It shall be the duty of the treasurer, in each and every year during the period in which he shall hold such office, to make a statement of his accounts, including all monies received by him, and the manner in which he has tendered or disbursed the same, which statement shall be verified by his oath, and published in the newspapers and posted in said village one week preceding each annual election.

15. All officers authorized to be appointed by the trustees under this act shall perform such duties as may be required of them, respectively, by the by-laws, rules, resolutions, orders, regulations and ordinances of the corporation.

16. It shall be the duty of the street commissioner, under the direction of the president and trustees, to superintend all the works, labor and improvements done [???] bestowed upon any of the streets, roads, lanes, [avenues], bridges, docks or sidewalks; to secure the materials for the same, employ the laborers, and to do and perform such other service as may be prescribed by this act or by the said trustees.

17. Vacancies in the office of president or trustees occasioned in any manner, may be filled at a special election, called and appointed by the trustees in office for the time being, and conducted in the same manner as an annual election. Vacancies in all other offices

shall be filled by appointment by the board of trustees. All appointments by the board of trustees under this act shall be by warrant, under the corporate seal, signed by the president or presiding officer of the board of trustees and the clerk. In case of a failure to elect a president or trustees at an annual election, or if from any cause there shall be no president or trustees, the clerk shall appoint the time and place for holding a special election in the usual manner, and appoint the inspectors of said elections. And in case there shall be no president, trustees, or clerk, any six inhabitants qualified to vote under this act shall appoint an election and inspectors thereof in the usual manner.

18. All officers, elected or appointed under this act shall, before entering upon the duties of their respective offices, take and subscribe the oath or affirmation of office prescribed by the constitution of this state. Such oath or affirmation may be taken before any person authorized to administer oaths, and shall be filed with the clerk of the village.

TITLE III
OF THE TRUSTEES-THEIR POWERS AND DUTIES

1. The trustees shall have the management and control of the finances, and of all the property, both real and personal, belonging to the corporation; and shall have power and authority, within said village, to make, establish, publish, alter, modify, amend and repeal rules, resolutions, regulations, ordinances, and by-laws for the following purposes, viz:

1st. To preserve peace and good order; to quell and prevent any noise, disturbances, riots and disorderly assemblages or meetings; to restrain and suppress disorderly houses, gaming houses, and instruments and [???]ces for the purposes of gaming.

2nd. To regulate auction sales.

3rd. To prohibit or regulate the rolling of hoops, playing at ball, flying of kites, sliding down hill on sleds, or any other amusements or practices having a tendency to annoy, or in any way injure or endanger persons passing on the street or sidewalks, or to frighten or interfere with teams, or horses, in said village, and to regulate or prevent the firing of guns, pistols, firearms, and the use, [???] of crackers, rockets, squibs and fireworks, or [???], in said village.

4th. To regulate or determine the time and place of bathing in any of the waters within the corporate bounds of said village or adjacent thereto, and to prevent the same.

5th. To restrain the running at large of cattle, horses, [???], mules, swine, sheep, goats, geese, and to authorize the distraining, impounding, and sale of the same, for any penalty incurred, and costs of proceedings, and to appoint one or two persons to drive any of the aforesaid animals, running at large, to the pound, and to determine their fees and duties; to establish and regulate public pounds; to appoint pound keepers, and to prevent the running at large of dogs owned or harbored by persons residing in said village, and tax the same.

6th. To prevent horse racing or immoderate riding or [???] within the limits of said village.

7th. To prevent and remove all encumbrances, obstructions and encroachments, from any cause whatever, in the public streets, alleys, docks, bridges, public areas or grounds, sidewalks or crosswalks of said village, and to cause the same to be removed, and the streets to be cleaned and unobstructed, and to prevent [riding], driving or leading horses, teams or cattle, with or without wagons, sleighs or carriages, or dumping or leaving any articles on any sidewalk or street in said village.

8th. To compel all persons to keep clean, and remove from the sidewalks, in front of the premises owned or occupied by them, all snow, ice and dirt.

9th. To compel the owner or occupant of any grocery, [????], tallow chandler shop, soap factory, tannery, stall, privy, sewer, slaughter house, skin factory, or other unwholesome house or place, to cleanse, remove, abate or discontinue the same whenever the same may be necessary for the health, comfort or convenience of the inhabitants of said village.

10th. To remove, destroy, prevent or abate nuisances; to regulate slaughter houses, to direct or prevent the use or location of the same, and to abate nuisances generally.

11th. To regulate the keeping and conveying of gunpowder and other combustible and dangerous materials.

12th. To regulate the ringing of bells, to erect [???] scales in said village, and to appoint weighers, measurers, and an examiner of weights and measures in said village.

13th. To sanction or prohibit, in their discretion, all exhibitions of any natural or artificial curiosities, caravans of animals, circuses, theatrical and other shows or exhibitions, or performances for money, within the bounds of said corporation. The said trustees, or a majority of them, may license any such exhibition or performance, on paying for the benefit of said corporation of not less than five or more than twenty dollars, in all cases where the amount is not specified by a vote of the board of trustees; but nothing in this section shall be construed to prevent the delivery of literary, historical or scientific lectures in said village, the use and exhibition of apparatus illustrating the same, and the receiving of money for the delivery of such lectures.

14th. To construct and regulate reservoirs, hydrants, water pipes, public pumps and wells, and to prevent the unnecessary use or waste of water of the same.

15th. To grade, pitch, level and repair, construct, make, amend or re-lay (or cause the same to be done) any street, lane, alley, road or highway, sidewalk, crosswalk, bridges, docks, sewers or aqueducts, either with plank, stone, brick, dirt or gravel, as said trustees may determine, and to provide for the planting or setting [???] protecting or removal, ornamental or shade trees in any public square, ground or street in said village.

16th. To survey the boundaries and streets of said village, establish the same, and make a map thereof.

17th. To enter and authorize others to enter in the day time, when it shall be necessary so to do, into any building in the said village, in which shall be a fireplace, chimney, stove or stovepipe, for the purpose of examining the condition of the same, and to make such regulations in regard thereto as a proper security against fires shall in their judgment require.

18th. To exercise all other powers conferred on them by this act, for any purpose whatever (to act as a board of health).

2. The trustees shall appoint a competent and suitable person to officiate as police constable, who shall hold his office during the pleasure of said trustees. It shall be the duty of said police constable to serve all papers of processes for or on account of the said trustees, or pertaining to the said corporation, to arrest all disorderly persons, or disturbers of the public peace; to see that the rules, regulations and by-laws of the said trustees, in relation to the police and the regulation of the officers of said corporation, are duly observed and enforced; to attend at fires and all unusual assemblages, to preserve order and to protect property; to use his utmost endeavors at all times to prevent or quell all riots, and [???] and every unlawful proceeding; and to do and perform all such other acts and duties, consistent with his office, which the president or trustees may direct, for such said service he shall receive such compensation as the said trustees may allow.

And the said police constable is hereby authorized and empowered to serve processes issuing from courts of justice and to perform the other duties pertaining to the office of a constable in the county of Westchester, the same as other constables elected by the people in the respective towns may do, and with like effect, and for such he shall receive the same fees allowed by law to [others] for similar services.

3. The trustees shall hold a meeting of their board for the transaction of public business on the first Monday of every month, at which the president of the village shall preside. In the absence of the president, they shall appoint one of their number to perform his duties; and in the absence of the clerk from any such meeting, [may] appoint any person to perform his duties for the time being. A majority of the trustees shall constitute a quorum for the transaction of business.

4. The trustees of said village may make, publish, ordain, amend and repeal all such ordinances, by-laws, and public regulations, not contrary to the laws of the state, as may be necessary to carry into effect the [powers] given to said trustees by this act, and enforce observance of all rules, regulations, resolutions, ordinances and by-laws made in pursuance of this act, by imposing penalties on any person or persons or corporations violating the same, not exceeding in any one case of violation [fifty] dollars, to be recovered with costs, in a civil action in any court having cognizance thereof. Every such ordinance or by-law, imposing any penalty or forfeiture for a violation of its provisions, shall, after the passage thereof be subscribed by the president and clerk, and published two weeks successively in the newspaper printed in such village; and proof of such publication, by the affidavit of the printer or publisher of said newspaper, taken before the president of said village, or any officer authorized to administer oaths, and filed with the clerk of the village, or any other competent proof of such publication, shall be evidence of the legal publication of such ordinances or by-law in all courts and places.

5. The trustees shall have power, from time to time, to prescribe the duties of the street commissioner, and all officers and persons appointed by them under this act, subject to the provisions of the same, and may remove all such persons, so appointed, at any time.

TITLE IV
OF THE ASSESSMENT, LEVYING AND COLLECTION OF TAXES

1. The trustees are authorized and empowered to raise money, by tax, to be assessed upon the estate, real and personal, within the bounds of the said corporation, and to be collected from the several owners and occupants thereof, for the purchase of any real or personal property for the use of the said village, and to defray the ordinary and contingent expenses of the said corporation; but no such tax shall be levied and collected to an amount exceeding one thousand dollars ($1,000), in any one year, until the same shall have authorized by a vote of a majority of the taxable inhabitants of said village, qualified to vote under this act, present at any annual election meeting, or at any special meeting duly called for that purpose.

2. Whenever any tax shall have been directed to be levied, the trustees shall apportion the same among the taxable inhabitants and corporations of the said village and the non-resident owners of property therein, in conformity, as nearly as practicable, with the provisions of law in respect to the assessment of taxes by town assessors; and when the assessment roll shall have been reviewed and completed, it shall be the duty of the trustees, immediately thereafter, to deliver the same to the village collector, with their warrant, under the hands of a majority of them, to be directed to

said collector, commanding him to levy and collect the amount of such tax in the same manner as warrants issued by the board of supervisors to the collectors of towns, and to make return thereof, and to pay over the money to the treasurer within thirty days after its receipt by the said collector of the village, or sooner if required by the trustees.

3. It shall be lawful for said trustees to issue new warrants, or to renew those which may be issued by them or their predecessors, for the collection of any tax, from time to time, so often as such warrants shall be returned uncollected, in whole or in part, during the time prescribed by law; but the renewal of any such warrant shall in no way affect the liability of the collector or street commissioner, or the sureties upon the bond of such collector or street commissioner.

4. The collector shall proceed to collect the amount of such tax, together with such fees or compensation for his services as the trustees by a by-law shall have provided, and after deducting his said fees or compensation, he shall pay the residue to the treasurer of the village, within thirty days from the receipt of said warrant by him (who shall give the collector a receipt for the same), and file the treasurer's receipt therefor with the clerk, together with his warrant and the tax list annexed thereto and the money, when collected and paid to the treasurer, shall be applied by the treasurer to the purposes for which such assessment was made, under the direction of the said trustees.

5. Whenever any person or corporation upon whose estate or property shall have been assessed, pursuant to the provisions of this act, any tax or highway work, payable in money, shall neglect or refuse to pay the same, and no personal property can be found whereon the same can be levied, the collector or street commissioner shall make return thereof to the trustees, who are authorized cause the land or estate on which such tax or highway work, payable in money, is assessed, to be sold at public auction for a term of time, for the payment of such tax giving six weeks notice of such sale, by advertisement in any newspaper published in said village, which notice shall contain a brief description of the premises, the amount of tax or highway work payable in money, requiring the owner or owners to pay the same by a day therein specified; and if such tax or highway work payable in money be not paid at the time and place specified in such notice, the real estate so advertised shall be sold under the direction of the trustees, by the collector, street commissioner, or some other person for that purpose appointed by the trustees, to the person who shall offer to take it for the shortest term for the payment of such tax or highway labor payable in money, and the interest thereof, and the expense of such notice and sale; but no such sale shall be made for a term longer than five years. The proceedings shall be discontinued at any time before sale, upon any person paying to the village treasurer the amount of such tax or

assessment, with the interest and printer's bill; and if the premises are sold, one dollar in addition to the interest and printer's bill may be charged for the expenses of such sale; and if the premises are not redeemed within one year from such sale, the trustees shall execute to the person or persons entitled thereto a lease of the premises so sold, under the corporate seal, and signed by the president for the time being, for the term for which the same were sold, to be computed from the expiration of one year from the day of such sale which lease shall be presumptive evidence that such tax or highway work payable in money was legally imposed, and of the regularity of the proceedings and sale, for which the trustees may charge the sum of one dollar, [upon] delivery thereof to the purchaser; and such lessee or lessees, his, her, or their legal representatives or assigns, may, by virtue of such lease, obtain possession of said premises in the manner prescribed by law in relation to persons holding over real estate sold under execution, and shall and may lawfully enjoy such premises during the term specified in such lease, against the owners thereof, and all persons claiming under them, and shall be at liberty, within thirty days of the expiration of said term, to remove all buildings and fixtures put on said premises during said term, in the right of said occupancy; certificates of such sale may be issued under the corporate seal and signed by the president, setting forth the facts and circumstances of said sale, and the time at which such purchaser will be entitled to such lease, and delivered to such purchaser.

6. The person or corporation in possession, as tenants, of any real estate, shall be liable to pay the taxes or highway work, payable in work or money, assessed thereon, and shall have the right to collect the amount of the owner, unless by agreement the occupant is bound to pay the same.

7. Every inhabitant of said village, having in his possession, or under his control, within the bounds of said incorporation, any real or personal property, as trustee, guardian, executor, or administrator, shall be deemed a taxable inhabitant to the amount thereof, within the meaning of this act, except as to the right of voting in any election, and may charge the tax, when paid, against the estate of which he is trustee, guardian, executor, or administrator.

TITLE V
OF HIGHWAYS, WALKS, STREETS, AND PUBLIC IMPROVEMENTS

1. The said village is hereby declared a separate road district, exempt from the superintendence of the commissioners of highways of the town of Yonkers; and the trustees of said village shall be commissioners of highways for the same, and shall possess all the powers given by law to the commissioners of highways. The street

commissioner shall possess all the powers and discharge all the duties, in his district, to and enjoined upon the overseers of the highways, in addition to the powers conferred upon him by this act, and such as shall be prescribed to him by said trustees from time to time, being accountable to the trustees as overseers of highways in towns are to commissioners. The said trustees may assess the highway work to be done by the taxable inhabitants and corporations in said village, in the manner, as far as applicable, prescribed in title four of this act; and may, in their discretion, require all or any portion that they deem proper of the said highway work to be paid in money at the rate of fifty cents for each day assessed; and may, by warrant, authorize the street commissioner to collect the same, with like power and authority as are given to collectors of towns for the collection of taxes. The commissioners of highways of the town of Yonkers shall hereafter have no jurisdiction within the corporate limits of said village.

2. The said trustees may allow the said street commissioner such compensation for his services as they shall deem proper, but not exceeding the sum of one dollar and fifty cents for each day's service. Such compensation may be paid out of the money received for highway labor, or from money raised for ordinary or contingent expenses, or from both, in their discretion.

3. All real estate situated within the bounds of said village shall be liable to be assessed for highway work, whether occupied or otherwise. And in case the highway work which shall at any time be assessed upon any real estate within said village, upon which there shall not be any actual resident, or any person residing in said village being the owner thereof, and the highway shall remain unpaid or not performed for ninety days after the assessment roll of such work shall have been delivered to the street commissioner, such real estate shall be sold pursuant to the provisions of title four of this act, as far as the same are applicable, and all provisions of title four of this act, as far as applicable, shall apply to this title.

4. The street commissioner shall, at any time when required by the trustees, render on account to them, in writing, of the receipt of all moneys by him, and the expenditure of the same, giving the details thereof, the names of the persons from whom such moneys may have been received, on what account, to whom paid, and for what purpose, which account shall be verified by his oath; and his neglect or refusal to render such account, as aforesaid, within ten days after such demand, shall be a forfeiture and breach of his official bond.

5. The board of trustees shall have power to lay out, make, and open streets in said village, and to alter, widen, contract or discontinue any street, alley, lane or highway in said village; they shall cause all streets, alleys, lanes or highways laid out by them to be surveyed, described and recorded in a book to be kept by the clerk, and the same, when opened and made, shall be public highways.

Whenever any street, alley, road or highway is laid out, altered or widened by virtue of this section, the damage arising to property by reason thereof, and the expense of such laying out, altering or widening of any street, alley, road or highway, shall be assessed and paid in the same manner as is provided by law for the laying out of roads in the several towns of the county of Westchester.

6. It shall be the duty of the owner and occupants of lots bounding on any of the streets in said village to construct, re-lay and keep in repair the sidewalks opposite their respective lots, in such time and manner, and of such materials as the trustees may by a by-law, resolution or ordinance for that purpose direct; and if any said owner or occupant shall refuse or neglect to contract, re-lay or repair the sidewalks opposite the lot or lots owned or occupied by him as aforesaid, when so directed to do by the trustees aforesaid, then in either case it shall be lawful for the trustees to cause such sidewalks to be so constructed, re-laid or repaired by the street commissioner, or some other person to be appointed by them, for and on account of the owner of such lots, and such owner shall be liable to pay the expense of such repair, relaying or construction; and all sums so expended upon such sidewalk, not exceeding fifteen dollars in any one year on every twenty-five feet of sidewalk, after being audited by the trustees, by a vote of their board shall thenceforth be an assessment or tax to that amount upon every such lot; and thereupon it shall be lawful for the trustees to issue to the collector their warrant, returnable in thirty days, for the collection thereof of the goods and chattels of the person liable to pay the same, and if such warrant shall be returned unsatisfied, in whole or in part, to advertise and sell such lot in the manner prescribed in title four of this act, as in cases for sale for the non-payment of taxes; and the purchaser or purchasers, owner or owners, and his, h[er], and their legal representatives, shall have the same rights and privileges as are given to them respectively in and by said title.

7. Whenever the occupant or lessee of any real estate in said village shall have been required, as above provided, to make, repair or construct any sidewalk, he may recover the expense incurred therefor of the owner of such lot, or set off the amount thereof against the claims for rent of the owners of said premises.

8. Whenever any sidewalk shall be required to be made or repaired, upon or adjoining any unoccupied lot of land, all the owner or owners of which shall be non-residents of said village or unknown, and such owners or owners shall neglect or refuse to construct or repair, after notice of such requirement shall have been published in any newspaper printed in said village for six weeks successively, it shall be the duty of the trustees to construct or repair such sidewalks, for and on account of such owner or owners, the expense of which shall be a lien or charge upon such lot, for which such lot may be advertised and sold, in the same manner and

with the same effect as is provided in this act in cases of sales for non-payment of taxes.

9. Whenever any real estate in said village is owned by two or more persons jointly, or as tenants in [common], a notice served on one of such persons shall be sufficient notice to all for any purposes requiring a notice under this act; and whenever the said owners shall reside out of the county of Westchester, it shall be sufficient to serve such notice on the occupant or lessee of such real estate.

TITLE VI
OF THE PREVENTION AND EXTINGUISHING OF FIRES

1. The trustees shall have power to prevent the dangerous construction and condition of chimneys, fireplaces, hearths, stoves, and stove-pipes, ovens, boilers, and apparatus used in any building or manufactory, and may cause the same to be removed or placed in a safe condition when considered dangerous, and to prevent the deposit of ashes in unsafe places. To require the inhabitants of said village to provide so many fire buckets, and in such manner and times as they shall prescribe, and to regulate the use of them in times of fire. To authorize the fire wardens, or other officers of the village, to keep away from the vicinity of any fire all idle or [sus]picious persons, and to compel all persons to aid in the extinguishment of fires and the preservation of property exposed to damage thereat; and generally to establish such regulations for the prevention or extinguishment of fires as they may deem expedient.

2. The trustees shall procure fire engines and other apparatus used in the extinguishment of fires, and have the charge and control of the same, and shall provide [for] and secure engine houses, or other places for keeping and preserving the same, and shall have power to organize fire, hook, hose, ladder, axe, and bucket companies, and to appoint a suitable and competent number of able and respectable inhabitants of said village as firemen, [to] take the care and management of the engines and other apparatus and implements used or provided for extinguishment of fire; to prescribe the duties of firemen, and to make rules and regulations for the government of the fire department. The members of the several fire, hook, hose, ladder, axe, and bucket companies, when organized under this section, shall have the power to select a chief engineer and one assistant engineer, a foreman and assistant foreman, and a clerk for each of their respective companies, and to select members to and fill any vacancies which may occur in their ranks, providing that no engine company shall exceed forty members, and no other company shall exceed thirty members at any one time. They may adopt by-laws for the government of their respective companies, and may impose fines and forfeitures for the violation of the same. They may

expel any member from their ranks for improper conduct or neglect of duty, but no expulsion shall be made unless a majority of all the members of the company concur in the same. During the time such companies shall remain duly organized, they shall have the custody of the engines and other apparatus pertaining to the fire department, subject to the authority and control of the president and trustees of said village.

3. The trustees shall be fire wardens, and shall have power, from time to time, to appoint such other fire wardens as they may deem necessary, and to prescribe their powers and duties.

4. The firemen enrolled by virtue of this act shall during the term of their service as such, be exempted from serving on juries, and in the militia, except in case of war, invasion, or insurrection; and a service of five years, as such firemen, shall forever exempt them from such jury or militia duty, excepting as aforesaid. The name of each fireman so enrolled shall be registered with the clerk of the village; and the evidence to entitle him to the exemptions provided in this section shall be the certificate of the said clerk, countersigned by the president of the village.

TITLE VII
MISCELLANEOUS PROVISIONS

1. All actions brought to recover any penalty or forfeiture under this act, or the ordinances, by-laws, rules, resolutions or regulations made in pursuance of it, shall be brought in corporate name; and in such action it shall be lawful to declare or complain generally for such penalty or forfeiture, stating the section of this act, or by-law, ordinance, rule, resolutions or regulations under which the penalty or forfeiture is claimed, and to give the special matter in evidence. The defendant may plead or answer, denying generally the allegations declared on or complained of, and give the special matter in evidence also.

2. The first process in any such action brought before a justice of the peace may be by summons or warrant, and execution may be issued immediately thereon on the rendition of judgment. If the defendant in any such action has no goods or chattels, lands or tenements, whereof the judgment can be collected, the execution shall require, where it shall appear that it was for a second offense, the defendant to be imprisoned in the jail of Westchester county, for a term not exceeding sixty days.

3. No person shall be an incompetent judge, justice, witness or juror, by reason on his being an inhabitant or officeholder in said village, in any action or proceeding in which the said village is a party or interested.

4. All oaths or affidavits, which are required or authorized by this act, may be taken before the president of said village; but the said president shall not be entitled to receive any fee for administering such oath.

5. All the estate, real or personal, vested in or belonging to or held in trust by the trustees of the village of Yonkers, at the time this act shall take effect as a law, shall continue to be, and is hereby declared to be vested in the said village.

6. All resignations of any officers under this act shall be made to the trustees, subject to their acceptance.

7. All fines, forfeitures and penalties, and all moneys received for licenses under this act, except for penalties for violations of the excise law, shall be paid to the treasurer of said village, and may be applied by said trustees to any purpose consistent with this act.

8. Special meetings of the inhabitants of said village may be called by the same persons, and in the same manner, as is provided for the calling of the annual meeting or elections in this act. The notice of such special meetings shall state the object of such meeting.

9. The president and trustees of the village of Yonkers are hereby constituted commissioners of excise, with sole power and authority, within the bounds of said village, to grant licenses to keepers of groceries, inns and taverns, being residents of their village, to sell strong, fermented spirituous liquors and wines, to be drank in their houses, or sold in quantities less than five gallons, under such provisions and restrictions as the said president and trustees may, from time to time, determine; but no such license shall be granted except upon the concurrence of a majority of the trustees elected, and the approval of the president of said village, nor until the person or persons applying for the same shall have produced satisfactory evidence that they possess the qualifications and accommodations to keep an inn or tavern, required by section 2 of chapter 22, part 1 of title 9 of the Revised Statutes, and until said person or persons shall have made and executed a bond to the people of this state, in the penal sum of two hundred and fifty dollars, with two good and sufficient sureties, to be approved by the said president and trustees, conditioned that such person or persons, during the time he or they shall keep such inn or tavern, will not suffer it to be disorderly; that they will not sell strong or spirituous liquors, of any kind, to persons who shall be, at the time, intoxicated, or who are known to be habitually intemperate, or suffer, permit or allow any cock-fighting, gaming, or playing with cards, dice, or any gaming table or instruments of gaming, or any game of hazard for money, liquor or other consideration whatsoever, in or about his or their said tavern, house or premises, or in any out-house, yard or garden belonging thereto, and that he or they will, in all things, conform to the statute in such case made and provided. Nor shall the said president and trustees

grant any such license until the person or persons applying therefor shall have first paid to the treasurer of said village a sum to be determined by the president and trustees, which shall not be less than five dollars in any one case.

10. Licenses, for the sale of strong spirituous liquors and wine, shall not be granted for a longer period than one year; and on the first Tuesday in May, in each and every year, all such licenses may be renewed, a new and satisfactory bond filed, and such sum of money paid to the treasurer for the same as the board of trustees shall determine, pursuant to the 9th section of title 7 of this act.

11. Every person who shall sell strong or spirituous liquors or wines, without the license named in the section last aforesaid, in any house, building, booth or tent, yard, street, highway or any other place within the limits of the corporation of Yonkers, shall forfeit and pay for each and every offense the sum of twenty five dollars; and it shall be the duty of the president and trustees of said village, or either of them, to prosecute for and recover the same, which, when so recovered, shall be paid to the treasurer of the village, to be paid to the overseers of the poor of the town of Yonkers, on their receipt, to be by them applied to the temporary relief of the poor of said town.

The bond received under the 9th section of this act shall be filed with the clerk, and upon the violation of any of its conditions, it shall be the duty of the president and trustees of said village to prosecute the same, under this act, and any sum of money received in such case shall be paid to the treasurer of the village, and by him turned over to the overseers of the poor of the town, on their receipt, and by them to be applied for the support of the poor of the town of Yonkers. And every person holding such license, who shall have violated any of the conditions of his said bond, shall forfeit his said license, and the same shall be declared void by the said president and trustees; but no person shall be subject to be prosecuted by virtue of the provisions of this title for selling [??]eglin, currant wine, cherry wine or cider.

12. The president and trustees are hereby empowered to act as a board of health, at all times to guard against the introduction of any malignant or infectious disease, and to adopt such measures as their judgment shall dictate to secure cleanliness and purity of atmosphere in the streets and alleys, and to promote the [???]atory condition of the village.

14. The said corporation shall possess the privileges and be subject to the restrictions contained in part 1, sec. 3, chap. 18 of the Revised Statutes, as far as they are applicable to such corporation.

15. This act is hereby declared a public act, and the [same] shall be construed favorably and benignly for any official purpose therein contained.

16. The Legislature may at any time hereafter alter, nullify, or repeal this act.

17. The inspectors named in the third section of the second title of this act shall, without unnecessary delay, give notice of a meeting of the electors of the territory described in the first title of this act, to be held at some convenient place therein, to be specified in such notice, for the purpose of determining whether such territory will be an incorporated village. At such meeting the polls shall be opened at six o'clock in the forenoon, and will be kept open until the setting of the sun, when they shall be closed; and the time of opening and closing the same shall be specified in such notice.

18. Such notice shall be published in the newspaper printed in such territory once in each week for three successive weeks previous to such meeting, and printed copies of such notice shall be posted in at least ten of the most public places in such territory, at least three weeks previous to such meeting.

19. Such inspectors shall preside and act as inspectors at such meeting; and all the laws of this state applicable to the election of town officers shall apply to such meeting and to all the proceedings thereat, so far as the same shall be applicable, and are consistent with the provisions of this act.

20. Every elector residing in such territory, and qualified to vote for town officers in the town of Yonkers, may vote at such meeting by a ballot having thereon the word "Yes," or the word "No."

21. Within ten days after such meeting, the inspectors presiding thereat shall cause a certificate of holding the same and of the canvass of the ballots given thereon, showing the whole number of such ballots, the number having thereon the word "Yes," and the number having thereon the word "No," together with a copy of the notice of holding such meeting, and an affidavit of posting and publishing the same as aforesaid, to be submitted to the county judge of the county of Westchester, who shall examine the same; and if from such examination he shall be satisfied that all the proceedings in respect to notifying and holding such meeting, canvassing the votes given thereat, and making such certificate, are legal, he shall endorse upon and annex to the paper so submitted to him a certificate to that effect.

22. If such judge shall be of the opinion that any of such proceedings were illegal, he shall make an order which shall be filed in the office of the county clerk of the county of Westchester, and recorded by him, directing another meeting of the electors of such territory to be held for the purpose of determining whether such territory shall be an incorporated village. The meeting so ordered shall be notified and held as provided in this act in respect to such previous meeting and the duties of such inspectors in relation thereto, and the proceedings thereat, shall apply to any subsequent meeting so ordered.

23. Whenever such judge shall have endorsed on or annexed to the papers so submitted to him such certificate, such papers, together with such certificate, shall be filed and recorded in such clerk's office; and such papers and certificate, or the record thereof, or a transcript from such record, certified by such clerk, shall be presumptive evidence of the fact therein stated.

22. If a majority of such ballots have thereon the word "No," the electors of such territory shall be deemed not to have assented to the incorporation thereof as a village, and this act shall be null and void; but if a majority of such ballots shall have thereon the word "Yes," the inhabitants of such territory shall, from the time of filing, as aforesaid, in the clerk's office, the papers so submitted to such judge, and the certificate so made by him, be a body politic and corporate, pursuant to the first title of this act.

23. This act shall take effect immediately.
(Note: the numbering above is the same as in the original.)
****

According to Thomas Astley Atkins the first election to incorporate the village of Yonkers was held sometime in August, 1853. He also reported that there were two main defects in the original charter. First, it allowed for only one police commissioner who was supposed to police the entire village all by himself. A second defect was that the board of trustees could only levy $1,000 in taxes. If more money was needed, the charter provided that it could only be raised with the consent of a majority vote of the taxable people. There may have been more arguments against the charter, but these two defects in the original charter, according to Atkins, were enough to change the vote of some village charter supporters to a "no," and send the charter down to defeat. (Atkins, p. 101.)

A third potential problem with the charter, and not mentioned by Atkins, was the holding of an election for village officers two weeks before the general vote on the charter's adoption. According to Title II section 2 of the original charter the election for village officers was to be held on Tuesday August 2, 1853. This date was repeated in section 3. However, in Title VII section 18 the yes/no vote on incorporation, after three weeks of public notification, was to be held, and it probably was, on August 16, 1853. It seems somewhat inconceivable that the intent of the State Legislature was to have Title II enforced without the rest of the charter being enforced until the yes/no vote, unless section 23 of Title VII is to be interpreted that the charter was in effect, and the yes/no vote would either just affirm the legislature's act, or rescind it. There are several plausible scenarios of what might have happened. First is that the election of officers did occur and was of no consequence because according to Title III section 3 the Board of Trustees was to hold their monthly meeting the first Monday of each month. Consequently, the first Board of Trustees meeting was not scheduled until September 5 by which time the charter had already been rescinded with no official action taken by the Board. Another scenario might have been that no notice of election for village officers was posted because the defeat of the charter was a foregone conclusion. If this was the action taken then it was in direct violation of an act of the State Legislature which directed that such notice be given and such election held. On the other hand, if the engrossed charter meant the last Tuesday in August for election of officers, errors did happen, then why hold the election for the yes/no vote? There are more possible scenarios, but the most significant point here is that there is an important gap missing in the history of Yonkers and hopefully more research will fill it.

Nonetheless the charter was defeated, and the defeat of the 1853 village charter was not because residents in the Getty Square area of Yonkers did not want to incorporate as a village, but rather because of the way the charter was written. Consequently, during 1854 and 1855 a new charter was developed and presented to the state legislature, and with the active support of men like Lemuel W. Wells, Robert Grant, Ethan Flagg, Charles C. Merchant, Ralph Shipman, Thomas C. Cornell, Samuel D. Rockwell, Henry W. Bashford, Thomas O. Farrington, Josiah Rich, W. H. Anderson, and Robert P. Getty it was passed by the state legislature April 12, 1855. After its passage it was immediately put into effect. (Town Records at Trevor Park Museum.)

The 1855 charter had some interesting differences between it and the 1853 charter. The 1853 charter, as discussed above, had a clause in it that called for a popular yes/no ratification vote, and elections for village officers be held less than two weeks after the passage of the act. The new charter did not call for a popular ratification vote, and it mandated that notice of village elections for officers be given immediately after its passage by the state legislature and that such notices run for six weeks. In the case of the new charter the act of the state legislature was sufficient to incorporate the village of Yonkers, and therefore no popular election for its adoption was necessary. The old charter appointed Robert P. Getty, William W. Woodworth, and Thomas C. Cornell as inspectors of the first village election under the new charter, while the 1855 charter appointed Thomas O. Farrington, John H. Myers, and Lawrence Post, Jr. as inspectors.

The 1853 charter directed village trustees to be elected for one-year terms, while the 1855 charter directed that the terms of trustees be for two years with "the first election under this act, six trustees shall be elected, the term of office of three of whom, (to be determined by lot), shall expire one year thereafter." Apparently William C. Waring, Frederick S. Gant, and Jacob Read won by lot the short one-year terms, while Lemuel Wells, Rueben Van Pelt, and Thomas O. Farrington won the two-year terms. This was deduced

60

from the fact that the latter three persons served a second year, while the first three named did not. Other possible explanations exist, such as resignations, but no evidence has been found at this point in time to suggest any other conclusion.

The second charter did resolve one of the shortcomings of the first charter by allowing for more than one constable. The second charter left the number of constables to the discretion of the Board of Trustees. However, one of the alleged defects of the first charter was not corrected in the second charter. The first charter restricted the amount of taxation in a single year to one thousand dollars, and the second charter stated that "no tax shall be levied and collected to an amount exceeding one thousand dollars in any one year," unless a majority of the voters voted for a higher tax. Consequently, if Atkins was right about the reasons for the defeat of the first charter, then the issue of constables was far more important a reason for its defeat than the ceiling on taxation. Even more curious though, is that the second charter was not mandated by the legislature to be voted on for ratification by the voters. This then raises the question of whether the amount of taxation was a popular concern, but not a concern to an elitist group who wrote the second charter which didn't need popular ratification.

Maybe even of more concern to the voters on the first charter was the role of street commissioner. The first charter called for only one street commissioner who was to have the same powers as an overseer of the highways. The first charter also made members of the Board of Trustees commissioners of the highways. The second charter, however, was quite different. It stated that the Board of Trustees were to appoint commissioners who were to be ratified by either "the county court of the county of Westchester," or by the state supreme court "at a special term held in the county."

Many, if not most, roads were private property that were maintained privately. Although it was rather expensive for private individuals to maintain roads for their private and business interest, the fact remained that they were private property. The concept of private property was so strongly embedded into the minds of Americans that men were willing to do physical battle in order to maintain the integrity of the concept. Consequently, giving up private property to a political entity was a serious matter not easily entrusted to a mere board of trustees and a street commissioner. Concerns of property owners along a given road were an equal and fair assessment of the cost of grading the road, an equal and fair assessment of damages to buildings and adjacent properties which included loss of trees, an equal and fair assessment of additional land taken, and an equitable assessment of the work that was done by the contractor. If politicians alone were to make these decisions, they may have been influenced by the wealth, power, and/or influence of one or more individuals along the line of the road. It must be remembered that when the national constitution was written it incorporated checks and balances as a result of a healthy distrust of government. People living during the 1850s were only removed from the writing of the constitution by a little more than seventy years, and they were very strong nationalists. Consequently, the rewriting of the section of the new charter dealing with roads, and having an impartial judiciary appoint the men who were to make the assessments, was an understandable event. Further, the rewriting of this section of the charter seems to have been just as important, if not a more important change than even the issue over constables. The importance of ceding roads to the village in an equitable manner remained an important and a hotly contested issue even after the new charter was adopted. To find support of this conclusion one only needs to look at the "Battle Over Main Street" and the time spent by the board of trustees haggling over roads in the minutes of the board meetings.

Whatever the definitive reasons were for the apparent general acceptance of the second charter, the fact remains that the first election under the new charter was held May 8, 1855. The election resulted in William Radford defeating Robert P. Getty 262 to 228 votes for village president. While the republican party was a true political entity by 1855, and even though voting for charter positions was supposed to be non-partisan, the strength of anti-democratic party Getty was very strong. He received 46.5% of the vote and that vote was a harbinger of an impending political shift in the newly created village which had rapidly become the economic, social, and political center of the entire town of Yonkers.

The first board of trustees consisted of Lemuel W. Wells, William C. Waring, Thomas O. Farrington, Rueben W. Van Pelt, F. S. Gant, and Jacob Read. The treasurer was John M. Stillwater, and the collector was Lyman F. Bradley.

While the 1855 charter was an improvement over the defeated 1853 charter, it was not permanently etched in stone. Like the original charter, it had some defects and limitations, and during its history it was amended several times. It was first amended on April 17, 1857 in order to increase the powers of the Board of Trustees. In 1860 new amendments were proposed which included extending the term of the president to two years, appointment of the clerk instead of electing him at a general election, power to bridge the Nepperhan River as necessary in order to connect streets with bridges and a drawbridge where the tidewater had to be crossed, make assessment districts as recommended by the Commissioners, to regulate docks and landing sites by ordinance, to divide the village into three wards, and to establish a lamp and watch district. (E-1/26/60 p.2, c.1,2.)

Chapter 4

Yonkers Politics

Politics during the 1850s saw critical national and local changes that dramatically impacted the entire world. During this period of time a national party died and a national party was born. A party divided conceded defeat to an upstart, and in three presidential elections between 1852 and 1860 two of the three presidents were elected with pluralities. During this period of time, the only president who was elected with a majority vote was Franklin Pierce in 1852, and he received only 50.95% of the total popular vote. Politics in the United States was in a frenzy.

The burning issue of the time was slavery, and the Whig Party was unable to satisfactorily address it. The Whig Party elected presidents in 1840, and 1848. However, 1852 was the last presidential election in which the Whigs would field a viable national candidate. In 1856 the Republican Party ran its first presidential candidate, John C. Fremont, who was defeated by James Buchanan. Four short years later the Republican Party nominated Abraham Lincoln for president and an eventual political victory. However, it was a bittersweet victory. While Lincoln took 59.4% of the vote in the Electoral College, he received a mere 39.78% of the popular vote. In other words 60.22% of the popular vote was cast against Lincoln. Even the Democratic Party was split in 1860. They fielded Stephen A. Douglas and John C. Breckinridge for the presidency. However, while their combined vote gave them almost a majority of the popular vote (48.58%), they were still far behind in the electoral college. A fourth candidate, John Bell, ran on the Constitutional Union ticket. He was strong enough to gain 12.64% of the vote. Consequently, the results of the 1860 election split the country; not down the middle, but rather into minority factions waiting to do battle.

Yonkers was not left out of the political turmoil of the 1850s. Village and town politics mirrored the national scene. When the Whig Party died nationally it also died in Yonkers. In the general elections of 1855 the Republican Party fielded its first candidates. In Westchester County the new Republicans fielded candidates who ran against hard Democrats, soft Democrats, and Americans. However, during the 1855 elections the Republican vote in Yonkers fell far short of their expectations. Republicans received 19.03%, hard

Democrats 39.10%, and Americans a respectable 37.54%. Only the soft Democrats trailed the Republicans. They received a mere 4.33%. According to the election returns Republicans were a small third party far out-distanced by hard Democrats and members of the American party.

However, in 1856 Republicans went head to head against the Democrats in the presidential election. The vote was much closer in Yonkers with Republicans receiving 38.7%, Democrats 39.7%, and Americans 21.6%. The Americans lost almost 16% of their 1855 vote while the Republicans increased their vote by 19.7%. The Republican Party in Yonkers, while gaining some Democratic votes, got their real boost from the Americans, and by 1857 the Americans became an insignificant political factor. However, during 1857 the remaining Americans who hadn't in the previous year defected to the Republican Party defected to the Democratic Party. The Republican vote fell a bit to 37.2% while the Democratic vote swelled with the new Americans to 61.3%. The remaining Americans received only 1.49% of the vote, and in 1858 they received only 2.8%, and 1858 proved to be their last year as an organized political party.

With the third party vote down to an insignificant level in 1857 and 1858 it meant that if Republicans were going to increase in numbers they had to look into the ranks of the Democratic Party and pull out those who felt a moral obligation, particularly on the slave issue, to join and vote Republican. In 1858 Yonkers Republicans saw their vote rise to a highly competitive 43.88%, and in 1859 it rose to 44.7%. However, the Democratic vote also increased in 1859 to 55.3%. The reason why both parties increased their percentage was that both split the remaining American Party votes. The Republicans picked up nearly 30% of the remaining American votes while the Democrats received 70%.

The rise of the Republican Party nationally led them to field Abraham Lincoln as a presidential candidate in 1860. However, the nomination of Lincoln was not an easy nomination. On January 26, 1860 the *Yonkers Examiner* published a list of possible Republican Party candidates for president and Lincoln was completely left off. However, by the time of the Republican convention in May, Lincoln had become a serious candidate for the nomination. On the first ballot he received 102 votes, second only to William H. Seward's 173 1/2 votes. On the second ballot Lincoln received 181, and on the third ballot he fell just 2 votes short of nomination. Before a fourth ballot could be taken the Ohio delegation announced that four of their members had switched to Lincoln. Other states began to follow Ohio and when all the changes were made Lincoln stood at 364 votes out of the 465 cast. The New York delegation stood behind their native U.S. Senator Seward, but after Lincoln was officially nominated they threw in the towel and gave their votes to Lincoln. (E-5/24/60 p.2, c.3)

The Democratic convention held in Baltimore was extremely divisive. Southern Democrats walked out, held their own convention and nominated John C. Breckinridge. Northern Democrats met again and nominated Stephen A. Douglas. Meanwhile a third political group of old line Whigs and Know Nothings, fearful of the break up of the union and the destruction of the Constitution, formed the Constitutional Union ticket headed by John Bell. With the Democratic Party mortally split, Republicans could taste victory. Even in Yonkers Republicans were pumped up for the coming presidential election.

However, in New York State the Democratic presidential electors chose not to split their vote and ran on the Union Ticket. This move gave the Democrats a semblance of order in the state, and would ensure that no votes against Lincoln would be split. If Lincoln was to win in New York he would have to win with a majority, and he did. In Yonkers however, the vote was very close. Lincoln took the town of Yonkers, on the strength of the Republican vote in the village, by only three votes. In the first election district, which comprised the village, Lincoln won with 553 votes (54.1%) to 469 votes (45.9%). In the second election district he lost 66 votes (31.9%) to 141 votes (68.1%). In the third election district he also lost 47 votes (47.0%) to 53 votes (53.0%). The final result therefore was Lincoln winning the town of Yonkers with 666 votes (50.1%) to 663 votes (49.9%). (E-11/8/60 p.2, c.2)

The 1860 general election dramatically changed the United States forever. No other election in our history had such a profound effect as this election, and in Yonkers the political winds of change, while not blowing anywhere near hurricane strength, were strong enough to show that the Republican Party was a political force that had to be dealt with. As noted above, in the presidential election Abraham Lincoln took the town of Yonkers by 3 votes. However, in the village his majority was 84 votes, demonstrating the political power of the village and the Republican Party.

While Lincoln won the town by 50.1%, the result of the gubernatorial race was different. Even though Edwin D. Morgan, the Republican candidate, won the town by 242 votes, he was only able to win it with a plurality of 49.8%. The lieutenant governor's race had similar results. However, in the canal commissioner's race the Republican candidate was able to take 50.6% of the town's vote. This race was a strange anomaly since the total number of votes cast in the town for canal commissioner were six more than for president.

However, the race for inspector of the state prisons returned the election to the previous pattern with the Republican candidate winning the town with a plurality of 49.2%. The race for Congress though saw the Republican candidate, Thomas Nelson, take 53.9% of the votes in the town, but the race for county treasurer, without a Democratic split, saw the Democratic candidate, Henry Willette, running on the Union ticket. He took 51.7% of the vote. The race for superintendent of the poor also saw the Democratic candidate take the town by 50.5%, while hometown boy William H. Lawrence, running for coroner on the Union ticket, took the town by 56.7%. In the race for Sessions the Democratic candidate won the town with 50.1%, while hometown boy Ethan Flagg, the Republican candidate for Assembly, took the town with 58.9% of the vote. The race for school commissioner was a split race with an additional two independent candidates running. One of the independent candidates was Jared M. Horton who was from South Yonkers in the second election district. While he did rather poorly overall he did take the second district with 67.8% of the vote. In this split race the Republican candidate was able to win with only 46% of the vote.

In the town of Yonkers, election district voting patterns were very clear. The village maintained a Republican majority, the second district was strongly Democratic, while the third district gave two Republicans a majority. Thomas Nelson, who was running for a seat in the United States House of Representatives, received 55.6% of the vote, while Ethan Flagg, who was running for the State Assembly, received 52% of the vote. Leaving out races with candidates from one of the three election districts, there was only a 3.8% swing vote in the village while district two had a 13.1% swing vote, and the third election district had a 16.2% swing vote. Meanwhile the town of Yonkers as a whole had a 13.4% swing vote. Even though the voting patterns in district two showed a double figure swing vote it remained staunchly Democratic giving the highest Republican only 44.8% of the vote.

Interestingly, the areas where manufacturing was centered gave a strong vote to Republicans, while the old line "hunker" farmers continued to vote Democratic. The strength of the Republican party in the town of Yonkers was in businessmen and laborers even though the laboring vote was probably slightly Democratic. The split laboring vote in the village of Yonkers with solid support from the business community allowed Republican candidates in every race to take the village. Again leaving out the race for assembly, where Ethan Flagg took the village with 63.5% of the vote, and the presidential election, the village gave winning percents to every Republican candidate of between 55.7% and 51.9%. However, in election district two, which was comprised of the eastern farming section of the town, even hometown boy Ethan Flagg could only muster 38.9% of the vote. Here, old line Democrats took a stand and the "hunkers" were victorious even though they were giving way in the rest of the town.

While the old line "hunkers" were giving way, racial prejudice was still rampant. Even though 54.1% of the voters in the village voted for Abraham Lincoln, they were solidly against changing the state constitution to allow black male suffrage. The village vote in favor of suffrage was only 7.9%, while the town was only 7.6%. Even more discouraging was that more than 53% of the voters who voted in the village didn't even care to cast a ballot on the issue. The rest of the town did a little better with about 35.4% not voting. It seems that Yonkers voters voted for Lincoln along party lines and not necessarily on issues. Certainly a large number of Yonkers residents were probably against the extension of slavery, and even against slavery, but they sure were not interested in extending the franchise to black males. Political bigotry and just plain old bigotry were still the rules of the day.

The victory of Lincoln had serious national repercussions, but in Yonkers the sage at the Republican *Yonkers Examiner* was blinded by an arrogant belief in his interpretation of the national constitution when he said "The Constitution with its broad shield of justice stands between them and aggression. Millions of honest patriots stand ready to defend their state rights when assailed, and therefore we are safe in saying - no overt act will ever drive the South into rebellion against Federal power." (E-11/8/60 p.2, c.2) However, by December 20, 1860 the publisher was saying "If secession follows the threats of the South, there will be civil war." (E-12/20/60 p.2, c.2)

Presidential elections made the blood of many Americans boil with passion. However, local politics and elections carried with them much of the same kind of passions. In Yonkers though, some of the passions of village election days were sometimes diminished by how the candidates for village president and trustees were chosen. Nominations, or what was called a primary, for village positions were made at an open village meeting, usually during the latter part of February, but prior to the general village election in early March. The 1857 village primary was quite interesting. Dr. Salmon Skinner called the meeting to order. Then C. H. Smith called for nominations to chair the meeting. Skinner, Rockwell, and Chamberlain were nominated, and Dr. Skinner won. Tellers for the nomination election were J. H. Jennings, J. J. Woodfine, and Thomas Smith. When nominations were taken for president William W. Woodworth, Robert P. Getty, and Thomas O. Farrington were put up for nomination. Getty hadn't asked to be nominated and didn't want to run against either of the other two nominees. When it came time to vote many of Getty's friends voted for another nominee with the result that Woodworth received 79 votes, Getty received 51 votes, and Farrington received only 6 votes.

The vote for nominations to the board of trustees for three seats up for election saw Ethan Flagg, and Robert Getty nominated by voice vote. The third seat, however, was contested primarily by Augustus W. Doren and James B. Kinslow. A secret ballot was taken and Doren beat Kinslow 69 to 56. Thomas Smith then motioned that the choice for trustees be made unanimous, and only a few negative voices responded. The meeting then went on to nominate a treasurer, a collector, and a clerk. Egbert Howland, Benjamin A. Starr, and William H. Post were each nominated by acclamation respectively to those positions. (E-2/26/57 p.2, c.1)

On Tuesday, March 5, 1857 the village general election was held. As expected Woodworth handily won with 389 votes to a scattering of only 8 votes. Ethan Flagg won election to the board of trustees with 396 votes, and so did Getty with 357 votes. However, the surprise of the election came with the votes cast for the third trustee seat up for election. The village primary nominee, Augustus W. Doren, was beaten by Henry F. Devoe, 210 votes to 208 votes. (E-3/5/57 p.2, c.2) It's not clear where Devoe politically came from, but the election demonstrated that a nomination at a village primary meeting was not necessarily tantamount to election at the general election.

The 1858 village election was not very hotly contested. Woodworth again easily won the presidency. Bailey Hobbs was returned to the board of trustees with the second highest vote total, 351. Only newcomer Leonard M. Clark with 352 votes out-polled Hobbs. The hot headed John Copcutt was also easily elected with 340 votes. However, the resignation of Henry F. Devoe from the board did cause one contested seat. This seat on the board was filled by Edward Underhill who beat James H. Monckton 170 votes to 127 votes. But, even in this election for a vacant seat there was no really heated contest since Underhill and Monckton were friends. In other positions the tranquility of the election also prevailed. Evart K. Baldwin beat Egbert Howland 251 to 99 for the treasure's position. Benjamin A. Starr for collector and William H. Post for clerk were uncontested. Starr received 350 votes and Post received 337 votes. (E-3/4/58 p.2, c.1)

For the most part the 1858 town elections were just as quiet as the village elections. The one exception was a close election for town clerk. William H. Post beat George L. Andrews 319 to 311. In other positions Augustus Van Cortlandt easily beat Ethan Flagg for Supervisor 557 to 282, James L. Valentine beat Thomas Smith for Justice of the Peace 515 to 320, Gilbert Taylor beat Abraham F. Vermilyea for commissioner of the highways 634 to 191, William G. Ackerman beat Joseph J. Bicknell for assessor for a regular term 634 to 192, Caleb F. Underhill beat Nathaniel Reynolds for assessor to fill a vacancy 649 to 184, William H. Lawrence and William McCabe beat William P. Littel and Frederick Gardineer for overseers of the poor 616 and 570 to 192 and 230. William H. Lawrence beat William N. Bailey for collector 677 to 163. There were fourteen candidates running to fill five constable positions. The winners with their total votes were William McCabe with 606, William H. Lawrence with 409, Edward Crisfield with 367, James Cuddy with 348, and Benjamin C. Nodine with 308. The losers with their total votes were John S.

Waterman with 294, John Archer with 257, John O'Meara with 243, Charles H. Smith with 240, Charles Gilchrest with 220, William P. Littel with 202, James Nodine with 177, and William N. Bailey and George W. Mold each with 161. The winning inspectors of election for election district number 1 were John Stevens with 640 votes and Leonard M. Clark with 635 votes. The losers were George P. Abbott with 178 and Henry B. Archer with 175. In election district number two the winners were William G. Ackerman with 635 and Caleb Van Tassell with 631. The losers were Charles Gilchrest with 185 and Frederick Gardiner with 179. In election district number three the winners were Caleb F. Underhill with 641 and William Dederer with 640. The losers were Abraham F. Vermilyea and Nathaniel Reynolds each with 176. According to the *Yonkers Examiner* the defeat of Thomas Smith for Justice of the Peace brought to a close the existence of the Know Nothing Party in Yonkers. (E-4/1/58 p.2 c.1,2)

In 1859 the village primary was held on Saturday, February 26. It was not widely publicized as to when the primary was going to be held. However, word of the primary meeting day and time had spread through the village by mouth, and apparently was known by most of the residents. Yet, when the doors of the Village Hall were opened, a little after 7 p.m., little more than a dozen men entered. However, in a little while that number swelled to at least 145.

Eventually the meeting was called to order and Isaac H. Knox was elected to chair the meeting without opposition. As he took the chair Thomas Smith entered the Hall and in no uncertain, and probably vulgar, terms told the people he was chairman last year and therefore chairman this year. After a verbal wrangle he was called to order, but in his final exhortation in this combative round he nominated Reuben W. Van Pelt for Village President. He then declared it carried, and asked all supporters of Van Pelt to leave the room, and meet at Hoyt's Hall. Nobody budged.

Finally, things were calmed down and two candidates, Van Pelt and Robert P. Getty, were nominated. John Copcutt was also nominated, but his name was withdrawn. Some confusion then ensued as to who could vote, which was eventually cleared up, and the balloting proceeded under the direction of Daniel Blauvelt and A. F. Gourlie. After all the ballots were cast, Getty was nominated with 77 votes. Van Pelt received 66 votes and Lyman Cobb 2 votes.

Other village officers who were nominated were James C. Bell, Ethan Flagg, Amos W. Gates for Trustees, William H. Post for Village Clerk, Benjamin A. Starr for Collector, and Evart K. Baldwin for Treasurer. While the vote for Trustees was being taken Smith once again urged followers of Van Pelt to leave, but once again nobody left. However, after the meeting adjourned some followers of Van Pelt did meet at Hoyt's Hall, and proceeded to nominate another ticket. Van Pelt was nominated for President, William Radford, John Stilwell, and John M. Purdy were nominated as Trustees, Lyman Cobb,

Jr. was nominated for Clerk, George L. Andrews was nominated for Collector, and Evart K. Baldwin was nominated for Treasurer. The counter ticket was declared the straight Democratic ticket.

Prior to this time only one slate of officers was presented to the voters. The village election was designed to keep partisan politics out of the election in order to select and elect the best possible people. With this election that goal was put to rest, and while partisan politics was always an underlying factor, it was with this election a clear issue.

There were only two full days, Sunday and Monday, between the primary nominations and the election. Getty and Van Pelt did not openly campaign against each other, but rumors and gossip about the candidates ran rampant throughout the village. Getty was accused of all sorts of sordid dealings, and Van Pelt was accused of being Smith's patsy.

On Monday evening the straight Democrats held a rally in Radford's Hall. The arrogant Thomas Smith in a speech in support of Van Pelt denounced the Young Men's Christian Association for holding a prayer meeting at the same time in Hoyt's Hall. To Smith the YMCA prayer meeting was nothing more than a meeting called to defeat him and his Democratic party. The editor of the *Yonkers Examiner* noted that Smith may very well have been right. In his speech, Smith continued to attack anything and everything that may have had a non-Democratic slant. He attacked the Yonkers Library Association and the Sabbatarian Committee. Smith was followed by James B. Kinslow who declared that any Democrat who didn't vote the straight Democratic ticket would be "excommunicated" from the party. Van Pelt and C. H. Chamberlain also spoke at the meeting.

On Tuesday, March 1, the largest number of voters in the short history of the village turned out. When the final count was completed 724 votes had been cast for President. Getty received 418, Van Pelt received 304, Lemuel W. Wells received 1, and 1 blank ballot was cast. Getty received 57.7% of the vote, which was a clear and decisive victory.

The vote for Trustees was just as decisive in its victory over Smith's Democrats. James C. Bell received a whopping 704 votes, while Flagg received 412 votes, and Gates received 424 votes. Smith's ticket did very poorly. Radford received 326 votes, Purdy received 298 votes, and Stilwell had nobody vote for him unless he was amongst a scattering of 7. Flagg, who received the lowest winning vote for Trustee, still managed a decisive victory with 56.9% of the total vote. The margin of victory of the other two winners was a decisive 58.6% for Gates and a staggering 97.9% for Bell.

The election for Clerk was close. Post was the incumbent and was on the right ticket, but he won over Cobb by a margin of only 10 votes, a bare majority of 50.6%. However, the Collector's election was not very close. Starr received 428 votes and Andrews received 353 votes. Post also received one vote for Collector. Consequently, Starr's majority was 65.4% of the total vote.

According to the *Yonkers Examiner* there was no great personal difference between Getty and Van Pelt. What made the difference was that Van Pelt let his name be used by Smith who was "as generally despised as he is universally detested." Whatever the reasons were for Getty's victory, three facts really standout as a result of this election. Many Democrats voted for a Republican, the margin of victory was decisive, and sharp partisan political lines were drawn for future elections. (E-3/3/59 p.2, c.1,2)

During the 1860 Village elections the nominating primary was held on Saturday, March 3, 1860 in the Village Hall and a slate of candidates was nominated. However, since the candidates who were nominated were a mixture of Republicans and Democrats, the Democrats held their own meeting at the Franklin House on Monday, March 6, 1860 on the very eve of the election. At this meeting they nominated an all-Democratic ticket that was entirely victorious on the next day.

The Democrat Thomas F. Morris in a rather close election beat Republican Robert P. Getty who was running as a Union candidate since he received the nomination at the regular primary meeting. The vote was 394 to 367. Morris received 51.8% of the vote and Getty received 48.2% of the vote. The Democratic slate for members of the Board of Trustees was swept into office with 54.9% of the vote. (E-3/8/69 p.2, c.1,2,3) The Republicans felt betrayed by the Democrats since it was the understanding in the past that a united ticket would be nominated and presented to the public. They hadn't learned from the village election of 1859.

However, it was a different story for the Republicans when it came to the 1860 Town elections that were held on Tuesday, March 27. On Saturday, March 17 they met at the Getty Lyceum and held their own organized meeting to nominate a Republican slate. At the meeting Ethan Flagg was nominated for Supervisor, William H. Post was nominated for Town Clerk, and a Republican was nominated for every position up for election including six Inspectors of Election for the three election districts. The year before Ethan Flagg was a candidate for Supervisor and "failed of election by about four votes." (E-3/22/60 p.2, c.3,4)

For the first time in the town's history the Republicans were organized and ready to fight. On Monday night, election eve, Republicans packed the hall in the Getty House. Horace Greeley was the speaker and "it exceeded any gathering of that enthusiastic year. We have never seen the Republicans of Yonkers so earnest in their work; a spirit of courage, faith and determination manifested itself in every face." Greeley spoke for an hour and "During his whole speech, his plain, simple, straight-forward and candid statement of the designs and creed of our party, was listened to with unabated interest. It was an argument so conclusive that it could not fail to do great good in confirming the wavering, and converting opponents."

The gloves were off and the campaigns were on. During the presidential election of 1856 Yonkers Republicans were quite active, but in this election it was the first time in the history of the town that there was going to be a clearly partisan town election with a true two-party system. The days of the old one party agrarian plutocratic Democratic "hunker" system was clearly over. All that remained was the short fight and the wait for the returns.

The wait was not a long one. On Thursday, March 27, a total of 1,167 votes were cast in the town of Yonkers for Supervisor. Ethan Flagg received 648 votes and Orrin A. Bills received 513 votes with 5 more votes going to Ethan Flagg with misspellings and one vote for Robert P. Getty. Taking the legal vote Flagg won by 135 votes. He received 55.5% of the vote. The voice of the Yonkers Republican Party, the *Yonkers Examiner*, rejoiced by saying "It is our privilege and pleasure today to announce the Election of the first Anti-Democratic Supervisor ever chosen in the Town of Yonkers since the creation of the world."

However, all was not joy for the Republicans. The Democrats won every other position up for election. In most cases though the margin of victory had to leave the Democrats a little nervous. Lyman Cobb, Jr. running for Town Clerk beat William H. Post with 54% of the vote, Charles R. Duesenberry for Justice of the Peace beat James H. Monckton with 51.5% of the vote, Thomas Radford running for Assessor beat Thaddeus Bell with 51.3% of the vote, James L. Valentine running for Commissioner of the Highways beat Joseph L. Bicknell with 53.4% of the vote, and William H. Lawrence running for Collector beat Evert K. Baldwin with a comfortable 60.5% of the vote.

There were two openings for Overseer of the Poor and Democrats won both seats. William H. Lawrence and William McCabe beat George W. Mold and William Smelt with 54.4% of the vote. There were five Constable positions that needed to be filled and all five were filled by Democrats. The Republican candidates were George W. Mold, William Smelt, John C. Boyd, John S. Brown, and Evert K. Baldwin. The Democratic candidates were William H. Lawrence, John Houston, William McCabe, John O'Meara, and Jacob Wackerly. They were all elected with a combined 54.4% of the vote.

During 1860 the town of Yonkers had three election districts. Each district had three inspectors of election positions of which two were filled during the town's general election and the third filled at the annual town meeting. Tradition, until 1859, was that the third position for inspector of elections was filled at the town meeting by the person who attained the third highest number of votes during the general election. This practice was continued in 1860, and it wasn't until October that the third inspectors were appointed.

At the 1860 general town election Democrats swept all six inspectors of elections positions. In the first election district the Republican candidates for inspector of elections were John M. Mason and William P. Mott while the Democrats fielded Abram Van Houten and Charles W. Chamberlain who garnered 54.6% of the vote. In the *Yonkers Examiner* of March 29 the vote was recorded as showing Mason beating Van Houten by one vote. However, there must have been a recount since Van Houten was recorded as the winner in the Town Record Book.

In the second election district the Republican candidates were Henry Farling and Joseph I. Bicknell while the Democratic candidates were Cornelius L. Purdy and Pembroke Lawrence. The Republicans did much better in this district. The Democrats won with only 50.7% of the vote.

In the third election district the Republican candidates were Odell Stevenson and Nathaniel Reynolds while the Democrats fielded Charles R. Dusenberry and William R. Dederer. The Democrats won this district with 52.8% of the vote. However, while losing this district the Republicans could claim a moral victory. The Republican strong hold was in the village and the first and second election districts split the village in half and included the northern two sections of the town, the third election district was completely outside the village. It included all the area south of Mount St. Vincent's, including the Mount, to the Harlem River and easterly to the Bronx River. There are some indications of some Republican strength in Kingsbridge and Spuyten Duyvil, but this was the territory of the old line Democrats. Consequently, while Republicans lost in all three election districts the margin of victory for the Democrats was hardly overwhelming. Also, the election indicated that Republicans had made strong inroads into the Democratic Party in all three election districts, and that they were strong enough to elect the Supervisor.

County wide the Republican party did quite well also. The county board of supervisors was comprised of 24 members. The Republicans elected 10, the Democrats 10, and the anti-Lecompton Democrats 4. As of 1860 37.5% of the board's membership was Republican with a strong split in the Democratic party. (E-3/29/60 p.2, c.1,2 and 4/5/60 p.2, c.3)

Coming back to the village the Democratic victory in the board of trustees meant some changes were called for. The police officers who were appointed by the board were usually the same as those elected in the town. The 1860 board appointments followed that practice, but with an interesting twist. At the April 2, 1860 meeting of the board the committee on police and prisons gave their report as to who the committee thought should be appointed policemen by the board. George W. Mold and William Smelt had both been town constables and village police officers for several years. They both ran for reelection in 1860 as town constables on the Republican ticket and both lost. They still went ahead and petitioned the board to be reappointed as village police officers. However, when the Democratic controlled committee reported to the board, their names were not endorsed for renomination. Ethan Flagg was upset by this move, and asked the committee why they were the only two left off the list and two newcomers, John Houston and Michael Tansey, were added to the list.

He went on to defend Smelt and Mold telling the committee that they had done an exceptionally good job as police officers for several years. John Wheeler, chairman of the police committee, responded to Flagg saying that the petitions were not rejected, but that they were being held back in case more police officers were needed. He went on to note that Houston was elected by the town and that in the case of Tansey he lived in an area of the town where a police officer was needed on Sundays.

Flagg was not fully convinced by these arguments, and his questioning seemed to insinuate that the committee's decision was based on politics. When the issue came to a vote his was the only vote against the appointments. In retrospect it seems quite clear that the recommendations and vote were both clearly political and traditional. However, Flagg did not really put up a fight, nor did he bluntly state that these appointments were political. His lack of fight might possibly have been because if the shoe was on the other foot his decision would also have been based on politics, especially since that had become the norm of the day. (E-4/5/60 p.2, c.5,6)

While elections had become highly politicized, there is little evidence of gerrymandering of election district boundaries even though gerrymandering had been a political practice in the United States since its inception. Late in 1860 the village of Yonkers was for the first time divided into wards. As the preamble to the division stated, the division came about as a consequence of having only one election district in the village for village elections. On a clear and mild day having only one place to vote was an inconvenience for voters living near the village boundaries. Walking was the normal means of transportation and the hills north of Getty Square meant that if a voter was to vote at the village hall on Palisade Avenue he would have quite a strenuous walk home. If the day was snowy, and it frequently snowed in early March, the walk could be dangerous.

Consequently, dividing the village into wards for election purposes was a logical decision based on geographical considerations. At first blush the actual boundaries of the wards also show no apparent influences of gerrymandering. The following are the ward boundaries as they were established in 1860:

Whereas great difficulty and inconvenience have arisen, heretofore, from the fact that there being but one Election District in the village of Yonkers.

And whereas, the village Charter provides for the division of said village into Wards.

Now therefore resolved, That in accordance with the provisions of Section 15, Title VII, of the Amended Charter, the said village of Yonkers be, and the same is hereby divided into three distinct Wards, as follows, viz.:

1st Ward - Bounded and described as follows: - Beginning at the intersection of Main Street with the easterly shore of the Hudson River, running then easterly along Main Street to Mechanic Street, thence easterly along Mechanic Street to Guion Street, thence along Guion Street to Davidson's Lane, thence along Davidson's Lane and in a line continuous therewith until the same connects with Maple Street, and thence along Maple Street to the easterly boundary line of the village. Thence southerly along the easterly boundary line of the village to the southerly line of the village, and thence westerly along the southerly line of the village to the easterly shore of the Hudson River, thence northerly along said easterly shore of the Hudson River to the place of beginning. All persons residing on the south side of Main and Mechanic Streets, Davidson's Lane, Maple Street and the line connecting Maple Street with Davidson's Lane, and east of Guion Street on said line, will be included in the first Ward.

2nd Ward - Beginning at a point where the line of the proposed bridge across the Nepperhan, connecting Warburton Avenue with Riverdale Avenue, intersects the northerly line of Main Street, and thence northerly along the said line of the proposed bridge to Dock Street to Broadway, thence northerly along Broadway to Ashburton Avenue, thence easterly along Ashburton Avenue to Oak Hill Avenue, thence northerly along Oak Hill Avenue, and in a line continuous therewith to the north line of the village, thence easterly along the northerly line of the village to the easterly line of the village, thence southerly along the easterly line of the village to Maple Street, thence westerly along Maple Street, and in a line continuous therewith, until the same connects with Davidson's Lane to Guion Street, thence along Guion Street to Mechanic Street, thence westerly along Mechanic Street to Main Street, and thence along Main Street to the line of the proposed bridge across the Nepperhan aforesaid. All persons residing on the southerly side of Dock Street and Ashburton Avenue, and on the easterly side of the proposed bridge, and Broadway and Oak Hill Avenue, and the line continuing said Oak Hill Avenue to the north line of the village, and on the northerly side of Maple Street, and the line connecting the same with Davidson's Lane; Davidson's Lane, Mechanic Street and Main Street, and westerly of Guion Street, on the said division line, will be included in the Second Ward.

3rd Ward - Beginning at a point where Main Street intersects the easterly shore of the Hudson River, and thence easterly along Main

Street to the line of the proposed bridge across the Nepperhan aforesaid, thence northerly along said line of proposed bridge to Dock Street, thence easterly along Dock Street to Broadway, thence northerly along Broadway to Ashburton Avenue, thence easterly along Ashburton Avenue to Oak Hill Avenue, thence northerly along Oak Hill Avenue, and in a line continuous therewith to the northerly line of the village, thence westerly along the northerly line of the village to the easterly shore of the Hudson River southerly to the place of beginning. All persons residing on the northerly side of Main Street, Dock Street, and Ashburton Avenue, and on the westerly side of said proposed bridge, Broadway, Oak Hill Avenue, and the line continuing said Oak Hill Avenue to the north line of the village, on said division line, will be included in the Third Ward. Dated, Yonkers, December 3, 1860. (E-12/6/60 p.3, c.1)

Village, town, county, state, and national politics during the 1850s were concerned with pivotal issues handmade to put their stamp on the future. Of course the national impact of the formation of the Republican Party during the 1850s, and the election of Lincoln in 1860, was the Civil War; a war that tore the United States apart. However, it was also a war that had serious ramifications at the local level. It took men from villages and towns, North and South, to fight the war, and all too frequently die in battle or in prisoner of war camps. The war also had an economic impact both nationally and locally. However, as January, 1861 approached, and the development of the coming storm was seen in uncertain politics, the future of life in the United States and in Yonkers would never be the same again.

Chapter 5

More Real Pillars of Yonkers and Some Others

This chapter contains micro-biographies of some of the most important people in Yonkers during the years 1853 through 1860. More important though, it contains micro-biographies of lesser-known residents of Yonkers who were just as important to the historical development of the town and especially the village. The micro-biographies, gleaned from original documents, the *Yonkers Examiner*, Brown's *1646 - 1922 Old Yonkers*, Allison's *The History of Yonkers*, and the 1860 United States Census, tell the social, economic, and political history of Yonkers in a very special way. Here we find the heartbreak of infant deaths as well as the joy of weddings; deaths from consumption and a variety of other diseases; the dangers of the railroad, drinking, fights, stabbings, and runaway horses; activities of the fire department, the Hatters Guard, and the Yonkers Library Association; and insights into the jury system.

At times some of the information may seem repetitive due to the number of people being in the same organizations, but in fairness to them this was unavoidable. Also, noting where the information was taken from in the context of the micro-biographies may seem to make some of them choppy. It was, nonetheless, necessary to compile them this way so others could also locate the information, verify its accuracy, and check to see if there is more information. In a few instances there is more information. The notations used are TRB for the Town Record Book, AVB for the Associated Village Documents, WWW for *Who Was Who in America*, and E- for the *Yonkers Examiner*. Information was taken from the 1860 United States Census and is noted by stating so. When information was taken from other sources, the author's surname is given followed by the page number(s).

In using the information from the 1860 census a certain amount of caution should be noted. There are several duplications of the same person and families. In a few instances the information is basically the same, but in most cases there are some small but significant differences. All too frequently ages and other information do not match with the 1850 census, and the spelling of a few names was made quite difficult due to the poor quality of the handwriting. Also, it appears that some known residents of Yonkers were not enumerated on the census, and apparently the first name Eliza was frequently used as an abbreviation for Elizabeth. An example of this is the name of Eliza Otis who was Elizabeth Otis wife of Elisha Graves Otis. On the other hand Ann Eliza Coe was listed in a legal advertisement as Eliza and apparently Eliza was her legal name and not shorthand for Elizabeth. One final note concerning historicity. The definitive and historically accurate history of Yonkers, New York has not been written yet. All secondary sources, and the 1860 United States Census, a primary document, contain errors and contradictions. However, the information given by Brown seems to be the least reliable.

Abbott, George P. On Saturday, September 5, 1857 he was elected at a Republican primary meeting to be a delegate to the Republican district convention. (E-9/10/57 p.2, c.6) During 1858 he was appointed an Inspector of Elections for Election District Number One. (TRB) On Monday, August 23, 1858 he was a delegate to the Westchester County Republican Party Convention at Durell's Hotel in Morrisania. (E-8/26/58 p.2, c.2) On Friday evening, September 17, 1858 he was elected to the executive committee of the Yonkers Republican Association. (E-9/23/58 p.2, c.1) On Tuesday, November 16, 1858, he was elected a vice president of a Republican Party meeting in Yonkers. (E-11/18/58 p.2, c.2) On Monday evening March 7, 1859 he was elected a manager of the Yonkers Library Association. (E-3/10/59 p.2, c.7) During 1859 he and L. J. Adams bought a grocery store on the corner of Broadway and Mechanic Street from W. and E. Hallock. (E-5/5/59 p.3, c.2) On Thursday, August 13, 1859 he was elected to the executive committee of the newly formed Republican Association at a Republican Town meeting. He was also chosen at the same meeting to be a delegate to the Assembly District Convention, and he was also chosen to be a delegate to the Republican County Convention. (E-10/20/59 p.3, c.1) During the early part of 1860 he and Adams advertised to rent their store. (E-1/12/60 p.3, c.1) On Monday evening March 26, 1860 he was elected one of thirty-two vice presidents of a Republican election rally meeting at the Getty House. (E-3/29/60 p.2, c.3) On Friday evening, August 10, 1860, he was elected a member of the executive committee of the Yonkers Republican Wide Awakes. (E-8/16/60 p.2, c.6) On Tuesday evening, September 11, 1860 he was elected to the executive committee of the Yonkers Republican Association for a five-month term. After the meeting was over the Republican Wide Awakes held a meeting and elected him 1st Lieutenant of the club. (E-9/13/60 p.2, c.2) (E-9/13/60 p.2, c.2) On the 1860 census he is listed as a 30-year-old grocer with a personal estate of $3,000. His wife F. I., probably Frances I., was also 30 years old and they had three children, Francis who was 7, George who was 3, and Anna who was 9 months old. A William I. G. who was a 23-year-old glazier with a personal estate of $3,000 also lived in their household. Also, a Lizzy Gore, who was 19 years old and probably a servant, lived in their household.

Ackerman, James In 1857 he owned a grocery store with Philip A. Deyo near Getty Square on the corner of Broadway and Dock Street. (E-5/28/57 p.2, c.2) He applied for a store license in 1858, (E-6/3/58 p.2, c.5) and he received his license. (E-6/24/58 p.2, c.5) During the latter part of 1858 he signed a petition to have a meeting of the taxpayers in School District #2 meet to reconsider the location of two new schools; one on the corner of Wood Place and Warburton Avenue, and the other on St. Mary's Street near the Catholic Church and school. (E-12/23/58 p.2, c.2) On the 1860 census he is listed as a 40-year-old grocer with $6,000 in real estate, and a personal estate of $1,000. His wife Mary was also 40, and they had two children at home who were; Martha who was 18, and Frederick who was 4. They had an Irish servant, Ellen, who was 17 years old.

Ackerman, John I. W. During the latter part of 1858 he signed a petition to have a meeting of the taxpayers in School District #2 meet to reconsider the location of two new schools; one on the corner of Wood Place and Warburton Avenue, and the other on St. Mary's Street near the Catholic Church and school. (E-12/23/58 p.2, c.2) On the 1860 census he is listed as a 45-year-old bookkeeper with $2,000 in real estate and a $1,000 personal estate. His wife Nancy was also 45 years old. They had six children. Lucy was 13, Margaret was 10, Mary was 10, Ella was 7, John W. was 15, and Freeman was 3 years old. Another J. Ackerman is listed on the 1860 census as a 30-year-old carpenter with $2,000 in real estate, and a personal estate of $500. His wife, Mrs. Ackerman, was 28 years old, and they had two children; Susan who was 4, and Jane who was 2.

Ackerman, John J. According to Brown he lived on Warburton Avenue during 1858, and built the first elevated railroad. Brown also published a picture of "J. P. Ackerly of Yonkers demonstrating that an elevated train would not fall off the track." (Brown, p.53,154) However, in *Famous First Facts* Charles T. Harvey is given credit for building the first elevated railroad in 1867 in New York City. (Kane, p.236)

Ackerman, John W. During 1858 he lived on Warburton Avenue. (Brown, p. 53) On Saturday afternoon, May 14, 1859, the yacht *Dream* was launched from Glenwood. He had the yacht built under the direction of H. O. Weed. (E-5/19/59 p.2, c.3)

Ackerman, William G. On March 10, 1857 he was elected a Director of the Bank of Yonkers. He either lived or had a business in Kingsbridge. (E-3/12/57 p.2, c.7) On Tuesday, October, 6, 1857 he was appointed a delegate to the Democratic County Convention. (E-10/8/57 p.2, c.2) On Tuesday, October 20, 1857 he married Caroline M. Stilwell, the daughter of John Stilwell. (E-10/22/57 p.2, c.7) On Tuesday evening December 29, 1857 a house which he owned in

Kingsbridge was burned to the ground. A family by the name of Jackson was renting the house from him. They were away on a Christmas visit when the fire occurred. All of the furniture and valuables belonging to the family were destroyed. The value of the house was estimated at $3,500 and was insured for $1,200. (E-12/31/57 p.2, c.5) On March 22, 1859 he was again elected a Director of the Bank of Yonkers. (E-4/7/59 p.2, c.5) On Monday, September 17, 1860 he was to serve on the Grand Jury of the Court of Sessions in Bedford. (E-8/30/60 p.3, c.1) During 1854 and 1855 he was Supervisor of the town of Yonkers. He was an Inspector of Elections for Election District Number Two from 1853 through 1855, and again during 1858. In 1858 he was also elected an Assessor during the town meeting. (TRB)

Achert, Nelson On July 22, 1858 he signed a petition calling for a meeting of eligible voters in School District #2 to decide if the school district should become a Union Free School District. (E-8/5/58 p.4, c.3) During 1859 he and S. Francis Quick were practical builders and joiners at 3, 5, and 7 Atherton Street near Dock Street. (E-5/26/59 p.3, c.2)

Adams, Clarissa She died June 17, 1857 at 66 years of age. Her husband was Platt Adams and they lived on Warburton Avenue. The funeral was held at their house on Saturday, June 20 at 3 p.m. (E-6/18/57 p.3, c.1)

Adams, Hawley On Tuesday, October, 6, 1857 he was appointed a delegate to the Democratic County Convention. (E-10/8/57 p.2, c.2)

Adams, L. J. During 1859 he and George Abbott bought a grocery store on the corner of Broadway and Mechanic Street from W. and E. Hallock. (E-5/5/59 p.3, c.2) During the early part of 1860 he and Abbott advertised to rent their store. (E-1/12/60 p.3, c.1)

Adams, Platt During 1860 he was asked to serve on a Grand Jury. (E-6/14/60 p.2, c.7) On the 1860 census he is listed as a 63-year-old gentleman with $12,000 in real estate, and a personal estate of $2,500. Frances may have been his wife or daughter (see Clarissa Adams). She was 40 years old. There were two Emilys in his household. One was 25 and the other was 11. His servant was Kate O'Donnell who was 24 years old and was from Ireland.

Agate, Joseph Sometime before March, 1857, he donated $25 to the Yonkers Library Association and as a result was made a life member. (E-3/12/57 p.2, c.5) During March, 1859 he was selected to serve as a petit juror during the court session beginning Tuesday, March 18, 1859. (E-3/3/59 p.3, c.1) On the 1860 census he is listed as a 41-year-old merchant with $150,000 in real estate, and a personal estate of $1,000. His wife Mary was 28 years old, and they had one child, Frederick, who was 6. They had a servant, a cook, a coachman, and what looks like a person who did the laundry.

Agnew, Charlotte On Wednesday, April 25, 1860, she was married by Rev. Seward to Charles R. Griffin. She was the eldest daughter of Professor J. H. Agnew. (E-5/24/60 p.3, c.3)

Agnew, J. Holmes During 1858 he was a professor. On Sunday, January 31, 1858 he gave a speech at the First Presbyterian Church. (E-1/28/58 p.2, c.6)

Agnew, Samuel J. During 1858 he lived in Yonkers and was an insurance and real estate broker in business with W. L. Seymour at 19 Nassau Street, NYC, in room No. 5. (E-3/11/58 p.3, c.7) On probably May 20, 1859 he was married at the Presbyterian Church to Mary Platt. J. Holmes Agnew was his father. (E-6/2/59 p.2, c.5)

Aiken, William On Wednesday, November 2, 1859, he won a cake basket in a target shooting contest at Weehawkan, New Jersey. He was a member of the Yonkers Hatters Guard. (E-11/3/59 p.2, c.6)

Ainsworth, Allen On Wednesday, November 2, 1859, he won a goblet in a target shooting contest at Weehawkan, New Jersey. He was a member of the Yonkers Hatters Guard. (E-11/3/59 p.2, c.6) During 1860 he won a Josephine gallery at a Yonkers Hatters Guard target shooting contest. (E-11/1/60 p.3, c.1) On the 1860 census he is listed as a 25-year-old hatter who lived in the same household as his 28-year-old brother whose wife was Sarah. She was 22 years old, and they had two children; Sarah Ann who was 4, and Allen who was 1.

Alcorn, William R. During 1860 he was a plumber and gas fitter on North Broadway. (E-6/21/60 p.3, c.3)

Allen, Charles M. During December, 1860 he was a member of a committee that was organized to run the second annual ball of Neptune Engine Company Number 3 that was to be held at the Getty Lyceum on January 24, 1861. (E-12/13/60 p.2, c.7)

Allen, R. L. In 1857 he lived in Yonkers and dealt in agricultural implements and seeds at 189 and 190 Water Street, NYC. (E-3/5/57 p.3, c.4)

Ambler, George W. On Wednesday, November 2, 1859, he won a pair of butter knives in a target shooting contest at Weehawkan, New Jersey. He was a member of the Yonkers Hatters Guard. (E-11/3/59 p.2, c.6)

Ames, Dyer On Sunday evening, June 27, 1857 he drowned in the Hudson River while taking a bath. He had lived in Yonkers at the Getty House for about two months. He went down to the river at eight o'clock and swam some distance down river with the tide. He ran into difficulty swimming back against the tide and William C. Oakley jumped into a boat and went after him. However, he went under before he could be reached. At the inquest Oakley testified that a Mr. Baxter had saved him Friday night when he got a cramp. He was 49 years of age and he was a good swimmer who thought he had gotten used to the tidal currents of the Hudson River. His body was not found until Wednesday floating face down in the water about forty rods below the lower dock. He was at one time a cashier at the Bank of Middletown, Connecticut, and became a financial agent for a company in Paris. When he returned to the United States he was cashier at the Farmers Bank of Bridgeport, Connecticut. He resigned that position and went to work for Adams and Company in Australia. At the time of his death he was president of a Vermont marble company. He left a widow and three children. The jury at the inquest ruled that it was an accidental death. (E-7/1/58 p.2, c.2)

Anderson, A. During the latter part of 1858 he signed a petition to have a meeting of the taxpayers in School District #2 meet to reconsider the location of two new schools; one on the corner of Wood Place and Warburton Avenue, and the other on St. Mary's Street near the Catholic Church and school. (E-12/23/58 p.2, c.2) On the 1860 census he is listed as a 58-year-old engraver with $3,000 in real estate, and a personal estate of $1,000. His wife Hester was also 58 years old, and they had two children; Lewis who was a 17-year-old carpenter's apprentice, and William who was 8 years old. Another A. Anderson is listed on the same census as a 21-year-old merchant with a personal estate of $1,000.

Anderson, E. O. During 1858 he lived in the Village of Yonkers. During November, 1858 the *Yonkers Herald* erroneously published his marriage to Miss Sarah A. Brown also a resident of the village. (E-11/25/58 p.2, c.1) Sometime during November, 1858 he lost a six-cylinder revolver patented in 1845. He offered a liberal reward for its return. (E-11/25/58 p.3, c.2) He and Sarah A. Brown finally were married for real on Tuesday, December 20, 1859 at the residence of her father, J. P. Brown in Glenwood. (E-12/22/59 p.2, c.6) On the 1860 census he is listed as a 21-year-old grocer with a personal estate of $4,000. His wife Sarah was 19 years old.

Anderson, Isaiah During the latter part of 1858 he signed a petition to have a meeting of the taxpayers in School District #2 meet to reconsider the location of two new schools; one on the corner of Wood Place and Warburton Avenue, and the other on St. Mary's Street near the Catholic Church and school. (E-12/23/58 p.2, c.2) He and his brother bought the harness and saddle business of Joseph Demerest on February 21, 1859. (E-3/10/59 p.3, c.4) On Thursday morning, January 19, 1860, he was on a coroner's jury to look into the death of Mrs. Field who died in a railroad accident at Tarrytown. He was listed as a harness maker. (E-1/26/60 p.2, c.5 see Foster Jenkins for more details) During 1860 he was also the Yonkers agent for Welling's Worm, Diuretic and Condition Powders. The powders were manufactured by Samuel G. Welling in New Rochelle. (E-8/30/60 p.3, c.4) On the 1860 census he is listed as a 37-year-old harness maker with a personal estate of $2,000. His wife Matilda was 35 years old, and they had three children; Henry who was 6, Mary who was 4, and William who was 2 years old. They also had an Irish servant, Hannah, who was 24 years old. A duplicate listing can be found on page 99 of the 1860 census. The only difference is the servant. She is listed as being 26 years old and her name was Hannah Cary.

Anderson, William H. During the latter part of 1858 he signed a petition to have a meeting of the taxpayers in School District #2 meet to reconsidered the location of two new schools; one on the corner of Wood Place and Warburton Avenue, and the other on St. Mary's Street near the Catholic Church and school. (E-12/23/58 p.2, c.2) During 1859 he advertised to sell a light top wagon with two seats. The wagon could be seen at the Factory, Dock Street. (E-8/9/59 p.3, c.4) On the 1860 census he is listed as a 38-year-old carriage maker. His wife was a 34-year-old milliner, and her name is not clear. She was from Massachusetts, and apparently her mother whose name is also unclear probably lived with them. She was 58 years old and was also from Massachusetts. A 3-year-old Aphelia and a 20-year-old carriage maker, Oscar, may have been his children. Edward Stephens and William Brown, both carriage makers, and a servant Mary who was 12 years old and another servant also lived in his household. Another William Anderson is on the 1860 census. He is listed as being a 33-year-old carpenter with a personal estate of $175. His wife was Mary and she was 30 years old, and they had two children; Maggie who was 2, and John who was 1 month old.

Anderson, William R. On May 10, 1854 he and his wife Irene L. sold land on Locust Street to William W. Woodworth. (E-6/3/58 p.4, c.4)

Andrews, E. (M.D.) During 1858 he advertised that on May 1st he was moving to the house next to the Reformed Dutch Church on South Broadway. (E-11/4/58 p.3, c.6)

Andrews, George L. (M.D.) During 1858 his office was at 8 Wheeler's Building. (E-9/9/58 p.3, c.3) He sold a product called Estarbrook's Condition Powders, that was supposed to cure all diseases of horses, cattle, and hogs. He also sold Estarbrook's Green Hoof Ointment that was supposed to cure all problems that a hoofed animal might have. (E-11/4/58 p.3, c.6) He was a druggist. (E-12/9/58 p.4, c.5) On Wednesday evening, December 14, 1859, at their annual meeting in Yonkers he was elected Junior Warden of Rising Star Lodge, No. 450, of F. & A.M. (E-12/15/59 p.2, c.5) On May 28, 1860 he became postmaster of the Yonkers Post Office. The *Yonkers Examiner* said he was a fine choice, but next year a new postmaster would be selected by a Republican president. (E-6/14/60 p.2, c.4 and Walton, p.130) He grew up in Connecticut. (E-6/21/60 p.2, c.4) On the 1860 census he is listed as a 37-year-old postmaster with $2,000 in real estate, and a personal estate of $1,000. His wife Bertha was 27 years old, and they had one 2-year-old child, Jenny. All three were born in Connecticut. During the 1859 town meeting he was elected a Justice of the Peace. (TRB)

Anstice, Henry During 1858 he lived on North Broadway next to a house that was on the corner of Glenwood Avenue, which he had renovated, and was for sale or to be rented. (E-5/27/58 p.3, c.2) He also had other property to sell on Nepperhan, Main, and Pine Streets. He was a real estate agent with offices on North Broadway and at 25 Nassau Street, NYC. (E-6/3/58 p.4, c.1 and E-8/5/58 p.4, c.2) On Monday, December 13, 1858 he became Senior Warden of the newly formed Episcopal Church on Mechanic Street. (E-12/23/58 p.2, c.3) During 1858 he bought the property next to his residence and made about $1,500 worth of improvements. (E-1/20/59 p.2, c.3) On June 28, 1859 he signed a letter addressed to Frederick A. Coe asking legal advice concerning a written promise of the Hudson River Railroad Company to construct a carriageway across the Nepperhan River near the draw bridge. (E-7/7/59 p.2, c.4) On April 9, 1860 he was elected a senior warden at St. Paul's Free Church. (E-4/12/60 p.2, c.6) On Friday, May 4, 1860, he was elected one of six members of the committee on Premiums for Plants and Flowers for the June exhibition of the newly formed Yonkers Horticultural Society. (E-5/17/60 p.3, c.3) On the 1860 census he is listed as a 50-year-old with $30,000 in real estate, and a personal estate of $2,500. His wife Mary was 40 years old, and they had four children; Henry, who was 17 and was a student, Anna who was 15, James who was 9, and [John] who was 6. A Mrs. Perkins lived with them, and they had a servant and a cook.

Appleton, W. H. Sometime before March 2, 1857 he donated 18 volumes to the Yonkers Library Association. (E-3/5/57 p.2, c.6)

Archer, Anthony B. During 1859 he was assistant foreman of Lady Washington Engine Company Number 2. (E-12/29/59 p.2, c.3) On Tuesday, January 3, 1860 he was elected foreman of Lady Washington Engine Company Number 2. (E-1/5/60 p.2, c.4)

Archer, Benjamin During 1856 he was a town Pound Master. (TRB)

Archer, C. D. During 1860 he was a carpenter who was in business with Samuel L. Smith on Bashford Street. (E-6/21/60 p.3, c.2)

Archer, Charles S. During 1857 he lived on Guion Street next to James W. Mitchell. He may have built Mitchell's house. (E-12/31/57 p.2, c.3,4) During 1858 he, John Squire, Jr., and Thomas O. Farrington owned a grocery store at 202 West Street, NYC. (E-9/9/58 p.3, c.7)

Archer, George During November, 1858 he was a member of the arrangement committee for the Second Annual Ball to benefit the widows and orphans of deceased Yonkers firemen. (E-11/25/58 p.2, c.7)

Archer, Henry B. On Wednesday, September 16, 1857 he married Mary Matilda Post. (E-9/17/57 p.2, c.7) On Monday, August 23, 1858 he was a delegate to the Westchester County Republican Party Convention at Durell's Hotel in Morrisania. (E-8/26/58 p.2, c.2) On

Friday evening, September 17, 1858 he was elected to the executive committee of the Yonkers Republican Association. (E-9/23/58 p.2, c.1) On Tuesday, November 16, 1858, he was elected a vice president of a Republican Party meeting in Yonkers. (E-11/18/58 p.2, c.2) On Thursday, August 13, 1859 he was elected a vice president of the newly formed Republican Association at a Republican Town meeting. At the same meeting he was also elected to the association's executive committee, and he was also chosen to be a delegate to the Assembly District Convention. (E-10/20/59 p.3, c.1) On Tuesday, January 3, 1860 he was elected one of two representatives of Lady Washington Engine Company Number 2. (E-1/5/60 p.2, c.4) On Friday evening, August 10, 1860, he was elected a member of the executive committee of the Yonkers Republican Wide Awakes. (E-8/16/60 p.2, c.6) On Tuesday evening, September 11, 1860 he was elected to the executive committee of the Yonkers Republican Association for a five-month term. After the meeting was over the Republican Wide Awakes held a meeting and elected him 2nd Lieutenant of the club. (E-9/13/60 p.2, c.2) On Thursday evening, October 25, 1860, he was one of eight secretaries at a Republican campaign meeting. (E-11/1/60 p.2, c.2)

Archer, John During November, 1858 he was a member of the arrangement committee for the Second Annual Ball to benefit the widows and orphans of deceased Yonkers firemen. (E-11/25/58 p.2, c.7) During December, 1860 he was a member of a committee that was organized to run the second annual ball of Neptune Engine Company Number 3 that was to be held at the Getty Lyceum on January 24, 1861. (E-12/13/60 p.2, c.7) During 1854 and again in 1859 he was a Constable. (TRB)

Archibald, Andrew During the week of January 30, 1860 he was in Kingsbridge and recognized the horse that was rented from John Wheeler and was not returned to him. He told Wheeler about it and eventually Wheeler had his property returned to him. (E-2/9/60 p.2, c.5)

Archibald, Jane M. On Thursday, November 18, 1858 she married Albert H. Speedling. (E-11/25/58 p.2, c.7)

Arnold, Edmund (M.D.) In 1857 he donated a very large and valuable collection of books to the Yonkers Library Association. (E-5/21/57 p.2, c.6) During 1858 he bought a house on Broadway next to the Dutch Church for $7,000. He then spent another $1,000 on renovations and moved in. (E-4/22/58 p.2, c.3) On Tuesday, August 17, 1858 he and sixteen other men wrote C. Jerome Hopkins a letter requesting him to give another piano concert at the Getty House. (E-8/19/58 p.2, c.4) During 1858 he made about $800 in improvements to his house. (E-1/20/59 p.2, c.3) On Sunday, March 13, 1857, his mother Elizabeth died at Sydenham, England. His father was the late W. R. Arnold, Esq. (E-4/7/59 p.2, c.5) His daughter Mary Whiting Arnold died on Thursday, August 15, 1859, at the age of 11 months and 4 days. His wife, and the mother of his daughter, was Eliza Arnold. (E-9/1/59 p.2, c.7) On the 1860 census he is listed as a 35-year-old physician with $15,000 in real estate, and a personal estate of $2,500. His wife Eliza was 30 years old, and they had two children; Edmund who was 4 years old, and Susan who was 6 months old. Eliza Brown, who was 21 was their nurse, and Bridget Hogan who was 16 was their servant. They were both born in Ireland.

Arthur, William H. Sometime between May 13, 1856 and March 5, 1857 he received $6.63 from the Village Treasurer. (E-3/5/57 p.3, c.1) During 1857 he owned a book store at 39 Nassau Street at the corner of Liberty St., NYC. On March 10, 1857 he was elected a Director of the Bank of Yonkers. (E-3/12/57 p.2, c.7) During the latter part of 1858 he signed a petition to have a meeting of the taxpayers in School District #2 meet to reconsider the location of two new schools; one on the corner of Wood Place and Warburton Avenue, and the other on St. Mary's Street near the Catholic Church and school. (E-12/23/58 p.2, c.2) On March 22, 1859 he was again elected a Director of the Bank of Yonkers. (E-4/7/59 p.2, c.5) On Tuesday morning, January 24, 1860 his daughter Kate died at the age of 1 year, 6 months, and 28 days. His wife was Catherine Arthur. (E-1/26/60 p.3, c.1) On Friday, May 4, 1860, he was elected one of five members of the committee on Premiums for Fruits for the June exhibition of the newly formed Yonkers Horticultural Society. (E-5/17/60 p.3, c.3) On the 1860 census he is listed as a 35-year-old bookstore owner with $15,000 in real estate, and a personal estate of $200. His wife Kate was 30 years old, and they had three children; Anna who was 10, Elizabeth who was 8, and James who was 6. Also living in his household was Jane Founney who was 50 years old. In addition to her there was a 20-year-old clerk, William Crawford, a 25-year-old seamstress, Elizabeth Harris, a 20-year-old servant, Ca[th] Gerald, a 55-year-old gardener, William Johnson who was born in Scotland, and a 6-year-old male by the name of Webster who was born in New York and may have been the gardener's son.

Atherton, Henry L. During 1860 he was selected to serve as a grand juror in the Court of Sessions that sat Monday, March 12, 1860. (E-3/8/60 p.2, c.5) On Friday, May 4, 1860, he was elected one of six members of the committee on Premiums for Plants and Flowers for the June exhibition of the newly formed Yonkers Horticultural Society. (E-5/17/60 p.3, c.3)

Atwater, William L. During 1858 he owned property on North Broadway near Lamartine Avenue. (E-10/7/58 p.4, c.5) On June 28, 1859 he signed a letter addressed to Frederick A. Coe asking legal advice concerning a written promise of the Hudson River Railroad Company to construct a carriageway across the Nepperhan River near the draw bridge. (E-7/7/59 p.2, c.4) During 1859 the New York State Supreme Court in a special session in Brooklyn named him one of three Commissioners appointed to open Irving Place. (E-7/7/59 p.2, c.4)

Atwood, W. L. In the early days of the Yonkers Library Association he was made a life member. (E-3/12/57 p.2, c.5)

Austice, H. Just before March 12, 1857 he donated $25 to the Yonkers Library Association and became a life member. (E-3/12/57 p.2, c.5) He lived on North Broadway and had clothing stolen from him. (E-4/9/57 p.2, c.2)

Austin, Alonzo On Saturday evening, February 6, 1858, he was run over by a wagon driven by two Germans who ran him over purposely. They were able to leave the village without being arrested. Austin received a bad cut on the head and was bruised. (E-2/11/58 p.2, c.6)

Austin, Daniel During 1853 he was a tavern keeper.

Austin, Eleazer On Monday, May 21, 1860 he died at the age of 62 years, 3 months, and 18 days. (E-5/24/60 p.3, c.3)

Austin, Jacob S. On Monday, September 17, 1860 he was to serve on the petit jury of the Court of Sessions in Bedford. (E-8/30/60 p.3, c.1)

Back, L. A. On the 1860 census he is listed as a 43-year-old blacksmith with $3,500 in real estate, and a personal estate of $800. His wife Rebecca was 40 years old, and they had four children; Henry who was 12, Louisa who was 9, Charles who was 7, and Frederick who was 4 years old. Rebecca who was 60, and Harriet who was 55 years old also lived with them.

Badde, Thomas W. During the early part of 1858 he owned land between Locust Street and Ashburton Avenue along a line that eventually became Woodworth Avenue. (E-1/7/58 p. 2, c.5)

Bailey, Nelson On Thursday evening, October 25, 1860, he was one of twenty-two vice presidents at a Republican campaign meeting. (E-11/1/60 p.2, c.2)

Bailey, William N. On Wednesday, September 10, 1857 he married Sarah Hallet. (E-9/17/57 p.2, c.7) During 1859 he was in the process of building two wood-frame cottages on Buena Vista Avenue next door to Dr. Chilton that cost about $3,500 each. He was his own builder. (E-1/12/60 p.2, c.1) On Monday evening March 26, 1860 he was elected one of several secretaries of a Republican election rally meeting at the Getty House. (E-3/29/60 p.2, c.3) On Tuesday evening, September 11, 1860 he was elected one of two vice presidents of the Yonkers Republican Association for a five-month term. (E-9/13/60 p.2, c.2) During December, 1860 he was a secretary of a committee that was organized to run the second annual ball of Neptune Engine Company Number 3 that was to be held at the Getty Lyceum on January 24, 1861. (E-12/13/60 p.2, c.7)

Baird, E. P. He was a member of the Yonkers Debating Society and a member of its Arrangement Committee. (E-3/15/57 p.2, c.7)

Baird, Henry M. (Rev.) Sometime, probably during the 1850s, he lived in Yonkers. Then he went to Princeton College, N.J., then to the University of New York to be a professor teaching Greek. (E-9/15/59 p.3, c.1) During 1860 he apparently came back to Yonkers and was a professor at the University of the City of New York. On Wednesday, August 15, 1860 he was married by Rev. Carter to Susan E. Baldwin. (E-8/16/60 p.2, c.7) On the 1860 census he is listed as a 28-year-old professor who was living with his father and mother. His father was Robert Baird who was a 61-year-old clergyman.

Baird, Sarah Ann On April 2, 1857 she married John Brown. (E-4/23/57 p.2, c.6)

Baker, N. Z. During 1857 he was the secretary of the Yonkers Cricket Club. (E-7/16/57 p.2, c.7)

Baldwin, Anson During the spring of 1857 he purchased property on the corner of Palisade and Ashburton Avenues and remodeled the house that was on the property. The venture cost him about $800. During the same year he built a three-story brick house on the west side of Palisade Avenue in the rear of his residence. The building cost $1,600. His business, Baldwin, Waring and Company, built two brick houses on their factory property for some employees of the business at a cost of $3,000. (E-12/31/57 p.2, c.3) During the early part of 1858 he either was elected or appointed president of the Yonkers Association for Improving the Condition of the Poor. (E-3/4/58 p.2, c.7) On March 1, 1858 he and his son, Hall F. Baldwin, bought the shares of William C. Waring and Chester C. Waring of the old Waring, Baldwin and Company and began the firm of A. Baldwin and Son. They manufactured wool hats. (E-3/4/58 p.3 c.5) On Tuesday, November 16, 1858, he was elected a vice president of a Republican Party meeting in Yonkers. (E-11/18/58 p.2, c.2) Also during 1858, he erected a green and grape house, and made other improvements at his residence on Locust Hill Avenue. The work cost him about $1,200. (E-1/20/59 p.2, c.3) During 1859 he added a billiard room, a 20' X 40' parlor, a number of bedrooms, and several other improvements including stained glass windows in the parlor that cost about $6,000. He also built a conservatory in his garden that could rival any in the country for $3,000. (E-1/12/60 p.2, c.2) On Monday evening March 26, 1860 he was elected one of thirty-two vice presidents of a Republican election rally meeting at the Getty House. (E-3/29/60 p.2, c.3) On May 1, 1860 he, Hall F. Baldwin and William C. Waring formed the Union Hat Factory. They made wool hats. (E-5/3/60 p.2, c.6) On Tuesday, May 8, 1860, he was elected one of two vice presidents of the newly formed Yonkers Horticultural Society. (E-5/17/60 p.3, c.3)

Baldwin, Carrie On Monday evening, December 26, 1859 she was married by Rev. Carter to Thomas S. Finin at her father's house. She was the daughter of Evert K. Baldwin. (E-12/29/59 p.2, c.6)

Baldwin, Ebenezer On the 1860 census he is listed as an 85-year-old gentleman with $3,000 in real estate, and a personal estate of $1,000. His wife Lydia was 73 years old. This is in conflict with the 1850 census where she is listed as being 68 years old. (See vol. 1.)

Baldwin, Evert K. He was a member of the Committee of Arrangements for the first annual Fire Department Fund Ball held to raise funds to help widows and orphans of deceased Yonkers firemen. The ball was held on Thursday evening, March 4, 1858. (E-2/18/58 p.3, c.5) During 1858 he was the village treasurer. (E-8/12/58 p.3, c.2) During 1858 and 1859 he was a member of the arrangement committee for the Second Annual Ball to benefit the widows and orphans of deceased Yonkers firemen. (E-11/25/58 p.2, c.7) He was a member of the firm Baldwin & Bradley, masons. During 1858 he built a brick house for himself on Broadway near Washington Street. The house cost about $4,000. (E-1/20/59 p.2, c.3) On Thursday evening, September 1, 1859 he was elected a representative of Hope Hook and Ladder Company. (E-9/8/59 p.3, c.1) On Wednesday, November 2, 1859, he was chosen as a judge of a target shooting match at Weehawkan, New Jersey, between the men of the Yonkers Hatters Guard. (E-11/3/59 p.3, c.6) On Thursday evening, September 1, 1859 he was elected Foreman of Hope Hook and Ladder Company. (E-9/8/59 p.3, c.1) On Thursday evening, September 1, 1859, at a fire department meeting he was appointed by the committee that was authorized to buy a new fire engine to be a member of that committee. (E-12/29/59 p.2, c.2) On Monday, September 3, 1860 he was to serve on the grand jury of the Court of Oyer and Terminer in White Plains. (E-8/30/60 p.3, c.1) On Monday evening, September 17, 1860, he was elected Treasurer of the Fire Department Fund Association. (E-9/20/60 p.2, c.7) On Thursday evening, October 25, 1860, he was one of twenty-two vice presidents at a Republican campaign meeting. (E-11/1/60 p.2, c.2) On the 1860 census he is listed as a 40-year-old mason with $8,000 in real estate, and a personal estate of $1,000. His wife Amelia was 35 years old, and they had four children; M. I. who was a 15-year-old female, Lora who was 7, Ida who was 5, and William who was 1.

Baldwin, Hall F. On March 1, 1858 he and his father, Anson Baldwin, bought the shares of William C. Waring and Chester C. Waring of the old Waring, Baldwin and Company and began the firm of A. Baldwin and Son. They manufactured wool hats. (E-3/4/58 p.3 c.5) On May 1, 1860 he, Anson Baldwin and William C. Waring formed the Union Hat Factory. They made wool hats. (E-5/3/60 p.2, c.6)

Baldwin, Susan E. On Wednesday, August 15, 1860 she was married by Rev. Carter to Henry M. Baird. She was the daughter of Anson Baldwin. (E-8/16/60 p.2, c.7)

Ball, Samuel On Wednesday, June 30, 1857 he bought a lot on Buena Vista Avenue for $535. (E-7/1/58 p.2, c.2)

Bangs, Francis N. During 1858 he lived on Warburton Avenue. (Brown, p.61) On Tuesday, January 31, 1860 he and seven others sent a letter to R. J. DeCordova asking him to visit Yonkers and deliver his humorous lecture on "Wall Street." (E-2/16/60 p.2, c.5) During March, 1860 he was elected as an alternate delegate to the Republican State Convention. (E-4/5/60 p.2, c.3) On Tuesday evening, September 11, 1860 he was elected to the executive committee of the Yonkers Republican Association for a five-month term. (E-9/13/60 p.2, c.2) On Saturday, September 29, 1860 he was a delegate to the Republican First Assembly District Convention that was held in Morrisania Hall, Morrisania. At the same convention he was chosen to represent Yonkers during the Congressional Convention. (E-10/4/60 p.2, c.2) On Thursday evening, October 25, 1860, he chaired a Republican campaign meeting. (E-11/1/60 p.2, c.2) On the 1860 census he is listed as a 31-year-old attorney who had a personal estate of $400. Also living in his household was Amelia who was 22, Emma who was 12, and William who was 1. There was also a cook and a nurse living in his household.

Barclay, John On Saturday night, September 8, 1860 he attempted to stab Henry Hetzelburg with a dagger. He was about 18 years old and he was sent to the county prison for defaulting on a fine and surety to keep the peace. (E-9/13/60 p.2, c.4)

Bard, E. H. Starting on Friday, October 9, 1857 he taught voice in the lecture room of the Presbyterian Church. (E-10/1/57 p.3, c.1)

Barker, Isaac N. On Monday night, December 17, 1860 he was installed as an officer into the Rising Star Lodge of Free and Accepted Masons as Tiler. (E-12/20/60 p.2, c.3)

Barnes, Sarah H. On Saturday, November 27, 1857 she married John E. Baxter. (E-12/2/58 p.2, c.6)

Barrett, E. During 1860 he won $2.50 at a Yonkers Hatters Guard target shooting contest. (E-11/1/60 p.3, c.1)

Barrett, E. L. (Rev.) During May of 1857 he donated about 12 volumes of books to the Yonkers Library Association. (E-5/21/57 p.2, c.6)

Barry, Samuel S. On June 28, 1859 he signed a letter addressed to Frederick A. Coe asking legal advice concerning a written promise of the Hudson River Railroad Company to construct a carriageway across the Nepperhan River near the draw bridge. (E-7/7/59 p.2, c.4)

Bartholomew, George H. During 1859 on Locust Hill Avenue he used a Grover and Baker noiseless sewing machine. (E-8/11/59 p.3, c.2) On Monday night, December 17, 1860 he was installed as an officer into the Rising Star Lodge of Free and Accepted Masons as Marshall. (E-12/20/60 p.2, c.3)

Bartlett, A. H. During the early part of 1857 he dissolved a business partnership with a Harvey. The business was in the Spuyten Duyvil section of Yonkers. (E-4/9/57 p.5, c.7)

Bashford, Andrew On the 1860 census he is listed as a 24-year-old postal clerk. He lived in the house of his mother Ester. According to the 1850 census he should have been 26 in 1860.

Bashford, Emma F. On Wednesday, February 8, 1860 she was married by Rev. Carter to William Dean of Tarrytown. (E-2/16/60 p.2, c.7)

Bashford, Ester A. She was postmistress of the Yonkers Post Office from May 31, 1848 to May 27, 1860. (E-6/14/60 p.2, c.4 and Walton, p.130) On the 1860 census she is listed as being 54 years old. Interestingly she is not listed as postmistress. Rather, her son Henry is listed as postmaster. Besides her sons who are noted separately in this section, there are also listed on the 1860 census as living in her household Emma Dean who was 22 years old, William Dean who was a 24-year-old stationery store owner with a personal estate of $2,000, and Kate Rock who was a 30-year-old servant from Ireland. Also in the household are a George and a John who probably weren't Bashfords, but rather they were probably related to Emma and William Dean. George was a clerk. There was also a John Coon who was 14 years old living in her household.

Bashford, Henry W. He was one of seven original members of Hope Hook and Ladder Company No. 1 when it was first formed on August 15, 1853. In 1855 he was elected during the town meeting to serve a full term as Justice of the Peace. (TRB) (E-12/29/59 p.2, c.2) During 1857 he owned a lumber yard at 13 Dock Street. (E-2/5/57 p.3, c.2) During the early days of the Yonkers Library Association he was made a life member. (E-3/12/57 p.2, c.6) On March 10, 1857 he was elected a Director of the Bank of Yonkers. (E-3/12/57 p.2, c.6) Also during 1857 he was a Director of the Yonkers Gas Light Company. (E-8/13/57 p.3, c.3) On Wednesday, July 29, 1857 he was again elected a director of the Yonkers Gas Light Company. (E-8/27/57 p.3, c.5) During the early part of 1858 he either was elected or appointed secretary of the Yonkers Association for Improving the Condition of the Poor. (E-3/4/58 p.2, c.7) During 1858 he was also a real estate and insurance agent. He was also a stock, note, and exchange broker as well as a general commission merchant. During 1858 he opened an office on the corner of Broadway and Main Street. (E-4/15/58 p.2, c.7) On Tuesday, August 17, 1858 he and sixteen other men wrote C. Jerome Hopkins a letter requesting him to give another piano concert at the Getty House. (E-8/19/58 p.2, c.4) During the latter part of 1858 he signed a petition to have a meeting of the taxpayers in School District #2 meet to reconsider the location of two new schools; one on the corner of Wood Place and Warburton Avenue, and the other on St. Mary's Street near the Catholic Church and school. (E-12/23/58 p.2, c.2) On February 15,

1859 he sold his lumber company at 13 Dock Street to Read, Speedling, & Company. (E-3/31/59 p.2, c.7) His old business was bought by Jacob Read, Alonzo P. Speedling, and John Nairn. E-4/7/59 p.2, c.3) On March 22, 1859 he was again elected a Director of the Bank of Yonkers. (E-4/7/59 p.2, c.5) During 1859 he was also an insurance agent for the Home Insurance Company that had their offices at 112 and 114 Broadway, NYC. (E-10/6/59 p.3, c.7) During 1860 he owned the Grove House which was apparently on the Hudson River at the foot of Locust Street. On Monday night, February 6, 1860 an arsonist set it on fire and it burned to the ground. The house was empty at the time and it was almost fully insured. The house was primarily used by people who rented it during the summer. The renters' furniture was totally destroyed, but also fully insured. (E-2/9/60 p.2, c.3) On the 1860 census he is listed as a 28-year-old postmaster. He lived in the household of his mother Ester.

Bashford, James During 1857 he owned a carriage factory on Mechanic Street next to the store owned by Joseph Rhodes. (E-6/18/57 p.3, c.3) On the 1860 census he is listed as a 57-year-old carriage maker with $8,000 in real estate and a personal estate of $2,000. His wife Elizabeth was 67 years old. (See Vol. 1)

Bashford, John During 1858 he lived on North Broadway and Bashford Avenue was named after him. (Brown, p.61) On an 1858 map of the village Bashford Street originally ran from Dock Street to Wells Avenue. Later most of the street was inside the confines of the Otis Elevator factory. Brown's little book was published in 1922 and while there may have been a Bashford Avenue he probably meant Street. According to Brown he owned a hotel on the dock, was a director of a Yonkers bank, and a portrait of his daughter, Joanna, was on one of the bills of the bank. (Brown, pp. 75-76) Brown is in conflict with Allison where Allison has the original John Bashford dying in 1848, which is apparently accurate. Also, according to Allison it was the daughter of the 1840s John Bashford who adorned "the bills of the Yonkers Bank until 1865." (Allison, p. 160) This John Bashford may have been a son of the John Bashford noted in Vol. I. On Thursday, August 13, 1859 he was chosen as a delegate to the Republican Assembly District Convention by the newly formed Republican Association at a Republican Town meeting. (E-10/20/59 p.3, c.1) During December, 1860 he was a member of a committee that was organized to run the second annual ball of Neptune Engine Company Number 3 that was to be held at the Getty Lyceum on January 24, 1861. (E-12/13/60 p.2, c.7)

Bate, David During 1857 he sold lumber and coal at 6 Dock Street with a man named Walsh. (E-3/5/57 p.3, c.5) By July 7, 1857 he became the sole owner of the business. (E-7/2/57 p.3, c.4) During the latter part of 1858 he signed a petition to have a meeting of the taxpayers in School District #2 to reconsider the location of two new schools; one on the corner of Wood Place and Warburton

Avenue, and the other on St. Mary's Street near the Catholic Church and school. (E-12/23/58 p.2, c.2) On Saturday morning, April 16, 1859 the schooner *Fairfax* on her way from Elizabethtown to Yonkers sank near Robbins' Reef while carrying fifty tons of coal he owned. A sudden wind caused the cargo to shift and the boat capsized. The coal was a total loss. (E-4/21/59 p.2, c.5) Sometime after July 2, 1857 he took into his lumber and coal business with him, as a partner, Jacob Steen. By October, 1859 the partnership was dissolved and Steen continued by himself in the business. Evidently, the loss of coal during April forced him into bankruptcy because he was sued on three separate days; August 1, September 3, and October 3 in the New York State Supreme Court. As a result of these suits the Westchester County Sheriff, William Bleakley, Jr., was to sell his property on Dock Street on December 8, 1859. (E-10/13/59 p.3, c.2)

Batten, Sylvester J. During 1857 he was a Director of the Yonkers Gas Light Company. (E-8/13/57 p.3, c.3) On Wednesday, July 29, 1857 he was again elected a director of the gas company. (E-8/27/57 p.3, c.5) On Wednesday, September 16, 1857 John Olmsted as president of the Bank of Yonkers sued him for $426.87 with interest dated back to April 10, 1857, and court costs. (E-9/24/57 p.3, c.2)

Baum, J. Late in 1857 he opened a clothing store in the Getty building in Getty Square. He was a tailor, and he sold ready-made clothing for men and boys. (E-12/3/57 p.3, c.3) By July, 1858 he moved his business to 5 Wheeler's Building. (E-7/1/58 p.3, c.3) During May, 1860 he moved from Getty Square to the Getty Block on North Broadway opposite Dock Street. (E-6/7/60 p.1, c.1) During 1860 he sold overcoats on sale for $3 to $15, frock coats for $3 to $12, pants for $2.50 to $6, and vests for $1.25 to $5. (E-8/2/60 p.4, c.3)

Baur, Augustus During 1859 he opened a dentist office in Radford's Building. He sold a 20-caret-gold plate for $3.00. He practiced in England, France, Germany, Boston, and New York. His office hours were from 8 a.m. to 6 p.m. He called his practice the Hudson River American, French and German Dental Establishment. (E-9/8/59 p.3, c.3)

Baxter, A. On Wednesday, June 30, 1857 he bought a lot on Hudson Street for $1,305. He bought another lot on the same day on Depot Street for $710. (E-7/1/58 p.2, c.2)

Baxter, John E. On Saturday, November 27, 1858, he married Sarah H. Barnes. (E-12/2/58 p.2, c.6)

Beal, Mary Anna (Miss) On Saturday, March 27, 1858 she died at the age of 31. She was formerly of Newark, New Jersey. (E-4/1/58 p.3, c.2.)

Beal, William During 1857 he was the superintendent of the Yonkers Gas Light Company. (E-8/27/57 p.2, c.5) On Thursday,

November 25, 1858 he lost his black and tan English terrier dog. The dog answered to the name "Tip," and could be returned at the gas company. (E-12/2/58 p.3, c.1) On Monday, December 13, 1858 he became Vestryman of the newly formed Episcopal Church on Mechanic Street. (E-12/23/58 p.2, c.2) Around August, 1859 the Library Association was incorporated and he became a member of the Board of Trustees. (E-8/14/59 p.2, c.4) On April 9, 1860 he was elected a Vestryman at St. Paul's Free Church. (E-4/12/60 p.2, c.6) On Friday evening, August 10, 1860, he was elected a member of the executive committee of the Yonkers Republican Wide Awakes. (E-8/16/60 p.2, c.6) On Thursday evening, October 25, 1860, he was one of eight secretaries at a Republican campaign meeting. (E-11/1/60 p.2, c.2) On the 1860 census he is listed as a 22-year-old in the gas works business. He lived in the household of Daniel Bates who was a 42-year-old lumber merchant with a personal estate of $2,500. Bates' wife was Ann who was 33 years old, and they had three children; Hannah who was 17, Margaret who was 15, and Martha who was 19. (See also David Bate.)

Bean, John During 1858 he was a Worshipful Master of the American Protestant Association Yonkers Lodge 31. (E-/8/12/58 p.3, c.1)

Beasley, L. H. On Wednesday, November 2, 1859, he won a vest pattern in a target shooting contest at Weehawkan, New Jersey. He was a member of the Yonkers Hatters Guard. (E-11/3/59 p.2, c.6)

Beers, William H. Early in 1858 he lost a terrier dog. The dog had a brown spot on each eye and answered to the name of Terry. (E-1/21/57 p.3, c.3) On Tuesday, August 17, 1858 he and sixteen other men wrote C. Jerome Hopkins a letter requesting him to give another piano concert at the Getty House. (E-8/19/58 p.2, c.4)

Belknap, Charles On the 1860 census he is listed as a 52-year-old contractor with $2,500 in real estate and a $500 personal estate. His wife Jane was 41 years old, and they had four children. Mary was 16, Ethelbert, who was a bookkeeper, was 17, William was 15, and Ida was 5 years old. They had a servant, Jane, who was 25 years old. She was from Ireland.

Bell, Agnes During 1859 she became the principal of a new school on Wood Place in the Union Free School District #2. (E-4/28/59 p.2, c.4)

Bell, Alonzo On March 2, 1857 he was elected President of the Yonkers Debating Society. (E-3/5/57 p.2, c.6) Also during 1857 he owned a stoneyard at 4 Dock Street where he sold flagging, curbing and gutter stones. (E-8/20/57 p.3, c.2) On Monday evening, March 1, 1858 he was again elected President of the Yonkers Debating Society. (E-3/4/58 p.2, c.2) However, on March 18, 1858 he addressed the Debating Society as its retiring president. (E-3/25/58 p.2, c.1) But, he was listed as the society's president during September, 1858. (E-9/2/58 p.2, c.6) On Tuesday, November 16, 1858, he was elected a secretary of a Republican Party meeting in Yonkers. (E-11/18/58 p.2, c.2) On Monday, February 14, 1859 he gave a lecture at the Lyceum on "Elements of Success." The editor of the *Yonkers Examiner* called him "our eloquent young friend." (E-2/10/59 p.2, c.1) On Monday evening March 7, 1859 he was elected secretary of the Yonkers Library Association. (E-3/10/59 p.2, c.7) On Monday evening, March 21, 1859, he delivered a speech before 400 members of the Yonkers Debating Society entitled "General Intelligence and the Education of Young Men." (E-3/24/59 p.2, c.2) On Thursday evening, October 25, 1860, he was one of eight secretaries at a Republican campaign meeting. (E-11/1/60 p.2, c.2) During December, 1860 he was also an agent for the Cosmopolitan Art Association which sold paintings. (E-12/13/60 p.3, c.1)

Bell, James C. During the early days of the Yonkers Library Society he was made a life member. (E-3/12/57 p.2, c.5) On March 10, 1857 he was elected a Director of the Bank of Yonkers. (E-3/12/57 p.2, c.7) On Monday afternoon, January 3, 1858, his two sons, Philip T. and Jonathan Wethered, were ice skating on a pond just north of Baldwin's factory with Victor MacFarlane, who was the son of Duncan MacFarlane, when one of his sons fell through the ice. The other son went after him and he also fell through the ice. Victor MacFarlane used a long pole furnished by Mr. Bell just in case such an incident were to occur and was able to get one of the boys out of the water. The other boy had gone under the ice and the ice had to be broken to rescue him. Both boys were unharmed. On Saturday, January 29, 1859 Victor was presented with a silver watch and gold charm by the two boys. The watch had an inscription on it with the names of the boys and the date January 3, 1859. (E-1/6/59 p.2, c.2 and E-2/3/59 p.2, c.2) During 1858 he made some improvements to his houses on Locust Hill Avenue and Palisade Avenue. The improvements cost about $1,500. (E-1/20/59 p.2, c.4) He came to Yonkers sometime during 1849. He was head of a wealthy banking firm in NYC. (E-3/10/59 p.2, c.1) On March 22, 1859 he was elected a Director of the Bank of Yonkers. (E-4/7/59 p.2, c.5) On the 1860 census he is listed as a 46-year-old banker with $50,000 in real estate, and a personal estate of $75,000. His wife H. Bell was 39 years old and they had five children; Philip who was 14, John who was 12, James who was 10, Lizzy who was 8, and Jacob who was 6. In their household they had a nurse, cook, and a servant. They were from Ireland, and they were H. Morrisey who was a 30-year-old nurse, Eliza Dorson who was a 40 year cook, and Jane King who was a 30-year-old servant. During 1859 and 1860 he was a member of the village Board of Trustees.

Bell, Stephen At his residence, on Saturday, April 7, 1860, he was married by Rev. Waters to Jeannette Terry. (E-4/19/60 p.2, c.7)

Bell, T. Jr. During 1857 he lived in Yonkers and was an auctioneer and real estate broker in NYC at 5 Beekman Street in the Park

Bank Building rooms 13 and 15. He also loaned money, was a dealer in stocks, and collected rents. (E-7/9/57 p.4, c.7)

Bell, Thaddeus During the early part of 1858 he owned land between Lamartine Avenue and Gold Street along a line that eventually became Woodworth Avenue. (E-1/7/58 p. 2, c.5) During the latter part of 1858 he signed a petition to have a meeting of the taxpayers in School District #2 meet to reconsider the location of two new schools; one on the corner of Wood Place and Warburton Avenue, and the other on St. Mary's Street near the Catholic Church and school. (E-12/23/58 p.2, c.2) During November, 1859 he was asked to serve as a juror for the petit jury of Westchester County. (E-11/24/59 p.3, c.1) During 1859 he built a house on Warburton Avenue near Union Place that cost $3,500. (E-1/12/60 p.2, c.3) On Friday evening, February 3, 1860, in the absence of the president he was appointed Chairman of a Yonkers Republican Association meeting. (E-2/9/60 p.2, c.5) On Tuesday evening, September 11, 1860 he was elected one of two vice presidents of the Yonkers Republican Association for a five-month term. (E-9/13/60 p.2, c.2) On Thursday evening, October 25, 1860, he was one of twenty-two vice presidents at a Republican campaign meeting. (E-11/1/60 p.2, c.2)

Bell, William Sometime before March 12, 1857 he donated $25 to the Yonkers Library Association and became a life member. (E-3/12/57 p.2, c.5) On Monday morning August 8, 1857 he had a horse run away from him. The horse ran down Broadway and was eventually stopped, but his wagon was completely destroyed. (E-8/13/57 p.2, c.6) During the spring of 1857 he built a stable, a carriage house, and several other out-buildings. They were built in an Italian design and they cost about $3,000. (E-12/31/57 p.2, c.3) During 1858 he added a greenhouse and made other improvements to his property costing about $2,000. (E-1/20/59 p.2, c.4) On Thursday evening, April 26, 1860, he was elected a trustee of the Yonkers Library Association. (E-5/3/60 p.2, c.3) On Friday, May 4, 1860, he was elected one of ten members of the executive committee of the newly formed Yonkers Horticultural Society. (E-5/17/60 p.3, c.3) On Friday, May 4, 1860, he was elected one of five members of the committee on Premiums for Fruits for the June exhibition of the newly formed Yonkers Horticultural Society. (E-5/17/60 p.3, c.3)

Benedict, Charles W. During 1858 he owned property on the west side of North Broadway near Lamartine Avenue. (E-10/7/58 p.4, c.5)

Bennett, Franklin T. He was a member of the Committee of Arrangements for the first annual Fire Department Fund Ball held to raise funds to help widows and orphans of deceased Yonkers firemen. The ball was held on Thursday evening, March 4, 1858. (E-2/18/58 p.3, c.5) During November, 1858 he was a member of the arrangement committee for the Second Annual Ball to benefit the widows and orphans of deceased Yonkers firemen. (E-11/25/58 p.2, c.7) During 1859 he was in business with Carlton E. Merrill. The business was dissolved on July 1, 1859, and he continued it under his name. (E-7/28/59 p.3, c.2) Their business was Bennett and Merrill's Yonkers and New York Express Company. (E-7/28/59 p.3, c.1,2)

Bennett, J. During 1860 he won a cup at a Yonkers Hatters Guard target shooting contest. (E-11/1/60 p.3, c.1)

Benson, John During 1857 he was a plumber, a tin and sheet iron worker, a locksmith, and a bell hanger. He also installed furnaces and heaters, and fixed speaking tubes with or without the patented Alarm Whistle. His shop was on Broadway opposite the Getty House. (E-2/5/57 p.3, c.2) On Monday evening March 26, 1860 he was elected one of thirty-two vice presidents of a Republican election rally meeting at the Getty House. (E-3/29/60 p.2, c.3) Sometime after February, 1857 he moved his shop to Main Street, and in 1860 he sold the business to C. Soame. (E-6/14/60 p.2, c.7) On the 1860 census he is listed as a 40-year-old landlord from England with a personal estate of $1,000. His wife Jane was also 40 years old, and they had at least four children; William who was 17, Mary who was 14, Jane who was 10, and John who was 7 years old. There were 12 males living in his tenement, and one female servant, Mary, who was from Ireland.

Benziger, W. During 1857 he taught German, oil painting, drawing, and music at the Yonkers Collegiate Institute. (E-6/23/59 p.3, c.3)

Bergman, S. During 1860 he won a cake basket at a Yonkers Hatters Guard target shooting contest. (E-11/1/60 p.3, c.1)

Berrian, John During 1856 a John L. Berrian was an Inspector of Elections for Election District Number Two. (TRB) During 1858 he was an anti-Lecompton Democrat who was appointed a vice president of a meeting in Morrisania Hall. (E-6/24/58 p.2, c.1)

Berrian, Richard During 1859 he was an Inspector of Elections for Election District Number Two. (TRB)

Berrian, S. During 1860 he won a cake basket at a Yonkers Hatters Guard target shooting contest. (E-11/1/60 p.3, c.1)

Berrian, W. During 1860 he won a box of cigars at a Yonkers Hatters Guard target shooting contest. (E-11/1/60 p.3, c.1)

Bertine, James On Monday evening March 26, 1860 he was elected one of several secretaries of a Republican election rally meeting at the Getty House. (E-3/29/60 p.2, c.3)

Berwick, James During the spring of 1857 he bought a small shanty-style house that was being built by J. H. Jennings. The house was opposite the house of W. H. Arthur before he moved it and enlarged it converting it into a comfortable little tenement. The upper floor was occupied by Miss Blair who used it as a school for small children. Moving and renovating the structure cost him about

$2,000. (E-12/31/57 p.2, 4.) On July 22, 1858 he signed a petition calling for a meeting of eligible voters in School District #2 to decide if the school district should become a Union Free School District. (E-8/5/58 p.4, c.3) During 1859 he built a brick house on Broadway near Irving Place that cost about $3,000. (E-1/12/60 p.2, c.2)

Bettner, George (Dr.) On Sunday, May 6, 1860 he died at the age of 50. He lived in Riverdale. (E-5/10/60 p.2, c.6)

Bettner, James E. (His name was spelled with one t in the article about the fire.) During 1860 he owned land on Riverdale Avenue. (E-1/19/60 p.3, c.2) On Thursday morning, December 13, 1860 his carriage house burned down. He lost two horses, several carriages, and harnesses. Thieves with a careless light were suspected. (E-12/20/60 p.2, c.3)

Bettner, James (Mrs.) She was the manager of a collection to help the Ladies of Mount Vernon Association make the grave of president George Washington a public shrine. No donation larger than a dollar was accepted. However, those who wanted to donate more could donate a dollar for each member of their family. (E-8/19/58 p.2, c.4) Later any amount could be donated. (E-9/9/58 p.2, c.4)

Bicker, Henry K. On Monday, January 4, 1858 he died of consumption in Yonkers. Emelia Sophia Bicker was his daughter. He may have lived in NYC. (E-1/7/58 p.2, c.7)

Bicknell, Joseph I. On Friday evening, September 17, 1858, he was elected one of six vice presidents of the Yonkers Republican Association. (E-9/23/58 p.2, c.1) On Monday, December 20, 1858 he visited a Mr. Bolton near Kingsbridge. While there he left his horse alone for a few minutes and a thief stole his saddle. (E-12/23/58 p.2, c.7) On Saturday evening, October 20, 1860, he was elected treasurer of the Spuyten Duyvil Republican Club at a meeting held at the Iron Foundry. (E-10/25/60 p.2, c.3) On Thursday evening, October 25, 1860, he was one of twenty-two vice presidents at a Republican campaign meeting. (E-11/1/60 p.2, c.2) During 1859 he was an Inspector of Elections for Election District Number Two. (TRB)

Bicknell, William J. In late 1858 he was selected as a juror for the petit jury for a Court of Sessions at Bedford. (E-12/2/58 p.2, c.3)

Bills,---- During 1857 he lived just south of the village. On Sunday evening August 9, 1857 he and Harvey Post had harnesses stolen from their out-buildings. (E-8/13/57 p.2, c.6)

Birdsall, Thomas W. He was to be a juror for the Petit Court at White Plains on June 21, 1858. (E-6/17/58 p.2, c.2) On Tuesday, August 17, 1858 he and sixteen other men wrote C. Jerome Hopkins a letter requesting him to give another piano concert at the Getty House. (E-8/19/58 p.2, c.4) On Monday, December 13, 1858 he became Vestryman of the newly formed Episcopal Church on

Mechanic Street. (E-12/23/58 p.2, c.3) On Monday evening March 26, 1860 he was elected one of thirty-two vice presidents of a Republican election rally meeting at the Getty House. (E-3/29/60 p.2, c.3) On the 1860 census he is listed as a 36-year-old gentleman with $10,000 in real estate, and a personal estate of $2,000. His wife Margaret was also 36 years old, and they had two children; Louisa who was 10, and Anna who was 8. They also had a cook and a servant.

Bishop, Dwight During 1858 he was a wholesale and retail seller of furniture at 394 Hudson Street, NYC. He lived in Yonkers on Prospect Hill. (E-5/13/58 p.3, c.1) On the 1860 census he is listed as a 52-year-old merchant. His wife Ann was 42, and they had three children; Maria who was 19, Clara who was 4, and Harry who was 3. They also had four servants.

Blacknell, J. I. On Tuesday, November 16, 1858, he was elected a vice president of a Republican Party meeting in Yonkers. (E-11/18/58 p.2, c.2)

Blackwell, James About 1847 he bought land between Ashburton Avenue and the Hudson River to Wicker Street for $150 an acre. He then laid out Warburton Avenue and some cross streets in order to divide the land into lots and sell them. He made a fortune doing this. (E-3/5/57 p.2, c.1) This may be James H. Blackwell. See below and Vol. 1 pp. 37-38.

Blackwell, James H. On Monday, June 21, 1858 he died at the age of 72. (E-6/24/58 p.2, c.7) He owned 51 acres of land just north of the village that had a view of the Hudson River and Long Island Sound. The property was opposite the property of C. H. Lilienthal, and was advertised for sale. Sidney S. Blackwell and Benjamin Brown were the executors of his will and they were selling the property. (E-3/8/60 p.3, c.1)

Blackwell, J. G. R. On Tuesday, September 21, 1858 sometime after 2 a.m. thieves who had broken into several houses in Yonkers stole his boat and sailed down the Hudson River. The boat was found just below Manhattanville. (E-9/23/58 p.2, c.4)

Blackwell, Joseph During 1858 he renovated his house next to the gas works. It cost him about $600. (E-1/20/59 p.2, c.5)

Blackwell, Sidney S. During the early part of 1858 he owned land between Lamartine Avenue and Gold Street along a line that eventually became Woodworth Avenue. (E-1/7/58 p.2, c.5) On the 1860 census a Sidney Blackwell is listed as a 47-year-old gentleman with $50,000 in real estate, and a personal estate of $15,000. His wife Eliza was 37 years old, and they had four children; Agnes who was 22, William who was a 20-year-old student, Mary who was an 18-year-old student, and Sidney who was a 17-year-old clerk. They had a cook, a servant, and a coachman.

Blauvelt, Daniel During 1854 he was a Constable for the town of Yonkers. (TRB) During 1857 he was the Chief Engineer of the Fire

Department. (E-10/29/57 p.2, c.2) He was a member of the Committee of Arrangements for the first annual Fire Department Fund Ball held to raise funds to help widows and orphans of deceased Yonkers firemen. The ball was held on Thursday evening, March 4, 1858. He was also Chairman of the committee. (E-2/18/58 p.3, c.5) At about 2 a.m. Tuesday, September 21, 1858 his house was broken into. The thieves stole a gold watch, about $30, and some silverware. He lived on Smith Street. (E-9/23/58 p.2, c.4) During November, 1858 he was a member of the arrangement committee for the Second Annual Ball to benefit the widows and orphans of deceased Yonkers firemen. (E-11/25/58 p.2, c.7) On Thursday, August 13, 1859 he was elected to the executive committee of the newly formed Republican Association at a Republican Town meeting. (E-10/20/59 p.3, c.1) Also, during 1859 he was again the chief engineer of the Yonkers Fire Department. (E-12/29/59 p.2, c.2) He worked as a mason during the construction of Underhill's brewery. (E-1/12/60 p.2, c.3) On Monday evening March 26, 1860 he was elected one of thirty-two vice presidents of a Republican election rally meeting at the Getty House. (E-3/29/60 p.2, c.3) During 1860 he was chairman of the Yonkers Temperance Society's Temperance Demonstration committee. (E-6/21/60 p.3, c.1) On Monday evening, September 17, 1860, he was elected president of the Fire Department Fund Association. (E-9/20/60 p.2, c.7) On the 1860 census he is listed as a 41-year-old mason with $2,500 in real estate, and a personal estate of $400. His wife Ann was 35 years old, and they had two children; Maria who was 19, and Daniel who was 14. During 1854 he was a town Constable.

Bleeker, George W. He lived in Yonkers for a period of time and then moved to Brooklyn where he was active in religion and politics. On Wednesday, November 23, 1859, he died at the age of 59. He was a family member of the Revolutionary War Bleekers. (E-12/1/59 p.2, c.4)

Bliven, Charles During 1860 he was selected to serve as a petit juror in the Court of Sessions that sat Monday, March 12, 1860. (E-3/8/60 p.2, c.5)

Bliven, Lottie On Wednesday, August 8, 1860, she was married by Rev. King to Charles L. Chadeayne. (E-8/16/60 p.2, c.7)

Bloomer, Elisha During the latter part of 1858 he signed a petition to have a meeting of the taxpayers in School District #2 meet to reconsider the location of two new schools; one on the corner of Wood Place and Warburton Avenue, and the other on St. Mary's Street near the Catholic Church and school. (E-12/23/58 p.2, c.2) During 1859 he built a brick stable for $3,500, renovated his wood-frame stable into a residence for $3,300, and made other improvements that cost $7,800. (E-1/12/60 p.2, c.3) On Friday, May 4, 1860, he was elected one of six members of the committee on Premiums for Vegetables for the June exhibition of the newly formed

Yonkers Horticultural Society. (E-5/17/60 p.3, c.3)

Bloomer, John On Friday night, December 9, 1859, his house on Warburton Avenue was burglarized. The thieves took silverware, a gold bracelet, and an overcoat. The overcoat was later found on the grounds of the Episcopal Church. (E-12/15/59 p.2, c.5)

Blute, John On Wednesday, November 2, 1859, he won a musket in a target shooting contest at Weehawkan, New Jersey. He was a member of the Yonkers Hatters Guard. (E-11/3/59 p.2, c.6) During 1860 he won a box of cigars at a Yonkers Hatters Guard target shooting contest. (E-11/1/60 p.3, c.1)

Bogardus, Romeyn On the morning of Thursday, June 3, 1858 he married Julia E. Radcliff. He was from NYC. (E-6/10/58 p.2, c.6) On the 1860 census he is listed as a 25-year-old butcher with a personal estate of $1,500. His wife Jane (see above) was 22 years old.

Bogle, Mary E. (Mrs.) On Sunday, December 12, 1858, she died at the age of 65. (E-12/23/58 p.2, c.7)

Boland, P. During 1860 he won $5 at a Yonkers Hatters Guard target shooting contest. (E-11/1/60 p.3, c.1)

Bolmer, Matthew A. On Thursday, August 13, 1859 he was chosen a delegate to the Republican County Convention by the newly formed Republican Association at a Republican Town meeting. (E-10/20/59 p.3, c.1) On Thursday morning, January 19, 1860, he was on a coroner's jury to look into the death of Mrs. Field who died in a railroad accident at Tarrytown. He was listed as a gentleman. (E-1/26/60 p.2, c.5 see Foster Jenkins for more details) On Monday evening March 26, 1860, he was elected one of thirty-two vice presidents of a Republican election rally meeting at the Getty House. (E-3/29/60 p.2, c.3) On Thursday evening, October 25, 1860, he was one of twenty-two vice presidents at a Republican campaign meeting. (E-11/1/60 p.2, c.2)

Bolmer, Manuel T. During 1857 he was a real estate broker. (E-7/9/57 p.3, c.6)

Bosworth, Caleb H. On Saturday, September 5, 1857 he was elected at a Republican primary meeting to be a delegate to the Republican district convention. (E-9/10/57 p.2, c.6) Sometime during the week of October 19, 1857 he fell three stories in an elevator at the Spuyten Duyvil foundry. He lived in Spuyten Duyvil. (E-10/29/57 p.2, c.4) During 1857 he was an Inspector of Elections for Election District Number Two. (TRB)

Bowers, Henry Jr. During 1858 he bought a wooden frame house on Warburton Avenue next to Shonnard's house for $7,100. (E-4/22/58 p.2, c.3) During the latter part of 1858 he signed a petition to have a meeting of the taxpayers in School District #2 meet to reconsider the location of two new schools; one on the corner of Wood Place and Warburton Avenue, and the other on St. Mary's Street near the Catholic Church and school. (E-12/23/58 p.2, c.2)

On Tuesday, April 17, 1860 his wife Amelia died at 32 years of age. The funeral was at St. John's Church, and she was buried in Greenwood. (E-4/19/60 p.2, c.7) On the 1860 census he is listed as a 40-year-old merchant with $18,000 in real estate, and a personal estate of $2,500. He had four children who were Henry age 11, Amelia age 6, Sarah age 2, and Ella who was 2 months old. Evidently his wife died during childbirth. A. H. Bowers who was 78 years old and was apparently his father was also in his household as well as a Mary Cooper who was 41 years old and who was from Connecticut. He also had a coachman, cook, two nurses, and a servant.

Bowler, A. During 1860 he won a tea pot at a Yonkers Hatters Guard target shooting contest. (E-11/1/60 p.3, c.1)

Bowler, George On Monday evening March 26, 1860 he was elected one of thirty-two vice presidents of a Republican election rally meeting at the Getty House. (E-3/29/60 p.2, c.3)

Bowles, Reuben During 1859 he renovated his residence on Oak Hill Avenue near Ashburton Avenue for about $1,500. The house was previously owned by Isaac Brown. (E-1/12/60 p.2, c.2)

Boyd, Carrie F. (Miss) During 1858 she and Miss Harriet E. Clapp owned a millinery business opposite the business of Ackerman and Deyo. They sold hats, veils, hosiery, gloves, laces, ribbons, combs, brushes, and other things. They did fashionable dressmaking. (E-5/20/58 p.2, c.7)

Boyd, Henry C. On Tuesday, December 7, 1858 he married Miss Harriet E. Clapp. (E-12/16/58 p.2, c.6)

Boyd, John C. During 1859 he opened the Excelsior Paint Store at 5 Baldwin's Buildings on North Broadway. (E-9/8/59 p.3, c.3) On the 1860 census he is listed as a 37-year-old painter with $1,700 in real estate and a personal estate of $250. His wife Jane was 25 years old. They had four children. Edward was 10, John was 4, Elizabeth was 2, and George was three months old.

Bradley, J. During 1860 he won a ton of coal at a Yonkers Hatters Guard target shooting contest. (E-11/1/60 p.3, c.1)

Bradley, Lyman F. During 1853 and 1854 he was a town Constable. On July 13, 1855 he was appointed an Overseer of the Poor, but he resigned that office on July 19, 1855. (TRB) During 1855, 1856, and 1857 he was a village police officer. Prior to February, 1857 he was Collector for the village. During 1858 he and Michael Keefe owned land on Williams Street. Court action was brought against them by Sanford Stedwell. As a result of the court action their land was to be sold at auction on October 23, 1858. (E-9/9/58 p.3, c.2) On Monday evening March 26, 1860 he was elected one of thirty-two vice presidents of a Republican election rally meeting at the Getty House. (E-3/29/60 p.2, c.3)

Bragdon, I. C. On July 22, 1858 he signed a petition calling for a meeting of eligible voters in School District #2 to decide if the school district should become a Union Free School District. (E-8/5/58 p.4, c.3)

Brennan, Michael On Wednesday, November 2, 1859, he won some silver spoons in a target shooting contest at Weehawkan, New Jersey. He was a member of the Yonkers Hatters Guard. (E-11/3/59 p.2, c.6) During 1860 he won a cup at a Yonkers Hatters Guard target shooting contest. (E-11/1/60 p.3, c.1)

Brevoort, Henry F. During 1857 he along with a Thompson bought a grocery store on the corner of Broadway and Getty Square from Thomas O. Farrington. (E-4/9/57 p.3, c.2) During 1859 they moved to the Radford Building on the bridge. (E-3/1059 p.3, 4) On May 23, 1860 he was married by Rev. Hulbert to Sarah A. Thompson in the home of her mother. (E-5/24/60 p.3, c.3) During December, 1860 he added a sidewalk to the Palisade Bridge. (E-12/13/60 p.2, c.5)

Brewer, Darius R. (Rev.) During September, 1858 he became the pastor of the Episcopal Mission Church. (E-9/9/58 p.2, c.6) Later the church became St. Paul's Church. (E-9/1/59 p.3, c.1) Bishop Clark of Rhode Island at the request of the Provisional Bishop of New York installed him into the rectorship of St. Paul's on April 22, 1860. (E-4/12/60 p.2, c.6) During April, 1860 he advertised for a married man to be a gardener or house keeper. (E-4/19/60 p.3, c.2) On Monday night, December 17, 1860 he was installed as an officer into the Rising Star Lodge of Free and Accepted Masons as Chaplain. (E-12/20/60 p.2, c.3)

Briggs, Isaac M. On Sunday evening, January 17, 1858 he married Sarah Anna Williams who was from Yonkers. Isaac was from Fordham. (E-1/28/58 p.2, c.6)

Brink, William H. During December, 1860 he was a member of a committee that was organized to run the second annual ball of Neptune Engine Company Number 3 that was to be held at the Getty Lyceum on January 24, 1861. (E-12/13/60 p.2, c.7)

Brommley, James On Wednesday, November 2, 1859, he won in a drawing a cup at a target shooting contest at Weehawkan, New Jersey. He was a member of the Yonkers Hatters Guard. (E-11/3/59 p.2, c.6) During 1860 he won a $6 pair of pants at a Yonkers Hatters Guard target shooting contest. (E-11/1/60 p.3, c.1)

Brown, B. During 1859 he built a wood-frame house on Broadway near his former residence for about $5,000. (E-1/12/60 p.2, c.2,3)

Brown, Benjamin During 1853, 1855, and 1857 he was a Pound Master. (TRB)

Brown, F. B. On Thursday, August 13, 1859 he was chosen as a delegate to the Republican Assembly District Convention by the newly formed Republican Association at a Republican Town meeting. (E-10/20/59 p.3, c.1)

Brown, George During 1860 he was a member of the Yonkers Temperance Society's Temperance Demonstration committee. (E-6/21/60 p.3, c.1)

Brown, John On April 2, 1857 he married Sarah Ann Baird. (E-4/23/57 p.2, c.6) During the latter part of 1859 he was a member of the arrangement committee for the fourth annual ball of Protection Fire Engine Company Number 1. (E-12/22/59 p.2, c.6) On Tuesday, January 3, 1860 he was elected assistant foreman of Lady Washington Engine Company Number 2. (E-1/5/60 p.2, c.4)

Brown, John During 1857 he was Secretary of the African Methodist Episcopal Zion Church. (E-7/9/57 p.2, c.7) On the 1860 census he is listed as a 33-year-old waiter with a $100 personal estate. His wife was Charlotta and she was 28 years old. Their children were Emma who was 13, Leonna who was 10, and Henrietta who was four years old.

Brown, J. D. During 1860 he left the firm of Brown and Ackerly and opened a carpentry shop on Wells Avenue between Broadway and Warburton Avenue. (E-4/19/60 p.3, c.2) On the 1860 census he was a 41-year-old master builder with $2,800 in real estate and a $1,000 personal estate. His wife Angeline was 35 years old. They had three children. George was 17 years old and is listed as an architect. Jane was 5 and Charles was 2 years old. Also, living in the household was a Sarah who was 21 years old.

Brown, Patrick During 1857 he applied for a license to operate a grocery store. (E-5/28/57 p.2, c.2) Apparently he was not granted a license. (E-6/4/57 p.2, c.4) On Tuesday, October, 6, 1857 he was probably appointed a delegate to the Democratic County Convention. (E-10/8/57 p.2, c.2) During 1858 he built a residence on Riverdale Avenue for about $1,000. (E-4/22/58 p.2, c.3) On October 7, 1858 he was one of 32 businesses to announce they were closing their businesses at 8 p.m. during the winter. (E-10/7/58 p.3, c.4) He may have been in business with an Ackerly. The business was dissolved by mutual consent and he sold his interest in it on January 3, 1860. (E-1/19/60 p.4, c.1)

Brown, Sarah A. (Miss) During 1858 she lived in the Village of Yonkers. During November, 1858 the *Yonkers Herald* erroneously published her marriage to E. O. Anderson, also a resident of the village. (E-11/25/58 p.2, c.1) Apparently they finally did get married on Tuesday, December 20, 1859 at the residence of her father, J. P. Brown in Glenwood. (E-12/22/59 p.2, c.6)

Bruce, John M. (Jr.) During 1859 he was building a large house on the Post Road just east of Mt. St. Vincent's. The paper speculated that "when finished the house will cost about $20,000." (E-1/12/60 p.2, c.1) He was selected to serve on the petit jury November 19, 1960 in the Circuit Court. (E-11/15/60 p.3, c.2)

Bryant, George During 1860 he was elected one of eight Lieutenants of the Yonkers Hatters Guard. (E-10/18/60 p.2, c.5) During

1860 he won $3.50 worth of beef at a Yonkers Hatters Guard target shooting contest. (E-11/1/60 p.3, c.1)

Bryant, S. During 1860 he won some English cheese at a Yonkers Hatters Guard target shooting contest. (E-11/1/60 p.3, c.1)

Buckhout, Henry During October, 1859 he and James B. Farrington owned a grain and feed business at 4 North Broadway in the Farrington Building. (E-10/13/59 p.3, c.2) The partnership was dissolved on May 10, 1860, and the business was continued by Farrington. (E-5/24/60 p.3, c.4)

Bucklin, Robert L. He was the first assistant foreman of Hope Hook and Ladder Company No. 1 when it was originally formed on August 15, 1853. (E-12/29/59 p.2, c.2) During 1857 he was the proprietor of the Getty House. He also donated $25 to the Yonkers Library Association in 1857 and became a life member. (E-3/12/57 p.2, c.5) He also operated a tavern which was probably at the Getty House. (E-5/28/57 p.2, c.2) On Monday, October 12, 1857 he was a delegate to the County Republican Convention. (E-10/15/57 p.2, c.3) In 1858 he received a hotel license. (E-6/17/58 p.2, c.6) During 1859 he was granted another hotel license. (E-8/11/59 p.2, c.7) On Saturday, August 20, 1859, he was appointed as an alternate delegate to the State Republican Convention. (E-8/25/58 p.2, c.3) On Thursday, August 13, 1859 he was appointed secretary for a Republican Town meeting. He was also elected to the association's executive committee, and he was also chosen at the same meeting to be a delegate to the Assembly District Convention. (E-10/20/59 p.3, c.1) On Tuesday, May 1, he retired from the Getty House. (E-5/3/60 p.2, c.3) On Tuesday evening, September 11, 1860 he was elected to the executive committee of the Yonkers Republican Association for a five-month term. After the meeting was over the Republican Wide Awakes held a meeting and elected him captain of the club. (E-9/13/60 p.2, c.2) On Saturday, September 29, 1860 he was a delegate to the Republican First Assembly District Convention that was held in Morrisania Hall, Morrisania. (E-10/4/60 p.2, c.2) On Thursday evening, October 25, 1860, he was one of twenty-two vice presidents at a Republican campaign meeting. (E-11/1/60 p.2, c.2) On Monday night, December 17, 1860 he was installed as an officer into the Rising Star Lodge of Free and Accepted Masons as Steward. (E-12/20/60 p.2, c.3)

Bunker, Benjamin F. During 1858 he built a paint store on the corner of Main Street and Buena Vista Avenue. The cost was estimated at $1,000. (E-1/20/59 p.2, c.4) During late February or early March, 1859 he opened another paint store on the corner of Main and Depot Streets opposite the Hudson River Railroad depot. (E-3/10/59 p.3, c.4) During 1859 he built a wood-frame house on the corner of Depot and Main Streets next door to his paint store that cost about $1,200. (E-1/12/60 p.2, c.1) On the 1860 census he is listed as a 64-year-old paint store owner with $10,000 in real estate and a personal estate of $1,500. His wife Jane was 54 years old.

Burchard, Horace During 1857 he was one of two principals at the Female Classical Seminary located on the Hudson River at Glenwood. (E-4/9/57 p.3, c.1 and 4/1/58 p.2, c.5)

Burns, Bethia On Wednesday, September 14, 1859 she was married by Rev. Seward to James McCleine. (E-9/22/59 p.3, c.4)

Burns, David During 1857 he operated the Yonkers Intelligence Office at the corner of Getty Square and Palisade Avenue. The business was an employment agency that supplied servants to households. He charged 25 cents per application. (E-2/19/57 p.5, c.3) During 1857 he supplied the Yonkers Library Association with the *Daily Tribune* without any charge. He also supplied the *Daily Herald* for a fee. (E-3/5/57 p.2, c.6) On October 15, 1857 his business was one of 33 businesses in Yonkers to announce they were closing their stores at 8 p.m. beginning on October 12, 1857 until March 27, 1858. (E-10/15/57 p.3, c.1) During 1858 he also owned the Periodical Depot at the same location as his employment agency. He was the sole agent for the New American Cyclopedia, A. Benton's abridged edition of the Congressional Debates, and Burton's Cyclopedia of Wit and Humor. (E-8/12/58 p.3, c.2.) During 1859 he moved his book store to Farrington's new building on Palisade Avenue. (E-9/1/59 p.2, c.4) On the 1860 census he is listed as a 47-year-old with $2,500 in real estate and a personal estate of $400. His wife Jane was 41 years old and they had five children; Jane who was 14, Amelia who was 12, Margaret who was 9, Wilmot who was 7, and George who was 5 years old. He and his wife were from Scotland, but all the children were born in New York.

Burns, J. During 1860 he won $2.50 at a Yonkers Hatters Guard target shooting contest. (E-11/1/60 p.3, c.1)

Burns, Jeremiah During 1857 he was either a dealer or a manufacturer of machinery and tools at 102 Broadway, NYC. He was a resident of Yonkers. (E-3/5/57 p.3, c.4) During the latter part of 1858 he signed a petition to have a meeting of the taxpayers in School District #2 meet to reconsider the location of two new schools; one on the corner of Wood Place and Warburton Avenue, and the other on St. Mary's Street near the Catholic Church and school. (E-12/23/58 p.2, c.2) On February 19, 1859, properties that he owned at 1, 3, 5, 7, 9, and 11 Nepperhan Street were to be sold because he owed $59.89 in taxes. (E-1/27/59 p.3, c.1,2,3) However, he paid his taxes. (E-2/3/59 p.3, c.1,2,3) During 1859 he won the contract to furnish the machinery for William C. Waring's new hat factory at Brewster's Station in Putnam County. He also was just about finished with a contract he had with Henry F. Devoe to furnish two horizontal high pressure engines with locomotive boilers. (E-2/10/59 p.2, c.4) On June 28, 1859 he signed a letter addressed to Frederick A. Coe asking legal advice concerning a written promise of the Hudson River Railroad Company to construct a carriageway across the Nepperhan River near the draw bridge. (E-7/7/59 p.2, c.4) During May, 1860 he was called on to serve on the petit jury. (E-5/31/60 p.3, c.3)

Bussard, Henri During 1858 he had a nursery on Waverly Street east of the District school house. (E-4/29/58 p.3, c.1)

Bussing, John He is listed on the 1860 census as a 70-year-old farmer with $25,200 in real estate, and a personal estate of $4,000. His wife Susan was also 70 years old, and three of their children lived with them. John was a 25-year-old farmer, Susan was 16, and Elijah was 11. A 30-year-old Irish laborer also is listed in his household. (See Vol. 1, p. 39.)

Cable, Isaac During 1858 he lived on Mechanic Street and made monuments and tombstones. (Brown, p. 57)

Caldwell, Adda (Miss) During 1859 she was a school teacher probably in Mount Vernon, but she was from Yonkers. (E-5/12/59 p.2, c.5)

Calum, Catherine Ann (Miss) On Tuesday, September 4, 1860, she died at the age of 32. Funeral services were held at the Presbyterian Church on Friday, September 7 at 1:30 p.m.. (E-9/6/60 p.2, c.7)

Campbell, Charles On Monday, September 17, 1860 he was to serve on the petit jury of the Court of Sessions in Bedford. (E-8/30/60 p.3, c.1) During 1859 he was an Inspector of Elections for Election District Number 3. (TRB)

Campbell, George C. During 1857 he was a house painter and he had a shop on Main Street below Broadway. (E-3/12/57 p.3, c.1) During December, 1860 he was a member of a committee that was organized to run the second annual ball of Neptune Engine Company Number 3 that was to be held at the Getty Lyceum on January 24, 1861. (E-12/13/60 p.2, c.7) On the 1860 census he is listed as a 28-year-old painter. His wife Ruth was also 28 years old, and they had one child, Fanny, who was one year old.

Campbell, J. R. During 1857 and 1858 he was a real estate broker and he had an office on the corner of Point Street and Ravine Avenue near the Glenwood Station. He also loaned money. (E-2/25/58 p.3, c.1)

Candee, E. W. He was made a life member of the Yonkers Library Association during its early years. (E-3/12/57 p.2, c.5) On Monday, December 13, 1858 he became Vestryman of the newly formed Episcopal Church on Mechanic Street. (E-12/23/58 p.2, c.3) On April 9, 1860 he was elected a Vestryman at St. Paul's Free Church. (E-4/12/60 p.2, c.6)

Candell, E.W. During 1857 he finished building a house on the west side of Palisade Avenue. He then sold the house to E. Clapp and built himself another house on an adjoining lot. (E-12/31/57 p.2, c.3)

Carbay, E. During 1860 he won a pair of boots at a Yonkers Hatters Guard target shooting contest. (E-11/1/60 p.3, c.1)

Cargill, Charles H. During 1853 he was a Constable. (TRB)

Cargill, Chloe (Mrs.) During 1860 she owned property on or near Prescott Street. (E-11/15/60 p.3, c.2)

Carpenter, Mrs. On May 4, 1857 she was to take over the boys first primary class for the school in the Village School District. (E-4/23/57 p.2, c.7) In 1859 she became the principal of a new school on Clinton Street in Union Free School District #2. (E-4/28/59 p.2, c.4)

Carpenter, Newton On Friday, May 4, 1860, he was elected one of five members of the committee on Premiums for Fruits for the June exhibition of the newly formed Yonkers Horticultural Society. (E-5/17/60 p.3, c.3)

Carpenter, S. W. During 1857 he was a member of the Masons. (E-8/20/57 p.3, c.1)

Carr, Robert On Saturday evening, December 25, 1858 he married Henrietta A. Huestis. They were married by Rev. V. M. Hulbert. (E-1/6/59 p.2, c.7)

Carry, John On Wednesday, November 2, 1859, he won in a drawing a writing desk at a target shooting contest at Weehawkan, New Jersey. He was a member of the Yonkers Hatters Guard. (E-11/3/59 p.2, c.6)

Carter, A. B. (Rev.) (Dr.) On Sunday evening, May 30, 1858 he held the first services of the Free Episcopal Church in the Mission Room on Mechanic Street. (E-6/3/58 p.2, c.4) On Tuesday, August 17, 1858 he and sixteen other men wrote C. Jerome Hopkins a letter requesting him to give another piano concert at the Getty House. (E-8/19/58 p.2, c.4) On the 1860 census he is listed as a 40-year-old clergyman with a personal estate of $300. His wife, C. G., was also 40 years old, and they had seven children; Maria who was 18, Hannah who was 16, Br[ach] who was 13, Mary who was 12, Cornelia who was 11, William who was 5, and Catherine who was 3. They had a nurse, Ann Henry, who was 30 years old, and a cook, Eliza Holt, who was also 30 years old. They were both born in Ireland.

Catlow, James During 1859 he was the Standard Bearer of the Yonkers Hatters Guard. On Wednesday, November 2, 1859 he went with the guard to Weehawken, New Jersey where the guard was involved in a shooting contest amongst themselves. (E-11/3/59 p.3, c.6)

Chadeayne, Charles L. On Wednesday, August 8, 1860, he was married by Rev. King to Lottie Bliven. (E-8/16/60 p.2, c.7)

Chadeayne, H. On Thursday evening, September 1, 1859, at a fire department meeting he was appointed to a committee that was authorized to buy a new fire engine. (E-12/29/59 p.2, c.2) On the 1860 census he is listed as probably 34 years old since it appears that a 3 was written over a 2. He had a personal estate of $2,000.

His wife Charity was 22 years old, and she had a personal estate of $2,000.

Chadeayne, Stephen C. During 1859 he owned the Broadway Boot and Shoe Store, and he hired J. K. Miller as the superintendent of the workman's department. (E-12/1/59 p.4, c.2)

Chamberlain, C. H. On Tuesday, October 6, 1857 he was appointed one of two secretaries at the Democratic electors of the Town of Yonkers meeting. (E-10/8/57 p.2, c.2)

Chamberlain, Charles W. On Monday evening March 7, 1859 he was elected a manager of the Yonkers Library Association. (E-3/10/59 p.2, c.7) During 1860 he was an Inspector of Elections for Election District Number One. (TRB)

Chambers, Lydia (Mrs.) During December, 1859, she was on the arrangement committee to give a benefit for their pastor John Taylor. The guest speaker was the Rev. Henry Highland Garnett, pastor of the Shiloh Presbyterian Church in NYC. Admission was 50 cents and the proceeds went to Rev. Taylor. Her husband Isaac was also on the committee. (E-12/8/59 p.3. c.2)

Chambers, Samuel W. He was the first foreman of Hope Hook and Ladder Company No. 1 when it was first formed on August 15, 1853. (E-12/29/59 p.2, c.2) During 1853 he was Town Clerk. (TRB)

Charl, Ellen On Wednesday, October 19, 1859 she was married by Rev. Seward to William Wharmby. (E-11/10/59 p.3, c.2)

Chase, George (Captain) Sometime prior to 1859 he lived in Yonkers. On Sunday, July 24, 1859 his eldest daughter Mary A. MacKay died at her residence on Howard Street in San Francisco of heart disease. Her husband was David MacKay, and her mother was Mary Chase. (E-9/1/59 p.3, c.1)

Chatterton, Abraham C. On Monday, June 20, 1859 he died in New York City. He was 23 years old and had moved to NYC from Yonkers. While living in Yonkers he was a member of Lady Washington Engine Company No. 2, and he was honored by its members. (E-6/23/59 p.2, c.6,7)

Chatterton, A. J. He was arrested along with Andrew Jones, and Joseph R. Hurd for an attack on a Flemish man. On Monday, December 14, 1857 they were released from jail on $500 bail and they were to appear at the next session of General Court. See Andrew Jones for an account of the incident. (E-12/17/57 p.2, c.1)

Chilton, James R. (Dr.) Prior to June, 1859 he lived on Buena Vista Avenue, but moved. (E-6/16/59 p.2, c.3) However, during the same year he renovated his house on Buena Vista Avenue and also built a stable on the property. The projects cost about $3,000. (E-1/12/60 p.2, c.1)

Choate, D. During 1858 he was an artist living a little west of the Episcopal Church. He dealt in ambrotypes, daguerreotypes, and leathertypes. He took pictures of sick and deceased people at their residences. (E-5/20/58) He called his business the United States Picture Gallery. (E-5/27/58 p.3, c.3)

Clapp, Everett On July 22, 1858 he signed a petition calling for a meeting of eligible voters in School District #2 to decide if the school district should become a Union Free School District. (E-8/5/58 p.4, c.3) On Tuesday, August 17, 1858 he and sixteen other men wrote C. Jerome Hopkins a letter requesting him to give another piano concert at the Getty House. (E-8/19/58 p.2, c.4) During 1858 he was building a brick house on the corner of Palisade Avenue and Railroad Avenue. The house cost about $12,000. (E-1/20/59 p.2, c.4) On Monday evening March 7, 1859 he was elected a manager of the Yonkers Library Association. (E-3/10/59 p.2, c.7) The New York State Supreme Court in a special session in Brooklyn named him one of three Commissioners appointed to open Irving Place. (E-7/7/59 p.2, c.4)

Clapp, Harriet E. (Miss) During 1858 she and Miss Carrie F. Boyd owned a millinery business opposite the business of Ackerman and Deyo. They sold hats, veils, hosiery, gloves, laces, ribbons, combs, brushes, and other things. They did fashionable dressmaking. (E-5/20/58 p.2, c.7) On Tuesday, December 7, 1858 she married Henry C. Boyd. (E-12/16/58 p.2, c.6)

Clark, Edward During 1860 he had a stable on Pine Street near Glenwood Avenue. He was selling two gentle goats that could be harnessed. A wagon, harness, whip and bells went along with the goats. (E-3/29/60 p.2, c.6)

Clark, Leonard M. During 1857 he was a sash and blind maker with a store on Nepperhan Street next to the Steam Planing Mill. (E-2/19/57 p.3, c.3) Also during 1857 he was a member of the Masons (E-8/20/57 p.3, c.1) On Tuesday, October, 6, 1857 he was appointed a delegate to the Democratic County Convention. (E-10/8/57 p.2, c.2) He lived on Willow Street. On Thursday evening August 25, 1859 his home was broken into by thieves, but nothing was taken. (E-9/1/59 p.2, c.4) On Wednesday, November 2, 1859, he was chosen as a judge of a target shooting match at Weehawkan, New Jersey, between the men of the Yonkers Hatters Guard. (E-11/3/59 p.3, c.6) On Wednesday evening, December 14, 1859, at their annual meeting in Yonkers he was elected Master of Rising Star Lodge, No. 450, of F. & A.M. (E-12/15/59 p.2, c.5) On the 1860 census he is listed as a 44-year-old sash and blind maker with $10,000 in real estate, and a personal estate of $2,000. His wife Rachel was also 44 years old, and they had four children; Henry who was an 18-year-old sash and blind maker, George who was 11, Sarah who was 8, and William who was 1. He also had a J. Nesbit who was a ship builder in his household as well as two women from France. During 1857 and 1858 he was an Inspector of Elections for Election District Number One. (TRB) During 1858, 1859 and 1860 he was a member of the village Board of Trustees.

Clark, Leonora M. On Wednesday, May 30, 1860 she was married by Rev. Seward to John Pierson of New York City at the house of her parents. She was the oldest daughter of Leonard M. Clark. (E-6/7/60 p.2, c.6)

Clarke, F. During 1859 he was secretary of the Yonkers Light Guard. (E-10/27/59 p.3, c.5)

Clarke, Jeremiah During 1857 he was a carpet fitter. (E-5/7/57 p.2, c.7) His shop was on the corner of Mechanic and Guion Streets. (E-3/11/58 p.3, c.3) He also manufactured carpets. (E-4/15/58 p.4, c.5) During 1859 he also sold umbrellas. (E-7/14/59 p.2, c.7)

Claus, Santa (Headquarters) At Cornell's, Mechanic Street, opposite the Getty House, Yonkers. Has the largest, cheapest and best assortment of confectionery, toys, &c., suitable for holiday presents, ever afforded for sale in Yonkers. All that he asks, is that persons desiring any article in his line will give him a call, when they will be sure to purchase. (E-12/17/57 p.3, c.1)

Cleveland, Cyrus W. Sometime before March 2, 1857 he donated 10 volumes to the Yonkers Library Association, and on March 2, 1857 he was elected a manager of the Association. (E-3/5/57 p.2, c.6) On Monday evening, March 1, 1858 he was again elected a manager of the Yonkers Library Association. (E-3/4/58 p.2, c.3) On Tuesday, August 17, 1858 he and sixteen other men wrote C. Jerome Hopkins a letter requesting him to give another piano concert at the Getty House. (E-8/19/58 p.2, c.4) During 1858 he moved a wood-frame building from one location on Broadway to another location on Broadway. He then renovated the building at a cost of $500, and sold it to Philip Flood as a residence. During the same year he built another wood-frame building on the old site of the previously moved building on Broadway near St. Mary's Street which cost about $5,000. (E-1/20/59 p.2, c.3) On Monday evening March 7, 1859 he was elected a manager of the Yonkers Library Association. (E-3/10/59 p.2, c.7) Around August, 1859 the Library Association was incorporated and he became a member of the Board of Trustees. (E-8/14/59 p.2, c.4) During 1859 he was a member of the Yonkers Circulating Library Association lecture committee. (E-12/22/59 p.2, c.6) During 1860 he owned land on Broadway near Guion Street. (E-3/29/60 p.2, c.6) On Tuesday, May 8, 1860, he was elected recording secretary of the newly formed Yonkers Horticultural Society. (E-5/17/60 p.3, c.3)

Cleveland, Mrs. She helped take up a collection to help the Ladies of the Mount Vernon Association make the grave of President George Washington a public shrine. No donation larger than a dollar was accepted. However, those who wanted to donate more could donate a dollar for each member of their family. Later any amount could be donated. (E-9/9/58 p.2, c.4)

Clintock, W. R. Mrs. During 1857 she was a dressmaker and milliner on Manor Place, Broadway. (E-2/5/57 p.3, c.2)

Coates, S. During 1857 he owned a portable gas heater manufacturing company. His office was at 376 Broadway, NYC. (E-6/18/57 p.3, c.3) During 1858 the inventory in his factory on Nepperhan Street was to be sold at auction. (E-8/5/58 p.4, c.3) On the 1860 census he is listed as a 50-year-old gentleman with $7,000 in real estate, and a personal estate of $5,000. His wife R. Coats (no e was discernible between the s and t) was 48 years old, and they had one servant. Also in their house was a Henry Coats who was a 52-year-old gentleman. He also had a servant. Another S. Coates is listed on the 1860 census also as a 50-year-old gentleman with $10,000 in real estate. His wife, Mrs. Coates, was 45 years old, and three other people, who were all from Ireland, also lived in their household. They were an Eliza who was 25, Jane Stone who was 60, and James Nugent who was 24 and is listed as a servant.

Cobb, C. S. During 1858 he owned a stationery business in the vestibule of the Getty House. He sold books, stationery, sheet music, periodicals, weekly papers, and steel engravings. (E-7/8/58 p.3, c.2)

Cobb, Lyman Jr. During 1857 he was principal of the Yonkers Female Seminary which was located 2 buildings north of the Presbyterian Church on Broadway. (E-4/30/57 p.3, c.4) An L. Cobb, Jr. sold Edge's premium fireworks at Riker's Express office 1 Manor Place, Broadway. (E-7/1/58 p.2, c.7) On Monday, March 7, 1859 he was elected secretary of the Yonkers Debating Society. (E-3/10/59 p.2, c.7) On April 9, 1860 he was elected a Vestryman at St. Paul's Free Church. (E-4/12/60 p.2, c.6) During 1859 and 1860 he was Town Clerk. (TRB) In 1860 he was also Village Clerk.

Cobb, Mrs. During 1857 she ran a school for girls. (E-2/19/57 p.2, c.1)

Coe, Eli On Monday, December 26, 1859, he was acting foreman of the old fire truck during a parade of the Yonkers Fire Department. (E-12/29/59 p.2, c.3)

Coe, Frederick A. Around March 5, 1857 he received $105 for fees as an attorney. (E-3/5/57 p.3, c.1) On March 10, 1857 he was elected an Inspector for the next election of the Bank of Yonkers. (E-3/12/57 p.2, c.7) During March of 1857 he was made a life member of the Yonkers Library Association. (E-3/19/57 p.2, c.6) On Saturday, September 5, 1857 he was elected at a Republican primary meeting to be a delegate to the Republican district convention. (E-9/10/57 p.2, c.6) On Tuesday evening, November 17, 1857 the horse and carriage of E. E. Hassee crashed into his carriage. (E-11/19/57 p.2, c.7) His wife was Ann Eliza Coe. (E-5/24/60 p.3, c.4) On the 1860 census he is listed as a 40-year-old attorney. His wife Anna (see above) was also 40 years old. They had four servants all from Ireland. They were Hannah Coe who was 20, Patrick Do[n] who was either 16 or 76, Bridget Deal?? who was 22, and Mary Dunn who was 25 years old. Clara is listed on the census as the last person in the household. She was 11 years old and may have been the daughter of the Coes' since she was born in New York.

Coe, Halsted C. During 1857 he worked as a mason on the Ferris building which was on the corner of Palisade Avenue and Locust Hill Avenue. (E-7/2/57 p.2, c.4) He was a member of the Committee of Arrangements for the first annual Fire Department Fund Ball held to raise funds to help widows and orphans of deceased Yonkers firemen. The ball was held on Thursday evening, March 4, 1858. (E-2/18/58 p.3, c.5) During 1858 he was the Assistant Foreman of the Hook and Ladder Company. On Friday night, May 7, 1858 he died after a six-day illness. The *Yonkers Examiner* noted "His loss will be severally felt by all who knew him. Punctual, straightforward and faithful in his business, amiable, kind hearted and generous as a friend, and prompt, liberal and disinterested in his performance of his duties as a citizen, he had won the respect of all, and had enrolled everyone who knew him among his steady friends." He was buried at Rockland Lake on Sunday, May 9, 1858. The services were preformed by Rev. V. M. Hulbert of the Reformed Dutch Church of Yonkers. (E-5/13/58 p.2, c.2) On July 22, 1858 he signed a petition calling for a meeting of eligible voters in School District #2 to decide if the school district should become a Union Free School District. He may have signed the petition before he died, or maybe his wife signed the petition. (E-8/5/58 p.4, c.3)

Coe, Halsted C. (Mrs.) During 1859 she advertised to rent an apartment on Irving Place, second house from Warburton Avenue, that was suitable for a small family. (E-3/31/59 p.4. c.3) On Monday, December 26, 1859, to show her affection, she presented the men of Hope Hook and Ladder Company with a wreath of artificial flowers after a parade of the Yonkers Fire Department. (E-12/29/59 p.2, c.3)

Coe, Richard W. During 1857 he was a dealer in flour, feed, and grain at 194 West Street, NYC. (E-3/5/57 p.3, c.4) See Montgomery, William for additional information.

Coffey, J. During the renovations of Hope Hook and Ladder Company Number 1's fire house he was a gas fitter. (E-9/13/60 p.2, c.2)

Coffee, Joanna During 1858 she, Michael Coffee, and Jeremiah Coffee owned land on Jefferson Street. Court action was brought against them by Ethan Flagg. As a result of the court action their land was to be sold at auction on October 33, 1858. (E-9/9/58 p.3, c.2)

Coffin, Henry M. During 1854 he was Sealer of Weights and Measures. (TRB)

Cogan, Terence During the early part of 1860 his land on Riverdale Avenue was to be sold by the Sheriff on March 1, 1860. (E-1/19/60 p.3, c.2)

Cogan, Thomas During July, 1859 he was elected Treasurer of Protection Fire Engine Company Number 1. (E-7/28/59 p.2, c.3) During the latter part of 1859 he was a member of the arrangement committee and also a member of the reception committee for the fourth annual ball of Protection Fire Engine Company Number 1. (E-12/22/59 p.2, c.6) On Monday evening, September 17, 1860, he was elected Treasurer of the Fire Department Fund Association. (E-9/20/60 p.2, c.7)

Coger, George W. During 1859 he was hired at Wakeman's hardware store to head the plumbing department. (E-6/9/59 p.2, c.4)

Coles, Mary On Thursday, June 23, 1859 she was married by Rev. Brewer to Thomas McRonald. (E-6/30/59 p.3, c.1)

Coleman, Timothy During 1860 he received a hotel license. (E-7/26/60 p.2, c.6)

Coleman, William T. Sometime before March 12, 1857 he donated $25 to the Yonkers Library Association and became a life member. (E-3/12/57 p.2, c.5) During 1857 he bought 6 acres of land from Shonnard at $3,000 per acre. (E-3/19/57 p.2, c.2) On Tuesday evening, November 17, 1857 the horse and carriage of E. E. Hassee crashed into his doing quite a bit of damage. However, he was not injured. (E-11/19/57 p.2, c.7) Later in December, 1857 the *Examiner* reported that he bought seven acres of land from Shonnard for $21,000. The land he purchased was on the west side of the Post road at the top of the hill north of the village. The land was covered with evergreens that were planted in 1811. Because of the trees he called the property the Evergreens. In the same year he commenced building a Gothic-style brick stable which cost about $4,500. He also put up fences, a green house, and made other improvements that cost an additional $4,000. See Shonnard for information on buildings that were on the land he purchased. (E-12/31/57 p.2, c.3) In late 1858 he was selected as a juror for the grand jury for a Court of Sessions at Bedford. (E-12/2/58 p.2, c.3) During 1858 he built several greenhouses, some other buildings, and was preparing the ground in order to build a house on Broadway. (E-1/20/59 p.2, c.4) During 1859 he continued to improve his property by putting up an iron fence and gate, and he added to a brick building that was used as a carriage house but was then to be used as a house for him until he built a permanent residence. The cost of the projects were estimated at $15,500. (E-1/12/60 p.2, c.2) On Tuesday, January 31, 1860 he and seven others sent a letter to R. J. DeCordova asking him to visit Yonkers and deliver his humorous lecture on "Wall Street." (E-2/16/60 p.2, c.5) On Saturday evening, March 3, 1860, he presided over a meeting to nominate candidates for the village election on March, 6. On Monday the 5th of March he was chairman of a Democratic Party meeting held in Farrington's Hall for the purpose of nominating a Democratic ticket for the village election.

(E-3/8/60 p.2, c.1,3) On Friday, May 4, 1860, he was elected one of ten members of the executive committee of the newly formed Yonkers Horticultural Society. (E-5/17/60 p.3, c.3) On Friday, May 11, 1860, his daughter Lillie Carrie Coleman died at the age of 2 years and 2 months. (E-5/24/60 p.3, c.3)

Colgate, James B. On Monday evening March 26, 1860 he was elected one of thirty-two vice presidents of a Republican election rally meeting at the Getty House. (E-3/29/60 p.2, c.3) He may have been the son of William Colgate the soap manufacturer. His son was James Boorman Colgate. (*Who Was Who in America*, p.115) On Thursday evening, April 26, 1860, he was elected a trustee of the Yonkers Library Association. (E-5/3/60 p.2, c.3) On Friday, May 4, 1860, he was elected one of six members of the committee on Premiums for Plants and Flowers for the June exhibition of the newly formed Yonkers Horticultural Society. (E-5/17/60 p.3, c.3) On Thursday evening, October 25, 1860, he was one of twenty-two vice presidents at a Republican campaign meeting. (E-11/1/60 p.2, c.2) On the 1860 census he is listed as a 42-year-old broker with $30,000 in real estate, and a personal estate of $2,000. His wife Susan was also 42 years old. A W. H. Colgate, probably his father as noted above, lived with them, and he was 74 years old. They had one daughter, Mary, who was 4 years old. They had 12 other people in their household all from Ireland. They had a gardener, his wife and three children, a coachman, a cook, and her daughter, a waiter, a seamstress, and two servants.

Condit, George L. During 1853 he was a tavern keeper. (TRB) During 1857 he was a hotel and tavern keeper. (E-5/28/57 p.2, c.3) Later he wrote a letter to the Village Board demanding an investigation into an accusation that his house was disorderly. This accusation cost him a tavern license. (E-5/28/57 p.2, c.3 and E-6/4/57 p.2, c.3) However, on October 15, 1857 he advertised that William F. Titus had no interest in the Nepperhan Saloon, and that he was the sole proprietor and would promptly settle any unpaid claims against the business. (E-10/15/57 p.3, c.1) He was a member of the Committee of Arrangements for the first annual Fire Department Fund Ball held to raise funds to help widows and orphans of deceased Yonkers firemen. The ball was held on Thursday evening, March 4, 1858. (E-2/18/58 p.3, c.5) During November, 1858 he was a member of the arrangement committee for the Second Annual Ball to benefit the widows and orphans of deceased Yonkers firemen. (E-11/25/58 p.2, c.7) On Tuesday evening, April 19, 1859, he was presented a silver trumpet by James B. Kinslow in behalf of the members of Engine Company Number 1, for six years of service as the Company's Foreman. (E-4/21/59 p.2, c.5) During 1859 he lived on Guion Street. On Tuesday evening, May 24, 1859 a lamp exploded while his wife was trying to refill it. Her left hand and arm were badly burned, and a child of hers was slightly injured. Little damage was done to the house. (E-5/26/59 p.2, c.5) During July, 1859 he was again elected Foreman of Protection Fire Engine Company Number 1. (E-7/28/59 p.2, c.3) During 1859 he was granted another hotel license. (E-8/11/59 p.2, c.7) On Thursday, August 13, 1859 he was elected a vice president of the newly formed Republican Association at a Republican Town meeting. He was also elected to the association's executive committee. (E-10/20/59 p.3, c.1) During the latter part of 1859 he was a member of the arrangement committee and also a member of the floor committee for the fourth annual ball of Protection Fire Engine Company Number 1. (E-12/22/59 p.2, c.6) During 1860 he received a hotel license. (E-7/26/60 p.2, c.6) On Thursday evening, October 25, 1860, he was one of twenty-two vice presidents at a Republican campaign meeting. (E-11/1/60 p.2, c.2)

Condon, Lawrence R. During 1857 he owned a grocery store. (E-5/28/57 p.2, c.2) On October 15, 1857 his business was one of 33 businesses in Yonkers to announce they were closing their stores at 8 p.m. beginning on October 12, 1857 until March 27, 1858. (E-10/15/57 p.3, c.1) He applied for a store license in 1858. (E-6/3/58 p.2, c.5) He received the license. (E-6/17/58 p.2, c.6) During 1859 he was granted another grocery license. (E-8/11/59 p.2, c.7) During 1860 he received another grocers license. (E-7/26/60 p.2, c.6) On the 1860 census he is listed as a 40-year-old grocer with $12,000 in real estate, and a personal estate of $2,000. His wife Mary was 35, and they had three children; Richard who was 6, William who was 4, and James who was 1. They also had a 25-year-old clerk, Philip, and a 20-year-old Kate living with them. Both of these two people were born in Ireland.

Conklin, Elijah On Monday, March 28, 1859 he suddenly died. He was buried on Thursday, April 28, 1859. Services were held at the Reformed Dutch Church. (E-4/28/59 p.2, c.4)

Connell, John On Wednesday, November 2, 1859, he won a pair of butter knives in a target shooting contest at Weehawkan, New Jersey. He was a member of the Yonkers Hatters Guard. (E-11/3/59 p.2, c.6)

Cooke, George (Rev.) Sometime during 1858 he bought the Yonkers Collegiate Institute and became its principal. He had twenty-five years in education and the last five years were as the president of the University of East Tennessee. (E-4/15/58 p.2, c.1) In 1858 he bought the house of George Gilroy on Riverdale Avenue for $12,000. (E-4/22/58 p.2, c.3) On Tuesday, August 17, 1858 he and sixteen other men wrote C. Jerome Hopkins a letter requesting him to give another piano concert at the Getty House. (E-8/19/58 p.2, c.4)

Coons, John W. During December, 1860 he was a member of a committee that was organized to run the second annual ball of Neptune Engine Company Number 3 that was to be held at the Getty Lyceum on January 24, 1861. (E-12/13/60 p.2, c.7)

Cooper, Cornelia K. Sometime during either late February or early March, 1859 she married Josiah Withington at Chestnut Cottage in Yonkers. He was from Boston. (E-3/3/59 p.3, c.3)

Cooper, Charles W. (Dr.) On Wednesday evening, December 14, 1859, at their annual meeting in Yonkers he was elected Senior Deacon of Rising Star Lodge, No. 450, of F. & A.M. (E-12/15/59 p.2, c.5) On Monday night, December 17, 1860 he was installed as an officer into the Rising Star Lodge of Free and Accepted Masons as S.W. (E-12/20/ 60 p.2, c.3)

Copcutt, John His father John Copcutt lived in Tarrytown and he was the original owner of the properties in Yonkers. (E-7/2/57 p.2, c.4) During the latter part of 1857 he put up a high board fence around the yard attached to his mahogany mill. Supposedly the fence was erected to stop thieves from stealing his mahogany lumber. (E-11/19/57 p.2, c.3) Sometime during the early part of 1858 he occupied the Logwood and Dye Mills of Mr. Russell. The mills adjoined his Mahogany Sawmill. (E-2/18/58 p.2, c.4) His father John B. died on Tuesday May 27, 1858 in Tarrytown at 81 years of age. (E-6/3/58 p.2, c.6) During 1858 he put up two brick buildings on his property on Hudson Street. They cost about $5,000. (E-1/20/59 p.2, c.3) During 1860 he had a machine shop and silk factory near Elm Street. (E-2/9/60 p.2, c.2) During May, 1860 he was putting up a new building on Main Street near Market Place. It was to be occupied by a blacksmith and a wheelwright. (E-5/17/60 p.2, c.4) During 1860 he built a brick factory on Main Street. It was alleged that the factory illegally encroached on Main Street by ten feet. (E-9/20/60 p.2, c.5) On the 1860 census he is listed as a 55-year-old mahogany dealer with $200,000 in real estate, and a personal estate of $5,000. His wife Rebecca was 44 years old, and they had six children; Anna who was 20, Rebecca who was 18, William who was 15, Mary who was 11, Ann who was 8, and John who was 5. They also had a cook and a servant. Both he and his wife were born in England, and all of the children were born in New York. During 1858, 1859, and 1860 he was a member of the village Board of Trustees.

Cornell, John During 1857 he sold fireworks in his store on Mechanic Street next to the store of Hollock and Page. He sold sky rockets, Roman candles, vertical wheels, fire crackers, and more. He delivered to any place in town and advertised that he had as good or better prices than in NYC. (E-6/18/57 p.3, c.3) See Santa Claus.

Cornell, Mrs During the latter part of 1858 she owned a candy store on Mechanic Street opposite the Getty House. She also sold toys. (E-12/23/58 p.3, c.1)

Cornell, Richard During 1857 he was a Trustee of the African Methodist Episcopal Zion Church. (E-2/5/57)

Cornell, Thomas C. During 1857 he was a real estate broker. (E-2/5/57 p.3, c.3) On March 10, 1857 he was elected a Director of the

Bank of Yonkers. (E-3/12/57 p.2, c.7) His office was located on the corner of Palisade Avenue and Mechanic Street. (E-6/18/57 p.3 c.3) On Wednesday, July 29, 1857 he was elected a director of the Yonkers Gas Light Company and at a later meeting in August of the same year he was elected president of the company. (E-8/27/57 p.3, c.5) On March 22, 1859 he was elected a Director of the Bank of Yonkers. (E-4/7/59 p.2, c.5) On Friday, May 4, 1860, he was elected one of three members of the arrangement committee for the June exhibition of the newly formed Yonkers Horticultural Society. (E-5/17/60 p.3, c.3)

Corsor, Sarah On Monday, February 15, 1858 she died at the age of 99. She was the widow of Benjamin Corsor. (E-2/18/58 p.3, c.5)

Cotton, David During 1857 he had a furniture store in Wheeler's Row. (E-5/14/57 p.3, c.5) During 1858 he bought three lots on Grinnell Street and Prospect Hill for $1,350. He built a house on one of them for about $2,000. (E-4/22/58 p.2, c.3) During 1858 he had a partnership with Augustus Gaul which on Friday, April 2, 1858 was dissolved. (E-5/13/58 p.2, c.7)

Costello, Joseph During 1858 he built a residence on St. Mary's Street for about $1,000. (E-4/22/58 p.2, c.3)

Costigan, Lewis At one time he was a police officer in Yonkers. Sometime, probably in August, 1857, he and ex-officer Duflon arrested Charles Bloom for burglarizing the store of Nicholas C. Blauvelt in Spring Valley. Bloom escaped and the two, probably bounty hunters, obtained an arrest warrant and gave it to police officer G. S. Myers of Haverstraw. The warrant was for the arrest of Bloom and George Many. Bloom was recaptured by Costigan and turned over to Myers. There is no mention of Many being arrested. (E-10/15/57 p.2, c.5) On Wednesday, November 4, 1857 he arrested a pickpocket on Chambers Street, NYC. While attempting to get the consent of John W. Ferdon, son of Mrs. Ferdon who was the person accosted, the thief escaped. Mrs. Ferdon was from Piermont, NY. (E-11/5/57 p.2, c.4)

Cowdrey, Clinton During 1857 he was a member of the Yonkers Debating Society and was a member of its Arrangement Committee. (E-3/5/57 p.2, c.7) On Monday evening, March 21, 1859, he read an essay before 400 members of the Yonkers Debating Society entitled "Benedict Arnold." (E-3/24/59 p.2, c.2)

Cowdrey, Frederick During March, 1860 he advertised that he was going to start a milk route. (E-3/8/60 p.2, c.7) On Thursday evening, October 25, 1860, he was one of eight secretaries at a Republican campaign meeting. (E-11/1/60 p.2, c.2)

Cowdrey, Peter A. Sometime during the 1850s he owned a farm about three miles east of the village near the farm of James Odell. Evidently he died sometime during 1859. (E-2/9/60 p.2, c.7)

Cowdrey, Samuel B. On Monday, August 23, 1858 he was a delegate to the Westchester County Republican Party Convention at

Durell's Hotel in Morrisania.

Coyne, C. During 1860 he won a pair of blankets at a Yonkers Hatters Guard target shooting contest. (E-11/1/60 p.3, c.1)

Cox, Harriet M. (Mrs.) On Monday, August 22, 1859, she died at the age of 27 years, 11 months, and 22 days. (E-9/1/59 p.2, c.7)

Cozzens, Frederick S. During 1857 he was a wine merchant at 73 Warren Street NYC. He sold Longfellow and Zimmerman's still Ohio wines. (E-3/5/57 p.3, c.4) In March of 1857 he received a life membership in the Yonkers Library Association for valuable donations and services as a lecturer. (E-3/12/57 p.2, c.5) On Monday evening, March 1, 1858 he was elected a manager of the Yonkers Library Association. (E-3/4/58 p.2, c.3) On Tuesday, May 8, 1860, he was elected president of the newly formed Yonkers Horticultural Society. (E-5/17/60 p.3, c.3) He is listed on the 1860 census as a 42-year-old merchant with $25,000 in real estate, and a personal estate of $2,000. His wife Susan was 38 years old, and they had four children; Fr[inch] who was 14, Horatio who was 13, Isabella who was 10, and Lucy who was 5. They had three servants from Ireland. His wife was Susan Meyers. He was a distinguished author who was the editor of the trade publication *Wine Press* from 1854 till 1861, and he wrote Yankee Doodle, 1847, Prismatics, 1853, The Sparrowgrass Papers, 1856, Acadia or A Month with the Bluenoses, 1859, and The Sayings of Dr. Bushwacker and Other Learned Men, 1867. He died December 23, 1869. (WWW, p. 125 and Brown, p. 55) He lived on Downing Street. (Brown, p.55)

Crabb, Henry During 1856 he was a town Constable. (TRB)

Craft, D. During 1860 he won $3 at a Yonkers Hatters Guard target shooting contest. (E-11/1/60 p.3, c.1)

Craft, J. W. During 1860 he won $10.00 at a Yonkers Hatters Guard target shooting contest. (E-11/1/60 p.3, c.1)

Craft, William H. On Thursday evening, August 19, 1858 he fell from the rope of Hose Company Number 2's Fire Truck and died almost instantly. The Coroner's jury ruled that he died from a sudden congestion of the lungs. He was 18 years old and the youngest son of John and Mary A. Craft. He was a member of the Fire Department and they eulogized him by saying "... we have lost an esteemed associate, the community at large a member, who, although young, already gave promise of a useful manhood, and his family an affectionate son and kind brother." (E-8/26/58 p.2, c.6 and p.3, c.1)

Crambert, George Until June, 1860 he ran a bakery at the corner of Mechanic and Guion Streets. His bakery, apartments, and stable were being offered to rent for $12 a month. (E-6/21/60 p.3, c.3)

Crambert, (Mrs.) On Saturday morning, September 11, 1858 she was going to get a pail of water. As she was crossing the stoop it gave way and she fell into the hole. She broke her leg, but it was noted that her leg may have been broken in the attempt to get her out. (E-9/16/58 p.2, c.5)

Crane, H. C. During 1859 he built a wood-frame house on the corner of Point Street and Glenwood Avenue that cost about $4,000. (E-1/12/60 p.2, c.2) On the 1860 census he is listed as a 30-year-old accountant with $50,000 in real estate and a personal estate of $200. His wife Jane was 27 years old and they had two children; William who was 7, and [Millie] who was 2 years old. Kate Francis, who was 20 years old and from Ireland, also lived with them probably as a servant.

Crassous, F. H. During the latter part of 1858 he signed with a B middle initial a petition to have a meeting of the taxpayers in School District #2 meet to reconsider the location of two new schools; one on the corner of Wood Place and Warburton Avenue, and the other on St. Mary's Street near the Catholic Church and school. (E-12/23/58 p.2, c.2) During 1860 he lived on Lamartine Avenue and he had a rowboat and sailboat for sale. (E-6/28/60 p.3, c.1)

Crawford, E. M. During December, 1860 he was a member of a committee that was organized to run the second annual ball of Neptune Engine Company Number 3 that was to be held at the Getty Lyceum on January 24, 1861. (E-12/13/60 p.2, c.7)

Crawford, Hannah (Mrs.) On Saturday, August 13, 1859, she died at the age of 88. More than likely she was the wife of Silas Crawford. (E-9/1/59 p.2,c.7 see also Vol. 1 p.42) Silas is listed on the 1860 census. His age was listed as 88, and he lived in the household of Benjamin Crawford who was a 47-year-old carpenter.

Crisfield, Edward During 1858 he was a town Constable. (TRB)

Crisfield, John B. On June 22, 1857 he filed a complaint with the Clerk of the County of Westchester against William W. Woodworth, Charles B. Huntington, his wife Caroline A. Huntington, William H. Halsey, Ethan F. Bishop, John W. Stuart, Amos S. Holbrook, and Thomas C. Cornell. His attorney was William W. Scrugham. (E-9/24/57 p. 3, c.2) The complaint made its way to the special term of the Supreme Court held in Brooklyn March 1, 1858. Apparently the complaint was over a little more than 13 acres of land that was conveyed to Woodworth February 13, 1853 and was to be sold at auction. (E-3/4/58 p.3, c.5) In 1853 he was an Inspector of Elections for Election District Number One. In 1855 he was Sealer of Weights and Measures. During the 1856 town meeting he was elected to a full term as a Justice of the Peace. In 1857 he was also a Pound Master. (TRB) His office as Justice of the Peace was in Flagg's Hall in the office of W. F. Groshon. (E-3/11/58 p.2, c.1 and p.3, c.1) On Monday, February 7, 1859 he brought a pair of oxen to the village. They weighed in at 4,350 pounds. One of them was to be killed and sold as prime meat for the "delight" of "the connoisseur and epicure." (E-2/10/59 p.2, c.2)

Crowell, Wallace L. During 1857 he owned the Glenwood Ship Yard. He had a 2-ton Brig and a rowboat for sale or for exchange of property. He was offering an eighth share for the Brig. (E-6/25/57 p.2, c.7) On June 13, 1860, his business, the Marine Railway or Dry Dock, was advertised for sale at auction. (E-6/14/60 p.2, c.7)

Crowley, John During early 1858 he was a fireman. On Saturday evening January 16, 1858 he was riding on Fire Engine Number One, which was summoned to a false alarm, when he slipped and fell. The engine ran over both of his knees. However, no bones were broken, but he was badly bruised. (E-1/28/58 p.2, c.6) During the latter part of 1859 he was a member of the arrangement committee for the fourth annual ball of Protection Fire Engine Company Number 1. (E-12/22/59 p.2, c.6) On Thursday evening, October 25, 1860, he was one of eight secretaries at a Republican campaign meeting. (E-11/1/60 p.2, c.2)

Cuddy, James During 1858 he was a town Constable. (TRB)

Cuddy, Thomas During 1858 he was a town Constable. (TRB)

Cummings, William J. On Wednesday, November 2, 1859 he went with the Yonkers Hatters Guard to Weehawken, New Jersey where the guard was involved in a shooting contest amongst themselves. He was a member of the guard. At the target shooting contest he won a silver watch. Also at the target shooting contest he won some pants. (E-11/3/59 p.3, c.6) During the latter part of 1859 he was a member of the arrangement committee for the fourth annual ball of Protection Fire Engine Company Number 1. (E-12/22/59 p.2, c.6) During 1860 he won a $6 pair of pants at a Yonkers Hatters Guard target shooting contest. (E-11/1/60 p.3, c.1)

Cunningham, Hannah On Saturday, July 16, 1859 she was married by Rev. Hulbert to John Pagan. (E-7/21/59 p.3, c.2)

Cunningham, Sarah On Friday, October 14, 1859, she was married by Rev. Seward to William Moore. (E-10/27/59 p.3, c.5)

Curley, E. A. During 1857 he was an evening school teacher. He taught on Monday, Tuesday, Wednesday, and Friday evenings between 7:30 and 9 p.m.. Five weeks tuition in the common branches and bookkeeping cost $2. Higher education cost more. His classroom was in the debating room at the Yonkers Library Association, Wheeler's Building. (E-2/5/57 p.3, c.3) Sometime during May of 1857 he donated 25 volumes to the library. (E-5/21/57 p.2, c.6)

Curran, Hugh During 1859 he built a wood-frame tenement building on Walnut Street that cost about $3,000. He was able to get most of the material for the building from the materials of old houses that were torn down to make way for Farrington's Building. (E-1/12/60 p.2, c.2) On Monday evening March 26, 1860 he was elected one of thirty-two vice presidents of a Republican election rally meeting at the Getty House. (E-3/29/60 p.2, c.3)

Curran, Mary Ann On Tuesday evening June 1, 1858 she married James Newell at St. John's Church. (E-6/3/58 p.2, c.6)

Curran, P. During the latter part of 1859 he was a member of the arrangement committee for the fourth annual ball of Protection Fire Engine Company Number 1. (E-12/22/59 p.2, c.6) During 1860 he won two shirts at a Yonkers Hatters Guard target shooting contest. (E-11/1/60 p.3, c.1)

Curran, T. During 1860 he won $3 at a Yonkers Hatters Guard target shooting contest. (E-11/1/60 p.3, c.1)

Curtice, Ebenezer During the early part of 1857 he was a resident of Yonkers who moved to the far west. He was the principal of Public School #2. (E-4/30/57 p.2, c.4) However, during 1860 an E. Curtice of Yonkers was secretary of the Westchester Educational Society. (E-7/19/60 p.2, c.3)

Cuthbert (Mrs.) On Tuesday, December 28, 1858, she was leaving the house of a Mr. Wilson when a dog startled her horses. The horses bolted and the carriage overturned. She and the children with her were only slightly injured. She was from Riverdale. (E-12/30/58 p.2, c.3)

Daley, T. J. During 1860 he won a castor at a Yonkers Hatters Guard target shooting contest. (E-11/1/60 p.3, c.1)

Danks, Eli He died on Wednesday, July 13, 1859, exactly one week after his wife Naomi. He was 81 years, 6 months, and 10 days old. This is in contradiction with the 1850 census. (E-7/14/59 p.2, c.6) They were married in 1800. The paper now says he was 82 and died on a Tuesday. However, if he listed his age correctly on the 1850 census, he was either 79 or 80 when he died. (E-7/21/59 p.3, c.1, also Vol 1. p.43.) William G. Ackerman was the executor of his will. (E-5/24/60 p.3, c.4)

Danks, Naomi On Wednesday, July 6, 1859 she died at 79 years of age. She was the wife of Eli Danks. Her funeral was Friday, July 8 at 2 o'clock from the Reformed Dutch Church. (E-7/7/59 p.2, c.7 also Vol. 1.)

Darby, S. J. During 1859 he opened a restaurant and candy store at 7 Wheeler's Block. He also was a caterer. (E-6/9/59 p.3, c.4)

Darke, Charles During 1860 he was asked to serve on a grand jury. (E-6/14/60 p.2, c.7 see also Vol. 1, p.43 for Charles Dark)

Davidson, John During July, 1859 he was elected Secretary of Protection Fire Engine Company Number 1. (E-7/28/59 p.2, c.3) On the 1860 census he is listed as a 45-year-old baker with $70,000 in real estate, and a personal estate of $6,000. His wife Anna was 40 years old, and they had eight children; John who was a 23-year-old baker, Isabella who was 18, David who was 16, Jane who was 14, Archibald who was 12, James who was 10, Robert who was 8, and Charles who was 4. The whole family was born in Scotland. They also had a servant and two gardeners.

Dederer, William R. From 1853 through 1856, and then again from 1858 through 1860, he was an Inspector of Elections in Election District Number Three. He lived in the northeast part of the town near Greenburgh. (TRB)

Delafield, Lewis L. On Saturday evening, October 20, 1860, he was elected secretary of the Spuyten Duyvil Republican Club at a meeting held at the Iron Foundry. (E-10/25/60 p.2, c.3)

Delancey, Thomas J. During 1855 he was an Inspector of Elections for Election District Number Two. (TRB)

De Long, Charles During 1857 he was the proprietor of the Yonkers Gymnasium. (E-7/9/57 p.2, c.2)

Demarest, Joseph During 1858 he owned a boot and shoe establishment. It was so successful that he moved to the Broadway House which had recently been remodeled. (E-11/4/58 p.2, c.6) On February 21, 1859 he sold the business to Isaiah Anderson and his brother. It was noted as a saddle and harness business. (E-3/10/59 p.3, c.4) However, he moved his boot and shoe store to the Broadway House. (E-3/10/59 p.3. c.5) On May 26, 1859 he advertised that he had a carriage, buggy, a light fancy wagon, and a Jagger Wagon for sale. Inquiries could be made at the Broadway Boot and Shoe Store. (E-5/26/59 p.3, c.2)

Denslow, Oliver C. During 1853 he was a tavern keeper. (Documents.) During 1857 he was a hotel and tavern owner. (E-5/28/57 p.2, c.2) He applied for a hotel license in 1858. (E-6/3/58 p.2, c.5) He received his license. (E-6/24/58 p.2, c.5) During 1859 he was granted another hotel license. (E-8/11/59 p.2, c.7) On the 1860 census he is listed as a landlord with real estate valued at $1,700 and personal wealth of $1,500. He was 66, his wife Hannah was 67, a daughter Olive was 36, and another daughter Mary was 25 years old. These ages are contradictory with the 1850 census. Also, Peter Dickerson who was a 25-year-old bartender from New York, Ann Foley who was a 25-year-old servant from Ireland, and Peter Garrison who was a 63-year-old laborer from Ireland were in his household. During 1853 he was Hog Warden. In 1854 he was an Assessor, and in 1857 he was reelected. In 1858 his assessment district included the village north to the Greenburgh line. (E-4/8/58 p.2, c.2) On April 28, 1860 he was appointed an Assessor. (TRB & AVD)

Denslow, Van Buren During 1857 he was an attorney with a practice at 229 Broadway, NYC. He also had an office in Flagg's Hall, Yonkers. (E-3/5/57 p.3. c.4) On Thursday, March 18, 1858 he read a poem entitled "Humbug," before the Debating Society. (E-3/25/58 p.2, c.1) On Monday evening, March 21, 1859, he delivered a forty-five minute hilarious lecture before 400 members of the Yonkers Debating Society entitled "Popping the Question." (E-3/24/59 p.2, c.2)

Derby, C. L. During 1858 he bought the house of a Sarony on Ravine Avenue for $16,000. (E-4/22/58 p.2, c.3)

Derby, James C. On March 2, 1857 he donated 40 volumes to the Yonkers Library Association. (E-3/5/57 p.2, c.6) Just before March 12, 1857 he received a life membership in the Yonkers Library Association. (E-3/12/57 p.2, c.5) Sometime before April 16, 1857 he donated 30 additional volumes to the Yonkers Library Association. (E-4/16/57 p.2, c.6) During 1858 he owned a mansion on Warburton Avenue in North Glenwood. (E-8/19/58 p.2, c.3) During the latter part of 1858 he signed a petition to have a meeting of the taxpayers in School District #2 meet to reconsider the location of two new schools; one on the corner of Wood Place and Warburton Avenue, and the other on St. Mary's Street near the Catholic Church and school. (E-12/23/58 p.2, c.2) During 1860 he was selected to serve as a petit juror in the Court of Sessions that sat Monday, March 12, 1860. (E-3/8/60 p.2, c.5) On Monday, September 3, 1860 he was to serve on the petit jury of the Court of Oyer and Terminer in White Plains. (E-8/30/60 p.3, c.1)

Desmond, Michael During 1858 he built a residence on Washington Street for about $1,000. (E-4/22/58 p.2, c.3)

Devoe, Daniel He died June 6, 1857 at 70 years of age. (E-6/18/57 p.3, c.1, also, see Vol. 1, p.44)

Devoe, Henry F. On March 10, 1857 he was elected a Director of the Bank of Yonkers. (E-3/12/57 p.2, c.7) During 1857 he was a lumber dealer at 320 West Street corner of Charlton, NYC. (E-3/12/57 p.3, c.2) Also during 1857 he had a steam sawmill on Dock Street, and shipped his lumber to NYC. (E-7/2/57 p.2, c.5) He was chosen in 1857 to serve on the Grand Jury at White Plains. (E-8/27/57 p.2, c.4) In late 1856 he finished a large building on Dock Street between Nepperhan Avenue and Dock Street. During 1857 he finished building a steam saw and planing mill near the railroad. The building cost about $3,000. He shipped lumber all over the world. (E-12/31/57 p.2, c.2) On Friday, April 30, 1858 his steam planing mill caught fire from sparks that ignited shavings which were stored in the same room. The fire department responded promptly and since the wind was from the southwest a large supply of lumber on the dock was not damaged. (E-5/6/58 p.2, c.4) He bought the entire dock from Nepperhan Street to the west end of Dock Street and the Woodworth Dock for $28,000. He built a brick building and put a steam engine, a boiler, and other machinery in it for $5,000. He purchased his lumber in Albany, brought it to Yonkers on Yonkers vessels to be cut, and then sent the lumber to New York City by Yonkers boats. On the same property he was erecting in 1858 another building to be used as stores, and above the stores apartments for his employees. During 1857 he built a forty-thousand-square-foot building at the dock on the east side of the Nepperhan River. He put steam power and other machinery in the building to be used by a diversity of businesses. It was to employ about 250 adult males. (E-11/4/58 p.2, c.5,6) During 1858 he built a block of three story wood-frame buildings on Dock Street outside of the railroad. They were to be used as stores and tenements. The estimated cost was $6,000. Also during the same year he put two steam engines, each producing 60 horsepower, in his manufacturing building. The cost was estimated at $10,000. (E-1/20/59 p.2, c.4) The steam engines and boilers were purchased from and made by Jeremiah Burns for Devoe's brick factory. (E-2/10/59 p.2, c.4) On March 22, 1859 he was elected a Director of the Bank of Yonkers. (E-4/7/59 p.2, c.5) On Thursday evening, February 9, 1860, a cold front moved through Yonkers bringing with it high winds. The winds partially tore off the roof of his residence on North Broadway. (E-2/16/60 p.2, c.5) During 1860 he was asked to serve on the petit jury. (E-6/14/60 p.2, c.7) On the 1860 census he is listed as a 45-year-old lumber merchant with $50,000 in real estate, and a personal estate of $2,000. His wife Sarah was 43 years old, and they had seven children; Jane who was 20, Elizabeth who was 18, Maria who 16, Henry who was 14, Martin who was 12, Frank who was 8, and Joanna who was 6. During 1857 he was a member of the village Board of Trustees. On February 1, 1859 he resigned from the Board, but was present on February 24 and March 1.

Devoe, Jacob M. During 1858 he had a tea and coffee store on the corner of Palisade and Locust Hill Avenues. He sold Oolong teas that ranged from 25 to 75 cents per pound. Extra fine Oolong tea sold at 48 cents per pound, superior gunpowder for 50 cents a pound, and English breakfast tea for 48 cents a pound. (E-8/5/58 p.3, c.3)

Devoe, M. C. (Mrs.) During 1859 she built a wood-frame house on Ashburton Avenue that cost about $3,000. (E-1/12/60 p.2, c.2)

Deyo, Philip A. During 1857 he owned a grocery store with James Ackerman near Getty Square at the corner of Broadway and Dock Street. (E-5/28/57 p.2, c.2) He applied for a store license in 1858. (E-6/3/58 p.2, c.5) He received his license. (E-6/24/58 p.2, c.5) During 1860 he was selected to serve as a petit juror in the Court of Sessions that sat Monday, March 12, 1860. (E-3/8/60 p.2, c.5) On the 1860 census he is listed as a 37-year-old grocer with no assets. His wife Louise was 36 years old, and they had one child, Andrew, who was 5 years old. They also had a 22-year-old servant, Bridget, who was from Ireland. Also, in the household was Ann Ernest who was 51 years old.

Diamond, D. I. During 1859 he donated to the Yonkers Library Association a bound copy of the *New York Times* from the beginning of the paper to just a few months before the donation. (E-4/14/59 p.2, c.4)

Dibble, William During 1858 he lived on Palisade Avenue. On Tuesday, November 16, 1858, his coachman was on his way to meet him at the depot when the horses bolted. Opposite Mr. Stevens' livery stable on North Broadway the coach overturned and the coachman broke his left arm. Eventually the runaway horses hit a team of oxen and their yoke was broken. The oxen could not be reyoked and they ran past Wheeler's Building, up Mechanic Street, and headed for their home at Mile Square. (E-11/18/58 p.2, c.5) On the 1860 census he is listed as a 48-year-old gentleman. His wife Isabel was 41 years old. They had a cook and a servant.

Dickinson, John During 1860 he was asked to serve on a grand jury. (E-6/14/60 p.2, c.7)

Didson, Simon During December, 1860 he was a member of a committee that was organized to run the second annual ball of Neptune Engine Company Number 3 that was to be held at the Getty Lyceum on January 24, 1861. (E-12/13/60 p.2, c.7)

Dietzel, Simeon On Wednesday, November 2, 1859, he won $5 in a target shooting contest at Weehawkan, New Jersey. He was a member of the Yonkers Hatters Guard. (E-11/3/59 p.2, c.6) During 1860 he won a pair of gilt shades at a Yonkers Hatters Guard target shooting contest. (E-11/1/60 p.3, c.1)

Digman, B. On Wednesday, November 2, 1859, he won a pair of boots and knives in a target shooting contest at Weehawkan, New Jersey. He was a member of the Yonkers Hatters Guard. (E-11/3/59 p.2, c.6) During 1860 he won a cigar stand at a Yonkers Hatters Guard target shooting contest. (E-11/1/60 p.3, c.1) On the 1860 census he is listed as a 33-year-old hatter. His wife Johanna was 26 years old, and they had one child, Mary, who was one year old.

Disbrow, J. P. During 1858 he lived on Broadway near St. Mary's Street. His property adjoined Cyrus Cleveland's property on the south, and was the old property of Judge Aaron Vark. During the same year he made some improvements to his property which cost about $1,000. (E-1/20/59 p.2, c.3) On Monday night, October, 24, 1859, his home was burglarized. The thieves took some lace curtains, an overcoat, and a few other clothes. (E-10/27/1859 p.2, c.4) On Thursday evening, April 26, 1860, he was elected a trustee of the Yonkers Library Association. (E-5/3/60 p.2, c.3) On Thursday evening, April 26, 1860, he was elected a trustee of the Yonkers Library Association. (E-5/3/60 p.2, c.3) On the 1860 census he is listed as a 48-year-old butcher with $42,000 in real estate, and a personal estate of $2,000. His wife Susan was 39 years old, and they had seven children; Mary who was 18, Josephine who was 16, Sarah who was 14, Thomas who was 11, Joseph who was 6, Charles who was 4, and Lucy who was 4 months old. They also had a cook.

Dobson, George (Captain) On Friday, February 12, 1858 he died in New York City at the age of 49. He lived in Yonkers. (E-2/18/58 p.3, c.5)

Dolson, A. J. (Mrs.) During 1857 she ran a school for girls. (E-2/19/57 p.2, c.2) Also during 1857 she ran a summer school. Board in full cost $125, while tuition was $10 for the first and second classes, $15 for the third, and $20 thereafter. (E-4/9/57 p.3, c.1) In 1858 she was one of two principals at the Female Classical Seminary on the Hudson River at Glenwood. (E-4/1/58 p.2, c.5)

Donaldson, During 1857 he lived on South Broadway. He had an office at 112 and 114 Duane Street, NYC. He sold horses and carriages. (E-8/13/57 p.4, c.6)

Donnelly, (Mrs.) During 1859 she lived on St. Mary's Street, and advertised for the return of a lost child's dress. (E-8/18/59 p.3, c.2)

Donnelly, W. During 1860 he won $5 at a Yonkers Hatters Guard target shooting contest. (E-11/1/60 p.3, c.1)

Donohue, John C. On Monday evening, March 1, 1858 he was elected a manager of the Yonkers Library Association. (E-3/4/58 p.2, c.3) During the latter part of 1859 he was a member of the arrangement committee for the fourth annual ball of Protection Fire Engine Company Number 1. (E-12/22/59 p.2, c.6) During the latter part of 1859 he was a member of the reception committee for the fourth annual ball of Protection Fire Engine Company Number 1. (E-12/22/59 p.2, c.6)

Donovan, Hugh On Wednesday, November 2, 1859, he won $5 in a target shooting contest at Weehawkan, New Jersey. He was a member of the Yonkers Hatters Guard. (E-11/3/59 p.2, c.6)

Dooley, Patrick During 1859 he lived at 9 Jefferson Street, and James C. Bell was foreclosing on his property. (E-6/23/59 p.3, c.1)

Doremus During 1858 he sold his house and lot on the corner of Jones Place and Ashburton Avenue to a Blackwell. (E-4/22/58 p.2, c.3)

Doren, Augustus W. During 1857 he had a coal and wood yard at 4 Dock Street. (E-7/9/57 p.3, c.6) On December 1, 1857 he was elected a Trustee for School District Number 2 to replace Salmon Skinner. (TRB and E-2/4/58 p.3, c.1) On Friday night, June 3, 1859 a harness set was stolen from his stable at the coal yard. (E-6/9/59 p.2, c.2) During 1860 he also sold plaster, poudrette, and Mape's super phosphate of lime to farmers and gardeners. (E-5/3/60 p.3, c.3)

Doren, J. On Wednesday, November 2, 1859, he won a silver pitcher in a target shooting contest at Weehawkan, New Jersey. He was a member of the Yonkers Hatters Guard. (E-11/3/59 p.2, c.6)

Dortic (Mr.) He lived opposite the Mansion House. On Sunday morning at about 6 a.m., June 12, 1859 his barn burned down. (E-6/16/59 p.2, c.3)

Doty, Gil On Monday, December 26, 1859, he was acting assistant foreman of the old fire truck during a parade of the Yonkers Fire Department. (E-12/29/59 p.2, c.3)

Doty, Oliver W. On Tuesday, May 1, 1860 he became the "mine host" of the Getty House to replace Robert L. Bucklin. He came to Yonkers from Poughkeepsie. (E-4/26/60 p.2, c.2) While in Poughkeepsie he managed the Forbes House. (E-5/3/60 p.2, c.3) During 1860 he received a hotel license. (E-7/26/60 p.2, c.6) He was a member of the Masons. On either Wednesday or Thursday, December 5 or 6, 1860 he died. He left a wife and children, and he was buried in Poughkeepsie. (E-12/13/60 p.2, c.6) On the 1860 census he is listed as a 44-year-old landlord with a personal estate of $100. His wife Jane was 40 years old, and they may have had four children. The listing on the census is the Getty House and they had 9 female servants from Ireland, 2 bartenders, 4 black waiters, and 2 black porters. They also had 24 residents.

Dougan, David On July 7, 1857 he married Jane Vail at the Presbyterian Church. (E-7/16/57 p.2, c.7)

Doughty, S. G. During the latter part of 1858 he signed a petition to have a meeting of the taxpayers in School District #2 meet to reconsider the location of two new schools; one on the corner of Wood Place and Warburton Avenue, and the other on St. Mary's Street near the Catholic Church and school. (E-12/23/58 p.2, c.2)

Douglas, Robert J. He was a member of the Committee of Arrangements for the first annual Fire Department Fund Ball held to raise funds to help widows and orphans of deceased Yonkers firemen. The ball was held on Thursday evening, March 4, 1858. (E-2/18/58 p.3, c.5) On July 22, 1858 he signed a petition calling for a meeting of eligible voters in School District #2 to decide if the school district should become a Union Free School District. (E-8/5/58 p.4, c.3) During the latter part of 1858 he signed a petition to have a meeting of the taxpayers in School District #2 meet to reconsidered the location of two new schools; one on the corner of Wood Place and Warburton Avenue, and the other on St. Mary's Street near the Catholic Church and school. (E-12/23/58 p.2, c.2) On Wednesday, August 15, 1860 he lost an election as trustee for school district number 2. He received 1 vote. (E-8/16/60 p.2, c.6) On the 1860 census he is listed as a Douglass. He was a 40-year-old merchant with $20,000 in real estate, and a personal estate of $2,000. His wife Eliza was 35 years old, and they had five children; Mary was 16, Ada was 14, Eliza was 11, Foster was 5, and Robert was 1. In his household there was also an Elizabeth Lux who was 70 years old followed by a Sarah who was 20 on the listing. Julia Smart, who was 25 and was from Ireland, was their servant. A Dora, who was 40 and also from Ireland, was their cook, and Michael O'Donnell, who was 43 and also from Ireland, was their gardener.

Downes, A. T. During November, 1858 he lived on the Post Road about a mile and a half south of the village. He had two sorrel ponies, each fourteen and half hands high, for sale. He also had a saddle horse for sale. (E-11/11/58 p.2, c.7)

Doyle, M. L. On October 7, 1858 he was one of 32 businesses to announce they were closing their businesses at 8 p.m. during the winter. (E-10/7/58 p.3, c.4)

Doyle, T. W. On October 15, 1857 his business was one of 33 businesses in Yonkers to announce they were closing their stores at 8 p.m. beginning on October 12, 1857 until March 27, 1858. (E-10/15/57 p.3, c.1)

Drake, James M. On March 2, 1857 he was elected a manager of the Yonkers Library Association. (E-3/5/57 p.2, c.6) Sometime during March of 1857 he donated $25 to the Yonkers Library Association and he became a life member. During 1857 he built his residence on Buena Vista Avenue. The house was a wood Tudor Gothic style and cost about $9,500. (E-12/31/57 p.2, c.2) During 1858 he was a member of the Lecture Committee of the Yonkers Library Association. (E-1/7/58 p.3, c.1) On Friday evening, September 17, 1858 he was elected treasurer of the Yonkers Republican Association. (E-9/23/58 p.2, c.1) He was a stock broker at 49 Merchants' Exchange with an entrance on Wall Street. He was in the business with a Carter. (E-11/4/58 p.3, c.7) On Tuesday, November 16, 1858, he was elected a vice president of a Republican Party meeting in Yonkers. (E-11/18/58 p.2, c.2) During 1860 he was a Commissioner who assessed the expenses of work on St. Mary's Street. (E-11/29/60 p.3, c.1) On the 1860 census he is listed as a 30-year-old broker with $10,000 in real estate, and a personal estate of $2,000. His wife Mary was also 30 years old, and they had three children; Henry who was 7, Hubert who was 4, and Bertha who was 1. He also had a cook and a nurse.

Duff, Anna C. On Thursday, October 20, 1859 she was married by Rev. Seward to Samuel J. Everett. (E-11/10/59 p.3, c.2)

Duff, A. D. During 1857 he was a carpenter and builder with an office on Warburton Avenue between Dock Street and Wells Avenue. (E-4/9/57 p.2, c.7)

Duff, Mary M. On Thursday, December 9, 1858 she married Gilbert H. Tompkins. (E-12/16/58 p.2, c.6)

Duff, James F. On Sunday, July 24, 1859 he was married by Rev. King to Matilda Thompson. (E-7/28/59 p.2, c.7)

Duffey, Lawrence During the Court of Session proceedings that began on Monday, March 12, 1860, he was convicted of selling liquor in Yonkers without a permit. He was fined $30 or 20 days in the county jail. (E-3/29/60 p.2, c.5)

Durell, Henry Prior to 1857 he was the proprietor of the Getty House. See Augustus Van Liew. (E-7/30/57 p.2, c.5)

Durkee, Julius A. On Friday, May 4, 1860, he was elected one of six members of the committee on Premiums for Vegetables for the June exhibition of the newly formed Yonkers Horticultural Society. (E-5/17/60 p.3, c.3)

Dusenberry, Charles During 1857 he was a real estate broker with an office probably in Tuckahoe. (E-4/9/57 p.3, c.7) On Tuesday, October, 6, 1857 he was appointed a delegate to the Democratic County Convention. (E-10/8/57 p.2, c.2) He is listed on the 1860 census as a 69-year-old farmer with $120,000 in real estate, and a personal estate of $25,000. His wife Sarah was 60 years old. There were four other people in his household. (See vol.1, p.45) Another Charles Dusenberry is also listed on the 1860 census as a 30-year-old farmer. His wife Emily was 25 years old, and they had two children; Jane who was 4, and Anna who was 2. They had two laborers, two servants, and a teacher and her daughter living in the household. During 1860 he was an Inspector of Elections for Election District Number Three. (TRB)

Dusenberry, James During 1860 he was an Inspector of Elections for Election District Number Three. (TRB)

Dwight, Timothy C. On Monday evening March 26, 1860 he was elected one of thirty-two vice presidents of a Republican election rally meeting at the Getty House. (E-3/29/60 p.2, c.3) His mother Electa Center Dwight died in Franklin, Louisiana on Thursday, May 31, 1860 at the age of about 80. She was the widow of Henry Edwin Dwight of Cooperstown, New York. Her brother Robert and sister Asa H. Center, both of whom had died, lived in New York City. She died at the residence of her son-in-law Dr. Lyman in St. Mary's Parish, Louisiana. (E-6/28/60 p.2, c.6) On Thursday evening, October 25, 1860, he was one of twenty-two vice presidents at a Republican campaign meeting. (E-11/1/60 p.2, c.2)

Dyckman, George D. During 1860 he was asked to serve on the petit jury. (E-6/14/60 p.2, c.7)

Eagan, Michael During 1858 he lived on Irving Place and he was a well digger. (Brown, p.63)

Eagan, Peter On Sunday evening, May 29, 1859 he was married by Rev. Seward to Jane Bell who was from Hastings. (E-6/2/59 p.2, c.5)

East, Willie A. He died at Archdale at the age of 5 years, one month, and eight days old on July 2, 1859. (E-7/14/59 p.2, c.6)

Eaton, Augustine In NYC, on Saturday at noon, January 21, 1860, he suddenly died at the age of 57 years, and 8 and a half months. He was formerly a resident of Yonkers. (E-1/26/60 p.3, c.1)

Edgar, William B. During 1857 he donated $25 to the Yonkers Library Association and became a life member. (E-3/12/57 p.2, c.5) He applied for a grocery store license and apparently he did not receive one. However, the documents for 1857 note that he was licensed. (E-5/28/57 p.2, c.2 and E-6/4/57 p.2, c.3,4) He applied for a store license in 1858. (E-6/3/58 p.2, c.5) He received the license. (E-6/17/58 p.2, c.6) During 1859 he was granted another grocery license. (E-8/11/59 p.2, c.7) On Thursday evening, September 1, 1859 he was elected to the Finance Committee and he also was elected a representative of Hope Hook and Ladder Company. (E-9/8/59 p.3, c.1) On Monday, January 30, 1860 his wife Jeanie Shankland Edgar died at the age of 25. (E-2/2/60 p.3, c.3) During 1860 he received a grocer's license. (E-7/26/60 p.2, c.6) On the

1860 census he is listed as a 33-year-old grocer with a personal estate of $100. On the same census he is again listed as a 35-year-old grocer with real estate worth $10,000. He was from Scotland and was a resident of the Getty House.

Edwards, Albert On September 13, 1859 the partnership between him and Edmund Y. Morris was dissolved. They owned the People's Grocery and Tea Store on Mechanic Street opposite the Getty House. (E-9/15/59 p.3, c.3)

Eickmeyer, Rudolph On Monday evening March 26, 1860 he was elected one of thirty-two vice presidents of a Republican election rally meeting at the Getty House. (E-3/29/60 p.2, c.3) On Thursday evening, October 25, 1860, he was one of twenty-two vice presidents at a Republican campaign meeting. (E-11/1/60 p.2, c.2) On the 1860 census he is listed as a 28-year-old machinist with a personal estate of $1,000. His wife Mary was 23 years old, and they had two children; Eva who was 2, and Lucy who was 1 month old.

Eller, William During 1860 he won $5.25 at a Yonkers Hatters Guard target shooting contest. (E-11/1/60 p.3, c.1)

Elting, Ezekiel J. During October, 1857 he operated a dry goods store with Vail. The store was in the Radford Building. (E-10/1/57 p.3, c.1 and Brown, p. 63) On the 1860 census he is listed as a 35-year-old merchant with $1,000 in real estate and a personal estate of $6,000. He was a resident of the Getty House.

Elwell, Seymour B. During August of 1857 he opened a cigar and tobacco store in the old store of William H. Post, in the Wheeler Building. (E-8/27/57 p.2, c.5)

Embree, J. On the 1860 census he is listed as a 39-year-old contractor with real estate worth $2,500, and a personal estate of $1,000. His wife Sarah was 31 years old, and an Agnes who was 21 lived with them. They probably had two children, Joseph 11, and Elizabeth, 4 years old.

Embree, Robert During 1855 he was a town Pound Master. (TRB) On Tuesday, January 31, 1860 he was married by Rev. King of the M. E. Church to Sarah E. Wood. (E-2/23/60 p.2, c.7) During 1860 he was a member of the Yonkers Temperance Society's Temperance Demonstration committee. (E-6/21/60 p.3, c.1)

English, William D. During 1857 he owned a grocery store with Turniss. (E-5/28/57 p.2, c.2) During the same year he applied for a hotel license but apparently he did not receive it. (E-6/4/57 p.2, c.3) In December, 1857 he opened a billiard saloon on the first floor of a building at the corner of Broadway and Wells Avenue. He had two tables, but was going to add a third soon. He also had chess, checkers, and backgammon boards along with newspapers devoted to sports. (E-12/31/57 p.3, c.2)

Everett, Samuel J. On Thursday, October 20, 1859 he was married by Rev. Seward to Anna C. Duff. (E-11/10/59 p.3, c.2)

Falon, Patrick On Wednesday, November 2, 1859, he won in a drawing a pair of boots at a target shooting contest at Weehawkan, New Jersey. He was a member of the Yonkers Hatters Guard. (E-11/3/59 p.2, c.6)

Farley, Charles During 1860 he was a member of the Yonkers Temperance Society's Temperance Demonstration committee. (E-6/21/60 p.3, c.1)

Farling, Henry On Monday evening March 26, 1860 he was elected one of thirty-two vice presidents of a Republican election rally meeting at the Getty House. (E-3/29/60 p.2, c.3)

Farrell, J. During 1860 he won a ring at a Yonkers Hatters Guard target shooting contest. (E-11/1/60 p.3, c.1)

Farrington, Isaac O. On Monday evening March 26, 1860 he was elected one of thirty-two vice presidents of a Republican election rally meeting at the Getty House. (E-3/29/60 p.2, c.3)

Farrington, James B. On March 2, 1857 he was elected secretary of the Yonkers Debating Society. He was also a member of the Society's Arrangement Committee. (E-3/5/57 p.2, c.6) During October, 1859 he and Henry Buckhout owned a grain and feed business at 4 North Broadway in the Farrington Building. (E-10/13/59 p.3, c.2) The partnership was dissolved on May 10, 1860, and the business was continued by Farrington. (E-5/24/60 p.3, c.4)

Farrington, Richard On May 14, 1860 he was appointed a town Pound Master. (TRB)

Farrington, Thomas O. For part of 1857 he owned a dry goods and perishables store at the corner of Getty Square and Broadway. He was also an insurance agent for the Merchant's Insurance Company which was located in the Ocean Bank Building corner of Fulton and Greenwich Streets, NYC. He also was an insurance agent for the Westchester Mutual Insurance Company. (E-1/29/57 p.4, c.4) He retired from the grocery business but apparently remained an insurance agent. He was in business for 25 years and "For much of that time he was the only merchant of this village." (E-6/18/57 p.3, c.7) During July of 1857 he and Moses B. Patterson examined the books of Rev. Tripp of the African Methodist Episcopal Zion Church and found them in order. (E-7/23/57 p.2., c.7) During the early part of 1858 he either was elected or appointed treasurer of the Yonkers Association for Improving the Condition of the Poor. (E-3/4/58 p.2., c.7) During 1858 he, John Squire, Jr., and Charles S. Archer owned a grocery store at 202 West Street, NYC. (E-9/9/58 p.3, c.7) On Monday evening, October 25, 1858 he chaired a Republican meeting held at the Lyceum. (E-10/28/58 p.2, c.3) On Tuesday, November 16, 1858, he was elected a vice president of a Republican Party meeting in Yonkers. (E-11/18/58 p.2, c.2) His residence was on South Broadway near Prospect Street. (E-4/14/59 p.3, c.3) During 1859 he built a building, called "Farrington's Building," on the corner of Palisade Avenue and Getty Square. He was the superintendent for the project that cost about $14,000. (E-1/12/60 p.2, c.1) On Saturday, April 21, 1860 his youngest son, Frank C., died of scarlet fever at the age of 2 years and 10 months. (E-4/26/60 p.2, c.6) On Friday, May 4, 1860, he was elected one of six members of the committee on Premiums for Plants and Flowers for the June exhibition of the newly formed Yonkers Horticultural Society. (E-5/17/60 p.3, c.3) On the 1860 census he is listed as a 52-year-old merchant with $10,000 in real estate, and a personal estate of $5,000. His wife Rebecca was 44 years old, and they had five children; James B. who was a 22-year-old merchant and is listed above, Mary who was 20 years old, Thomas who was a 17-year-old clerk, Alice who was 12, and Samuel who was 6. A Mrs. Lawrence who was 64 years old, and two servants also lived in their household. During 1855 and 1856 he was a member of the village Board of Trustees. During 1857 and 1858 he was a Village Assessor. (AVD)

Farrou, John On Wednesday, November 2, 1859, he won a tea pot in a target shooting contest at Weehawkan, New Jersey. He was a member of the Yonkers Hatters Guard. (E-11/3/59 p.2, c.6)

Ferguson, Hugh H. On Wednesday, November 2, 1859, he won a china set in a target shooting contest at Weehawkan, New Jersey. He was a member of the Yonkers Hatters Guard. (E-11/3/59 p.2, c.6) During 1860 he won two barrels of potatoes at a Yonkers Hatters Guard target shooting contest. (E-11/1/60 p.3, c.1)

Ferris, O. C. During 1857 he had a building under construction on the corner of Palisade Avenue and Locust Hill Avenue. The building was to have an entrance on both streets and its estimated cost was $7,000. (E-7/2/57 p.2, c.5) The building contained stores and tenements. Later in the year the estimate for its construction was between $5,000 and $6,000. (E-12/31/57 p.2, c.4)

Fillmore, George H. During 1857 he became a professor at the Yonkers Collegiate Institute. Previously he was a professor of mathematics at Newton University in Baltimore, Maryland. He became part owner of the institute with M. N. Wisewell. (E-10/29/57 p.3, c.1) However, later in the year an advertisement noted that the partnership had not been consummated and that it was postponed. (E-12/31/57 p., c.7) On Thursday, March 18, 1858 he read an essay entitled "Human Inequalities," before the Debating Society. The editor of the *Yonkers Examiner* thought he should have delivered it a little more forcibly. (E-3/25/58 p.2, c.1)

Finin, Thomas S. On March 2, 1857 he was elected vice president of the Yonkers Debating Society. (E-3/5/57 p.2., c.6) On Monday evening, March 1, 1858 he was elected secretary of the Yonkers Debating Society. (E-3/4/58 p.2, c.2) On Thursday, March 18, 1858 he delivered a speech before the Debating Society and was loudly cheered. (E-3/25/58 p.2, c.1) On Tuesday, November 16, 1858, he was elected a secretary of a Republican Party meeting in Yonkers. (E-11/18/58 p.2, c.2) On Monday, March 7, 1859 he was elected president of the Yonkers Debating Society. (E-3/10/59 p.2, c.7) On Monday evening, March 21, 1859, he delivered a speech before 400 members of the Yonkers Debating Society entitled "The Featme of the Age." (E-3/24/59 p.2, c.2) During 1859 he bought the clothing business of Benjamin A. Starr at 15 North Broadway. During August, 1860 he advertised that his clothing business was at 5 South Broadway. (E-4/28/59 p.2, c.5 & 8/23/60 p.3, c.5) On Monday evening, December 26, 1859 he was married by Rev. Carter to Carrie Baldwin at her father's house. (E-12/29/59 p.2, c.6) He was a member and secretary of the Republican Young Men of Yonkers and at a meeting on Tuesday evening, July 31, 1860, resolutions were adopted to form the Republican Wide Awakes of Yonkers club. (E-8/2/60 p.2, c.3) On Friday evening, August 10, 1860, he was elected a member of the executive committee of the Yonkers Republican Wide Awakes. (E-8/16/60 p.2, c.6) On Saturday, September 29, 1860 he was a delegate to the Republican First Assembly District Convention that was held in Morrisania Hall, Morrisania. (E-10/4/60 p.2, c.2) On Thursday evening, October 25, 1860, he was one of eight secretaries at a Republican campaign meeting. (E-11/1/60 p.2, c.2) On Monday night, December 17, 1860 he was installed as an officer into the Rising Star Lodge of Free and Accepted Masons as secretary. (E-12/20/60 p.2, c.3)

Fisher, Charles On Thursday evening, May 19, 1859 he was married by Rev. Brewer to Mary Colwell. She was from Poughkeepsie. (E-5/26/59 p.2, c.7) During the latter part of 1859 he was a member of the arrangement committee for the fourth annual ball of Protection Fire Engine Company Number 1. (E-12/22/59 p.2, c.6)

Fisher, George On May 24, 1860 he advertised that he had two milk cows for sale. He evidently lived on Spring Street. (E-5/24/60 p.3, c.4)

Fisher, Hiram During 1858 he lived on the farm of the late Abraham Valentine. On Wednesday night, probably August 25, 1858, a horse was stolen from his pasture. The thieves also took a new harness from the stable. Hugh Quinn lived nearby and the thieves took a wagon with a standing top from him. They were tracked to Mount Vernon at the railroad depot and then down 4th Avenue toward NYC. (E-9/2/58 p.2, c.6)

Fisher, Rosetta On June 6, 1857 she married Albert Rogers at the Presbyterian Church. (E-6/18/57 p.3, c.1)

Fitch, O. M. Sometime during April of 1857 he donated 12 volumes to the Yonkers Library Association. (E-4/16/57 p.2, c.5)

Fitzgerald, Thomas Sometime during the Spring of 1857 he left Yonkers and moved to Beekmantown, Mount Pleasant. While in Yonkers he lived near the Engine House of Company No. 1. Also, while living in Yonkers he was sent to jail several times for beating his wife. One day during the week of November 9, 1857 in a fit of drunkenness he beat and stamped his wife to death. Before dying she gave birth to a stillborn child whose limbs were broken and crushed. She died shortly afterward at the County House. (E-11/26/57 p.2, c.4 and 12/10/57 p.3, c.1) He had been arrested frequently for beating his wife and was a suspect in her death. He then married a nineteen-year-old and apparently returned to Yonkers. On Sunday night, November 21, 1858, he was again arrested for an assault on his housekeeper. His wife was also arrested even though she got into the fight in an apparent attempt to break it up. Justice Groshon sentenced them both to sixty days in the county jail. (E-11/25/58 p.2, c.2)

Fitzpatrick, William During 1858 he built a wood-frame house on Willow Street worth about $1,400. (E-1/20/59 p.2, c.5)

Flagg, Ethan He came to Yonkers about 1844. (E-10/4/60 p.2, c.5, also see Vol. 1) During 1857 he was a real estate broker and was an Inspector of the Village Election. (E-2/5/57 p.3, c.3) During March of 1857 he donated $25 to the Yonkers Library Association and became a life member, and during the same month he was elected President of the Yonkers Savings Bank. (E-3/12/57 p.2, c.5 and 7) On March 12, 1857 he was elected a Director of the Bank of Yonkers. (E-3/12/57 p.2, c.7) During August of 1857 he was noted as a director of the Yonkers Gas Light Company. (E-8/13/57 p.3, c.3) On Saturday, September 5, 1857 he was elected at a Republican primary meeting to be a delegate to the Republican district convention. (E-9/10/57 p.2, c.6) During 1857 he was the Republican candidate for the New York State Assembly. (E-10/15/57 p.2, c.1) He lost the election for the Assembly to Abraham B. Tappan 861 votes to 1,392 votes. (E-11/5/57 p.2, c.2) During 1857 he put a glass front on his store on the corner of Palisade Avenue and Mechanic Street along with other improvements that cost about $2,000. During the same year he owned about five acres of land on a corner of Palisade and Ashburton Avenues. In the same year he built a stone fence along the street frontage with a recessed gateway that was designed by Thomas C. Cornell. The improvement cost about $3,000. He planned to build a mansion on the site. (E-12/31/57 p.2, c.3) During 1858 he was president of the Yonkers Savings Bank. (E-7/8/58 p.3, c.1) On Monday, August 23, 1858 he was a delegate to the Westchester County Republican Party Convention at Durell's Hotel in Morrisania. At that convention he was elected an alternate to the State Convention. (E-8/26/58 p.2, c.2) On Friday evening, September 17, 1858 he was elected to the executive committee of the Yonkers Republican Association. (E-9/23/58 p.2, c.1) On Tuesday, November 16, 1858, he was elected a vice president of a Republican Party meeting in Yonkers. (E-11/18/58 p.2, c.2) During 1858 he built a gardener's cottage, a barn, a stable, erected 900 feet of stone fence, did grading in preparation for another building, and built a grapery on his grounds on Oak Hill Avenue for about $5,900. (E-1/20/59 p.2, c.3) On March 22, 1859 he was elected a Director of the Bank of Yonkers. (E-4/7/59 p.2, c.5) His wife was Julia B. Flagg. (E-4/14/59 p.3, c.3) On Thursday, August 13, 1859 he was chosen a delegate to the Republican County Convention by the newly formed Republican Association at a Republican Town meeting. (E-10/20/59 p.3, c.1) On Wednesday, September 5, 1860, a new stonedigger and wall-laying machine was to be demonstrated on his farm. (E-8/30/60 p.2, c.5) He was still president of the Yonkers Savings Bank during 1860. (E-9/20/60 p.2, c.7) During 1860 he ran for the State Assembly and lost to Dr. McDermott by forty-nine votes. In the district he took Yonkers and West Farms, but lost Eastchester and Westchester to McDermott, and he lost Morrisania to Pierce Tallman. He took Yonkers with 58.8% of the vote, lost Eastchester with 31.9% of the vote, lost Westchester with only 20.3% of the vote, lost Morrisania with 33.2% of the vote, and won West Farms by a plurality of only 37.1% of the vote. In the town of Yonkers he won the village with 63.5% of the vote, lost the second election district with only 38.9% of the vote, and he won the third election district with 52.1% of the vote. (E-11/8/60 p.2, c.2) On the 1860 census he is listed as a 39-year-old gentleman. His wife Julia was 27 years old, and they had two children; Wilbur who was 2, and Martha who was 1. He had a cook, Bridgette Riley who was 21, and a nurse, Mary Rooney who was 19. Both were from Ireland. His 68-year-old mother also lived in the household. In 1856 and again in 1857 he was an Inspector of Elections for Election District Number One. During 1857 he resigned from that position. From 1857 through 1860 he was a member of the village Board of Trustees, and in 1860 he was elected Supervisor. (TRB and AVD)

Flagg, Levi W. (M.D.) During March 1857 he donated $25 to the Yonkers Library Association and became a life member. (E-3/12/57 p.2., c.5) On July 22, 1858 he signed a petition calling for a meeting of eligible voters in School District #2 to decide if the school district should become a Union Free School District. (E-8/5/58 p.4, c.3) On Tuesday, August 17, 1858 he and sixteen other men wrote C. Jerome Hopkins a letter requesting him to give another piano concert at the Getty House. (E-8/19/58 p.2, c.4) During 1858 he made improvements to his buildings on the corner of Broadway and Hudson Street. The buildings were occupied by the Yonkers Collegiate Institute. The improvements cost him about $3,500. (E-1/20/59 p.2, c.3) On March 22, 1859 he was elected an Inspector of Election for next year's board of directors election for the Bank of Yonkers. (E-4/7/59 p.2, c.5) On the 1860 census he is listed as a 43-year-old physician with $10,000 in real estate, and a personal estate of $2,500. His wife Charlotta was 38 years old, and they had five children; Howard who was 11, Mary, who was 9, Lucy who was 5, George who was 3, and Robert who was 1. They had three servants and a cook.

Fletcher, Martha Jane On Thursday, August 4, 1859, she died at the age of 1 year, 7 months, and 24 days. (E-9/1/59 p.3, c.1)

Flewelling, Stephen He was to be a juror for the Petit Court in White Plains on June 21, 1858. (E-6/17/58 p.2, c.2)

Flood, Peter On Saturday, January 1, 1858, he received a slight knife wound when he apparently tried to stop a fight between two men who had been drinking heavily. The fight occurred in the flats and the combatants were finally separated at the corner of Prospect Street and Broadway. (E-1/6/59 p.2, c.1)

Flood, Philip On Wednesday, June 30, 1857 he bought a lot on South Broadway for $1,170. (E-7/1/58 p.2, c.2) He bought the lot and house on Broadway from Cyrus Cleveland. (E-1/20/59 p.2, c.3)

Foote, William C. Prior to August of 1857 he was principal of Oak Grove Female Seminary. On October 5, 1857 he was to open a select school for a limited number of young ladies. (E-8/27/57 p.2, c.2) During 1858 he built a wood-frame school house on Broadway at the top of Lamartine Avenue. It cost him about $2,000. (E-1/20/59 p.2, c.3) On the 1860 census he is listed as a 45-year-old teacher with $15,000 in real estate, and a personal estate of $2,500. His wife Hannah was 44 years old. A G. Davis and Sophia were also listed in his household. Both were 75 years old. A clergyman and cook are also listed, as well as Helen Foot who was 15 years old and was probably William Foote's daughter. The census taker spelled his name Foot.

Forrest, Edwin During 1857 he owned land that was next to land owned or previously owned by John Crisfield. (E-3/4/58 p.3, c.5)

Foster, Peter H. During 1857 he loaned money and mortgaged buildings. He was also a real estate agent, and his office was at 289 Broadway, NYC. (E-3/5/57 p.3, c.4)

Fowler, Benjamin On Wednesday, December 22, 1859 he died. He was 86 years old. (E-12/29/59 p.2, c.6, see also Vol. 1, pp. 47,48) Isaac V. Fowler and Caleb Fowler were executors of his will. (E-7/19/60 p.3, c.2) In 1853 and again in 1855 he was a Pound Master. (TRB)

Fowler, Caleb He is listed on the 1860 census as a 55-year-old farmer with $18,000 in real estate, and a personal estate of $12,000. There were eight people in his household including a farm laborer, a servant, and four laborers. (See vol.1, p.48.)

Fowler, Gilbert During 1856 he was a Pound Master. (TRB)

Fowler, Isaac V. On Monday, September 3, 1860 he was to serve on the grand jury of the Court of Oyer and Terminer in White Plains. (E-8/30/60 p.3, c.1) During 1859 he was an Assessor. (TRB)

Fowler, Vermilyea During 1857 he was a Pound Master. (TRB)

Fox, George During 1857 he lived in a house on School Street. The house was for sale. (E-4/9/57 p.3, c.7)

Francis, George W. During the early days of the Yonkers Library Association he was given a life membership. (E-3/12/57 p.2, c.5) He was a teacher of things of "practical utility." (E-5/4/57) During the early part of 1859, and probably 1858, he sold Wright's Little Champion Gas Burners. The burners were supposed to save 15 to 20 percent in gas, and it seems they gave off less of a flicker then other gas burners. (E-1/6/59 p.2, c.3) During 1860 he bought the flour and grain business on the corner of Main and Mill Streets from E. B. Knox. (E-9/27/60 p.2, c.7) On the 1860 census he is listed as a 60-year-old teacher with $6,000 in real estate, and a personal estate of $1,000. His wife Martha was 57 years old, and they had two children; Mary who was 25, and Kellog who was 24. They also had an Irish servant. During 1853 and 1856 he was the town's Superintendent of Schools. (TRB)

Franklin, James H. He was a member of the Committee of Arrangements for the first annual Fire Department Fund Ball held to raise funds to help widows and orphans of deceased Yonkers firemen. The ball was held on Thursday evening, March 4, 1858. (E-2/18/58 p.3, c.5) During the latter part of 1859 he was a member of the arrangement committee and also a member of the floor committee for the fourth annual ball of Protection Fire Engine Company Number 1. (E-12/22/59 p.2, c.6)

Franklin, Richard L. During May, 1860 he was called on to serve on a the grand jury. (E-5/31/60 p.3, c.3)

Frazier, George During 1860 he and a Curran owned the Yonkers Blue Stone Yard. The stone was used for flagging. The yard was on the corner of Wells Avenue and River Street and he was the manager. (E-3/8/60 p.2, c.7) On the 1860 census he is listed as a 27-year-old stone yard owner with $2,000 in real estate, and a personal estate of $1,000. His wife Margaret was 28 years old, and they had three children; Isaac who was 6, Eliza who was 2, and George who was 1. Both he and his wife were born in Ireland, and their children were born in New York.

Fredenburgh, Abraham During 1857 he built a Gothic-style brick cottage on the west side of Warburton Avenue on the corner of Locust Street. The building cost about $3,000. (E-12/31/57 p.2, c.3) On July 22, 1858 he signed a petition calling for a meeting of eligible voters in School District #2 to decide if the school district should become a Union Free School District. (E-8/5/58 p.4, c.3) During the latter part of 1858 he signed a petition to have a meeting of the taxpayers in School District #2 meet to reconsider the location of two new schools; one on the corner of Wood Place and Warburton Avenue, and the other on St. Mary's Street near the Catholic Church and school. (E-12/23/58 p.2, c.2) During 1859 he owned a blue stone yard at the rear of the Franklin House. (E-6/30/59 p.3, c.3) He bought the property on Warburton Avenue from Frederick Coe and Ann Eliza Coe on December 9, 1858. During May, 1860 the property and house was to be sold at auction. His name was spelled Fradenburgh in the newspaper. (E-5/24/60 p.3, c.4) On the 1860 census he is listed as a 45-year-old stone yard owner with a personal estate of $2,000. His wife was Eliza and she was 40 years old. They had two children. Harriet who was 9, and Herbert who was 2 years old. In addition to their children there is listed an additional female and three males in their household.

Freeland, (Mrs.) At about 2 A.M. Tuesday, September 21, 1858 thieves attempted to enter her house on Warburton Avenue. The thieves tried to pry the door open, but couldn't. (E-9/23/58 p.2, c.4)

Friend, Emma R. On Monday, December 12, 1859 she was married at her fathers residence by Rev. Hulbert to Stephen L. Van Wart. (E-12/22/59 p.2, c.6)

Fuller, William C. On Wednesday, December 12, 1860, he was married by Rev. Seward to Mary M. Gale. (E-12/13/60 p.2, c.7)

Furniss, Alfred During 1857 he had a store to let on the northwest corner of North Broadway and Wells Avenue. (E-7/9/57 p.3, c.6) He boarded at Mrs. Woolcox's house on Smith Street. A Henry Field, a painter, also boarded there, and feeling sorry for him Furniss loaned him some money and other necessities. On Monday morning, April 11, 1859 Field rifled his and James Furniss's trunk and took cash, gold, and silver from them. (E-4/14/59 p.2, c.4)

Furniss, James During 1858 he built a cottage on Smith Street worth about $800. (E-1/20/59 p.2, c.5) He boarded at Mrs Woolcox's house on Smith Street. A Henry Field, a painter, also boarded there, and feeling sorry for him Furniss loaned him some money and other necessities. On Monday morning, April 11, 1859 Field rifled his and Alfred Turniss's trunk and took cash, gold, and silver from them. (E-4/14/59 p.2, c.4)

Furniss, Thomas During 1857 he had a workshop on Irving Place. He was a carpenter who made air-tight doors and windows. (E-12/31/57 p.3, c.3) On Monday, December 13, 1858 he became Vestryman of the newly formed Episcopal Church on Mechanic Street. (E-12/23/58 p.2, c.3) On April 9, 1860 he was elected a Vestryman at St. Paul's Free Church. (E-4/12/60 p.2, c.6) On the 1860 census he is listed as a 30-year-old carpenter with $2,000 in real estate, and a personal estate of $500. His wife Eliza was 29 years old, and they were both born in England. They had at least one child; Sarah who was 6 years old. A 16-year-old George is also listed, and he was a carpenter. The latter two were born in New York.

Gaffney, John During 1857 he owned a store on Mechanic Street. (E-4/9/57 p.3, c.2) During 1857 he applied for a grocery license and apparently did not receive it. (E-5/28/57 p.2, c.2 and E-6/4/57 p.2, c.3,4) On October 15, 1857 his business was one of 33 businesses in Yonkers to announce they were closing their stores at 8 p.m. beginning on October 12, 1857 until March 27, 1858. (E-10/15/57 p.3, c.1) During 1859 he was granted a grocery license. (E-8/11/59 p.2, c.7) On Monday evening March 26, 1860 he was elected one of thirty-two vice presidents of a Republican election rally meeting at the Getty House. (E-3/29/60 p.2, c.3) During 1860 he received a grocer's license. (E-7/26/60 p.2, c.6) On the 1860 census he is listed as being 47 years old with $2,500 in real estate, and a personal estate of $1,000. His wife Mary was 40 years old and they had four children, James who was 15, Robert who was 13, William who was 11, and George who was 8 years old. He, his wife, and their children were all born in Ireland.

Gale, Henry During the latter part of 1858 he signed a petition to have a meeting of the taxpayers in School District #2 meet to reconsider the location of two new schools; one on the corner of Wood Place and Warburton Avenue, and the other on St. Mary's Street near the Catholic Church and school. (E-12/23/58 p.2, c.2) He lived on Warburton Avenue near Lamartine Avenue. On Thursday evening August 25, 1859 his home was broken into by thieves, and they stole his watch. (E-9/1/59 p.2, c.4) On the 1860 census he is listed as a 43-year-old carpenter with a personal estate of $1,500. His wife Mary was 39 years old and their children were Josephine who was 21, Mary who was 19, George who was 14, William who was 12, Ida who was 10, and Frank who was 2. Twenty-four-year-old Ann Proce who was born in Ireland was their servant.

Gale, Mary A. On Wednesday, December 12, 1860, she was married by Rev. Seward to William C. Fuller. She was the second daughter of Henry Gale. (E-12/13/60 p.2, c.7)

Gallaudet, Thomas (Rev.) He was a professor in the New York Institute for the Deaf and Dumb. On Monday evening, July 11, 1859, he visited Yonkers and attended a service at St. John's. He signed the service for the deaf and dumb of Yonkers. He also gave an address to the congregation. (E-7/7/59 p.3, c.1) This must have been the son of Thomas Hopkins Gallaudet who raised money for the first Free American School for the Deaf during 1817 at Hartford, Ct. Thomas Hopkins died in 1851. (See *Who Was Who in America*.)

Gallena, Mr. During 1859 he renovated his house on Clinton Street. The renovation cost about $900. (E-1/12/60 p.2, c.1)

Galvin, Michael On Wednesday, November 2, 1859, he won some pants in a target shooting contest at Weehawkan, New Jersey. He was a member of the Yonkers Hatters Guard. (E-11/3/59 p.2, c.6)

Gant, F. S. During 1855 he was a member of the village Board of Trustees. (AVD)

Gardener, David During 1857 he was a Trustee of the African Methodist Episcopal Zion Church. (E-2/5/57) Sometime during July 1857 he resigned his position in protest of alleged missing funds ascribed to Rev. Tripp. (E-7/23/57 p.2, c.7) On Monday, August 9, 1857 thieves from NYC broke into his house near Fairy Grove and stole a gold watch and chain, a beautiful fan from China, and a coat and vest. The house was ransacked. The family was not at home during the robbery. (E-8/12/58 p.2, c.1) During December, 1859, he was on the arrangement committee to give a benefit for their pastor

John Taylor. The guest speaker was the Rev. Henry Highland Garnett, pastor of the Shiloh Presbyterian Church in NYC. Admission was 50 cents and the proceeds went to Rev. Taylor. (E-12/8/59 p.3. c.2)

Gardener, T. A. On Monday evening, March 21, 1859, he delivered a speech before 400 members of the Yonkers Debating Society entitled "The Lesson of Franklin's Life." (E-3/24/59 p.2, c.2)

Garrison, Edward During 1855 he was a Constable. (TRB)

Garrison, Hyatt L. During 1857 he was Captain of the sloop *Benjamin Franklin*. (E-5/14/57 p.2, c.7) On July 22, 1858 he signed a petition calling for a meeting of eligible voters in School District #2 to decide if the school district should become a Union Free School District. (E-8/5/58 p.4, c.3) During the latter part of 1858 he signed a petition to have a meeting of the taxpayers in School District #2 meet to reconsider the location of two new schools; one on the corner of Wood Place and Warburton Avenue, and the other on St. Mary's Street near the Catholic Church and school. (E-12/23/58 p.2, c.2) His house, on or near Locust Street, was entirely destroyed by a fire set by an arsonist on Monday night, February 6, 1860. The house was insured for about half of its value. (E-2/9/60 p.2, c.3) On the 1860 census he is listed as a 35-year-old sloop captain with $2,500 in real estate, and a personal estate of $500. His wife Sophia was also 35 years old, and they had two children; Edward who was 7, and Howard who was 2. Their servant was Mary Donahue who was 20 years old and she was from Ireland.

Garrison, John During 1853 he was a Commissioner of the Highways. (TRB)

Garrison, William H. During 1859 he and George Gaylor owned land on Atherton Street. (E-10/13/59 p.3, c.2) He died sometime in June or July, 1860. Joseph Peene and Henry P. See were executors of his will. (E-7/26/60 p.3, c.2)

Gates, Amos W. (Dr.) During 1859 and 1860 he was a member of the village Board of Trustees. (AVD)

Gaul, Augustus During 1858 he was a cabinetmaker and upholsterer over Radcliff's provision store at 3 Wheeler's Building. (E-4/29/58 p.3, c.1) Prior to that he was in business with David Cotton. The business was dissolved Friday, April 2, 1858. (E-5/13/58 p.2, c.7) During February, 1860 he moved his furniture store to North Broadway opposite the Baptist Church. (E-3/1/60 p.2, c.7) On the 1860 census he is listed as a 35-year-old cabinetmaker who was from Germany. His wife M[inie] was also 35 years old, and they had two children; Eliza who was 4, and Margaret who was 2 years old.

Gault, Abner C. On Wednesday, November 2, 1859 he went with the hatters guard to Weehawken, New Jersey where the guard was involved in a shooting contest amongst themselves. At the target shooting contest he won a set of spoons. (E-11/3/59 p.3, c.6) During

December, 1860 he was a member of a committee that was organized to run the second annual ball of Neptune Engine Company Number 3 that was to be held at the Getty Lyceum on January 24, 1861. (E-12/13/60 p.2, c.7)

Gault, M. During 1860 he won $7.50 at a Yonkers Hatters Guard target shooting contest. (E-11/1/60 p.3, c.1)

Gaylor, George During 1859 he and William H. Garrison owned land on Atherton Street. He also owned by himself another parcel of land that was next to the parcel he owned with Garrison. (E-10/13/59 p.3, c.2)

Gesner, Charles On Sunday, October 25, 1857 he was at Fairy Grove with several other boys. One of the boys had a bottle of hartshorn and asked him to rub some of it on his feet. Instead of giving Charles the bottle he threw the contents into Charles' face causing him to lose his sight for two days. [Hartshorn is an ammonium carbonate.] (E-10/29/57 p.2., c.4)

Getler, Francis (Mrs.) Prior to 1859 she was in business with H. Ehart on Wells Avenue between Broadway and Warburton Avenue. The business partnership was dissolved January 31, 1859 when Francis took sole possession of it. (E-2/3/59 p.2, c.7) During 1858 she had a confectionery and ice cream store at 2 Manor Place. She also sold fireworks. (E-7/1/58 p.2, c.7) She also sold fruits, nuts, French confectionery, and toys. (E-8/26/58 p.4, c.5) On Thursday, September 10, 1857 her son, who was about five years old, fell down a bank on the east side of Scrugham's office on Manor Place, and broke his right arm. (E-9/17/57 p.2, c.1 see also E-12/23/58 p.3, c.1) Some of the things she advertised to sell for Christmas were hobby horses, drums, fancy boxes, all kinds of dolls dressed and undressed, pedal wagons, hose carts, firemen and soldier caps, bedsteads with or without bedding, boys sleighs and sleds, toy tubs, wash boards and pails, willow wagons and cradles, all kinds of dancing jacks, whips, body parts for dolls, guns, swords, French barking dogs, rabbit drummers, furniture, Christmas ornaments, and of course candy. (E-12/15/59 p.3, c.2)

Getty, Moses D. During 1857 he was a 1st Lieutenant at the Yonkers Collegiate Institute. (E-8/13/57 p.2, c.3) On Sunday, March 20, 1858 he was in the woods about a mile from his father's house when he slipped at the top of a ledge and fell ten feet and hit his head on a rock, which apparently knocked him out. His companions ran to his father's house for help. When help reached him he was brought home and attended to. He received a concussion which healed rapidly. (E-3/24/59 p.2, c.3)

Getty, Robert A. During 1857 he was a 2nd Lieutenant at the Yonkers Collegiate Institute. (E-8/13/57 p.2, c.3)

Getty, Robert P. During February 1857 he served on the Lecture Committee of the Yonkers Lyceum. (E-2/5/57) On March 2, 1857 he was elected a Manager of the Yonkers Library Association. (E-

3/5/57 p.2., c.7) In the early days of the Yonkers Library he received a life membership, and on March 10, 1857 he was elected a Director of the Bank of Yonkers. (E-3/12/57 p.2, c.5 and p.2 c.7) He was president of the Yonkers Gas Light Company during 1857 and served in that position until August, 1857 when Thomas C. Cornell was elected president. (E-7/2/57 p.3, c.3 and E-8/27/ p.3, c.5) On Wednesday, July 29, 1857 he was elected a director of the Yonkers Gas Light Company. (E-8/27/57 p.3, c.5) During August of 1857 he was asked to serve on the Petite Jury at White Plains, and he was a 1st District Commissioner of the Republican Party. (E-8/27/57 p.2, c.1 and c.2) During 1857 he was a District Commissioner of the first and second districts of the Republican Assembly Convention. (E-9/3/57 p.2, c.6) On Saturday, September 5, 1857 he was elected at a Republican primary meeting to be a delegate to the Republican district convention. On Tuesday, September 8, 1857 he was elected by acclamation to be a delegate to the Republican State Convention by the Republican First Assembly District Convention. (E-9/10/57 p.2, c.6,5) During March, 1857 he bought the Baldwin buildings from Ebenezer Baldwin for $10,000. He glassed in the first story of the buildings and sectioned them into store fronts. The remodeling cost about $3,000. Also during 1857 he moved some old wooden buildings from the corner of Broadway and Main Street to a vacant lot on the corner of Adams Street (Riverdale Avenue) and Washington Streets where he converted them into tenements. The work cost about $5,000. During 1857 he also built several Philadelphia-style three-story brick buildings on the corner of Broadway and Main Street. These buildings cost about $12,000. (E-12/31/57 p.2, c.2,3) On Monday evening, March 1, 1858 he was elected a manager of the Yonkers Library Association. (E-3/4/58 p.2, c.3) During 1858 he was a member of the Finance Committee of the Yonkers Savings Bank. (E-7/1/58 p.3, c.6) On July 22, 1858 he signed a petition calling for a meeting of eligible voters in School District #2 to decide if the school district should become a Union Free School District. (E-8/5/58 p.4, c.3) On Friday evening, September 17, 1858 he was elected to the executive committee of the Yonkers Republican Association. (E-9/23/58 p.2, c.1) During 1859 he erected an eighty foot high observatory on the hill east of his house at a cost of about $400. (E-1/20/58 p.2, c.5) He was trained as a cooper's apprentice and eventually he was able to make more barrels and better barrels than anyone else in the shop. (E-3/10/59 p.2, c.1) On Monday evening March 7, 1859 he was elected a manager of the Yonkers Library Association. (E-3/10/59 p.2, c.7) On March 22, 1859 he was elected a Director of the Bank of Yonkers. (E-4/7/59 p.2, c.5) Around August, 1859 the Library Association was incorporated and he became a member of the Board of Trustees. He was also elected to the association's executive committee. (E-8/14/59 p.2, c.4) On Thursday, August 13, 1859 he was chosen to be a delegate to the

Republican County Convention by the newly formed Republican Association at a Republican Town meeting. (E-10/20/59 p.3, c.1) During 1859 he built a greenhouse on his property that was worth about $1,500. (E-1/12/60 p.2, c.1) On Tuesday, January 31, 1860 he and seven others sent a letter to R. J. DeCordova asking him to visit Yonkers and deliver his humorous lecture on "Wall Street." (E-2/16/60 p.2, c.5) On Monday evening March 26, 1860 he was elected president of a Republican election rally meeting at the Getty House. (E-3/29/60 p.2, c.3) On Thursday evening, April 26, 1860, he was elected a trustee of the Yonkers Library Association. (E-5/3/60 p.2, c.3) During 1860 he built 5 new stores on South Broadway in Getty Square. (E-5/17/60 p.2, c.4) On Friday, May 4, 1860, he was elected one of ten members of the executive committee of the newly formed Yonkers Horticultural Society. (E-5/17/60 p.3, c.3) On Wednesday, August 15, 1860 he lost an election as trustee for School District Number 2. He received 65 votes. (E-8/16/60 p.2, c.6) He is listed on the 1860 census as a 60-year-old inspector of pork with $100,000 in real estate, and a personal estate of $2,500. His wife Rebecca was 47 years old, and they had ten children; Harriet who was 22, Daro who was a 20-year-old clerk, Rebecca who was 18, Robert who was 16, Moses who was 14, William who was 12, John who was 10, Ellen who was 8, Mary who was 4, and Emma who was 2. Eliza West was their 40-year-old laundress, Mary North was their 21-year-old cook, and Katie Short was their 20-year-old servant. All three were from Ireland. During 1857 and 1858 he was a member of the village Board of Trustees. (AVD)

Getty, S. Emmett On Thursday, September 10, 1857 he was a member of the Yonkers Debating Society, and opened a debate on "Ought our present Usury Laws to be abolished?" (E-9/17/57 p.2, c.5) On Thursday, March 18, 1858 he delivered a speech before the Debating Society entitled "The Enthusiast." (E-3/25/58 p.2, c.1) On Monday, December 13, 1858 he became Vestryman of the newly formed Episcopal Church on Mechanic Street. (E-12/23/58 p.2, c.3) During 1859 he was in the process of building a brick Gothic cottage on the hill south of Mr. Robins' house. (E-1/20/59 p.2, c.4) On Wednesday, February 16, 1859, he married a Paddock. The page is torn where her first name was. (E-2/17/59 p.2, c.7)

Gilchrist, Charles During 1856 he was a Pound Master. In 1857 he was an Inspector of Elections for Election District Number Two. (TRB)

Gilday, Patrick On Sunday, July 8, 1860, while eating dinner, he choked to death on some meat. He was about 34 years old, and was a quarryman on the east side of North Broadway opposite the Wheeler Building. He was married and a native of Ireland. (E-7/12/60 p.2, c.4)

Giles, William O. During 1860 he was selected to serve as a petit juror in the Court of Sessions that sat Monday, March 12, 1860. (E-3/8/60 p.2, c.5)

Gilroy, George During 1857 he owned a paint store located in Getty Square. (E-5/14/57 p.3., c.7) During 1858 he sold his house on Riverdale Avenue to Rev. Cooke for $12,000. (E-4/22/58 p.2, c.3) He was a trustee of the Yonkers Savings Bank. On October 26, 1858 he died at the age of 43. He was buried from the Universalist Church on Beekman Street on Thursday October 28, and he was buried in Cyprus Hill Cemetery. (E-10/28/58 p.3, c.1) Also see (E-12/23/58 p.2, c.3) because his painting advertisement continued to run in the *Yonkers Examiner*. Ellen C. Gilroy was probably his wife and she was an executrix of his will, and Robert P. Getty was an executor of his will. (E-9/29/59 p.3, c.3) On December 12, 1859 his son W. P. M. Gilroy died at the age of 1 year, 7 months and 10 days. (E-12/29/59 p.2, c.6)

Giroud, Victor During 1859 he opened a jewelry store on Dock Street opposite Warburton Avenue. He was also a watch maker who received several awards for his watches. (E-5/12/59 p.2, c.3) During 1859 he moved to Farrington's Building and put up a public clock. (E-9/1/59 p.2, c.4) His residence was on Broadway opposite the Methodist Church. (E-10/18/60 p.2, c.6) During 1860 he evidently closed his business and was selling show cases from his home. The week before he advertised that watches and jewelry that he had fixed could be picked up at his residence. (E-10/18/60 p.3, c.3) During November, 1860 he was sued by William Bancroft, James H. Redfield, and James Rice for a total of $285.38 plus interest from March 16, 1860 and court costs. (E-11/1/60 p.3, c.3)

Gleeson, John On Saturday, November 26, 1859 he died of a heart attack on Hog Hill. He was a native of Ireland. (E-12/1/59 p.2, c.1)

Godwin, Joseph H. During 1858 he was an anti-Lecompton who was appointed a vice president of a meeting in Morrisania Hall. (E-6/24/58 p.2, c.1) On Saturday, August 20, 1859, he was appointed a delegate to the State Republican Convention. (E-8/25/58 p.2, c.3) On Monday evening March 26, 1860 he was elected one of thirty-two vice presidents of a Republican election rally meeting at the Getty House. (E-3/29/60 p.2, c.3) On Thursday evening, October 25, 1860, he was one of twenty-two vice presidents at a Republican campaign meeting. (E-11/1/60 p.2, c.2)

Goetschius, George H. During 1857 he owned a market on Manor Place. (E-4/23/57 p.2, c.7) On Friday evening, September 17, 1858 he was elected the permanent secretary of the Yonkers Republican Association. (E-9/23/58 p.2, c.1)

Golden, John During 1853 he was a Pound Master and in 1856 he was a Constable. (TRB)

Goodman, Alexander During December, 1860 he was a member of a committee that was organized to run the second annual ball of

Neptune Engine Company Number 3 that was to be held at the Getty Lyceum on January 24, 1861. (E-12/13/60 p.2, c.7)

Goodman, Samuel During 1859 he built a wood-frame house somewhere near Alexander Logue's new frame house and near Jefferson Street that cost $1,600. (E-1/12/60 p.2, c.1)

Goodman, Simon On Wednesday, November 2, 1859, he won in a drawing a goblet at a target shooting contest at Weehawkan, New Jersey. He was a member of the Yonkers Hatters Guard. (E-11/3/59 p.2, c.6)

Gorman, Patrick On Tuesday morning, December 10, 1857, he stopped at Samuel Graham's bar on the Flats for a drink of liquor. When Graham asked him to pay, Gorman refused and he threatened to shoot him. Justice Thomas Smith granted a warrant for his arrest and he was fined $100. He was also served with a peace warrant to stay at peace with Samuel Graham for one year. (E-12/10/57 p.3, c.2)

Gouch, L. A. During 1858 he was an architect with an office in the Radford Building. He also had an office in NYC. (E-6/17/58 p.3, c.2)

Gourlie, Archibald T. (His middle initial was F. 8/19/58) On Tuesday, August 17, 1858 he and sixteen other men wrote C. Jerome Hopkins a letter requesting him to give another piano concert at the Getty House. (E-8/19/58 p.2, c.4) On Monday evening March 26, 1860 he was elected one of thirty-two vice presidents of a Republican election rally meeting at the Getty House. (E-3/29/60 p.2, c.3) During 1860 he was selected to serve on the grand jury which sat November 19, 1960 in the Court of Oyer and Terminer. (E-11/15/60 p.3, c.2) On the 1860 census he is listed as a 45-year-old broker with $10,000 in real estate, and a personal estate of $25,000. His wife Susan was 30 years old, and they had four children; Isabel was 14, John was 8, Eliza was 6, and Robert was 2. A Mrs. Minor, who was 52 years old, lived with them.

Grafton, N. W. On October 15, 1857 his business was one of 33 businesses in Yonkers to announce they were closing their stores at 8 p.m. beginning on October 12, 1857 until March 27, 1858. (E-10/15/57 p.3, c.1)

Granger, Thomas On Monday, January 17, 1859, he married Miss Mary E. Odell. (E-2/3/59 p.2, c.5) They lived on Palisade Avenue. On Saturday, February 25, 1860, their son John Thomas Granger died of convulsions at the age of 3 months and 3 weeks. (E-3/1/60 p.2, c.6)

Grant, Fielding S. During 1855 he was appointed to a town committee to secure a permanent lockup. (TRB)

Grant, Robert Sometime between May 13, 1856 and March 5, 1857 he received $1,000 from the Village Treasurer. (E-3/5/57 p.3, c.1) This probably occurred late February or early March of 1857 and was for the sale of his fire engine. During 1857 he was a Director of the Yonkers Gas Light Company. (E-8/13/57 p.3, c.3) On Wednesday, July 29, 1857 he was once again elected a director of the gas company. (E-8/27/57 p.3, c.5) On Monday evening, March 1, 1858 he was elected a manager of the Yonkers Library Association. (E-3/4/58 p.2, c.3) On Friday evening, September 17, 1858 he was elected one of six vice presidents of the Yonkers Republican Association. (E-9/23/58 p.2, c.1) He had a farm near Archdale, and he owned a wood-frame building on it which he rented. The building caught fire on Thursday afternoon, October 28, 1858, which was caused by children playing with matches. The building, which was estimated at $500, was completely destroyed. (E-11/4/58 p.2, c.2) On Tuesday, November 16, 1858, he was elected a vice president of a Republican Party meeting in Yonkers. (E-11/18/58 p.2, c.2) On Monday evening March 7, 1859 he was again elected a manager of the Yonkers Library Association. (E-3/10/59 p.2, c.7) On Monday evening March 26, 1860 he was elected one of thirty-two vice presidents of a Republican election rally meeting at the Getty House. (E-3/29/60 p.2, c.3) On the 1860 census he is listed as a 55-year-old owner of a morocco factory. Both he and his wife Ann, who was 45 years old, were from Scotland. Their son John was 15 years old.

Grantham, Thomas On Friday, September 23, 1859 he stole a silver watch from the vest of a worker at the stone yard on the dock. The vest was hanging up in a shed. He was arrested and was sent to White Plains for three months. (E-9/29/59 p.3, c.1)

Greeley, Horace On Monday evening May 11, 1857 he visited Yonkers to lecture on the topic "Reform and Reformers" at the library. Admission was 25 cents. (E-5/7/57 p.2, c.6) On Monday evening, October 25, 1858 he spoke for an hour on the issue of slavery at the Yonkers Lyceum. (E-10/28/58 p.2, c.3)

Greenleaf, Augustus W. During March of 1857 he donated $25 to the Yonkers Library Association and became a life member. (E-3/12/57 p.2, c.6) During the latter part of 1858 he signed a petition to have a meeting of the taxpayers in School District #2 meet to reconsider the location of two new schools; one on the corner of Wood Place and Warburton Avenue, and the other on St. Mary's Street near the Catholic Church and school. (E-12/23/58 p.2, c.2) During 1858 he built a stable and a greenhouse. (E-1/20/59 p.2, c.5)

Greenwood, B. On Saturday, September 29, 1860 he was a delegate to the Republican First Assembly District Convention that was held in Morrisania Hall, Morrisania. (E-10/4/60 p.2, c.2) On the 1860 census he is listed as a 37-year-old grocer with a personal estate of $4,000. His wife was Salome and she was 35 years old. They had at least two children; Benjamin who was 13, and L. G. who was an 11-year-old female. Also, a Mary L. who was 22 lived in their household.

Grevert, John During 1859 he and John H. Jordon operated the Blue Stone Yard on the Dock. They furnished blue stone and employed the "best mechanics." (E-6/23/59 p.3, c.1) The stone yard was next to the brown stone yard on the Dock that was operated prior to this time by Houghtaling & Bell, but by this time was in business as Bell and Company. The blue stone yard was operated by John Grevert and John H. Jordon under the firm name of John Grevert & Co. (E-8/4/59 p.3, c.5)

Gridley, Miss Beginning May 4, 1857 she taught 2nd primary boys at the school in the village district. (E-4/23/57 p.2, c.7)

Griffin, Adaline (Miss) During December, 1859, she was on the arrangement committee to give a benefit for their pastor John Taylor. The guest speaker was the Rev. Henry Highland Garnett, pastor of the Shiloh Presbyterian Church in NYC. Admission was 50 cents and the proceeds went to Rev. Taylor. (E-12/8/59 p.3. c.2)

Griffin, Charles R. On Wednesday, April 25, 1860, he was married by Rev. Seward to Charlotte Agnew. (E-5/24/60 p.3, c.3)

Griffin, Julius During December, 1859, he was on the arrangement committee to give a benefit for their pastor John Taylor. The guest speaker was the Rev. Henry Highland Garnett, pastor of the Shiloh Presbyterian Church in NYC. Admission was 50 cents and the proceeds went Rev. Taylor. (E-12/8/59 p.3, c.2)

Griffin, King At about 3 a.m. Thursday, May 10, 1860 his barn was set on fire by an arsonist. He lost a lot of hay, a wagon, and a few other things in the fire. The fire department responded, but there was no water nearby. (E-5/17/60 p.2, c.4) His property was on the south side of School Street just south of Guion Street and east of South Broadway and probably went as far south as the current Chauncey Place or Park Hill Avenue. (E-9/20/60 p.3, c.2) On the 1860 census he is listed as a 64-year-old with real estate worth $2,000, and a personal estate of $200. Living in his household was Elizabeth who was 24, Isaac who was 33, Eliza who was 15, Rebecca who was 17, Ad[riene] who was 22, and Mary who was 10. The listings and his age do not match the 1850 census. (See vol. 1)

Griffin, Lydia On Wednesday, August 10, 1859, she died at the age of 63. She was the wife of King Griffin. On the 1850 census she is listed as being 47 years old. (E-9/1/59 p.3, c.1 See also Vol. 1 p.50)

Griffin, William During 1857 he was a Trustee of the African Methodist Episcopal Zion Church. (E-7/9/57 p.2, c.7) On Sunday, December 27, 1857 he married Ellen Robinson. The marriage ceremony was performed by Rev. Tripp. (E-1/7/58 p.2, c.6)

Griffing, A. (Mrs.) During 1857 she made considerable improvements to her house on Locust Hill Avenue that cost about $1,700. (E-12/31/57 p.2, c.3)

Grimes, Samuel During 1859 he built a wood-frame house on

Washington Street near Jefferson Street that cost about $1,600. (E-1/12/60 p.2, c.1)

Grimshaw, Joseph On Wednesday, November 2, 1859, he won $5 in a target shooting contest at Weehawkan, New Jersey. He was a member of the Yonkers Hatters Guard. (E-11/3/59 p.2, c.6) His wife was Ann. On Saturday evening, February 25, 1860, she took a walk along Palisade Avenue and fell injuring herself. Upon returning home she said nothing about the fall and went to bed later in the evening. On Sunday morning Joseph went to wake his wife, but she had died. The cause of death was a rupture of the abdomen. (E-3/1/60 p.2, c.5)

Groshon, William F. During 1857 he was a lawyer in Yonkers. (E-2/5/57 p.2, c.3) On Tuesday, August 17, 1858 he and sixteen other men wrote C. Jerome Hopkins a letter requesting him to give another piano concert at the Getty House. (E-8/19/58 p.2, c.4) During 1853 and again in 1857 he was elected a Justice Peace. (TRB)

Groot, Philip W. During 1858 he and his wife Deborah owned property on North Broadway near Lamartine Avenue. The property was sold at auction on September 9, 1858. (E-10/7/58 p.4, c.5)

Grow, Galusha A. On Monday, August 30, 1858 he wrote a letter to William Cauldwell stating that he would address a meeting in Tarrytown in support of Congressman John B. Haskin. He lived in the Glenwood section of the town. (E-9/9/58 p.2, c.2)

Guion, Gilbert Sometime during the early part of 1860 he died. The administrators of his will were Jane Lawrence and Thomas. O. Farrington. (E-4/5/60 p.3, c.3)

Gummerson, D. During the latter part of 1859 he was a member of the arrangement committee for the fourth annual ball of Protection Fire Engine Company Number 1. (E-12/22/59 p.2, c.6)

Habern, Moses During 1857 he was a Trustee of the African Methodist Episcopal Zion Church. (E-2/5/57) Also during 1857 he operated a whitewashing and wall cleaning business. During July 1857 as a Trustee of the church he signed a protest letter that contained allegations of missing money by Rev. Tripp. (E-7/23/57 p.2, c.6) During December, 1859, his wife was on the arrangement committee to give a benefit for their pastor John Taylor. The guest speaker was the Rev. Henry Highland Garnett, pastor of the Shiloh Presbyterian Church in NYC. Admission was 50 cents and the proceeds went Rev. Taylor. Moses was also on the committee. (E-12/8/59 p.3, c.2)

Hagany, J. B. (Rev.) During March of 1857 he received a life membership in the Yonkers Library Association for his valuable donations or as a lecturer. (E-3/12/57 p.2, c.6) During 1856 and 1857 he was pastor of the Methodist Church. On may 10, 1857 he preached his last sermon in Yonkers and was transferred somewhere else. (E-5/14/57 p.2, c.5)

Hahner, Andrew On Wednesday, October 10, 1860 his stable behind Anthony Imhoff's shop caught fire. It was quickly put out, but the second story was badly damaged. (E-10/11/60 p.2, c.4)

Haley, Thomas On Wednesday, November 2, 1859, he won a cake basket in a target shooting contest at Weehawkan, New Jersey. He was a member of the Yonkers Hatters Guard. (E-11/3/59 p.2, c.6) During 1860 he won $5 at a Yonkers Hatters Guard target shooting contest. (E-11/1/60 p.3, c.1)

Hallet, Sarah On Wednesday, September 16, 1857 she married William N. Bailey. (E-9/17/57 p.2, c.7)

Hall, Miss During 1857 she ran a school for females. (E-2/19/57 p.2, c.2) The school taught modern languages, drawing, music, dance, and other accomplishments. It was located on Broadway opposite the Episcopal Church. (E-9/3/57 p.3, c.1)

Haller, S. B. On October 15, 1857 his business was one of 33 businesses in Yonkers to announce they were closing their stores at 8 p.m. beginning on October 12, 1857 until March 27, 1858. (E-10/15/57 p.3, c.1)

Halliohan, Thomas On Wednesday, November 2, 1859, he won in a drawing a History of the United States at a target shooting contest at Weehawkan, New Jersey. He was a member of the Yonkers Hatters Guard. (E-11/3/59 p.2, c.6)

Hallock, George M. During 1857 he owned a grocery store with James H. Page on Mechanic Street. His middle initial may have been N. (E-5/21/57 p.3, c.5) He applied for a store license in 1858. (E-6/3/58 p.2, c.5) He received the license. (E-6/17/58 p.2, c.6) On November 27, 1859 his property at 3 and 5 Clinton Street was to be sold at auction by the Sheriff. (E-11/24/59 p.3, c.3)

Halloran, E. On Tuesday, October 6, 1857 he was appointed a delegate to the Democratic County Convention. (E-10/8/57 p.2, c.2)

Halloran, John Sometime in late January, 1860 he received an appointment to the Metropolitan Police Force. (E-2/2/60 p.3, c.1)

Halor[n], Edward On Tuesday, September 1, 1857 he was elected as a James Buchanan delegate to the County Democratic Convention to be held at West Farms on September 2, 1857. (E-9/3/57 p.2, c.7)

Hamlin, Frederick V. During 1859 he built a brick stable and carriage house on Glenwood Avenue that cost about $3,800. (E-1/12/60 p.2, c.3) On Friday, May 4, 1860, he was elected one of three members of the decoration committee for the June exhibition of the newly formed Yonkers Horticultural Society. (E-5/17/60 p.3, c.3) On the 1860 census he is listed as a 35-year-old clothing store owner who was born in Ireland. His wife Kate, who was born in New York, was also 35 years old. They had two children; Frederick who was 11, and Walter who was 7. Also in his household was Robert who was 25, and Sarah who was 28. They both were from Ireland

and may have been his brother and sister. Also, Mary Herman is listed. She was 35 years old, and was born in New York.

Hampson, Charles On Wednesday, November 2, 1859, he won a barrel of flour in a target shooting contest at Weehawkan, New Jersey. He was a member of the Yonkers Hatters Guard. (E-11/3/59 p.2, c.6) On the 1860 census he is listed as a 34-year-old hatter with a personal estate of $150. His wife Mary was also 34 years old, and they had two children; Ann who was 6, and Charles who was 4. The children were born in New York, and he and his wife were born in England.

Hampson, E. During 1860 he won a sheep at a Yonkers Hatters Guard target shooting contest. (E-11/1/60 p.3, c.1)

Hampson, F. During 1860 he won a barrel of flour at a Yonkers Hatters Guard target shooting contest. (E-11/1/60 p.3, c.1) On the 1860 census he is listed as a 42-year-old hatter with a personal estate of $100. His wife Martha was 40 years old, and they had six children; Eli who was 19 and a hatter, Thomas who was 17, Frank who was 12, Henry who was 8, Alice who was 6, and John who was 1. He, his wife, and their two oldest children were born in Ireland. The remaining children were born in New York.

Hampson, Henry On Wednesday, November 2, 1859, he won some silver spoons in a target shooting contest at Weehawkan, New Jersey. He was a member of the Yonkers Hatters Guard. (E-11/3/59 p.2, c.6) During 1860 he won a silver watch at a Yonkers Hatters Guard target shooting contest. (E-11/1/60 p.3, c.1)

Hampson, John During the latter part of 1857 he sold Isabella and Catawba vines. He also did pruning for a reasonable price. His business was on Palisade Avenue. (E-11/5/57 p.3, c.1) Sometime before February, 1859 he moved his business to Main Street. (E-1/27/59 p.3, c.1) On Wednesday, November 2, 1859, he won a castor in a target shooting contest at Weehawkan, New Jersey. He was a member of the Yonkers Hatters Guard. (E-11/3/59 p.2, c.6) During 1860 he won a pair of boots at a Yonkers Hatters Guard target shooting contest. (E-11/1/60 p.3, c.1)

Hampson, S. During 1860 he won a chess board at a Yonkers Hatters Guard target shooting contest. (E-11/1/60 p.3, c.1)

Hampson, Thomas During November, 1858 he was a member of the arrangement committee for the Second Annual Ball to benefit the widows and orphans of deceased Yonkers firemen. (E-11/25/58 p.2, c.7) During 1859 he was a Lieutenant in the Yonkers Hatters Guard. On Wednesday, November 2, 1859 he went with the guard to Weehawken, New Jersey where the guard was involved in a shooting contest amongst themselves. At the target shooting contest he won a pair of silver knives. (E-11/3/59 p.3, c.6) On Wednesday evening, December 14, 1859, at their annual meeting in Yonkers he was elected Tiler of Rising Star Lodge, No. 450, of F. & A. M. E-12/15/59 p.2, c.5) On Monday evening March 26, 1860 he was elected one of thirty-two vice presidents of a Republican election rally meeting at the Getty House. (E-3/29/60 p.2, c.3)

Hampson, William H. During 1859 he was a Lieutenant in the Yonkers Hatters Guard. On Wednesday, November 2, 1859 he went with the guard to Weehawken, New Jersey where the guard was involved in a shooting contest amongst themselves. At the target shooting contest he won a castor. He also won a vest at the contest. (E-11/3/59 p.3, c.6) During 1860 he was again elected one of eight Lieutenants of the Yonkers Hatters Guard. (E-10/18/60 p.2, c.5) During 1860 he won a $7 pair of pants and a castor at a Yonkers Hatters Guard target shooting contest. (E-11/1/60 p.3, c.1)

Hannigan, T. During 1860 he won a $6.50 pair of pants at a Yonkers Hatters Guard target shooting contest. (E-11/1/60 p.3, c.1)

Harbor, T. R. On Thursday, August 13, 1859 he was chosen a delegate to the Republican County Convention by the newly formed Republican Association at a Republican Town meeting. (E-10/20/59 p.3, c.1)

Hardy, (Miss) During 1858 she ran the millinery department of the Millinery and Dressmaking Establishment of Miss Livington's. (E-6/3/58 p.2, c.7)

Harney, John During 1859 he and his brother built two wood-frame tenements on Clinton Street at the foot of Washington Street that cost about $1,600. (E-1/12/60 p.2, c.1)

Hasbrouck, Washington Before 1857 he ran the Yonkers Collegiate Institute. (E-7/2/57 p.2, c.3)

Hasse, Ernest E. During 1857 he was a member of the Masons. (E-8/20/57 p.3, c.1) On Tuesday evening, November 17, 1857 he was driving his carriage down Broadway near the Presbyterian Church when he collided with the carriage of Frederick A. Coe. His horse then bolted down the street and ran into the carriage of W. T. Coleman. Coleman's carriage was severely damaged and the horse was badly cut, but no one was injured. (E-11/19/57 p.2, c.7) During 1859 and 1860 he was granted a hotel license. (E-8/11/59 p.2, c.7 &7/26/60 p.2, c.6)

Hatch, John Davis During 1857 he advertised to accept bids for building a house at Glenwood. He had an office at room 32 in the Bank of Commerce, Nassau Street, NYC. An architect on Ashburton Avenue drew up the plans for the house. (E-7/9/57 p.2, c.7) During 1858 he was an architect and superintendent with an office on the corner of Getty Square and Main Street over the post office. He was also a member of the American Institute of Architects. (E-8/26/58 p.3, c.3) On Friday, May 4, 1860, he was elected one of three members of the decoration committee for the June exhibition of the newly formed Yonkers Horticultural Society. He is listed on the 1860 census as a 34-year-old architect with a personal estate of $2,000. His wife Anna was 31 years old. A 22-year-old servant from Ireland,

Bridget Halley, also lived in their household. Both he and his wife were born in England.

Hatfield, F. During 1860 he won $5 at a Yonkers Hatters Guard target shooting contest. (E-11/1/60 p.3, c.1)

Hawes, C. C. On Friday night, December 4, 1857 there was an attempted burglary at his house. He heard the thieves and woke up. On hearing him the thieves ran away. They were assumed to be the same thieves that robbed Isaac Knox. (E-12/10/57 p.3, c.2)

Hawes, Charles R. Apparently he was killed in a train accident in Cincinnati sometime during November, 1859. (E-11/24/59 p.2, c.2) The accident occurred on Monday probably November 21 and he died on Wednesday, November 23. He was buried Tuesday, November 29 from the Presbyterian Church. He was a Mason. (E-12/1/59 p.2, c.4) He died in Seymour, Indiana and he was 47 years, 7 months, and 9 days old. His father was the late Peter Hawes of NYC. (E-12/1/59 p.3, c.2) The *Yonkers Examiner* said of him that "He was a man, faithful in every relation of life, and to every duty of the citizen, and his death fills with profound sorrow every heart by whom he was known." (12/1/59 p.2, c.4)

Hawes, Gardener S. During 1857 he was the Secretary for the Yonkers Library Association. (E-7/16/57 p.2, c.7) During 1858 he was a member of the Lecture Committee of the Yonkers Library Association. (E-1/7/58 p.3, c.1) On Monday evening, March 1, 1858 he was elected once again secretary of the Yonkers Library Association. (E-3/4/58 p.2, c.3) On Tuesday, January 31, 1860 he and seven others sent a letter to R. J. DeCordova asking him to visit Yonkers and deliver his humorous lecture on "Wall Street." (E-2/16/60 p.2, c.5) On Tuesday evening, September 11, 1860 he was elected to the executive committee of the Yonkers Republican Association for a five-month term. (E-9/13/60 p.2, c.2) On Thursday evening, October 25, 1860, he was one of twenty-two vice presidents at a Republican campaign meeting. (E-11/1/60 p.2, c.2)

Hawkes, Jenny Mrs. On Thursday evening, March 25, 1858 at the Presbyterian Church she was married by Reverend Seward to Conway Pilson. (E-4/1/58 p.3, c.2)

Hawkins, Joseph S. On March 22, 1859 he was elected a Director of the Bank of Yonkers. (E-4/7/59 p.2, c.5) On Friday, May 4, 1860, he was elected one of six members of the committee on Premiums for Vegetables for the June exhibition of the newly formed Yonkers Horticultural Society. (E-5/17/60 p.3, c.3) On the 1860 census he is listed as a 56-year-old merchant with $10,000 in real estate, and a personal estate of $2,000. His wife Eliza was 46 years old, and they had four daughters; Anna who was 21, Elizabeth who was 19, Mary who was 17, and Amelia who was 15. A Mary Benson, who was a 17-year-old black, was also in his household.

Hawks, Henry S. On Monday evening March 26, 1860 he was elected one of thirty-two vice presidents of a Republican election rally meeting at the Getty House. (E-3/29/60 p.2, c.3)

Haynes, James B. On Monday, February 22, 1858 he married Sarah J. Lyon of Yonkers. He was from Greenburgh. (E-2/25/58 p.2,3)

Hazelton, John C. On Monday evening March 26, 1860 he was elected one of thirty-two vice presidents of a Republican election rally meeting at the Getty House. (E-3/29/60 p.2, c.3) During 1860 he was selected to serve on the petit jury November 19, 1960 in the Circuit Court. (E-11/15/60 p.3, c.2)

Helwick, Frederick He had a business on Devoe's dock. On Wednesday, October 27, 1858 a fire was started in his business. A passerby sounded the alarm and put the fire out before the fire department arrived. (E-11/4/58 p.2, c.2) During 1859 he was granted a grocery license. (E-8/11/59 p.2, c.7)

Henderson, Susan (Mrs.) During December, 1859, she was on the arrangement committee to give a benefit for their pastor John Taylor. The guest speaker was the Rev. Henry Highland Garnett, pastor of the Shiloh Presbyterian Church in NYC. Admission was 50 cents and the proceeds went to Rev. Taylor. (E-12/8/59 p.3, c.2)

Hennebergher, John On Wednesday, November 2, 1859, he won a cake basket in a target shooting contest at Weehawkan, New Jersey. He was a member of the Yonkers Hatters Guard. (E-11/3/59 p.2, c.6)

Henry, William On Wednesday, November 2, 1859, he won $3 in a target shooting contest at Weehawkan, New Jersey. He was a member of the Yonkers Hatters Guard. (E-11/3/59 p.2, c.6) During 1860 he won a clock at a Yonkers Hatters Guard target shooting contest. (E-11/1/60 p.3, c.1) On the 1860 census he is listed as a 45-year-old hatter with a personal estate of $200. His wife A[ngirsta] was 39 years old, and they had three children; Rebecca who was 14, Sarah who was 5, and William who was 1. He, his wife, and Rebecca were born in Germany. The other two children were born in New York.

Herriot, George (Dr.) During 1858 he built a wood-frame cottage on South Broadway south of Kellinger's for about $2,000. (E-1/20/59 p.2, c.5) During 1859 he built five wood-frame cottages on South Broadway near Spring Street for about $3,000 each. (E-1/12/60 p.2, c.1) His property was near the current Herriot Place. (E-9/11/60 p.3, c.2)

Hibbard, Timothy R. During 1853 he owned land on Guion Street. (TRB) On February 2, 1857 he and his wife Jane Ann protested against widening Guion Street.

Hill, Thomas W. During 1859 he renovated the interior of John Copcutt's mansion. He was a student of the Royal Academy, Vernon Gallery, and a member of the British Society of Artists. (E-8/4/59 p.2, c.2) On Tuesday, January 3, 1860 his wife Susannah Lytecia Hill died at the age of 60 years and 6 months. (E-1/5/60 p.2, c.7)

During June, 1860 he decorated the front of Darby's saloon in Alhambra style. He completed his education with Owen Jones of London who did the decoration of the Alhambra Court of the Crystal Palace at Sydenham. (E-7/19/60 p.2, c.6) During December, 1860 he was a member of a committee that was organized to run the second annual ball of Neptune Engine Company Number 3 that was to be held at the Getty Lyceum on January 24, 1861. (E-12/13/60 p.2, c.7)

Hilliard, William On Wednesday, November 2, 1859, he won a set of tea spoons in a target shooting contest at Weehawkan, New Jersey. He was a member of the Yonkers Hatters Guard. (E-11/3/59 p.2, c.6)

Hindley, J. During 1860 he won something undecipherable at a Yonkers Hatters Guard target shooting contest. (E-11/1/60 p.3, c.1)

Hirst, Hugh On Wednesday, November 2, 1859, he won in a drawing a Josephine Gallery at a target shooting contest at Weehawkan, New Jersey. He was a member of the Yonkers Hatters Guard. (E-11/3/59 p.2, c.6)

Hitchcock, L. During 1857 he owned an ice cream and soda store on Broadway above the Baptist Church. (E-6/18/57 p.2, c.7)

Hobbs, Bailey During 1857 he made suits for men. (E-7/2/57 p.3, c.2) On October 15, 1857 his business was one of 33 businesses in Yonkers to announce they were closing their stores at 8 p.m. beginning on October 12, 1857 until March 27, 1858. (E-10/15/57 p.3, c.1) On Monday evening, March 1, 1858 he was elected a manager of the Yonkers Library Association. (E-3/4/58 p.2, c.3) On July 22, 1858 he signed a petition calling for a meeting of eligible voters in School District #2 to decide if the school district should become a Union Free School District. (E-8/5/58 p.4, c.3) On Monday, August 23, 1858 he was a delegate to the Westchester County Republican Party Convention at Durell's Hotel in Morrisania. (E-8/26/58 p.2, c.2) On Friday evening, September 17, 1858 he was elected one of six vice presidents of the Yonkers Republican Association. (E-9/23/58 p.2, c.1) On Tuesday, November 16, 1858, he was elected a vice president of a Republican Party meeting in Yonkers. (E-11/18/58 p.2, c.2) On Thursday morning, November 18, 1858 his store was broken into and nearly five hundred dollars of property was stolen. The thief was caught near Fort Washington and convicted. (E-11/25/58 p.2, c.4) His name was Karl Foster and he was sentenced to four years and six months in the State Prison. (E-12/2/58 p.2, c.5) On Monday evening March 7, 1859 he was elected vice president of the Yonkers Library Association. (E-3/10/59 p.2, c.7) On March 22, 1859 he was elected an Inspector of Election for next year's board of directors election for the Bank of Yonkers. (E-4/7/59 p.2, c.5) Around August, 1859 the Library Association was incorporated and he became a member of the Board of Trustees. (E-8/14/59 p.2, c.4) On Thursday morning, January 19, 1860, he was on a coroner's jury to look into the death of Mrs. Field who died in a railroad accident at Tarrytown. He was listed as a merchant tailor. (E-1/26/60 p.2, c.5 see Foster Jenkins for more details) (E-/2/23/60 p.2, c.2) On the 1860 census he is listed as a 42-year-old merchant with $14,000 in real estate, and a personal estate of $2,500. His wife Sarah was 35 years old, and they had one child, Zelia, who was 15. They had two servants. From 1856 through 1859 he was a member of the village Board of Trustees. During February, 1860 he declined to run again for the Board of Trustees. (AVD)

Hobbs, C. Miss Beginning on May 4, 1857 she was to teach a girls primary class at the school in the Village District. (E-4/23/57 p.2, c.7)

Hobbs, John During 1857 he was apparently a book seller to schools for two large publishing houses. He wrote a very interesting letter to the editor published May 11, 1857. (E-5/11/57 p.2, c.3) On July 22, 1858 he signed a petition calling for a meeting of eligible voters in School District #2 to decide if the school district should become a Union Free School District. (E-8/5/58 p.4, c.3) On Wednesday evening, August 18, 1858 he was elected a trustee for School District #2. (E-8/26/58 p.2, c.4) He was also the Clerk for the Board of Education in District #2. (E-10/7/58 p.3, c.4) He lived somewhere along the Croton Aqueduct and part of the entrance to his home was fenced off by the Croton Aqueduct Department. (E-10/14/58 p.2, c.5) During 1860 he was again a trustee and clerk for school district #2. (E-8/9/60 p.2, c.1) On Wednesday, August 15, 1860 he was again elected a trustee for school district #2. He received 92 votes. (E-8/16/60 p.2, c.6) On Tuesday, October 9, 1860 he was clerk of a school board meeting. (E-10/11/60 p.2, c.3) On the 1860 census he is listed as a 55 year bookstore owner with $4,000 in real estate, and a personal estate of $1,000. His wife Susan was also 55 years old. (See Vol. 1, p.51. Their ages on the 1850 and 1860 do not match.)

Hodges, Mary A. On Tuesday, November 8, 1859, she was married by Rev. King to James B. Odell. (E-11/10/59 p.3, c.2)

Hoffman, James F. During 1857 he was a wholesale grocer at 98 Pearl Street, NYC. (E-3/5/57 p.3, c.4) Prior to January 28, 1858 he lived on the corner of Warburton Avenue and Union Place. He advertised to rent his house. On the grounds he grew pears, cherries, grapes and raspberries sufficient for family use. He also had a fine view of the Hudson River. (E-1/28/58 p.3, c.2)

Hoffman, S. B. Probably during the early part of December, 1857 he bought the drug store in the Getty House from Robert J. Topolis. (E-12/31/57 p.3, c.2)

Hogan, Ann Nora On Monday afternoon, July 25, 1859 she was playing near the shanties on Hudson Street with some other children. They were burning sticks and her dress caught on fire. She was so badly burned that she died around midnight. She was about five years old. (E-7/28/59 p.2, c.4)

Hogeland, Jonathan During 1853 he was a Pound Master. (TRB)

Holberton, George During 1857 he owned a tavern, and was licensed as an innkeeper. (E-5/28/57 p.2, c.2. Documents.) During 1857 he applied for a hotel and tavern license and apparently he did not receive it. (E-6/4/57 p.2, c.3,4) In 1858 he received a hotel license. (E-6/17/58 p.2, c.6)

Holland, Joseph On Wednesday, November 2, 1859, he won a C[lims] sheep in a target shooting contest at Weehawkan, New Jersey. He was a member of the Yonkers Hatters Guard. (E-11/3/59 p.2, c.6)

Homans, Benjamin He lived in Yonkers sometime before November, 1858. On November 15, 1858 his only daughter Mary W. was married in Cincinnati by Rev. C. M. Butler to William H. Hood. (E-11/25/58 p.2, c.7)

Hommans, Edward C. During 1857 he was an Adjutant at the Yonkers Collegiate Institute. (E-8/13/57 p.2, c.3)

Hommans, J. During 1857 he advertised to sell a half Durham cow for $75, a Morgan horse and light carriage for $350 at Warburton Avenue, Glenwood. (E-8/13/57 p.4, c.4)

Hommans, J. S. During 1857 he donated 5 volumes to the Yonkers Library Association.

Hopkins, Anna On Thursday, April 21, 1859, she married Sidney S. Peck. They were married by Rev. V. M. Hulbert. (E-4/28/59 p.2, c.4) She and her husband lived with her 73-year-old mother. (See Peck, Sidney S.)

Hopp, William On Wednesday, November 2, 1859, he won in a drawing a barrel of potatoes at a target shooting contest at Weehawkan, New Jersey. He was a member of the Yonkers Hatters Guard. (E-11/3/59 p.2, c.6)

Horton, David During March, 1859 he was selected to serve as a petit juror during the court session beginning Tuesday, March 18, 1859. (E-3/3/59 p.3, c.1) On the 1860 census he is listed as a 60-year-old farmer with $20,000 in real estate. His wife Elizabeth was 61 years old, and apparently they still had six children living at home; Phebe who was 35, Johanna who was 33, Lewis who was a 24-year-old farmer, Sarah who was 24, William who was a 22-year-old farm laborer, and Mary who was 16. They also had a servant and a laborer living in their household. (See Vol. 1, pp. 51,52.) During 1853, 1855, and 1857 he was a Pound Master. During 1854 he was an Inspector of Elections in Election District Number One, and in 1859 he was a Commissioner of the Highways. (TRB)

Horton, Jared M. During 1858 he was one of three County School Commissioners. He was from South Yonkers. (E-1/28/58 p., c.7) On Wednesday night, August 25, 1858 thieves tried to enter his house. He heard them and the thieves were scared away. He followed them and saw them trying to enter the house of Mr. J. Govaert. They were carrying guns on their shoulders. He approached them and asked them what they were doing. For his troubles he was knocked down by a blow from the gun of one of the thieves. (E-9/2/58 p.2, c.5) During 1856 he was an Inspector of Elections for Election District Number Two. (TRB)

Houston, John During July, 1859 he was elected Assistant Foreman of Protection Fire Engine Company Number 1. (E-7/28/59 p.2, c.3) During the latter part of 1859 he was a member of the arrangement committee and also a member of the floor committee for the fourth annual ball of Protection Fire Engine Company Number 1. (E-12/22/59 p.2, c.6) During 1860 he was a Constable. (TRB)

Howarth, J. On Wednesday, November 2, 1859, he won a pair of boots in a target shooting contest at Weehawkan, New Jersey. He was a member of the Yonkers Hatters Guard. (E-11/3/59 p.2, c.6) During 1860 he won a pair of blankets at a Yonkers Hatters Guard target shooting contest. (E-11/1/60 p.3, c.1)

Howe, W. W. He moved to Yonkers in 1859. He was the author of the *Pasha Papers*. (E-8/18/59 p.2, c.6)

Howell, David During the latter part of 1859 he was a member of the arrangement committee and also a member of the floor committee for the fourth annual ball of Protection Fire Engine Company Number 1. (E-12/22/59 p.2, c.6)

Howland, Egbert During 1856 and 1857 he was the Village Treasurer. (E-2/5/57 p.3, c.1) Also during 1857 he was a cashier at the Bank of Yonkers. (E-2/19/57 p.3, c.3) He is listed on the 1860 census as a 60-year-old bank cashier. His wife Mary was 55 years old, and they had four children; James who was a 23-year-old teller, Susan who was 21, Ray who was 19, and Emily who was 17. They had a servant and a gardener.

Howlett, George On Wednesday, September 14, 1859 at 2 a.m., his only daughter Emma Leverette Howlett died at the age of 22 months. His wife was also Emma. (E-9/22/59 p.3, c.4)

Hoyt, Anson B. During 1854, 1855, and 1856 he was the Town Clerk. (TRB) During 1857 he operated a dry goods store with his brother George V. The store was on Broadway near the bridge. (E-2/19/57 p.5, c.4) Also during 1857 he was building a two-story wood-frame building over the Nepperhan River between the Broadway House and Wheeler's Building. William H. Post rented from him after the building was completed. (E-6/25/57 p.2, c.5) In 1858 he and his brother moved their store to Mechanic Street in the old store front of Benjamin A. Starr. (E-4/22/58 p.2, 3) During May, 1858 he renovated his store on Broadway. The renovation cost about $6,000. (E-1/20/59 p.2, c.3) On Wednesday, May 4, 1859, he was married to Martha Jane Stilwell by Rev. V. M. Hulbert in her residence. She was the daughter of John Stilwell. (E-5/5/59 p.3, c.1) During November, 1859 he was asked to serve as a juror for the grand jury of Westchester County. (E-11/24/59 p.3, c.1) On Thursday morning, January 19, 1860, he was on a coroner's jury to look into the death of Mrs. Field who died in a railroad accident at Tarrytown. He was listed as a merchant. (E-1/26/60 p.2, c.5 see Foster Jenkins for more details) He is listed on the 1860 census as a 27-year-old merchant. His wife Martha was 25 years old. Also in his household was a Mrs. Ackerman, who was 60 years old, and an Irish servant by the name of Bridget Flynn who was 24 years old.

Hoyt, Beldon During 1859 he renovated his house on South Broadway that cost about $2,400. (E-1/12/60 p.2, c.1)

Hoyt, George W. During 1857 he operated a dry goods store with his brother Anson B. (E-2/19/57 p.5, c.4)

Hoyt, N. B. During 1857 he occupied a three-story brick building owned by MacFarlane on the north corner of Main Street and Mill Lane. (E-7/2/57 p.2, c.5)

Hoyt, William H. In 1853 he was licensed as a tavern keeper. (Documents.) During 1857 he still owned a tavern. (E-5/28/57 p.2, c.2) However, he apparently did not receive a license during June of 1857. He owned the Yonkers Hotel, and on Wednesday June 3, 1857 the steamer *Edwin* landed at Yonkers as a violent thunder storm was commencing. He opened his parlors for the passengers saving them from possible injury. (E-6/4/57 p.2, c.6) On Thursday, May 20, 1858 upon the complaint of the Westchester County Board of Excise he was tried in violation of the Law for the Suppression of Intemperance for selling liquor and wine without a license. There were six members on the jury and a judge. His attorney was Reuben W. Van Pelt of Yonkers. Andrew Jones, Joseph R. Hurd, Michael Taney, Peter Flood, and George Holberton were witnesses for the prosecution. All the witnesses except George Holberton refused to answer any direct questions concerning the sale of liquor purchased by themselves or by others. The jury found him innocent. However, the prosecution was going to appeal. He lived on Dock Street apparently in the hotel he owned. (E-5/27/58 p.2, c.2,3) On the 1860 census he is listed as a 36-year-old landlord with real estate worth $7,000 and a net worth of $1,000. His wife Caroline was 30 years old. They had three sons and a daughter; Jerome was 12, Monterville was 10, Peter was 9 years old, and Margaret was 11 years old. They also had a 17-year-old servant from New York by the name of Hannah in their household. Also, listed in the household is William Wilkerson who was a 23-year-old bartender from New York, and Edward Doubring who was a 45-year-old carpenter also from New York.

Hubbard, Reuben (Rev.) On Thursday, February 10, 1859, he died in Cortlandt County at the age of 80. At the age of 15 he joined the Methodist Society and became a preacher. Later, he became an Episcopalian and was ordained about 1808. He was pastor of churches in Maryland, Connecticut, and New York. He lived in

Yonkers for eight to ten years with his family in semi-retirement. About two weeks before his death he went to Cortlandt to take part in services at a church he helped to found. The trip and the weather aggravated a health problem he already had, which caused his death. (E-2/24/59 p.2, c.4 and E-2/17/59 p.2,3)

Huestis, Henrietta A. On Saturday evening, December 25, 1858 she married Robert Carr. She was the daughter of William H. Huestis, and they were married by Rev. V. M. Hulbert. (E-1/6/59 p.2, c.7)

Huestis, J. T. During 1857 he was a pharmacist who sold wholesale and retail drugs. His pharmacy was on the corner of Warburton Avenue and Dock Street. He also sold powders for horses manufactured by S. G. Welling in New Rochelle. (E-2/5/57 p.3, c.2) On Wednesday, September 23, or 16, 1857 his drug store was broken into and some clothing belonging to his clerk was stolen. (E-9/24/57 p.2, c.6) Late in the year of 1857 he retired, and sold his drug store to Dr. G. P. Reevs. (E-12/31/57 p.2, c.7 and p.4, c.7)

Huestis, William H. On Saturday evening, December 25, 1858 his daughter Henrietta A. married Robert Carr. (E-1/6/59 p.2, c.7) On the 1860 census he is listed as a 54-year-old tailor with $2,000 in real estate and a $1,000 personal estate. His wife Dianeta was 47 years old and they had two sons and two daughters. George was 13, Mary Jane was 11, James was 9, and Fanny was 1 year old. He probably had a tenement because there are 12 others listed in his household who were all working people, and except for a 25-year-old female servant from Ireland, they were all males. Another William Huestis is also listed on the census as a 28-year-old merchant with $5,000 in real estate, and a personal estate of $2,500. His wife Isabella was 30 years old, and they had two children; William who was 3, and Andrew who was 2. He also had a nurse and a cook. This latter William may have been the son of the first William.

Hughes, John During 1859 he owned land on South Broadway probably south of Prospect Street. (E-4/14/59 p.3, c.3)

Hulbert, V. M. (Rev.) During 1857 he lived in the village. On Monday March 3, 1857 he gave a lecture on The Philosophy of Instinct. Also during March 1857 he received a life membership in the Yonkers Library Association. (E-3/12/57 p.2, c.3 and p.2, c.5) During April of 1857 his brother, F. R. Hulbert, was killed trying to get on the rear car of a Hudson River Railroad freight train. He fell under the wheels and the car ran over his thighs. He died in the hospital in severe agony. (E-4/30/57 p.2, c.5) On July 22, 1858 he signed a petition calling for a meeting of eligible voters in School District #2 to decide if the school district should become a Union Free School District. (E-8/5/58 p.4, c.3) On Tuesday, August 17, 1858 he and sixteen other men wrote C. Jerome Hopkins a letter requesting him to give another piano concert at the Getty House. (E-8/19/58 p.2, c.4) On Thursday, January 19, 1860, he testified at a coroner's inquest that he was a passenger on a train leaving Tarrytown and that he felt no brakes were put on just before a collision with a freight train that killed a Mrs. Field. He was the pastor of the Dutch Reformed Church. (E-1/26/60 p.2, c.6) On the 1860 he is listed as a 42-year-old clergyman with $4,000 in real estate, and a personal estate of $2,000. His wife Jane was 37 years old, and they had four children; Kate who was 15, Samuel who was 12, May who was 8, and Stephen who 6. They also had a servant.

Huntington, Charles B. During April, 1858 his eight-acre lot on Riverdale Avenue was foreclosed and sold at auction to Thomas C. Cornell for $4,738. The lot originally cost $24,000. (E-4/22/58 p.2, c.4)

Hurd, Joseph R. On Tuesday, October, 6, 1857 he was appointed a delegate to the Democratic County Convention. (E-10/8/57 p.2, c.2) He was arrested along with Andrew Jones, and A. G. Chatterton for an attack on a Flemish man. On Monday, December 14, 1857 they were released from jail on $500 bail and they were to appear at the next session of General Court. See Andrew Jones for an account of the incident. (E-12/17/57 p.2, c.1) During 1859 he was a lientenant in the Yonkers Hatters Guard. On Wednesday, November 2, 1859 he went with the guard to Weehawken, New Jersey where the guard was involved in a shooting contest amongst themselves. (E-11/3/59 p.3, c.6) During 1860 he was again elected one of eight lientenants of the Yonkers Hatters Guard. (E-10/18/60 p.2, c.5) During 1860 he won a set of silver spoons at a Yonkers Hatters Guard target shooting contest. (E-11/1/60 p.3, c.1) On the 1860 census he is listed as a 33-year-old hatter with a personal estate of $400. His wife Kate was 32 years old, and they had two children; Joseph who was 6, and Graham who was 5. He, his wife, and children were all born in Connecticut.

Huth, A. During 1860 he won a pair of boots at a Yonkers Hatters Guard target shooting contest. (E-11/1/60 p.3, c.1)

Hyatt, George He is listed on the 1860 census as a 60-year-old farmer with $5,000 in real estate, and a personal estate of $1,000. His wife Margaret was 57 years old. In their household was a 21-year-old Sarah, a 30-year-old carpenter, Franklin, 2-year-old Josephine, and 29-year-old Sarah Little who was a teacher. (See vol.1, p.53)

Hyatt, Richard W. During 1860 he was selected to serve on the petit jury that sat November 19, 1960 in the Circuit Court. (E-11/15/60 p.3, c.2)

Hyde, Jane (Mrs.) On Thursday, August 11, 1859, she was married by Rev. Brewer at Oaklawn, Yonkers to Paul Lepper of Quebec. She was the niece of Richard Walsh. (E-8/18/59 p.2, c.7)

Hynard, Zalmon S. On Monday evening March 26, 1860 he was elected one of thirty-two vice presidents of a Republican election rally meeting at the Getty House. (E-3/29/60 p.2, c.3) During 1856 he was elected a town Pound Master. On May 10, 1860 he was elected by the village Board of Trustees to be the village Pound Master. On May 8, 1860 he was appointed a town Pound Master. (TRB and AVD)

Iles, William His son William died Tuesday, January 10, 1860, at the age of 2 years, 8 months, and 22 days. The young boy was a twin. His wife was Maria. (E-1/12/60 p.2, c.7)

Imhof, A. During 1859 he built a wood-frame store and tenement building on the south side of Dock Street near Broadway that cost about $1,300. (E-1/12/60 p.2, c.1)

Inlay, John On Wednesday, November 2, 1859, he won a coffee pot in a target shooting contest at Weehawkan, New Jersey. He was a member of the Yonkers Hatters Guard. (E-11/3/59 p.2, c.6)

Ireland, Henry He owned and lived in a large house on the corner of Warburton and Lamartine Avenues for at least a part of 1857. During September, 1857 he advertised to rent a part or the whole house. (E-9/24/57 p.3, c.2) During 1858 he advertised to sell the house and land. If he couldn't sell it he was going to rent it out furnished for one and a half or three years. He would take for part of the payment a farm of ten to twenty acres. It is not clear whether the part payment was for buying or renting the house. (E-11/4/58 p.4, c.3) During the latter part of 1858 he signed a petition to have a meeting of the taxpayers in School District #2 meet to reconsider the location of two new schools; one on the corner of Wood Place and Warburton Avenue, and the other on St. Mary's Street near the Catholic Church and school. (E-12/23/58 p.2, c.2)

Isaac, John During 1859 he had a fruit store on Dock Street. The store was recently opened in Yonkers, but he had 15 years experience in the business. (E-5/12/59 p.3, c.1) He was a grocer. (E-12/22/59 p.2, c.7) On the 1860 census he is listed as a 35-year-old grocer with a personal estate worth $1,000. His wife Sarah was 31 years old and she was from England. There is a John Isaacs on the 1860 census who was 34 years old and also a grocer. He lived in the household of L. H. Bodine.

Isaacs, Edward During 1857 he was a Trustee of the African Methodist Episcopal Zion Church. (E-2/5/57) He resigned as Trustee in July 1857 as a protest over the alleged missing money by Rev. Tripp. (E-7/23/57)

Jackson, James During 1857 he owned a tavern. (E-5/28/57 p.2, c.2) During May of 1857 he applied for a hotel and tavern license and apparently did not receive it. (E-6/4/57 p.2 c.3,4) His tavern was on Dock Street and he must have been relicensed because on Wednesday, October 14, 1857 a laborer was passing his tavern who was invited in by some people who were inside the tavern. The laborer was asked to buy a round of drinks for everyone. However, he refused because he had no money. He was then asked to pawn his hat, and he refused that. The laborer was then thrown out on the street and some of the people in the tavern threw rocks at him. One rock hit him in the head and caused a serious injury. The laborer was saved by some residents of the neighborhood. (E-10/15/57 p.2, c.2) During early November, 1857, he had most of his chickens stolen from him in several separate burglaries. (E-11/12/57 p.2, c.3) He applied for a hotel license in 1858. (E-6/3/58 p.2, c.5) During 1859 he was granted a hotel license. (E-8/11/59 p.2, c.7) On Wednesday, November 2, 1859, he was chosen as a judge of a target shooting match at Weehawkan, New Jersey, between the men of the Yonkers Hatters Guard. (E-11/3/59 p.3, c.6) On Friday night, December 9, 1859, his bar was broken into and some pennies and an overcoat were taken. (E-12,15,59 p.2, c.5) During 1860 he received a hotel license. (E-7/26/60 p.2, c.6) A James Jackson is listed on the 1860 census as a 34-year-old hatter with real estate valued at $3,000, and a personal estate of $1,500. His wife was Hannah and she was 25 years old. Also, he probably, in the least, had a tenement, if not a hotel because also listed in his household were 13 other people from a variety of countries. Two were females and the rest were males.

Jenkins, J. Foster (M.D.) On March 3, 1857 he was elected a manager of the Yonkers Library Association. (E-3/5/57 p.2, c.6) During May of 1857 he donated 20 volumes to the Library. (E-5/14/57) On Monday evening, March 1, 1858 he was again elected a manager of the Yonkers Library Association. (E-3/4/58 p.2, c.3) On Tuesday, August 17, 1858 he and sixteen other men wrote C. Jerome Hopkins a letter requesting him to give another piano concert at the Getty House. (E-8/19/58 p.2, c.4) On Monday, December 13, 1858 he became Junior Warden of the newly formed Episcopal Church on Mechanic Street. (E-12/23/58 p.2, c.3) During November, 1859 he moved his residence to the northwest corner of Buena Vista Avenue and Prospect Street. His office was on North Broadway south of the Baptist Church. (E-11/24/59 p.3, c.2) On Thursday, January 19, 1860, he testified at a coroner's inquest that he was a passenger on a train leaving Tarrytown that collided with a freight train killing a Mrs. Anna H. Field, and that he attended to her. She received a compound fracture of two bones in the left leg, a lacerated wound on the upper part of the left thigh, and bruises on her head and left arm. He did not consider the injuries serious. There were no internal injuries serious enough to cause her death, and he supposed her death was caused by shock and loss of blood. She was left on the train even though he advised the people with her that she should stay in Tarrytown. They thought she would be better off in New York with her friends. However, they did stop in Yonkers where she was taken off the train, brought to the Getty House, where she died at about 7 p.m.. She had just married Thomas W. Field of Brooklyn in Kingston at 10 o'clock that morning, and apparently they were returning to Brooklyn when the accident occurred. Three others also died in the accident. They were Mrs. Tilley, Mr. Erwin, and Mr. Coey. (E-1/26/60 p.2, c.6 also E-2/2/60 p.2, c.6,7) On April 9, 1860 he was elected a junior warden at St. Paul's Free Church. (E-4/12/60 p.2, c.6) On Friday, May 4, 1860, he was elected one of five members of the committee on Premiums for Fruits for the June exhibition of the newly formed Yonkers Horticultural Society. (E-5/17/60 p.3, c.3) On Monday night, December 17, 1860 he was installed as an officer into the Rising Star Lodge of Free and Accepted Masons as a member of the standing committee. (E-12/20/60 p.2, c.3)

Jennings, Gould J. During 1859 he owned land on the corner of Lake Avenue and Broadway. His land was bounded by Sampson Simpson's, Edward F. Shonnard, and J. H. Jennings. It was to be sold at auction by the Sheriff on Thursday, October 6, 1859. (E-8/25/59 p.3, c.5)

Jennings, J. H. During 1857 he was an insurance agent for St. Mark's Fire Insurance Company. He was also a realtor at the corner of Broadway and Wells Avenue. (E-2/19/57 p.4, c.4) Also during 1857 he acted as a teller during a meeting to nominate a village president. (E-2/26/57 p.2, c.1) On Saturday, September 5, 1857 he was elected at a Republican primary meeting to be a delegate to the Republican district convention. (E-9/10/57 p.2, c.6) During the early part of 1858 he owned land between Locust Street and Ashburton Avenue along a line that eventually became Woodworth Avenue. (E-1/7/58 p. 2, c.5)

Johnson, Edward During 1858 he was an upholsterer at 3 Wheeler's Building. (E-4/15/58 p.2, c.7) During the 1856 town meeting he was elected a Justice of the Peace to fill a vacancy. (TRB)

Johnson, Elias During 1857 he was notified to serve on the Grand Jury at White Plains. (E-8/27/57 p.2, c.4)

Johnson, Harriet Augusta On Thursday afternoon, April 26, 1860, she was killed by a runaway horse and wagon opposite the post office. The horse and wagon belonged to a baker named Eberspeckers who left the horse unhitched while delivering bread. He was convicted of being criminally culpable in not securing his horse. She was a "little girl," and her funeral was at St. John's Episcopal Church. (E-5/3/60 p.2, c.2) She was the daughter of the late Edward and Harriet Augusta Johnson. When she died she was 9 years, 2 months, and 2 days old. (E-5/3/60 p.2, c.5)

Johnson, Isaac, G. At the 1856 town meeting he was elected a Justice of the Peace to fill a vacancy. (TRB)

Johnson. Nathan P. He was a young man in the dry goods business in New York City. He came to Yonkers on Sunday, September 5, 1858 to spend some time with friends and stayed at the Getty House. On leaving the upstairs dining room he tripped on the stairs and fell down about five stairs hitting his temple. The blow knocked him unconscious. He was attended to by Drs. Jenkins, Gates, and

Arnold, but at about 3 o'clock in the morning he died. It was thought that his mother and sisters lived in Hartford, Ct. (E-9/9/58 p.2, c.7)

Johnston, Edward Sometime before May, 1860 he and his wife Harriet died. On Thursday, April 26, 1860, their daughter died suddenly at the age of 9 years, two months and two days. (E-5/3/60 p.2, c.5) See Harriet Augusta Johnson above. This was the obituary and the family name was spelled Johnston. In an associated article it was spelled Johnson.

Jones, Alfred During the latter part of 1858 he signed a petition to have a meeting of the taxpayers in School District #2 meet to reconsider the location of two new schools; one on the corner of Wood Place and Warburton Avenue, and the other on St. Mary's Street near the Catholic Church and school. (E-12/23/58 p.2, c.3) He lived on Jones Place where he built a house sometime between 1851 and 1853. Jones Place ran northerly from Ashburton Avenue to Lamartine Avenue. It is now part of Woodworth Avenue. His house was the first on Jones Place, hence the street was named after him. (E-4/21/59 p.2, c.5)

Jones, Andrew On Tuesday evening, December 8, 1857 he was in front of the Broadway House with his fighting dog and several other men when a poor Flemish vagrant came by inquiring if he could talk with the Poor Master in order to stay the night. One of the men pushed the inquirer down and let the dog loose on him. The dog fastened himself to the leg of the man who dragged the dog more than 30 feet to the residence of Nicholas Rost where the dog let loose of his leg. He was treated by Doctors Upham and Andrews in the house of Rost, and they said he would be crippled for life. (E-12/10/57 p.2, c.4) Jones was arrested along with A. G. Chatterton, and Joseph R. Hurd. On Monday, December 14, 1857 they were released from jail on $500 bail and they were to appear at the next session of General Court. (E-12/17/57 p.2, c.1) On Thursday, May 20, 1858 he was a witness for the prosecution in a trial against William H. Hoyt for violating the Law for the Suppression of Intolerance. He was a carpenter living in Yonkers, and he refused to testify that he drank, or personally saw anyone else drink liquor at Hoyt's tavern. He took the 5th Amendment and the Judge decided to put him in jail. However, he said "I have seen men come in there and drink, but I would not be willing to swear what they drank." He was then asked if he heard what the men ordered. He answered that "They called for soda water, sarsaparilla, lemonade, gin, brandy, and wine, but I can't swear they got it." When he was asked it he drank any gin, brandy, or wine he refused to answer because it might degrade him, and he was upheld by the Judge. This set the tone for all the rest of the witnesses for the prosecution except one. Hoyt was acquitted. (E-5/27/58 p.2, c.3)

Jones, Henry During 1860 he was an agent for Smith's Freight Boat Company. (E-5/3/60 p.2, c.6)

Jones, J. S. During 1860 he won a set of spoons at a Yonkers Hatters Guard target shooting contest. (E-11/1/60 p.3, c.1)

Jones, L. M. During 1857 he was an Ensign at the Yonkers Collegiate Institute. (E-8/13/57 p.2, c.3)

Jordan, E. (Miss) During 1859 she was a dressmaker who lived on Dock Street next to the milliner's. She used a Wheeler and Wilson sewing machine. (E-9/22/59 p.3, c.5)

Jordon, John H. During 1859 he and John Grevert operated the Blue Stone Yard on the Dock. They furnished blue stone and employed the "best mechanics." (E-6/23/59 p.3, c.1)

Joyce, A. On Wednesday, November 2, 1859, he won a water pitcher in a target shooting contest at Weehawkan, New Jersey. He was a member of the Yonkers Hatters Guard. (E-11/3/59 p.2, c.6)

Joyce, John On Friday, September 11, 1857 he fell off scaffolding and broke his right wrist. He was a carpenter employed by Messrs. Akert and Quick, and he was working on the house of C. M. Odell. (E-9/17/57 p.2, c.4)

Joyce, Joseph S. He came to Yonkers to live with a relative sometime during 1859. He owned a hat manufacturing business in Orange, New Jersey that went out of business during the 1857 Panic. He became ill and traveled to the South, but his health worsened, hence he came to Yonkers. On Monday, December 5, 1859 he died. He was a Mason. (E-12/15/59 p.2, c.5)

Keeler During 1857 he owned with his son a boot and shoe store on the corner of Mechanic Street and Broadway. (E-2/19/57 p.2, c.6)

Keeler, Abraham G. On Tuesday, November 20, 1860, his wife Sarah died at the age of 77 years and 10 months. Abraham had died sometime before his wife. She was buried in Danbury, Connecticut. (E-11/29/60 p.2, c.7)

Keeler, Albert On Tuesday, February 25, 1857 his son broke two bones in his left arm above the wrist while sliding down Locust Hill Avenue when he ran into a telegraph pole. He was eight years old. (E-2/25/58 p.2, c.6 see also vol. 1 p.54)

Keeler, James During 1860 he was a practical garment dyer. He also cleaned clothing for men. His business was behind the Eagle Hat Factory on Palisade Avenue. (E-9/27/60 p.2, c.7) On the 1860 census he is listed as a 35-year-old dyer with a personal estate of $400. His wife Louisa was 36 years old, and they had four children; John who was 12, James who was 9, Louisa who was 7, and George who was 3. His brother John, who was a 23-year-old dyer, lived in his household. Everyone in his household was born in England.

Keeler, Samuel On December 6, 1854 a red and white cow wandered onto his property. (TRB)

Kellam, James H. On Friday, September 25, 1857 he died in Boston. He was born in Belfast Maine. While in Yonkers he was a Street Commissioner, the Clerk of the Marine Court, and he was a merchant with a business on Front Street, NYC.

Kelley, William (In 1860 Kelly) On Wednesday, November 2, 1859, he won a $5 gold pen in a target shooting contest at Weehawkan, New Jersey. He was a member of the Yonkers Hatters Guard. (E-11/3/59 p.2, c.6) During 1860 he won $5 at a Yonkers Hatters Guard target shooting contest. (E-11/1/60 p.3, c.1)

Kellinger, Dewitt C. During 1853 he was licensed as a tavern keeper. (TRB)

Kellinger, Joanna (Miss) On Saturday morning, September 11, 1858 she was riding in a carriage with her brother past Hobb's store when a shaft on the axle broke loose. She was thrown from the carriage and knocked unconscious for a half hour. Her brother was not hurt. (E-9/16/58 p.2, c.4)

Kellinger, Sarah During 1854 she was licensed as a tavern keeper. (TRB)

Kellogg, Dwight On Friday, August 19, 1859 he died at the age of 62. (E-9/1/59 p.3, c.1)

Kellogg, J. Q. During 1859 on Broadway he/she used a Grover and Baker noiseless sewing machine. (E-8/11/59 p.3, c.2)

Kellogg, S. T. During 1859 on Broadway he/she used a Grover and Baker noiseless sewing machine. (E-8/11/59 p.3, c.2)

Kelly, Daniel During December, 1859, his wife was on the arrangement committee to give a benefit for their pastor John Taylor. The guest speaker was the Rev. Henry Highland Garnett, pastor of the Shiloh Presbyterian Church in NYC. Admission was 50 cents and the proceeds went Rev. Taylor. He was also on the committee. (E-12/8/59 p.3, c.2)

Kelly, John On Wednesday, November 2, 1859, he won in a drawing a card basket at a target shooting contest at Weehawkan, New Jersey. He was a member of the Yonkers Hatters Guard. (E-11/3/59 p.2, c.6)

Kemp, N. During the latter part of 1859 he was a member of the arrangement committee for the fourth annual ball of Protection Fire Engine Company Number 1. (E-12/22/59 p.2, c.6) During 1860 he won $5 at a Yonkers Hatters Guard target shooting contest. (E-11/1/60 p.3, c.1)

Kemp, W. During 1860 he won $5 at a Yonkers Hatters Guard target shooting contest. (E-11/1/60 p.3, c.1)

Kent, L. On Wednesday, November 2, 1859, he won one ton of coal in a target shooting contest at Weehawkan, New Jersey. He was a member of the Yonkers Hatters Guard. (E-11/3/59 p.2, c.6)

Kerrigan, James On Tuesday, September 4, 1860, he died at apparently 60 years of age. (E-9/6/60 p.2, c.7)

Ketchum, David C. He was a partner of John T. Waring and Charles E. Waring in the hat manufactory of J. T. Waring and Co. On December 1, 1860 the partnership was dissolved and he left the business. (E-12/13/60 p.3, c.1)

Key, Edward Mrs. During 1857 she lived on the corner of Prospect and Grinnell Streets. She advertised that she would educate a few Yonkers children for $8 a quarter. Also, she would board two little girls and educate them for $100 a quarter. (E-6/4/57 p.2, c.2)

Kiffen, Alfred On Thursday, November 10, 1859, he died at the age of 4 years, 6 months, and 26 days at Spuyten Duyvil. (E-12/1/59 p.3, c.2)

King, L. H. (Rev.) On Sunday, May 15, 1859, he preached his first sermon as pastor of the Methodist Church. (E-5/19/59 p.2, c.3) He is listed on the 1860 census as a 38-year-old Methodist clergyman who had a personal estate of $1,000. His wife Amanda was also 38 years old, and they had three children; Lidia who was 12, John who was 8, and Carey who was 1. Mary Foley, who was a 30-year-old from Ireland, was their servant.

Kinsley, Hudson On June 28, 1859 he signed a letter addressed to Frederick A. Coe asking legal advice concerning a written promise of the Hudson River Railroad Company to construct a carriageway across the Nepperhan River near the drawbridge. (E-7/7/59 p.2, c.4)

Kinsley, William H. (Dr.) Before March 2, 1857 he donated 74 volumes to the Yonkers Library Association. He was also a member of the Yonkers Lyceum Lecture Committee, and a member of the Yonkers Debating Society serving as a member of the Arrangement Committee. (E-3/5/57 p.2., c.6) During March of 1857 he received a life membership in the Yonkers Library Association. (E-3/12/57 p.2, c.5) On Monday evening, March 1, 1858 he was elected vice president of the Yonkers Debating Society. (E-3/4/58 p.2, c.2) On Thursday, March 18, 1858 he recited a poem entitled "A Settler Revived; or Yonkers Two Hundred and Fifty Years Ago," before the Debating Society. (E-3/25/58 p.2, c.1) During 1858 he owned a wholesale drug store at 11 Gold Street between Maiden Lane and John Street, NYC. On Monday, March 7, 1859 he was elected vice president of the Yonkers Debating Society. (E-3/10/59 p.2, c.7) On the 1860 census he is listed as a 33-year-old druggist. He was living in the family of a Kinsley who was a 63-year-old physician. The older Kinsley had $15,000 in real estate, and a personal estate of $2,000. His wife was Fanny and she was 59 years old. Thomas Long, who was 25 years old and was from Scotland, was their gardener, and Ellen McCloskey, who was also 25 years old and was from Scotland, was their servant.

Kinslow, James B. During 1857 he was summoned as a juror for the Court of General Sessions at White Plains. (E-6/25/57 p.2, c.6) Also during 1857 he built a three-story Italian-style brick building with a basement in the grove between Ravine Avenue and the Hudson River just north of Sarony's house. The structure cost him about $10,500. (E-12/31/57 p.2, c.3) The house was still being built during the early part of 1858. On Monday morning January 4, 1858 his contractor discovered that a large quantity of tin, worth about

$25, had been stolen. (E-1/7/58 p.2, c.1) During the latter part of 1859 he was a member of the reception committee for the fourth annual ball of Protection Fire Engine Company Number 1. (E-12/22/59 p.2, c.6) On the 1860 census he is listed as a 37-year-old employee of the custom house with $20,000 in real estate, and a personal estate of $2,000. His wife Jane was 37 years old, and they had two children; William who was 14, and Mary who was 9. Also in his household was a P. and an Ann Flanagan. P. Flanagan was 67 years old and Ann was 60 years old. They also had a servant and coachman.

Knapp, Matilda S. During 1860 she owned land on Broadway near Guion Street. (E-3/29/60 p.2, c.6) On the 1860 census she is listed as being 40 years old. Her husband was 40 years old and was a hackman (taxi driver) who had $2,000 in real estate and a personal estate of $1,000. They had three children; Caroline who was 9, Mary who was 6, and William who was 4 years old. In the same household two men, by the name of John, both from Scotland, one 48 and the other 55 years old, lived with them. Another male, Geb from New York was 50 years old, also lived in the same household.

Kniffin, L. On Wednesday, November 2, 1859, he won a barrel of flour in a target shooting contest at Weehawkan, New Jersey. He was a member of the Yonkers Hatters Guard. (E-11/3/59 p.2, c.6)

Kniffin, W. H. During 1858 he was a wholesale and retail dealer in tea, coffee, sugar, flour, and other provisions at 438 Greenwich Street, near Canal Street, and at 720 Greenwich Street, on the corner of Charles Street, NYC. He was formerly in business with a Fowler. (E-4/1/58 p.3, c.6)

Knight, Abraham During November, 1859 he was called on to serve as a petit juror for the Court of Sessions in White Plains that was held on December 6, 1859. (E-12/1/59 p.2, c.7)

Knowles, William During 1860 he was elected one of eight lieutenants of the Yonkers Hatters Guard. (E-10/18/60 p.2, c.5)

Knowlton (Mr.) During 1857 he built a brick house on the east side of Buena Vista Avenue almost opposite the residence of Josiah Rich. The house cost about $6,500. (E-12/31/57 p.2, c.3)

Knowlton, James On Friday, May 4, 1860, he was elected one of three members of the arrangement committee for the June exhibition of the newly formed Yonkers Horticultural Society. (E-5/17/60 p.3, c.3)

Knox, E. B. During 1860 he sold the flour and grain business on the corner of Main and Mill Streets to George W. Francis. (E-9/27/60 p.2, c.7) On the 1860 census he is listed as a 35-year-old feed store owner with a personal estate of $20,000. His wife Harriet was 34 years old, and they had one child; George who was 7 years old. Also, living in his household was Lucy Long who was 14 years old, and Andrew Long who was 35 years old. Another E. B. Knox is listed on the same census as being a 36-year-old with no occupation, but he had $3,000 in real estate and a personal estate of $2,500. He was apparently married to a H. A. who was 37 years old and they had two children; George who was 7, and Elenora who was 11 years old.

Knox, Isaac H. On May 14, 1857 he advertised to sell a 4-year-old dark brown horse. The horse was alleged to be kind in either single or double harness and could trot inside 4 minutes. He had an office on Warburton Avenue. (E-5/14/57 p.3, c.5) During August of 1857 he was notified to serve as a juror on the Grand Jury at White Plains. (E-8/27/57 p.2, c.4) On Friday, December 6, 1857 his house was burglarized. There was no evidence of forced entry and his dog was apparently given chloroform. Knox and his wife were sleeping and the thieves entered the bedroom and stole a watch and all of his clothes. They also entered the kitchen, made themselves a chicken sandwich, and drank a bottle of wine. On learning of the theft Knox went down to the train station and questioned the conductor who told him a suspicious man got on with a couple of bundles at Hastings. He then told Constable Little about the theft and about the suspicious man even though he thought there was no connection between the man and the theft. However, Little did think there was a connection and he boarded the train. He approached the suspect and told him he wanted to search him. The man obliged, but on the way back to his seat he ran off the train at Fort Washington. Little ran after him and followed his tracks for about two miles, but lost him. The bags left behind by the man proved to contain some of the items stolen from Knox. (E-12/10/57 p.2, c.4) During the latter part of 1858 he signed a petition to have a meeting of the taxpayers in School District #2 meet to reconsider the location of two new schools; one on the corner of Wood Place and Warburton Avenue, and the other on St. Mary's Street near the Catholic Church and school. (E-12/23/58 p.2, c.3) On Thursday evening, April 26, 1860, he was elected a trustee of the Yonkers Library Association. (E-5/3/60 p.2, c.3) On Tuesday, May 8, 1860, he was elected corresponding secretary of the newly formed Yonkers Horticultural Society. (E-5/17/60 p.3, c.3) On Friday, May 4, 1860, he was elected one of ten members of the executive committee of the newly formed Yonkers Horticultural Society. (E-5/17/60 p.3, c.3) On Friday, May 4, 1860, he was elected one of three members of the arrangement committee for the June exhibition of the newly formed Yonkers Horticultural Society. (E-5/17/60 p.3, c.3) During 1860 he was the secretary of the Yonkers Savings Bank. (E-9/20/60 p.2, c.7) On the 1860 census he is listed as a 34-year-old merchant with $6,000 in real estate, and a personal estate of $1,500. His wife A. I. was 32 years old, and they had two children; Charles who was 8, and Sarah who was 2. A 32-year-old Mrs. Betts was in their household, and they had one servant, one coachman, and one cook all of whom were from Ireland.

Kusta, Gustav On October 15, 1857 his business was one of 33 businesses in Yonkers to announce they were closing their stores at 8 p.m. beginning on October 12, 1857 until March 27, 1858. (E-10/15/57 p.3, c.1) On the 1860 census he is listed as a 33-year-old boot maker with a personal estate of $1,000. His wife Mary was 30 years old, and they had four children; Adolph who was 7, Edward who was 6, Charles who was 4, and Oscar who was 4 months old. He and his wife were born in Germany. All the children were born in New York.

Lachaume, Jules During 1857 he was a landscape gardener and nurseryman. He had a greenhouse on Ashburton Avenue. (E-5/7/58 p.2, c.7) Sometime during May, 1858 he wrote a letter to the Board of Commissioners of Central Park describing how he would landscape the park. In the letter he said "...it will be an eternal honor to me to have been of some use to my adoptive country." His plan was lengthy and included "... a small lake, forming a river, at the foot of Vista Rock... The supply of water to the above lake should come through a subterranean pipe, from the reservoir's surplus... A waterfall could be started from an enormous rock nearby, and a basin dug at the foot of it; the water coming out of the basin might supply two little streams: the first one going east, and the other west, and both, running through grass, and trees, and shrubs, would add to the charms of that spot." His design included 40- to 80-feet high trees to border the roads. He expected the trees to live between 200 and 300 years. He suggested willow, poplar, catalpa, atlantus, American, panlownia, walnut and tulip trees. He also suggested smaller 20- to 50-feet high tress that would live between 60 to 70 years. The suggestions included birch, mulberry paper, judas, beech, magnolia, sophora, mountain ash, and locust trees. He divided a map into four parts: the Parade Grounds, the Vista Rock, the Botanical Gardens, and the Lake. The first would cost $573,299, the second $123,018, the third $131,840, and the fourth $352,962 for a total of $1,181,119. He wrote that it could cost a lot less if the park was divided into small lots and the work contracted out. (E-5/27/58 p.1, c.4,5,6)

Lages, Henry During 1858 he owned a saloon. (E-8/19/58 p.2, c.4) During 1860 he received a hotel license. (E-7/26/60 p.2, c.6) During 1860 he owned a hall on Mechanic Street opposite the Getty House. (E-4/12/60 p.2, c.4) During 1860 he rented for one dollar per evening his hall, called the Humboldt Hall, to the Yonkers Evening School. (E-10/25/60 p.2, c.5) On the 1860 census he is listed as a 30-year-old beer saloon owner with a personal estate of $1,000. His wife Louisa was 27 years old, and they had four children; Henry who was 8, Frank who was 6, John who was 4, and Louisa who was 2 years old.

Lalley, James On Wednesday, June 30, 1857 he bought a lot on Hudson Street for $460. (E-7/1/58 p.2, c.2)

Lawrence, Alexander B. During 1859 he was foreman of Lady Washington Engine Company Number 2. (E-12/29/59 p.2, c.3)

Lawrence, Charles During December, 1860 he was a member of a committee that was organized to run the second annual ball of Neptune Engine Company Number 3 that was to be held at the Getty Lyceum on January 24, 1861. (E-12/13/60 p.2, c.7)

Lawrence, Cornelius B. During 1857 he owned the Village Market on the corner of Broadway and Main Street. (E-2/5/57 p.3, c.2) By April 9, 1857 he moved to the Centre Market on Mechanic Street opposite the Getty House. He sold cattle, sheep, calves, and more. He also had wagons that delivered throughout the village. (E-4/9/57 p.4, c.5) On one of those deliveries an Irish woman on Hog Hill complained that one of his delivery boys short-changed her 1 cent. Evidently the argument drew a large crowd and a "general uprising" occurred. The boy ran off leaving the horse and wagon. Officers Waterman and Little recovered the horse and wagon but they were unable to find the ring leaders "of the mob." (E-6/14/57 p.2, c.6) On October 15, 1857 his business was one of 33 businesses in Yonkers to announce they were closing their stores at 8 p.m. beginning on October 12, 1857 until March 27, 1858. (E-10/15/57 p.3, c.1) On Tuesday, November 24, 1857 a boy driving his wagon in Getty Square carelessly crashed into the carriage of William H. Lawrence. (E-11/26/57 p.2, c.4) On Wednesday, November 2, 1859, he was chosen as a judge of a target shooting match at Weehawkan, New Jersey, between the men of the Yonkers Hatters Guard. (E-11/3/59 p.3, c.6) He moved his store during February, 1860 to the corner of Mechanic Street and Getty Square. He rented the store. (E-3/1/60 p.2, c.5) During December, 1860 he was chairman of a committee that was organized to run the second annual ball of Neptune Engine Company Number 3 that was to be held at the Getty Lyceum on January 24, 1861. (E-12/13/60 p.2, c.7) On the 1860 census he is listed as a 34-year-old butcher with a personal estate of $1,500. A Mrs. Van Pelt who was 58 years old lived with him. He had two children; Isabella who was 9, and Cornelius who was 4. He also had a 20-year-old female servant.

Lawrence, Frederick On October 15, 1857 his business was one of 33 businesses in Yonkers to announce they were closing their stores at 8 p.m. beginning on October 12, 1857 until March 27, 1858. (E-10/15/57 p.3, c.1) On the 1860 census he is listed as a 33-year-old butcher with a personal estate of $375. His wife Louise was 30 years old, and they had five children; Frederick who was 10, Amelia who was 8, [Janetta] who was 7, Bertha who was 3, and William who was one year old. Also, Kate Brown was their servant.

Lawrence, Justus During 1857 he was an insurance agent for the Manhattan Life Insurance Company with an office in the Getty House. (E-2/5/57 p.3, c.3) On Friday evening, September 17, 1858 he was elected to the executive committee of the Yonkers Republican

Association. (E-9/23/58 p.2, c.1) On Tuesday, November 16, 1858, he was elected a vice president of a Republican Party meeting in Yonkers. (E-11/18/58 p.2, c.2) On Monday evening March 7, 1859 he was elected a manager of the Yonkers Library Association. (E-3/10/59 p.2, c.7) Around August, 1859 the Library Association was incorporated and he became a member of the Board of Trustees. (E-8/14/59 p.2, c.4) On Thursday, August 13, 1859 he was elected treasurer of the newly formed Republican Association at a Republican Town meeting. (E-10/20/59 p.3, c.1) During 1859 he was a member of the Yonkers Circulating Library Association lecture committee. (E-12/22/59 p.2, c.6) On Monday evening March 26, 1860 he was elected one of several secretaries of a Republican election rally meeting at the Getty House. (E-3/29/60 p.2, c.3) On Thursday evening, April 26, 1860, he was elected a trustee of the Yonkers Library Association. (E-5/3/60 p.2, c.3) On Wednesday, August 15, 1860 he lost an election as trustee for school district number 2. He received 70 votes. (E-8/16/60 p.2, c.6) On Tuesday evening, September 11, 1860 he was elected treasurer of the Yonkers Republican Association for a five-month term. (E-9/13/60 p.2, c.2) On Saturday, September 29, 1860 he was a delegate to the Republican First Assembly District Convention that was held in Morrisania Hall, Morrisania. (E-10/4/60 p.2, c.2) On the 1860 census he is listed as a 42-year-old agent with $8,000 in real estate and a personal estate of $2,000. His wife Clara was 30 years old. Their servant was Bridget McKe[n]ly who was 25 years old and from Ireland.

Lawrence, Pembroke During 1860 he was an Inspector of Elections for Election District Number Two. (TRB)

Lawrence, Richard During 1857 he donated about 100 books to the Yonkers Library Association. (E-4/16/57 p.2, c.5) Sometime after April 16, 1857 but before May 14, 1857 he donated an additional 61 books to the library. (E-4/16/57 p.2, c.5) On Wednesday, June 30, 1857 he bought a lot on Hudson Street for $660. (E-7/1/58 p.2, c.2) During 1858 he built a large hennery and other outbuildings on his property on Riverdale Avenue. The work cost about $2,500. (E-1/20/59 p.2, c.5) On Friday, May 4, 1860, he was elected one of six members of the committee on Premiums for Plants and Flowers for the June exhibition of the newly formed Yonkers Horticultural Society. (E-5/17/60 p.3, c.3) He is listed on the 1860 census as a 49-year-old merchant with $30,000 in real estate, and a personal estate of $50,000. He had two children. One was James B. who was a 17-year-old student, and the other was Isabella who was 14. He had three servants.

Lawrence, Samuel Sometime during 1859 he died intestate. (E-6/23/59 p.2, c.3) He lived at 136 Warburton Avenue in a 14-room house. The house and property were to be auctioned March 7, 1860. (E-2/16/60 p.2, c.7)

Lawrence, William H. On Tuesday, September 1, 1857 he was elected as a James Buchanan delegate to the County Democratic Convention to be held at West Farms on September 2, 1857. (E-9/3/57 p.2, c.7) On Wednesday, October 14, 1857 he was nominated at a Democratic Convention to run for Coroner. (E-10/15/57 p.2, c.7) On Tuesday, November 24, 1857 a wagon of Cornelius Lawrence driven by a boy in Getty Square crashed into his carriage. (E-11/26/57 p.2, c.4) During 1857 he was a county constable and Deputy Sheriff. (E-12/31/57 p.2, c.6 and 1/28/58 p.3, c.1) On July 22, 1858 he signed a petition calling for a meeting of eligible voters in School District #2 to decide if the school district should become a Union Free School District. (E-8/5/58 p.4, c.3) He was coroner from 1857 to 1860. (E-10/18/60 p.2, c.6 and earlier papers) He was listed on the 1860 census as a 51-year-old coroner with $3,000 in real estate, and a personal estate of $1,000. His wife Maria was 45 years old, and they had eight children; Harriet who was 23, William who was a 19-year-old clerk, James who was 17, Isabela who was 11, Annett who was 9, Sidney who was 7, Cecil who was also 7, Arthur who was 5, and Eugene who was 2. From 1853 through 1860 he was an Overseer of the Poor, the town Collector, and a Constable. During 1857 he was elected to a three-year term of office as a Commissioner of the Highways. (TRB. Also, see vol. 1, p.55)

Leeds During 1857 he and his brothers were plasterers with an office on North Broadway north of Dock Street. (E-4/9/57 p.5., c.7)

Leeds, George On August 10, 1858 his only child Edith died at the age of 5 months and 25 days. He and his wife lived on North Broadway. (E-8/12/58 p.3, c.1) On Monday evening March 7, 1859 he was elected a manager of the Yonkers Library Association. (E-3/10/59 p.2, c.7) Around August, 1859 the Library Association was incorporated and he became a member of the Board of Trustees. (E-8/14/59 p.2, c.4) On Thursday evening, April 26, 1860, he was elected a trustee of the Yonkers Library Association. (E-5/3/60 p.2, c.3) During 1860 he was secretary of the Yonkers Temperance Society's Temperance Demonstration committee. (E-6/21/60 p.3, c.1) On Saturday, September 29, 1860 he was a delegate to the Republican First Assembly District Convention that was held in Morrisania Hall, Morrisania. (E-10/4/60 p.2, c.2)

Lent, Benjamin On Saturday, October 22, 1859 he died. He was working at Floyd's Neck, on Long Island, for Messrs. Mann and Keeler. He wasn't feeling well and went to bed early. Two other workers also went to bed at about the same time, but were awakened in about an hour by the smell of smoke. They found Lent sitting upright in a chair with his clothes on fire. They threw water on him, but he was dead. A lamp next to him was overturned and his clothes caught fire from the lamp. He did not struggle to put the flames out. Consequently, he probably had a heart attack, slumped into the chair overturning the lamp, and died. (E-10/27/59 p.3, c.4)

Leonard, Charles H. During 1859 he owned a fruit store. (E-6/9/59 p.2, c.4)

Lettree, G. During 1860 he won 500 cigars at a Yonkers Hatters Guard target shooting contest. (E-11/1/60 p.3, c.1)

Lettree, J. On Wednesday, November 2, 1859, he won $10 in a target shooting contest at Weehawkan, New Jersey. He was a member of the Yonkers Hatters Guard. (E-11/3/59 p.2, c.6)

Lilienthal, C. H. During March of 1857 he donated $25 to the Yonkers Library Association and became a life member. (E-3/12/57 p.2, c.5) On Monday, July 19, 1858 his youngest son James Pollock died. He was 1 year, 11 months and 4 days old. He was buried at Greenwood Cemetery. His wife was P. S. Lilienthall. (E-7/22/58 p.3, c.1) During 1858 he owned property on Broadway just north of the village line. On the property he built a gate-lodge, probably a power station, a poultry house, and other improvements costing about $10,000. (E-1/20/59 p.2, c.3) On June 28, 1859 he signed a letter addressed to Frederick A. Coe asking legal advice concerning a written promise of the Hudson River Railroad Company to construct a carriageway across the Nepperhan River near the draw-bridge. (E-7/7/59 p.2, c.4) On Friday, May 4, 1860, he was elected one of ten members of the executive committee of the newly formed Yonkers Horticultural Society. (E-5/17/60 p.3, c.3) He is listed on the 1860 census as a 48-year-old tobacconist with $300,000 in real estate, and a personal estate of $10,000. His wife Susan was 30 years old, which is a contradiction to the above, and they had four children; Henry who was 8, Susan who was 6, Hennrietta who was 2, and Ida who was 3 months. They also had a nurse, two servants, a cook, a teamster, and a laborer, the laborer's wife, and their child.

Lillienthal, S. During 1857 he built his residence on the Post Road on Blackwell's Hill. He owned about five acres of land that went from the Post Road to the Hudson River. He bought the land in 1855 from James H. Blackwell and Benjamin Brown for $50,000. The house, a large brick Gothic-style, also cost $50,000. (E-12/31/57 p.2, c.2)

Little, A. (Miss) On May 4, 1857 she was to reopen the Oak Hill Seminary for girls. (E-4/957 p.2, c.7) However, on May 14, 1857 her house, which was known as the Oak Hill Seminary, was being advertised to rent, and on June 4, 1857 her house and property was advertised for sale. (E-5/14/57 p.3, c.5 and E-6/4/57 p.2, c.6)

Littel, Willian P. During 1860 he owned property on Oliver Avenue. (E-11/15/60 p.3, c.2) On the 1860 census he is listed as Wm. P. Little. He was a 32-year-old mason with a personal estate of $400. His wife Lydia was a 31-year-old dressmaker. Their daughter, Mary, was 7 years old. During 1855, 1857, and 1858 he was a Constable. In 1858 he was also a town and village Pound Master. (TRB & AVD)

Livermore, A. A. (Rev.) During 1857 he was a member of the Liberal Christian Church. Beginning with June 6, 1857 he preached every Sunday at 10:30 a.m. in the Hall at the corner opposite the Episcopal Church. (E-6/18/57 p.3, c.1) On the 1860 census he is listed as a 48-year-old clergyman with $80,000 in real estate and a personal estate of $1,000. His wife, E. D. was 50 years old, and they had one child, Catherine, who was 13 years old.

Livingston, (Miss) During 1858 she owned a millinery and dressmaking shop at 4 Manor Place. Mrs. J. B. Thomas from NYC and New Orleans was in charge of the dressmaking department. (E-5/27/58 p.3, c.1) The millinery department was run by Miss Hardy. (E-6/3/58 p.2, c.7) During 1859 she moved her business next door to the Baptist Church on North Broadway. (E-5/19/59 p.2, c.3 and p.2, c.7) She sold clothes from Madame Demarest's, Broadway, New York, which was the first premium emporium for Paris, London, and New York fashions. (E-8/4/59 p.3, c.1)

Livingston, E. On October 15, 1857 his business was one of 33 businesses in Yonkers to announce they were closing their stores at 8 p.m. beginning on October 12, 1857 until March 27, 1858. (E-10/15/57 p.3, c.1)

Loyd, Joseph During 1860 he received a grocer's license. (E-7/26/60 p.2, c.6)

Logue, Alexander During 1858 he bought the Pacific Hotel, renovated it, and renamed it the Hudson Hotel and Dining Saloon. He advertised that his rates were reasonable and diners could have their meals on the European plan. The hotel was near the railroad station and boat landings. (E-4/8/58 p.3, c.3) He applied for a hotel license in 1858. (E-6/3/58 p.2, c.5) He received the license. (E-6/17/58 p.2, c.6) On Monday, June 28, 1858 he bought at an auction a lot on South Broadway on the corner of Prospect Street that went back to Jefferson Street. The lot had 25 feet on South Broadway, 87 1/2 feet on Prospect Street, and about the same on Jefferson Street. He bought the lot for $1,550. (E-7/1/58 p.2, c.2) During 1859 he was granted another hotel license. (E-8/11/59 p.2, c.7) During the latter part of 1859 he was a member of the arrangement committee and also a member of the reception committee for the fourth annual ball of Protection Fire Engine Company Number 1. (E-12/22/59 p.2, c.6) During 1859 he built a brick building for a restaurant on the corner of Broadway and Prospect Street. The project cost about $3,800. (E-1/12/60 p.2, c.1) On the 1860 census he is listed as a 30-year-old landlord with $5,500 in real estate, and a personal estate of $1,000. His wife Mary was also 30 years old, and they had four children; Mary who was 10, John who was 7, Catherine who was 5, and Emma who was 3. They had one servant, Kate Haggerty, who was 20 years old. He and his wife were born in Ireland, and their children were all born in New York.

Lord, William On Wednesday, November 2, 1859, he won a castor in a target shooting contest at Weehawkan, New Jersey. He was a member of the Yonkers Hatters Guard. (E-11/3/59 p.2, c.6) During 1860 he won $5 at a Yonkers Hatters Guard target shooting contest. (E-11/1/60 p.3, c.1)

Luce, James C. (Capt.) During 1857 he donated a map of Liverpool on rollers, the Plan of Constadt in a frame, and a painting of the Harbor of Constadt in a frame to the Yonkers Library Association. (E-5/14/57 p.2, c.6) Also during 1857 he was president of the Yonkers Republican Association. (E-9/3/57 p.2, c.6) He also donated a globe of the world to the Yonkers Library Association. The globe was made by Wyld in London, and it cost about $150. (E-9/17/57 p.2, c.5) His son Robert F. died on Friday, May 28, 1858 in St. Joseph, Missouri. About two weeks prior to his death he left Yonkers with some friends to go west because of health. He arrived in St. Joseph on the 26th. He was 22 years old. He died at the Planter's House of consumption. He was buried in Wareham, Massachusetts. James Luce was Captain of the ship *Arctic* which was lost at sea not long before the death of his son. There was no mention that he had died. (E-6/17/58 p.2, c.5)

Ludlow, Thomas W. During 1857 he donated $25 to the Yonkers Library Association and became a life member. (E-3/12/57 p.2, c.5) During 1859 he built two wood-frame houses on South Broadway. One was done in Italian style while the other was done in Gothic style. The cost was estimated to be $10,000. (E-1/12/60 p.2, c.1) On Friday, May 4, 1860, he was elected one of ten members of the executive committee of the newly formed Yonkers Horticultural Society. (E-5/17/60 p.3, c.3) During 1860 he wrote a letter to the *Journal of Commerce* defending slavery. (E-8/2/60 p.2, c.2) On the 1860 census he is listed as a 60-year-old gentleman. His wife Frances was also 60 years old. Living in their household was a person working in express, a cook, three servants, and a coachman. It appears that the person working in express was a C. James Ludlow, and Isabella Ludlow who was 62 was also in their household. A 29-year-old black man by the name of Peter Grany was also in their household. (See *Who Was Who* p.324)

Ludlow, Thomas W. Jr. On Friday, May 4, 1860, he was elected one of six members of the committee on Premiums for Plants and Flowers for the June exhibition of the newly formed Yonkers Horticultural Society. (E-5/17/60 p.3, c.3) He is listed on the 1860 census as a 31-year-old gentleman with a personal estate of $4,000. His wife Frances was 21 years old, and they had two children; Thomas who was 3, and James who was 1. They also had a servant, a cook, and a nurse.

Lynch, (Rev. Mr.) During 1857 he was a Roman Catholic priest at St. Mary's. On Tuesday, September 8, 1857 he attended a cornerstone-laying ceremony at Fonthill (Mt. Saint Vincent) for a new chapel. (E-9/10/57 p.2, c.1)

Lyon, Charles During 1860 he owned property on Prescott Street and another parcel of land on Webster Avenue. (E-11/15/60 p.3, c.2)

Lyon, David On Thursday evening, October 25, 1860, he was one of eight secretaries at a Republican campaign meeting. (E-11/1/60 p.2, c.2)

Lyon, E. During 1858 he had a bay horse for sale. The horse stood 15 hands and was about 8 years old. Inquiries were made at Seely's Livery Stable, Mechanic Street. (E-6/17/59 p.3, c.2)

Lyon, Sarah J. On Monday, February 22, 1858 she married James B. Haynes of Greenburgh. The paper had her as a Mrs. (E-2/25/58 p.2, c.3)

Lyons, Terence During 1859 he built a wood-frame house and store on Jefferson Street that was next to the building of Patrick Ryan. The project cost about $800. (E-1/12/60 p.2, c.1)

Macadam, George He was reported by the *Yonkers Examiner* on February 2, 1857 to be a member of the Lecture Committee of the Yonkers Lyceum. He donated 12 volumes to the Yonkers Library Association, and on March 3, 1857 he was elected a manager of the library. (E-3/5/57 p.2, c.6) He was born Monday, September 16, 1816 and died Sunday, March 29, 1857. His friends erected a monument for him that cost several hundreds of dollars "In the cemetery, laying just beyond the Nepperhan." [St. John's Cemetery.] On the marble monument there was in the middle oaken leaves and acorns. On the monument was written "ERECTED To the memory of GEORGE MACADAM. By his friends and fellow Townsmen as a tribute of Respect for his excellence as a Man, and for his disinterested labors in behalf of the Community of which he was an honored Member." (E-11/19,57 p.2, c.5)

MacFarlane, Duncan During 1857 he owned the Broadway Ice Cream Saloon. He also served cakes and pastries. (E-7/2/57 p.3, c.4) On October 15, 1857 his business was one of 33 businesses in Yonkers to announce they were closing their stores at 8 p.m. beginning on October 12, 1857 until March 27, 1858. (E-10/15/57 p.3, c.1) During 1857 he owned a three-story brick building on the north corner of Main Street and Mill Lane. The building was occupied by N. B. Hoyt. (E-7/2/57 p.2, c.5) The building cost about $2,000. In the same year he also built or renovated several inexpensive buildings on the opposite side of Main Street and also built some inexpensive tenements for about an additional $1,000. (E-12/31/57 p.2, c.3) On Saturday morning, June 12, 1858 sometime between 8:15 and 8:30 he lost a roll of bank bills as he was walking from his store to the depot. He offered a $10 reward for the return of the money. (E-6/24/58 p.2, c.7) On July 22, 1858 he signed a petition calling for a meeting of eligible voters in School District #2 to decide if the school district should become a Union Free School District. (E-8/5/58 p.4, c.3) On Friday night, December 9, 1859 his store was broken into and $30 was taken. (E-12/15/59 p.2, c.5)

MacFarlane, H. On Wednesday, June 30, 1857 he bought a lot on Washington Street for $300. (E-7/1/58 p.2, c.2)

MacFarlane, Mrs. William During the later part of 1858 she had a sewing machine business on Mechanic Street opposite the Getty House. She sold Taggot and Farr's sewing machines for $30 each. The stitches were guaranteed not to unravel even if every fourth stitch was cut. (E-12/2/58 p.3, c.1)

MacFarlane, William On Tuesday evening, September 11, 1860 he was elected to the executive committee of the Yonkers Republican Association for a five-month term. (E-9/13/60 p.2, c.2)

Machin, Aaron On Thursday evening, October 25, 1860, he was one of twenty-two vice presidents at a Republican campaign meeting. (E-11/1/60 p.2, c.2)

Mahr, Bridget During the Court of Sessions proceedings that began on Monday, March 12, 1860, she was convicted of selling liquor in Yonkers without a license. She was fined $30 or 20 days in the county jail. (E-3/29/60 p.2, c.5)

Maiden, R. During 1860 he won $5 at a Yonkers Hatters Guard target shooting contest. (E-11/1/60 p.3, c.1)

Major, Henry He built three brick dwellings on the upper part of Palisade Avenue during the early part of 1857. They cost between $18,000 and $20,000. (E-12/31/57 p.2, c.1) He built a wood-frame house in the same area during 1858 for about $3,000. (E-4/22/58 p.2, c.3)

Majory, William J. During 1853 and 1854 he was an Inspector of Elections for Election District Number Two. (TRB)

Malden, W. During 1860 he won a family Bible at a Yonkers Hatters Guard target shooting contest. (E-11/1/60 p.3, c.1)

Malloy, James During November, 1859 both he and his wife came down with a fever and they were attended to by Dr. Arnold. The medical treatment didn't work and Malloy decided to treat both himself and his wife with old sure-fire cures. On Thursday, November 24, 1859, he took a large dose of laudanum, which was a preparation made up of mostly opium, and the effects of the drug caused him to go on a rampage. He wanted to kill Dr. Arnold since he thought Arnold was killing his wife. On Friday he went to see Father Lynch at St. Mary's Roman Catholic Church, and again threatened to kill Arnold. Father Lynch called officer Archer who helped to calm Malloy down, and he was allowed to go home. When he got to his house on Morgan Street he learned that his wife was at the house of Mrs. Pollock across the street. He went there and when Mrs. Pollock opened the door he stabbed her with a pocket knife eight times and at least once in the face. He also attacked a Mrs. Hill, who also lived in the same house, stabbing her eleven times. He left the house and headed to St. Mary's Church apparently to attack Father Lynch. On the way there he came across Mrs. Edward Underhill and one of her sons who was twelve years old. He stabbed her in the face near the nose. The blade went through the teeth, into the tongue, and broke off. He ran off to St. Mary's rectory where he jumped through a window. While Father Lynch and he were fighting, Malloy was captured, and was sent to the jail in White Plains where he got into more trouble because of his aggressiveness. Father Lynch was unhurt, and the wounds the ladies received were not severe. However, Mrs. Pollock "received a stab in the groin, which causes some uneasiness to her friends." (E-12/1/59 p.2, c.5) While in jail, Dr. Arnold did not attend to him. Another Yonkers doctor did and claimed Malloy was insane. (E-12/8/59 p.2, c.4) His trial began on Friday, December 9 and lasted through Saturday and into Monday. He was acquitted on the grounds of insanity. The paper thought the verdict proper and supposed he would be put in an asylum. (E-12/15/59 p.2, c.5)

Malone, Philip During 1857 he owned a cooperage at Peter F. Peek's Mills. He also had a branch office at 239 West 16th Street, NYC. (E-7/16/57 p.3, c.3) On Tuesday, September 1, 1857 he was elected as a James Buchanan delegate to the County Democratic Convention to be held at West Farms on September 2, 1857. (E-9/3/57 p.2, c.7)

Malony, Biddy According to an anonymous letter to the editor the village Board of Trustees made her keep her pig out of the streets. The author was annoyed that poor Biddy's pig was forced off the streets, but rich Squire "What-d'ye-call-him's cows" were not. (E-9/24/57 p.2, c.7)

Malthie, W. D. Prior to 1859 he was a resident in Yonkers. However, he still owned property on Hudson Street between Clinton and Grinnell Streets. On Saturday morning, October 1, 1859 about thirty boys gathered on Hudson Street and tore down his picket fence. Apparently the boys wanted the wood to burn during the winter. (E-10/6/59 p.2, c.6)

Mangin, John During 1860 he was the agent for the Hudson River Railroad in Yonkers. On Friday afternoon, September 14, 1860 his son drowned in the Nepperhan River just above the drawbridge. (E-9/20/60 p.2, c.3)

Mankin, Henry A. On Tuesday, January 17, 1860 he died of consumption. He was 24 years old. (E-1/19/60 p.2, c.7)

Mann, William During November, 1858 he was a member of the arrangement committee for the Second Annual Ball to benefit the widows and orphans of deceased Yonkers firemen. (E-11/25/58 p.2, c.7)

Manning, John W. During 1857 he owned land on Locust Street. On July 10, 1858 his land was to be auctioned off. (E-5/20/58 p.2, c.1)

Mapes, Julia Ann On Wednesday, November 23, 1859, she died at the age of 35 years, 9 months, and 26 days. (E-12/1/59 p.3, c.2)

Martin, E. M. Jr. On Monday, December 13, 1858 he became Vestryman of the newly formed Episcopal Church on Mechanic Street. (E-12/23/58 p.2, c.3) On April 9, 1860 he was elected a Vestryman at St. Paul's Free Church. (E-4/12/60 p.2, c.6)

Mason, John M. On March 3, 1857 he was elected a manager of the Yonkers Library Association. (E-3/5/57 p.2, c.6) He also donated $25 to the library and became a life member. (E-3/12/57 p.2, c.5) On Saturday, September 5, 1857 he was elected at a Republican primary meeting to be a delegate to the Republican district convention. (E-9/10/57 p.2, c.6) During 1857 he was a member of the executive committee of the Republican party. (E-10/1/57 p.2, c.7) On Tuesday, October 6, 1857 he was elected as a delegate to the Republican County Convention. (E-10/8/57 p.2, c.3) During 1858 he was chairman of the Lecture Committee of the Yonkers Library Association. (E-1/7/58 p.2, c.7) On Monday evening, March 1, 1858 he was elected vice president of the Yonkers Library Association. (E-3/4/58 p.2, c.3) On Friday evening, September 17, 1858 he was elected president of the Yonkers Republican Association. (E-9/23/58 p.2, c.1) Again in 1858 he was elected a member of the Westchester County Republican Executive Committee. (E-10/21/58 p.2, c.6) On Tuesday, November 16, 1858, he was elected a vice president of a Republican Party meeting in Yonkers. (E-11/18/58 p.2, c.2) During the latter part of 1858 he signed a petition to have a meeting of the taxpayers in School District #2 meet to reconsider the location of two new schools; one on the corner of Wood Place and Warburton Avenue, and the other on St. Mary's Street near the Catholic Church and school. (E-12/23/58 p.2, c.3) On Monday evening March 7, 1859 he was elected president of the Yonkers Library Association. (E-3/10/59 p.2, c.7) Around August, 1859 the Library Association was incorporated and he became a member of the Board of Trustees. (E-8/14/59 p.2, c.4) During August, 1859 he was elected a Trustee of the school district in the village. (E-8/18/59 p.2, c.6) On Saturday, August 20, 1859, he was appointed a delegate to the Judicial Republican Convention. (E-8/25/58 p.2, c.3) On Thursday, August 13, 1859 he was elected president of the newly formed Republican Association at a Republican Town meeting. He was also chosen at the same meeting to be a delegate to the Assembly District Convention. (E-10/20/59 p.3, c.1) On Thursday evening, April 26, 1860, he was elected a trustee of the Yonkers Library Association. (E-5/3/60 p.2, c.3) On Tuesday evening, September 11, 1860 he was elected president of the Yonkers Republican Association for a five-month term. (E-9/13/60 p.2, c.2)

Mather, Charles L. During 1859 he owned a cottage on Buena Vista Avenue. He advertised to rent the cottage until April 1, 1860 when evidently he was going to return to spend the summer. He could be reached either at the cottage or the Astor House in NYC. (E-10/13/59 p.3, c.4) On Tuesday, January 31, 1860 he and seven others sent a letter to R. J. DeCordova asking him to visit Yonkers and deliver his humorous lecture on "Wall Street." (E-2/16/60 p.2, c.5) On Tuesday, May 8, 1860, he was elected treasurer of the newly formed Yonkers Horticultural Society. (E-5/17/60 p.3, c.3) On Friday, May 4, 1860, he was elected one of three members of the music committee for the June exhibition of the newly formed Yonkers Horticultural Society. (E-5/17/60 p.3, c.3)

Matthews, James On Wednesday, November 2, 1859, he won a castor in a target shooting contest at Weehawkan, New Jersey. He was a member of the Yonkers Hatters Guard. (E-11/3/59 p.2, c.6) During 1860 he won a barrel of flour at a Yonkers Hatters Guard target shooting contest. (E-11/1/60 p.3, c.1)

Mayo, Sylvanus On Friday, May 4, 1860, he was elected one of six members of the committee on Premiums for Vegetables for the June exhibition of the newly formed Yonkers Horticultural Society. (E-5/17/60 p.3, c.3) On the 1860 census he is listed as a 35-year-old broker with $8,000 in real estate, and a personal estate of $5,000. His wife Maria was also 35 years old, and they had three children; Maria who was 6, Emily who was 5, and Kate who was 3. He was born in Massachusetts, and everyone else was born in New York.

McCabe, William He was a member of the Committee of Arrangements for the first annual Fire Department Fund Ball held to raise funds to help widows and orphans of deceased Yonkers firemen. The ball was held on Thursday evening, March 4, 1858. (E-2/18/58 p.3, c.5) During November, 1858 he was a member of the arrangement committee for the Second Annual Ball to benefit the widows and orphans of deceased Yonkers firemen. (E-11/25/58 p.2, c.7) During 1859 he was Secretary and a lieutenant in the Yonkers Hatters Guard. On Wednesday, November 2, 1859 he went with the guard to Weehawken, New Jersey where the guard was involved in a shooting contest amongst themselves. At the target shooting contest he won a silver caster. (E-11/3/59 p.2, c.6) During the latter part of 1859 he was a member of the arrangement committee and also a member of the floor committee for the fourth annual ball of Protection Fire Engine Company Number 1. (E-12/22/59 p.2, c.6) During 1860 he was again elected one of eight lieutenants and secretary of the Yonkers Hatters Guard. (E-10/18/60 p.2, c.5) During 1860 he won a cup of molasses and a pair of vases at a Yonkers Hatters Guard target shooting contest. (E-11/1/60 p.3, c.1) During 1858, 1859, and 1860 he was a town Constable. During 1858 and 1860 he was elected an Overseer of the Poor. (TRB)

McCall, Thomas On Wednesday, November 2, 1859, he won in a drawing a cup at a target shooting contest at Weehawkan, New Jersey. He was a member of the Yonkers Hatters Guard. (E-11/3/59 p.2, c.6) During 1860 he won a tea pot at a Yonkers Hatters Guard target shooting contest. (E-11/1/60 p.3, c.1)

McCleine, James On Wednesday, September 14, 1859 he was married by Rev. Seward to Bethia Burns. (E-9/22/59 p.3, c.4)

McElrone, Hugh During 1857 he was a hotel and tavern owner. (E-5/28/57 p.2, c.2) On Tuesday, October, 6, 1857 he was appointed a delegate to the Democratic County Convention. (E-10/8/57 p.2, c.2) He applied for a hotel license in 1858. (E-6/3/58 p.2, c.5) He received the license. (E-6/17/58 p.2, c.6) During 1859 he was granted another hotel license. (E-8/11/59 p.2, c.7) On Thursday, December 22, 1859, he was married by Rev. Donnelly at the Catholic Church on 31st Street in NYC to Eliza McCarty who was from NYC. (E-12/29/59 p.2, c.6) During 1860 he received a hotel license. (E-7/26/60 p.2, c.6)

McFarlane, William During 1860 he was a member of the Yonkers Temperance Society's Temperance Demonstration committee. (E-6/21/60 p.3, c.1) He is listed on the 1860 census as a 28-year-old silk manufacturer with a personal estate of $10,000. His wife Jane was 23 years old, and they had two children; Emma who was 3, and William who was 6 months old. He and his wife were from Scotland, and the children were born in New York. Joan Short who was 50 years old also lived with them.

McGrath, Dennis During 1853 and 1857 he was licensed as a grocer. (TRB) During 1857 he owned a grocery store. (E-5/28/57 p.2, c.2) He applied for a store license in 1858. (E-6/3/58 p.2, c.5) He received his license. (E-6/24/58 p.2, c.5) During 1859 he was granted another grocery license. (E-8/11/59 p.2, c.7)

McGrath, Hugh On Tuesday, September 1, 1857 he was elected as a James Buchanan delegate to the County Democratic Convention to be held at West Farms on September 2, 1857. (E-9/3/57 p.2, c.7)

McKenzie, John R. On July 17, 1855 he was appointed a Constable. (TRB)

McLain, John On Monday, December 26, 1859, he put up a banner across Mechanic Street in front of his store welcoming visiting firemen who paraded with men of the Yonkers Fire Department. (E-12/29/59 p.2, c.4) During 1860 he was the Yonkers agent for Aurora Oil which was an oil burned in lamps. One dollar of this oil was comparable to $3.16 worth of lard oil, $9.46 worth of burning fluid, and $4.74 worth of sperm oil. (E-3/1/60 p.3, c.1) During the renovations of Hope Hook and Ladder Company Number One's fire house he and Conway Pilson were painters. (E-9/13/60 p.2, c.2)

McRonald, Thomas On Thursday, June 23, 1859 he was married by Rev. Brewer to Mary Coles. (E-6/30/57 p.3, c.1)

McRone, Bernard On Saturday morning, October 9, 1858 he took the boat *Broadway* to New York. When the boat was near Fort Washington he took a walk along a section of the boat where there wasn't a railing. At that point he "took a fit" fell down, and rolled towards the edge. Several men came to his rescue, but they could only grab his coat. He fell into the water and immediately sank and drowned. He was a tinsmith who lived in Yonkers for sometime. (E-10/14/58 p.2, c.4)

McSweeney, J. On October 15, 1857 his business was one of 33 businesses in Yonkers to announce they were closing their stores at 8 p.m. beginning on October 12, 1857 until March 27, 1858. (E-10/15/57 p.3, c.1)

Mead, Abraham B. During the latter part of 1858 he signed a petition to have a meeting of the taxpayers in School District #2 meet to reconsider the location of two new schools; one on the corner of Wood Place and Warburton Avenue, and the other on St. Mary's Street near the Catholic Church and school. (E-12/23/58 p.2, c.3) On Monday evening March 26, 1860 he was elected one of thirty-two vice presidents of a Republican election rally meeting at the Getty House. (E-3/29/60 p.2, c.3) On the 1860 census he is listed as a 50-year-old carpenter with $4,000 in real estate, and a personal estate of $1,000. His wife Sally was also 50 years old.

Meakin, W. During 1860 he won $5 at a Yonkers Hatters Guard target shooting contest. (E-11/1/60 p.3, c.1)

Meeker, George H. On Thursday, August 13, 1859 he was chosen a delegate to the Republican Assembly District Convention by the newly formed Republican Association at a Republican Town meeting. (E-10/20/59 p.3, c.1) During 1859 he was a lieutenant in the Yonkers Hatters Guard. On Wednesday, November 2, 1859 he went with the guard to Weehawken, New Jersey where the guard was involved in a shooting contest amongst themselves. At the target shooting contest he won some blankets. (E-11/3/59 p.3, c.6) On the 1860 census he is listed as a 37-year-old hatter from Connecticut with a $300 personal estate. His wife Mary was 30 years old, and she was from Ireland. They had four children; Catherine was 8, George was 4, Frederick was 3, and William was one-year-old.

Meeker, Ward On Wednesday, June 30, 1857 he bought a lot on Grinnell Street for $1,400. (E-7/1/58 p.2, c.2)

Melah, Valentine During 1857 he owned a boot and shoe store on Dock Street. (E-2/19/57 p.2, c.1) On October 15, 1857 his business was one of 33 businesses in Yonkers to announce they were closing their stores at 8 p.m. beginning on October 12, 1857 until March 27, 1858. (E-10/15/57 p.3, c.1) He applied for a hotel license in 1858. (E-6/3/58 p.2, c.5) He received his license. (E-6/24/58 p.2, c.5) During 1859 he was granted another hotel license. (E-8/11/59 p.2, c.7) During 1860 he operated the Manor Place Exchange and Billiard Saloon on Dock Street. (E-6/21/60 p.3, c.3) During 1860 he received a hotel license. (E-7/26/60 p.2, c.6) On the 1860 census he is listed as a 53-year-old landlord with real estate valued at $8,000 and a personal estate of $2,000. He was from Italy.

Also in his household was an Edmund who was 21 years old and a bartender, and a 30-year-old servant, Bridget, who was from Ireland.

Mercer, Charles (Capt.) During 1859 he was Captain of the schooner *Fairfax*. On Saturday morning, April 16, 1859, he was transporting fifty tons of coal belonging to David Bate from Elizabethtown to Yonkers, when a sudden wind caused the cargo to shift and the schooner to capsize. The coal was a total loss, but it was thought that the schooner could be raised. (E-4/21/59 p.2, c.5)

Merchant, Charles C. During 1857 he owned a dry goods store at 449 Broadway between Howard and Grant Streets, NYC. (E-3/5/57 p.3, c.4) The Supreme Court in a special session in Brooklyn named him one of three Commissioners appointed to open Irving Place. (E-7/7/59 p.2, c.4) On Tuesday, January 31, 1860 he and seven others sent a letter to R. J. DeCordova asking him to visit Yonkers and deliver his humorous lecture on "Wall Street." (E-2/16/60 p.2, c.5) During 1856 and 1857 he was a member of the village Board of Trustees.

Merrill, Carlton E. On Monday, October 12, 1857 he was a delegate to the Republican First Assembly District convention. (E-10/15/57 p.2, c.3) On Tuesday, November 16, 1858, he was elected a vice president of a Republican Party meeting in Yonkers. (E-11/18/58 p.2, c.2) During 1859 he was in business with Franklin T. Bennett. The business was dissolved on July 1, 1859, and Bennett continued the business under his own name. Their business was Bennett and Merrill's Yonkers and New York Express Company. (E-7/28/59 p.3, c.1,2)

Messenger, James A. During 1858 he owned a grocery store on the corner of Broadway and Wells Avenue. He delivered free of charge to any part of the village. (E-8/5/58 p.3, c.3)

Meyers, John H. During 1853, 1855, and 1857 he was an Inspector of Elections for Election District Number One. (TRB)

Migy, (Mrs.) Evidently during 1857 she ran the Yonkers Seminary for Young Ladies which was a music school. (E-2/5/57 p.3, c.3) Apparently the school was closed and she advertised to sell a Gilbert piano with an Eolian attachment "6 1/2 octaves." (E-6/4/57 p.2, c.5) The eolian was some kind of wind attachment. On the 1860 census she is listed as a 40-year-old teacher with $5,000 in real estate, and a personal estate of $1,000. She had one child, Matilda, who was 14 years old.

Miles, Francis S. During 1857 he lived in a house on North Broadway which had 12 rooms, gas throughout, inside water, and heated by a furnace. The house was on 12 acres of land that had grapes, cherries, currants, and other fruit. He was moving to the West and was willing to sell it cheap at $5,500, with a $2,000 down payment. (E-4/9/57 p.3, c.7) However, if this is the same person he was elected a Director of the Yonkers Gas Light Company, and was served notice to serve on a petit jury at White Plains. (E-8/13/57 p.3, c.3 and E-8/27/57 p.2, c.4) On Wednesday, July 29, 1857 he was again elected a director of the gas company. (E-8/27/57 p.3, c.5) Also during 1857 he built a small wood-frame cottage on Locust Street that cost him about $2,500. The house was his residence. (E-12/31/57 p.2, c.2) During the latter part of 1858 he signed a petition to have a meeting of the taxpayers in School District #2 meet to reconsider the location of two new schools; one on the corner of Wood Place and Warburton Avenue, and the other on St. Mary's Street near the Catholic Church and school. (E-12/23/58 p.2, c.3) During 1858 he made about $700 in improvements to his house in Archdale. During 1859 he was building a brick house on Bell Place. The house cost about $7,000. (E-1/20/59 p.2, c.3) During 1859 the business he was in with his brother S. Miles was dissolved. His brother evidently lived in Elbridge, NY. (E-5/26/59 p.3, c.2) On Thursday evening, February 9, 1860, a cold front moved through Yonkers bringing with it high winds. The winds partially tore off the roof of his residence on Baldwin Place. (E-2/16/60 p.2, c.5)

Miles, James During 1857 he was a driver for a Seeley. On Monday, December 14, 1857 his horse became frightened and he was thrown from the carriage. The carriage then ran over his legs. He received only a few bruises. (E-12/17/57 p.2, c.6) On his way back from Mount Vernon on Wednesday, November 24, 1858, his horses, harnessed to a carriage of Seeley, bolted on top of Valentine Hill. The axle broke but the horses continued toward the village until they hit a rock in front of Rev. Mr. Hubbard's residence. He was thrown from the carriage and was severely bruised, but he did not receive any broken bones and apparently no internal injuries. (E-11/25/58 p.2, c.3) On the 1860 census he is listed as a 34-year-old livery stable owner with a personal estate of $500, and he and his wife Sarah, who was 26 years old, were from Ireland. They had three children. Emma was 4, James was 2, and William was one year old. All the children were born in New York.

Miller, D. Henry (Rev.) He lived in Yonkers prior to 1860 and was to return to give a lecture at the Yonkers Library Association on Monday, March 12, 1860. (E-3/8/60 p.2, c.4)

Miller, James K. During 1857 he and his partner C. T. Sleight were manufacturers and sellers of boots and shoes at No. 7 Wheeler Building. (E-4/16/57 p.3, c.7) The partnership broke up by June 4, 1857 and he was in business by himself. (E-6/4/57 p.2, c.7) On October 15, 1857 his business was one of 33 businesses in Yonkers to announce they were closing their stores at 8 p.m. beginning on October 12, 1857 until March 27, 1858. (E-10/15/57 p.3, c.1) On the 1860 census he is listed as a 40-year-old shoe maker with a $300 personal estate. His wife Mary was 35 years old, and they had four children; Amy who was 20, Archibald who was a 17-year-old clerk, Frank who was 15, and Ada who was 6 years old.

Milne, John During 1857 he built an Italian-style two-story brick house with a basement on the corner of Locust Hill Avenue and Ashburton Avenue that cost about $2,600. He either sold the house upon completion or rented it. (E-12/31/57 p.2, c.3)

Minturn, Robert During 1857 his sister Miss Mary Minturn died in Naples, Italy after catching the flu in Florence. (E-3/19/57 p.2, c.4)

Mitchell, George W. On Tuesday, January 3, 1860 he was elected secretary of Lady Washington Engine Company Number 2. (E-1/5/60 p.2, c.4) On Monday evening, September 17, 1860, he was elected a Trustee of the Fire Department Fund Association. He was also elected secretary of the association at the same meeting. (E-9/20/60 p.2, c.7)

Mitchell, James W. During 1857 he built a two-story wood-frame house for himself on Guion Street next to Charles Archer. The building cost him about $6,000. (E-12/31/57 p.2, c.3) During 1858 he was the pro tem secretary of Lady Washington Fire Engine Company #2. (E-8/26/58 p.3, c.2) On Saturday morning, August 13, 1859, at about 4 a.m. thieves entered his house and stole $70. He chased them, but couldn't catch them. (E-8/18/59 p.2, c.5) During November, 1859 he was asked to serve as a juror for the petit jury of Westchester County. (E-11/24/59 p.3, c.1) On the 1860 census he is listed as a 60-year-old carpet manufacturer with $6,000 in real estate, and a personal estate of $1,000. His wife Sarah was 46 years old, and they had eight children; George who was a 22-year-old machinist, James who was 20, Benjamin who was 15, Samuel who was 13, Alice who was 11, Agnes who was 9, Sarah who was 6, and Elizabeth who was 2. He was born in Scotland. Everyone else was born in New York including a 16-year-old servant, Mary Perry.

Moffat, Jane On Tuesday, March 16, 1857 she died at the age of 38 years, 3 months. She was the wife of John Moffat, and the eldest daughter of David and Marion Stewart. (E-3/19/57 p.2, c.7)

Moffat, John During 1857 he owned a feed store near a bend in the Nepperhan River just east of the Hudson River. (E-11/11/58 p.2, c.5) During the latter part of 1858 he signed a petition to have a meeting of the taxpayers in School District #2 meet to reconsider the location of two new schools; one on the corner of Wood Place and Warburton Avenue, and the other on St. Mary's Street near the Catholic Church and school. (E-12/23/58 p.2, c.3) On Thursday evening, September 1, 1859, at a fire department meeting he was appointed by the committee that was authorized to buy a new fire engine to be a member of that committee. (E-12/29/59 p.2, c.2) On Thursday evening, September 6, 1860 he was elected treasurer of Hope Hook and Ladder Company Number 1. (E-9/13/60 p.2, c.2) On the 1860 census he is listed as a 34-year-old store keeper with a personal estate of $2,500. He and his wife Jane had three children; James who was 12, Mary who was 10, and Ellen who was 7 years old. Also, in his household was Julia Union who was 24 years old and probably a servant. She was from Ireland.

Mold, George W. He was a member of the Committee of Arrangements for the first annual Fire Department Fund Ball held to raise funds to help widows and orphans of deceased Yonkers firemen. The ball was held on Thursday evening, March 4, 1858. (E-2/18/58 p.3, c.5) On Friday evening, September 17, 1858 he was elected one of six vice presidents of the Yonkers Republican Association. (E-9/23/58 p.2, c.1) On Tuesday, November 16, 1858, he was elected a vice president of a Republican Party meeting in Yonkers. (E-11/18/58 p.2, c.2) On Thursday, August 13, 1859 he was chosen a delegate to the Republican Assembly District Convention by the newly formed Republican Association at a Republican Town meeting. He was listed as C. W. Mold. (E-10/20/59 p.3, c.1) During 1859 he was an Overseer of the Poor. (TRB)

Molinaor, During 1857 he owned the Broadway Market on Manor Place. (E-7/23/57 p.2, c.7) Sometime in early November, 1857, meat was stolen from the market. (E-11/12/57 p.2, c.3)

Monckton, James H. On July 22, 1858 he signed a petition calling for a meeting of eligible voters in School District #2 to decide if the school district should become a Union Free School District. (E-8/5/58 p.4, c.3) On Wednesday evening, August 18, 1858 he was elected trustee for School District #2. (E-8/26/58 p.2, c.4) During the winter of 1858 and 1859 he held an evening school in carpentry. Apparently he owned a brick shop on Morgan Street. (E-9/23/58 p.3, c.1) On Wednesday, August 15, 1860 he was again elected a trustee for School District Number 2. He received 94 votes. (E-8/16/60 p.2, c.6)

Monlun, H. Early in 1857 he built a wood-frame house on the east side of Riverdale Avenue just west of the residence of Dortic. The house cost about $6,000. (E-12/31/57 p.2, c.2) During 1860 he was a member of the Yonkers Temperance Society's Temperance Demonstration committee. (E-6/21/60 p.3, c.1)

Montgomery, William On March 2, 1857 he was elected a manager of the Yonkers Library Association. (E-3/5/57 p.2, c.6) He donated $25 to the Yonkers Library Association and became a life member. (E-3/12/57 p.2, c.7) On March 10, 1857 he was elected an Inspector for the next election of the Bank of Yonkers. (E-3/12/57 p.2, c.7) During 1857 he was co-owner with George D. Lund of the Yonkers Machine Works, incorporated as William Montgomery and Company, with an office at 229 Broadway at the corner of Barclay Street, NYC. They manufactured steam engines and boilers, shafts, pulleys, and machinist tools as well as other items. On Wednesday, November 4, 1857 he was elected the secretary of the Yonkers Bible Society. (E-11/12/57 p.2, c.5) On Wednesday, April 7, 1858 the co-partnership in the William Montgomery and Company was mutually dissolved. (E-4/15/58 p.2, c.6) On Tuesday, November 16, 1858, he was elected a vice president of a Republican Party meeting in Yonkers. (E-11/18/58 p.2, c.2) The dissolution of the business went into litigation. (E-2/3/60 p.2, c.2) On the 1860 census he is listed as a 40-year-old machinist with a personal estate of $5,200. His wife Sarah was 37 years old, and they had six children; James who was 16, Lucy who was 14, Margaret who was 11, Mary who was 9, Elizabeth who was 3, and William who was one year old. In his household there also were Hannah Riley who was 25 and she was born in Ireland, R. W. Coe who was 35 and had a personal estate of $1,000, his wife Elmira who was 29 years old, their daughter Mary L. Coe who was 11, George Platt who was 34, Matthew F. Rowe who was editor of the *Yonkers Examiner* and was 30, and Rose McClanly who was born in Ireland and was 23 years old.

Moore, (Mr.) During 1858 he was superintendent of the Baptist Sunday School. The school celebrated its fourth anniversary on June 20, 1858. They had 91 members, but only about 40 were in attendance. (E-6/24/58 p.2, c.4)

Moore, E. C. On Monday evening March 26, 1860 he was elected one of several secretaries of a Republican election rally meeting at the Getty House. (E-3/29/60 p.2, c.3) On Thursday evening, April 26, 1860, he was elected a trustee of the Yonkers Library Association. (E-5/3/60 p.2, c.3) On the 1860 census he is listed as a 32-year-old gentleman with $15,000 in real estate and a personal estate of $2,000. His wife Mary was 28 years old, and they had three children; William who was 5, Edward who was 3, and Charles who was 2 years old. Their cook was Mary who was 25 and from Ireland. They also had a servant, Ann, who was 26 years old, and a coachman, Michael, who was 25 years old. They were both from Ireland. In their household there was also a Clarabella who was probably 6 years old.

Moore, William On Friday, October 14, 1859, he was married by Rev. Seward to Sarah Cunningham. (E-10/27/59 p.3, c.5)

Morehouse, A. On Wednesday, November 2, 1859, he won some pants in a target shooting contest at Weehawken, New Jersey. He was a member of the Yonkers Hatters Guard. (E-11/3/59 p.2, c.6) On the 1860 census he is listed as a 45-year-old hatter with $3,000 in real estate and a personal estate of $250. His wife Mary was 47 years old and they had three children; Mary who was 14, Samuel who was 12, and Benjamin who was 11 years old.

Morgan, F. A. On October 15, 1857 his business was one of 33 businesses in Yonkers to announce they were closing their stores at 8 p.m. beginning on October 12, 1857 until March 27, 1858. (E-10/15/57 p.3, c.1)

Morgan, H. L. On Monday, May 17, 1858 a bay horse with a short tail and a white foot entered his premises. (E-5/20/58 p.2, c.7)

Morris, Edmund Y. On September 13, 1859 the partnership between him and Albert Edwards was dissolved. They owned the

People's Grocery and Tea Store on Mechanic Street opposite the Getty House. (E-9/15/59 p.3, c.3) He continued to operate the business after the dissolution of the partnership. (E-9/22/59 p.3, c.4) During 1859 he moved his grocery store to the Farrington Building. (E-10/13/59 p.2, c.7) On Tuesday, January 3, 1860 he was elected treasurer of Lady Washington Engine Company Number 2. (E-1/5/60 p.2, c.4) On Monday evening March 26, 1860 he was elected one of thirty-two vice presidents of a Republican election rally meeting at the Getty House. (E-3/29/60 p.2, c.3) During 1860 he received a grocer's license. (E-7/26/60 p.2, c.6) On the 1860 census he is listed as a 30-year-old grocer with a personal estate of $3,000. He was born in England. His wife Kate was 29 years old, and they had two children; Mary who was 9, and Albert who was 2. His wife and children were all born in New York.

Morris, Thomas F. On Monday evening, March 1, 1858 he was elected a manager of the Yonkers Library Association. (E-3/4/58 p.2, c.3) On Tuesday, August 17, 1858 he and sixteen other men wrote C. Jerome Hopkins a letter requesting him to give another piano concert at the Getty House. (E-8/19/58 p.2, c.4) During November, 1858 he was a member of the arrangement committee for the Second Annual Ball to benefit the widows and orphans of deceased Yonkers firemen. (E-11/25/58 p.2, c.7) On Monday, December 13, 1858 he became Vestryman of the newly formed Episcopal Church on Mechanic Street. (E-12/23/58 p.2, c.3) On Thursday evening, September 1, 1859 he was elected Foreman of Hope Hook and Ladder Company. (E-9/8/59 p.3, c.1) On Thursday evening, September 1, 1859, at a fire department meeting he was appointed by the committee that was authorized to buy a new fire engine to be a member of that committee. (E-12/29/59 p.2, c.2) On Tuesday, January 31, 1860 he and seven others sent a letter to R. J. DeCordova asking him to visit Yonkers and deliver his humorous lecture on "Wall Street." (E-2/16/60 p.2, c.5) At the annual village Charter Election Tuesday, March 6, 1860 he was elected village president by defeating Robert P. Getty 394 to 367. He was the head bank teller for the Metropolitan Bank. He was a member of the Democratic Party. (E-3/8/60 p.2, c.1,3) On April 9, 1860 he was elected a Vestryman at St. Paul's Free Church. (E-4/12/60 p.2, c.6) On Friday, May 4, 1860, he was elected one of three members of the music committee for the June exhibition of the newly formed Yonkers Horticultural Society. (E-5/17/60 p.3, c.3) On Thursday evening, September 6, 1860 he was elected foreman of Hope Hook and Ladder Company Number 1. (E-9/13/60 p.2, c.2) On the 1860 census he is listed as a 30-year-old bank teller. His wife Emma was also 30 years old and they had three children; L. M. who was a 7-year-old male, G. who was a 5-year-old male, and Walter who was one-year-old. Their servant was Catherine Doty who was 30 years old and from Ireland.

His mother Catherine Morris, who was 56 years old, also lived with them, and a Clara Van Ran who was 28 also lived with them.

Motram, G. Jr. During 1860 he won one barrel of flour at a Yonkers Hatters Guard target shooting contest. (E-11/1/60 p.3, c.1)

Mott, Abram C. On Tuesday, November 16, 1858, he was elected a secretary of a Republican Party meeting in Yonkers. (E-11/18/58 p.2, c.2) On Wednesday evening, December 14, 1859, at their annual meeting in Yonkers he was elected Secretary of Rising Star Lodge, No. 450, of F. & A.M. (E-12/15/59 p.2, c.5) On Monday night, December 17, 1860 he was installed as an officer into the Rising Star Lodge of Free and Accepted Masons as J.W. (E-12/20/60 p.2, c.3) On February 28, 1859 he was appointed village Clerk pro tem. (TRB)

Mott, Anson B. During 1857 he was an insurance agent. (E-4/7/57 p.3, c.7)

Mott, William P. During 1857 he was an agent for Leeds Brothers in NYC. He sold India Rubber Roofing for the North River Roofing Company. He was also a builder and a house mover with an office on North Broadway. (E-3/5/57 p.2, c.7 and p.3, c.1) During November, 1858 he was a member of the arrangement committee for the Second Annual Ball to benefit the widows and orphans of deceased Yonkers firemen. (E-11/25/58 p.2, c.7) On June 28, 1859 he signed a letter addressed to Frederick A. Coe asking legal advice concerning a written promise of the Hudson River Railroad Company to construct a carriageway across the Nepperhan River near the drawbridge. (E-7/7/59 p.2, c.4) During December, 1860 he moved his business to the corner of Guion Street and Elm Street. (E-12/20/60 p.2, c.7)

Mottram, George On Wednesday, November 2, 1859, he won $5 in a target shooting contest at Weehawkan, New Jersey. He was a member of the Yonkers Hatters Guard. (E-11/3/59 p.2, c.6)

Mulholland, James While in NYC on Tuesday, June 22, 1854 he tried to stop a team of runaway horses and he had his left knee fractured. (E-6/24/58 p.2, c.4)

Muller, William F. On May 24, 1860 he advertised that he had a piano for sale. He apparently lived on Broadway opposite the Methodist Church. (E-5/24/60 p.3, c.4) On the 1860 he is listed as a 39-year-old music teacher from Germany who had $10,000 in real estate and a personal estate of $2,000. His wife L. was 34 years old and also from Germany. They had four children; Herman and William were both 10, Johanna was 5, and Lizzetta was 4 years old. Ellen Black was their 20-year-old servant. William Labvincier, from France, who was a 33-year-old professor of language and had a personal estate of $250, also lived in their household.

Murphy, C. During 1860 he won a pair of pants worth $6 at a Yonkers Hatters Guard target shooting contest. (E-11/1/60 p.3, c.1)

Murphy, Mary H. (Miss) During 1860 she was a seamstress who used a Wheeler and Wilson sewing machine. (E-4/12/60 p.2, c.7)

Myers, John Henry He was an Inspector of the Village Election March 2, 1857. (E-3/5/57) Sometime in August or September he bought the coal yard owned by A. W. Doren on Dock Street opposite Anderson's carriage factory. He also sold wood, lime, lath, plaster, and lumber. (E-9/24/57 p.3, c.2) During 1859 he lived with his wife Susan on Academy Street. He owed $1,856 on his property to Charlotte Myers, also of Yonkers, who started foreclosure proceedings on December 28, 1859. (E-12/29/59 p.2, c.7)

Myers, John K. On Friday, May 4, 1860, he was elected one of six members of the committee on Premiums for Vegetables for the June exhibition of the newly formed Yonkers Horticultural Society. (E-5/17/60 p.3, c.3)

Myers, K. On Monday evening March 26, 1860 he was elected one of thirty-two vice presidents of a Republican election rally meeting at the Getty House. (E-3/29/60 p.2, c.3)

Nairn, John On February 15, 1859 he, Jacob Read and Alonzo P. Speedling bought the lumber and coal business of Henry W. Bashford. (E-4/7/59 p.2, c.3) On the 1860 census he is listed as a 40-year-old lumber merchant. He and his wife, Janitta who was 35 years old, were from Scotland. A Robert Clark who was 18 years old, and also from Scotland, lived with them.

Nairn, (Mrs.) During 1859 on Broadway she used a Grover and Baker noiseless sewing machine. (E-8/11/59 p.3, c.2)

Narburst, S. During 1860 he won a pair of boots at a Yonkers Hatters Guard target shooting contest. (E-11/1/60 p.3, c.1)

Nesbit, Robert W. In 1858 he received a hotel license and was licensed as a grocer. (E-6/17/58 p.2, c.6, and TRB) On Monday, December 13, 1858 he became a Vestryman of the newly formed Episcopal Church on Mechanic Street. (E-12/23/58 p.2, c.3) During 1859 he was granted a grocery license. (E-8/11/59 p.2, c.7)

Neubauer, Jacob During 1857 he owned a haircutting and shaving saloon at the Getty House. He charged 18 cents for an adult male haircut, and 12 1/2 cents for a child's haircut. He opened at 6 a.m. and closed at 9 p.m.. He also sold wigs for men and women, toupees, curls, and braids. (E-2/5/57 p.3, c.2)

Neville, Robert During 1859 he built a brick house on Wood Place that cost $1,200. (E-1/12/60 p.2, c.3) On the 1860 census he is listed as a 40-year-old teamster with $2,000 in real estate, and a personal estate of $1,000. His wife Catherine was 36 years old and they had at least two children; Sarah who was 9, and Robert who was 2. Agnes Bell, who was a 20-year-old teacher, also lived with them, and a Martha who was 5 years old is also listed on the census after Bell.

Nevins, Thomas During 1860 he was elected one of eight lieutenants of the Yonkers Hatters Guard. (E-10/18/60 p.2, c.5) During 1860 he won a barrel of potatoes and a barrel of apples at a Yonkers Hatters Guard target shooting contest. (E-11/1/60 p.3, c.1)

Newcomb, H. L. During 1857 he was one of the principals at the Yonkers Collegiate Institute. (E-2/5/57 p.3, c.3)

Newell, James On Tuesday evening June 1, 1858 he married Mary Ann Curran at St. John's Church. (E-6/3/58 p.2, c.6)

Newman, Benjamin On Thursday, August 13, 1859 he was elected to the executive committee of the newly formed Republican Association at a Republican Town meeting. He was also chosen at the same meeting to be a delegate to the Assembly District Convention. He was listed as F. Newman. He was also chosen at the same meeting to be a delegate to the Assembly District Convention. (E-10/20/59 p.3, c.1) On Wednesday, November 2, 1859 he went with the guard to Weehawken, New Jersey where the guard was involved in a shooting contest amongst themselves. At the target shooting contest he won a barrel of flour. (E-11/3/59 p.3, c.6) On Tuesday evening, September 11, 1860 he was elected to the executive committee of the Yonkers Republican Association for a five-month term. (E-9/13/60 p.2, c.2) On Thursday evening, October 25, 1860, he was one of twenty-two vice presidents at a Republican campaign meeting. (E-11/1/60 p.2, c.2) During 1860 he won a cup and a set of spoons at a Yonkers Hatters Guard target shooting contest. (E-11/1/60 p.3, c.1) On the 1860 census he is listed as a 34-year-old hatter with a personal estate of $100. His wife Rebecca was 36 years old, and they may have had one son, Charles, who was 14 years old.

Nisbett, R. W. During 1860 he manufactured soda water, sarsaparilla, lemon soda, and mineral water at his factory at the head of Mechanic Street. (E-5/3/60 p.2, c.4,6)

Nodd, R. During 1860 he won $2.50 at a Yonkers Hatters Guard target shooting contest. (E-11/1/60 p.3, c.1)

Nodine, Abigail She is listed on the 1860 census as a 16-year-old living in the household of John Austin who was a 67-year-old farmer with $10,000 in real estate, and a personal estate worth $1,000. She was born in New York.

Nodine, Benjamin He is listed on the 1860 census as a 29-year-old mason with $1,000 in real estate, and a personal estate of $1,500. His wife Emeline was also 29 years old, and they had five children; James who was 11, Mary who was 9, William who was 8, Julia who was 6, and Jeannie who was 3. James Hall, who was a 23-year-old mason, also lived in his household. (See Vol. 1, pp. 59-60.)

Nodine, Benjamin C. Sometime between May 13, 1856 and March 5, 1857 he received $100.61 from the Village Treasurer. (E-3/5/57 p.3, c.1) From 1856 through 1858 he was a Constable. (TRB) On June 15, 1857 he was appointed a Village Pound Master by the village Board of Trustees.

Nodine, C. On the 1860 census he is listed as a 23-year-old wheelwright. His wife Mary was 20 years old.

Nodine, Clark On the 1860 census he is listed as a 55-year-old master mason with $2,500 in real estate and a personal estate of

$4,000. His wife Catherine was 49 years old. There were 12 other people in their household which was probably a small tenement building. He was born in New York.

Nodine, Clark He is listed on the 1860 census as an 83-year-old living in the household of Benjamin Curser who was a 56-year-old farmer. Clark was born in New York.

Nodine, Dennis On the 1860 census he is listed as a 60-year-old farm laborer with $2,500 in real estate, and a personal estate of $400. His wife Kate was 45, and they had one child, Charles, who was 16 years old. Dennis was born in New York.

Nodine, Elizabeth On Monday, June 20, 1859, she was married by Rev. Brewer to Samuel Orme. (E-6/23/59 p.2, c.6)

Nodine, Isaac On the 1860 census he is listed as a 28-year-old hatter. His wife was probably Caroline who was 26 years old. They lived in the household of Clark and Catherine Nodine. He may have been the son of Clark. He was born in New York.

Nodine, Isaac C. He was a member of the Committee of Arrangements for the first annual Fire Department Fund Ball held to raise funds to help widows and orphans of deceased Yonkers firemen. The ball was held on Thursday evening, March 4, 1858. (E-2/18/58 p.3, c.5) During 1859 he was secretary of Fire Protection Engine Company No. 2. (E-10/27/59 p.3, c.5) During the latter part of 1859 he was a member of the arrangement committee for the fourth annual ball of Protection Fire Engine Company Number 1. (E-12/22/59 p.2, c.6) On Monday evening March 26, 1860 he was elected one of several secretaries of a Republican election rally meeting at the Getty House. (E-3/29/60 p.2, c.3) On Friday evening, August 10, 1860, he was elected a member of the executive committee of the Yonkers Republican Wide Awakes. (E-8/16/60 p.2, c.6) During 1860 he won a castor at a Yonkers Hatters Guard target shooting contest. (E-11/1/60 p.3, c.1)

Nodine, James During 1858 he owned a lot near Dr. Amos W. Gates that was near Mechanic Street. (E-6/3/58 p.3, c.1) He is listed on the 1860 census as a 50-year-old farmer with $2,500 in real estate, and a personal estate of $1,000. His wife Sarah was 52 years old, and they had six children; George was a 30-year-old laborer, Amanda was 28, William was a 20-year-old laborer, Agnes was 16, Hester was 13, and Alfred was 10. James was born in New York. In 1858 he unsuccessfully ran for town constable. (E-4/1/58 p.2, c.1,2) During 1853 he was an Overseer of the Poor and a Constable. (TRB)

Nodine, Martha On February 1, 1859 she died at 77 years of age. She was the wife of Clark Nodine. The funeral was held at Benjamin Curser's house on Saw Mill River Road at 1 p.m. February 3, 1859. (E-2/3/59 p.2, c.5)

Nodine, Mrs. On the 1860 census she is listed as being 67 years old with $2,500 in real estate, and a personal estate of $100. The census listed her as a separate family, but she was living in the same dwelling house as J. Waters who was a 40-year-old grocer with a personal estate of $1,000. He and his wife Mahala, who was 32 years old, had a 7-year-old son, Edwin. Also, he, his wife, and son were all born in England. Mrs. Nodine may have owned the building where they lived, as well as the grocery store.

Nodine, O. He is listed on the 1860 census as a 30-year-old teamster with a personal estate of $200. His wife Susan was 25 years old, and they had one child, Frederick, who was one year old. O., his wife, and son were all born in New York.

Nodine, Peter On November 13, 1858 a lawsuit was filed against him by William Shaw and Conway Pilson for $205.82 with interest. (E-11/25/58 p.3, c.2) On March 28, 1859 he and his wife Abigail had the land they owned on Guion Street foreclosed. At least some of the land he bought from Ethan Flagg and his wife Julia B. Flagg. The plaintiff was Jane Weaver, and her attorneys were from the firm of Carpenter and Brace at 15 Nassau Street, NYC. Apparently he owed Weaver $442.24 on the mortgage. (E-4/14/59 p.3, c.3) During 1860 he won a castor at a Yonkers Hatters Guard target shooting contest. (E-11/1/60 p.3, c.1)

Nodine, Peter He is listed on the 1860 census as a 16-year-old laborer who was born in Ireland. He lived in the household of 35-year-old David James who was born in New York. In the same household there were four additional laborers who were born in Ireland and an agent who was born in New York.

Nodine, Theodore He is listed on the 1860 census as a 31-year-old teamster with $2,000 in real estate, and a personal estate of $400. His wife Kate was 28 years old, and they had three children; Elizabeth who was 9, Oscar who was 7, and Theodore who was 2. He was born in New York.

North, T. M. On Monday evening March 26, 1860 he was elected one of several secretaries of a Republican election rally meeting at the Getty House. (E-3/29/60 p.2, c.3) On Saturday evening, October 20, 1860, he was elected vice president of the Spuyten Duyvil Republican Club at a meeting held at the Iron Foundry. (E-10/25/60 p.2, c.3) On the 1860 census a Thomas North is listed as a 34-year-old attorney with $20,000 in real estate, and a personal estate of $2,000. His wife Mary was 29 years old, and they had two children; Mary who was 9, and Henry who was 4. Possibly his 67-year-old mother, Julia A., and 50-year-old Mary Clark, also lived in his household. He also had a cook and a servant, and one more person living in his household. He was born in Connecticut.

Norton, G. B. On Saturday, September 5, 1857 he was elected at a Republican primary meeting to be a delegate to the Republican district convention. (E-9/10/57 p.2, c.6) On the 1860 census he is listed as a 60-year-old sawyer with $3,500 in real estate, and a personal estate of $7,000. His wife Hester was 50 years old.

Oakley, Charles M. During December, 1860 he was a member of a committee that was organized to run the second annual ball of Neptune Engine Company Number 3 that was to be held at the Getty Lyceum on January 24, 1861. (E-12/13/60 p.2, c.7)

Oakley, John B. On the 1860 census he is listed as a 42-year-old butcher with a personal estate of $450. His wife Abigail was 38 years old and they had two children, John who was 7, and Catherine who was 17 years old. On Sunday, January 15, 1860, their adopted son Charles B. Oakley died of scarlet fever at the age of 4 years, 10 months, and 10 days. (E-1/26/60 p.3, c.1)

Oakley, Marvin R. On Wednesday, April 18, 1860 he was married by Rev. Seward to Maria E. Williams. (E-5/24/60 p.3, c.3)

Oakley, Solomon, W. On Sunday, September 25, 1859 he was married by Rev. L. H. King at the Methodist Episcopal Church to Mary J. Whitett. (E-10/20/59 p.3, c.1) On the 1860 census he is listed as a 41-year-old butcher with $1,600 in real estate and a personal estate of $8,000. His wife Mary was 35 years old. They had ten people living in their household and some of them might have been his or her children from a previous marriage.

Oakley, T. W. He advertised to sell one and a half acres of land on Oak Hill Avenue. The land was suitable to divide into lots. (E-9/17/57 p.3, c.1)

O'Brien, M. On Wednesday, November 2, 1859, he won in a drawing an order of meat at a target shooting contest at Weehawkan, New Jersey. He was a member of the Yonkers Hatters Guard. (E-11/3/59 p.2, c.6)

O'Connell, John Some time just before March 28, 1859 he suddenly died. He was a member of the Yonkers Catholic Library Association. (E-3/31/59 p.2, c.5)

O'Connor, Michael On Wednesday, November 2, 1859, he won a cup in a drawing at a target shooting contest at Weehawkan, New Jersey. He was a member of the Yonkers Hatters Guard. (E-11/3/59 p.2, c.6)

Odell, Ann D. On Tuesday, December 4, 1860, she was married by Rev. Carter to Samuel M. Raisbeck in her father's house. Her father was C. M. Odell. (E-12/6/60 p.2, c.6)

Odell, Cornelius On Saturday morning, December 15, 1860 his house on Saw Mill River Road a few miles from the village burned down. Earlier in the day a chimney had caught fire on the second floor, but was supposedly put out. Later, the chimney collapsed and fire spread throughout the house. They were able to save most of their furniture and clothing, but everything else was lost. He was insured for $3,000, but the estimated loss was $7,000. (E-12/20/60 p.2, c.3) He is listed on the 1860 census as a 62-year-old gentleman with $25,000 in real estate, and a personal estate of $10,000. His daughter Ann was 33, and his son William was 20. There were three laborers in his household. (See vol.1, p.62.)

Odell, Jacob On Wednesday, April 27, 1859, he married Sarah H. Seymour at St. John's Church. (E-4/28/59 p.2, c.4)

Odell, James B. On Tuesday, November 8, 1859, he was married by Rev. King to Mary A. Hodges. (E-11/10/59 p.3, c.2)

Odell, Jonathan During 1857 he sold bibles and was a manager for the Westchester County Bible Society. (E-7/957 p.2, c.6) On Wednesday, November 4, 1857 he was elected chairman of the Yonkers Bible Society. (E-11/12/57 p.2, c.5) In late 1858 he was selected as a juror for the petit jury for a Court of Sessions at Bedford. (E-12/2/58 p.2, c.3) During 1859 he lived about one and half miles south of the village. Also, he advertised to hire two servants; one as a chamber maid, and the other as a cook. (E-9/8/59 p.3, c.3)

Odell, Joshua During 1858 he lived near the corner of Jackson Avenue and Saw Mill River Road about two miles from Hastings. On Saturday, August 7, 1858 the underside of a carriage containing Miss Anna B. Lyell, Mrs. Lyell, and Mrs. Phebe A. Dean broke while coming down the hill on Jackson Avenue near Saw Mill River Road. The horse bolted and dragged the carriage down the hill and into a tree. The women were thrown from the carriage and Miss Lyell and Mrs. Dean were killed. Mrs. Lyell received a broken arm and other injuries. Miss Lyell's neck was broken, and Mrs. Dean had a badly fractured skull. She lived for a few minutes after the accident. All of the dead and injured were taken care of in his house. (E-8/12/58 p.2, c.5)

Odell, Mary E. On Monday, January 17, 1859, she married Thomas Granger. (E-2/3/59 p.2, c.5) They lived on Palisade Avenue. On Saturday, February 25, 1860, their son John Thomas Granger died of convulsions at the age of 3 months and 3 weeks. (E-3/1/60 p.2, c.6)

O'Hanlin, T. During 1860 he won $5 at a Yonkers Hatters Guard target shooting contest. (E-11/1/60 p.3, c.1)

Oliver, Thomas During 1857 he was a real estate agent with an office at the Getty House. (E-4/9/57 p.3, c.7) During 1858 he and Benjamin Townsend owned land on or near Laurel Street which was south of Guion Street. The land was to be put up for auction at the County Court House in White Plains, March 13, 1858. (E-1/28/58 p.3, c.1) On January 26, 1859 his mother-in-law, who lived with him, died. Her name was Mary Corsa, she was 83 years old, and the widow of Andrew Corsa of Fordham. Her funeral was held on Friday, January 28 at the Reformed Dutch Church in Yonkers. (E-1/27/59 p.2, c.6)

Olmstead, L. J. During 1852 and 1853 he was a surveyor who lived in Kingsbridge. (TRB)

Olmsted, John C. On March 10, 1857 he was elected a Director and President of the Bank of Yonkers. (E-3/12/57 p.2, c.7) He was also a real estate agent. (E-4/9/57 p.3, c.7) On Wednesday, September 16, 1857 he sued Sylvester S. Battin as president of the Bank of

Yonkers for $426.87 plus interest back to April 10, 1857, and court cost. The attorney for the bank was William W. Scrugham. (E-9/24/57 p.3, c.2) On Tuesday, June 8, 1858 he donated 14 volumes to the Yonkers Library Association. (E-6/17/58 p.2, c.3) On Tuesday, August 17, 1858 he and sixteen other men wrote C. Jerome Hopkins a letter requesting him to give another piano concert at the Getty House. (E-8/19/58 p.2, c.4) In late 1858 he was selected as a juror for the grand jury for a Court of Sessions at Bedford. (E-12/2/58 p.2, c.3) On Monday evening, March 21, 1859, he delivered a speech before 400 members of the Yonkers Debating Society entitled "The True Hero." (E-3/24/59 p.2, c.2) On March 22, 1859 he was again elected a Director of the Bank of Yonkers. At the next meeting of the board of directors he was unanimously elected President of the Bank of Yonkers. (E-4/7/59 p.2, c.5) On the 1860 census he is listed as a 45-year-old bank president with $10,000 in real estate, and a personal estate of $1,000. A Mrs. Olmsted who was 44 years old is also listed. (See Lucy F.) He had five children; John who was a 21-year-old student, Rebecca who was 19, William who was 17, Hubert who was 15, Lucy who was 11, and ???? a 2-year-old female. Also, in the household was [L.] G. Olmsted who was a 40-year-old female. Mary Hayes, who was also 40 years old and was from Ireland, was their servant.

Olmsted, John Jr. During 1857 he was a sophomore at Williams College and he was a prize speaker at a moonlight exhibition August 4, 1857. (E-4/30/57 p.2)

Olmsted, Lucy F. On Wednesday, June 30, 1858 she died at 26 years of age. Her funeral was Thursday afternoon at the Presbyterian Church. She was the wife of John C. Olmsted. (E-7/1/58 p.2, c.7)

O'Meara, C. During 1860 he won two tons of coal and apparently two cords of wood at a Yonkers Hatters Guard target shooting contest. (E-11/1/60 p.3, c.1)

O'Marra, Charles On Wednesday, November 2, 1859 he went with the guard to Weehawken, New Jersey where the guard was involved in a shooting contest amongst themselves. At the target shooting contest he won a cake basket. (E-11/3/59 p.3, c.6) During 1860 he was elected one of eight lieutenants of the Yonkers Hatters Guard. (E-10/18/60 p.2, c.5)

O'Marra, John During 1859 he was a lieutenant in the Yonkers Hatters Guard. On Wednesday, November 2, 1859 he went with the guard to Weehawken, New Jersey where the guard was involved in a shooting contest amongst themselves. At the target shooting contest he won a cake basket. (E-11/3/59 p.3, c.6) During 1860 he was again elected one of eight lieutenants of the Yonkers Hatters Guard. (E-10/18/60 p.2, c.5) On the 1860 census he is listed as a 29-year-old hatter with a personal estate of $100. His wife Maria was 25 years old, and they had three children; Mary who was 5, Elizabeth who was 4, and John who was 8 months old. He and his wife were born in Ireland, and the children were born in New York.

O'Meara, John During 1860 he won a ton of coal and apparently a cord of wood at a Yonkers Hatters Guard target shooting contest. (E-11/1/60 p.3, c.1) During 1860 he was a constable. (TRB)

Orme, Samuel On Monday, June 20, 1859, he was married by Rev. Brewer to Elizabeth Nodine. (E-6/23/59 p.2, c.6)

Ormes, John On Wednesday, November 2, 1859, he won two cups in a drawing at a target shooting contest at Weehawkan, New Jersey. He was a member of the Yonkers Hatters Guard. (E-11/3/59 p.2, c.6)

Ormes, Luke On Thursday, August 19, 1858 he died at the age of 36. (E-8/26/58 p.3, c.1)

Osthaus, H. On Tuesday evening, August 17, 1858 he was in the saloon of H. Lages with George Wicke. The two had argued at a German picnic in Dobbs Ferry a few weeks earlier and they got into an argument again which became a fight. However, the fight was broken up and they agreed to be friends. At 9:30 he decided to go home and invited Wicke with him even though Wicke lived in the Flats and Osthaus lived on Irving Place in the opposite direction to Wicke's house. Near Doctor Skinner's house a new argument and fight broke out. While both men were struggling on the ground Osthaus took out a jack knife and stabbed Wicke in the shoulder once and the chest twice. The wounds were not deep but he bled profusely. Wicke was taken to a nearby drugstore where his wounds were dressed. Osthaus went home and got his gun and went looking for Wicke. He was arrested by Waterman, and taken to jail. However, Wicke declined to prosecute and he was released. (E-8/19/58 p.2, c.4)

Otis, Charles Rollin During the early part of 1858 he was a fireman of Engine Company Number 1 from which he resigned a little while before April 8, 1858. (E-4/8/58 p.2, c.3) During the early part of 1859 he advertised to sell a 4-year-old Black Hawk mare. The horse was kept near the bedstead factory. (E-1/27/59 p.3, c.1) On the 1860 census a C. Otis is listed as a 25-year-old foundry worker or owner. He lived in the household of a clerk. He was a son of Elisha Graves Otis.

Otis, Elisha Graves In early 1857 he purchased about 4 acres of land between Riverdale Avenue and the Hudson River. The land was owned by a Vark. (E-3/19/57 p.2, c.2) On Friday evening, September 17, 1858 he was elected chairman of the Yonkers Republican Association. (E-9/23/58 p.2, c.1) He owned a cannon that was used by the Yonkers Republican Artillery Company. He loaned the cannon to Republicans in Dobbs Ferry and when it came back on Tuesday November 2, 1858, it stayed at the railroad depot overnight. During the night political rivals spiked it. He was going to shoot the cannon once for a Republican victory, but on learning that the gun was spiked decided to fire it one hundred times. (E-11/4/58 p.2, c.7) On

Tuesday, November 16, 1858, he was elected a vice president of a Republican Party meeting in Yonkers. (E-11/18/58 p.2, c.2) On Thursday, August 13, 1859 he chaired a Republican Town meeting. (E-10/20/59 p.3, c.1) He wrote a letter to the editor of the *Yonkers Examiner* that was published December 1, 1859, defending himself against a political attack from the *Yonkers Herald* which said he was unfair to his workers. In the letter Otis said he was "a practical working man myself for thirty years: my education was principally obtained in a mechanic shop; my diploma was written upon an anvil, with a sledge hammer for a pen." He noted that his sympathies were with laborers and that he was in favor of reducing the work day to eight hours. He invited all other shops in Yonkers with 25 to 30 employees to reduce the working hours in Yonkers to nine hours, and once that was accomplished lower the working hours to eight. He also noted that he owned sixty lots between Riverdale Avenue and the Hudson River. (E-12/1/59 p.2, c.6) Sometime probably during November, 1859 he was arrested in Charleston, Virginia. [That was before West Virginia was created as a result of the Civil War.] The authorities thought he might have been a northerner like John Brown who was going to seize a fort. However, he was released and he returned to Yonkers. (E-12/8/59 p.2, c.3) In a humorous and sarcastic letter to the editor he explained his arrest in Virginia by saying he spent "Three days and three nights in the great Virginian Whale's Belly. The Maniac armed with a pocket knife and spy glass, and breathing out threatening and slaughter, invades the Old Dominion, takes possession of Alexandria, Mount Vernon, Leesburgh, Hillsborough, the Blue Ridge, the Shenandoah Ford, and arriving at Charlestown, that renowned city surrenders without the firing of a gun." He went on to describe the taking of Alexandria by stating "Arrived at Alexandria, I was magnified into five hundred men, and the military called out. A battle ensued, short but decisive. Modesty forbids my recounting my various exhibitions of courage and lofty daring - suffice it to say that in fifteen minutes from the firing of the first gun, Alexandria had fallen. The maniac and I, had met the enemy and they were ours." He went on to describe other glorious victories including the fall of Charlestown. "With the proud air of a conqueror we ensconced ourselves in Room No. 13, little dreaming that within the next twenty four hours we should be a prisoner of war in the same room, surrounded by scores of fierce men armed with revolvers and drawn swords, and thirsting for the blood of a Black Republican Abolitionist" was his first description of his capture. However, it seems that his captures were not quite that bad because it gave him a chance to preach Republicanism, the consequences of war, and "many other questions were discussed in a frank and friendly spirit for thirty six hours, without a single exhibition of ill feeling on either side. I was everywhere treated with entire courtesy and respect by the people of the South... I spent a week of unalloyed pleasure, and returned to Yonkers imbued with feelings of the highest respect and esteem for the people of the South." He then went on to lash out at Northerners who supported slavery with "principals emanating only from their pockets - not from their heads nor their hearts." [Apparently he was never arrested.] (E-12/15/59 p.2, c.6,7) He manufactured steam elevators, several different types of hoisting machines, and he did shafting and machine work. He also had an office at 307 Broadway, NYC, near Duane Street. In an advertisement he noted that ten men had been killed during the year in NYC by the rope of their elevator breaking. His elevator was the first safety elevator where if the hoisting rope broke the platform would not fall. By the end of 1859 he had sold elevators in New York City, Brooklyn, Jersey City, Boston, Hartford, Nagatuck at Goodyear's rubber factory, Brewster at W. T. Waring's hat factory, Philadelphia, Baltimore, Charleston, Savannah, New Orleans, Cincinnati, Chicago, Peoria, Syracuse, Little Falls, Cohoes, Albany, Kinderhook, and Newburgh. He warranteed his steam hanging machines to save his customer 50% or no sale. His biggest market was New York City. (E-12/15/59 p.3, c.2) Concerning workers he was good to his word. He advertised for employers in Yonkers to join him in reducing the work day to nine hours. (E-12/15/59 p.3, c.1) On the 1860 census he is listed as a 49-year-old machinist with $6,000 in real estate, and a personal estate of $5,000. His wife was Elizabeth who was also 49 years old, and they had three children; Carey who was 26, Morton who was a 20-year-old machinist, and Julia who was a 19-year-old dressmaker. In his household there were three blacksmiths, a machinist, two carpenters, and a servant. He was born in Halifax, Vermont on August 8, 1811. His wife's maiden name was Elizabeth Boyd. During the period 1838 to 1845 he manufactured wagons and carriages. He eventually moved to Albany, New York where he invented a turbine water wheel. In 1851 he was a master mechanic at a bedstead factory in Bergen, New Jersey. In 1852 he invented railroad trucks and brakes. When he came to Yonkers, around 1853, he was in charge of installing machinery for a factory. (WWW, p.389) In 1853 he invented the first safety elevator, and in 1857 he invented the first elevator fully enclosed for the transportation of passengers. The first invention was originally installed September 20, 1853 at 275 Hudson Street, New York City. The second invention was originally installed in the store at the corner of Broadway and Broome Streets, New York City. (Kane, p.236) Later in 1857 he patented a steam plow, and in 1858 he patented a baking oven. (WWW)

Otis, Horatio N. During the latter part of 1858 he signed a petition to have a meeting of the taxpayers in School District #2 meet to reconsider the location of two new schools; one on the corner of Wood Place and Warburton Avenue, and the other on St. Mary's Street near the Catholic Church and school. (E-12/23/58 p.2, c.3) His wife's name was Margaret B. On Thursday evening, January 19,

1860, their son Horatio D. died at the age of 1 year and 8 months. (E-1/26/60 p.3, c.1) On Monday night, December 17, 1860 he was installed as an officer into the Rising Star Lodge of Free and Accepted Masons as a member of the standing committee. (E-12/20/60 p.2, c.3) On the 1860 census he is listed as a 40-year-old secretary of the Erie Railroad with $100,000 in real estate, and a personal estate of $10,000. His wife Margaret was 35 years old, and they had two children; Bradford who was five, and Margaret who was 4 months old. They had two servants who were both from Ireland. One servant was Ann who was 20 years old, and the other servant was Agnes who was 15 years old.

Packer, Mrs. She owned a store on Dock Street. During August of 1857 she sold tickets for a Methodist Episcopal Sunday school trip to Mount Pleasant. (E-8/20/57 p.2, c.6)

Paddock, Obed S. During 1847 he and his brother Vincent rented a pine sawmill from John Copcutt. He originally lived on Walnut Hills which eventually was passed on to Flagg and then Montgomery. (E-3/19/57 p.2, c.2)

Paddock, Vincent During 1847 he and his brother Obed S. rented a pine sawmill from John Copcutt. (E-7/9/57 p.2, c.4)

Paddock, Walter H. During the latter part of 1858 he and Daniel M. Terry bought the grocery store on Broadway and Ashburton Avenue from White & Richmond. (E-12/16/58 p.3, c.1) During 1860 the partnership was dissolved by mutual consent and he continued the business under his name. (E-4/5/60 p.3, c.3) During 1860 he received a grocer's license. (E-7/26/60 p.2, c.6)

Pagan, John On Saturday, July 16, 1859 he was married by Rev. Hulbert to Hannah Cunningham. (E-7/21/59 p.3, c.2)

Page, James H. He was one of seven members of Hope Hook and Ladder Company No. 1 when it was first formed on August 15, 1853. (E-12/29/59 p.2, c.2) During 1857 he and George N. Hallock owned a grocery store on Mechanic Street. (E-5/21/57 p.3, c.5) He applied for a store license in 1858. (E-6/3/58 p.2, c.5) On Thursday evening, September 1, 1859, at a fire department meeting he was appointed to a committee that was authorized to buy a new fire engine. (E-12/29/59 p.2, c.2) On the 1860 census he is listed as a 27-year-old milkman. He may have been married to Mary Page who was 19 years old. They lived in the household of Henry Dank who was a 40-year-old fish market owner.

Palmer, A. Judson (M.D.) On Tuesday, October 5, 1858 he married Miss M. D. Sinderen at her house in New Lots, Long Island. They were married by Rev. John M. Van Buren. (E-10/7/58 p.3, c.2)

Palmer, Joseph H. On Thursday March 17, 1859 his wife Hannah Maria died at the age of 28. (E-3/24/59 p.2, c.7) On Friday night, March 23, 1860, one of his cows strayed away from the steamboat landing. He lived on Saw Mill River Road one mile from the village. He delivered fresh milk to several villages. (E-3/29/60 p.2, c.6 and p.3, c.6) During 1860 he was one of three vice presidents of the Westchester Educational Society. (E-7/19/60 p.2, c.3)

Palmer, Rosalinda H. (Miss) During 1858 she was hired by the Yonkers Collegiate Institute to teach ten boys, who were seven to twelve years old, in the school's primary department. She was from Worcester, Massachusetts. (E-4/15/58 p.2, c.7) On Monday, October 11, 1858 she was going to open a Latin School for Boys in the hall over Hoyt's store. She may still have been connected with the Collegiate Institute. (E-9/16/58 p.2, c.7)

Parks, Gorham Jr. He advertised that he was a referee for a State Supreme Court authorized auction of land, lots, tenements, hereditaments, and appurtenances of Rich, Scrymser, and Woodworth along Grinnell Street. (E-9/24/57 p.3, c.2) During 1858 he lived in a house that was bought by Henry Anstice. (E-1/20/59 p.2, c.3)

Parnell, C. A. During 1859 he was a cabinetmaker and upholsterer at the Getty House, Mechanic Street. The business was formerly owned by E. Johnson. (E-3/10/59 p.3, c.4)

Partridge, William T. On Monday evening March 7, 1859 he was elected a manager of the Yonkers Library Association. (E-3/10/59 p.2, c.7)

Patterson, Catherine A. (Kate) On May 4, 1857 she became the assistant principal of the girls department of the school in the village school district. She was also the wife of Moses B. Patterson the principal. (E-4/23/57 p.2, c.7)

Patterson, Moses B. On May 4, 1857 he became principal of the school in the village school district. He was from West Farms. (E-4/23/57 p.2, c.7 and E-4/30/57 p.2, c.4) During July of 1857 he and Thomas O. Farrington examined the books of Rev. Tripp and found them to be correct. (E-7/23/57 p.2, c.7) At a meeting of the First Assembly District School Teachers Association held at Williams Bridge on Saturday, June 19, 1858 he was elected vice president of the association. (E-6/24/59) On July 22, 1858 he signed a petition calling for a meeting of eligible voters in School District #2 to decide if the school district should become a Union Free School District. (E-8/5/58 p.4, c.3) On Sunday, July 29, 1860, his only child Kate died. His wife was Catherine A. Patterson. (E-8/2/60 p.2, c.7) On the 1860 census he is listed as a 36-year-old teacher with a personal estate of $1,000. His wife Kate was 33 years old, and they had one child, Kate, who was 2 months old.

Peake, Ella Louise She died in Yonkers on Sunday, July 31, 1859 at the age of 5 months and 10 days. She was the daughter of Henry Peake of New York City. (E-8/4/59 p.3, c.1)

Pearce, Helen On Thursday, August 30, 1860, she died at the age of 19 years and 9 days in Glenwood. (E-9/13/60 p.2, c.7)

Pearce, Nelson On Monday, August 30, 1860, he died at the age of 19 years and 9 days in Glenwood. (E-9/6/60 p.2, c.7)

Pease, Mr. During 1858 he did some renovations to his house on North Broadway that cost $900. (E-1/20/59 p.2, c.5)

Peck, Aaron On Wednesday, July 14, 1858 he was elected a director of the Yonkers Gas Light Company. (E-8/26/58 p.3, c.2)

Peck, John B. During the latter part of 1858 he signed a petition to have a meeting of the taxpayers in School District #2 meet to reconsider the location of two new schools; one on the corner of Wood Place and Warburton Avenue, and the other on St. Mary's Street near the Catholic Church and school. (E-12/23/58 p.2, c.3) During May, 1860 he was called on to serve on a grand jury. (E-5/31/60 p.3, c.3) On the 1860 census he is listed as a 30-year-old merchant with $4,000 in real estate, and a personal estate of $1,500. His wife Anna was 25 years old, and they had two children; James who was 4, and Mary who was 1. They also had a cook and a servant.

Peck, Sidney S. During 1857 he sold hats at a store on Dock Street which was 3 doors from Broadway. (E-2/5/57 p.3, c.2) On October 15, 1857 his business was one of 33 businesses in Yonkers to announce they were closing their stores at 8 p.m. beginning on October 12, 1857 until March 27, 1858. (E-10/15/57 p.3, c.1) Sometime in the early part of May, 1858 he moved his hat shop to the Getty House. (E-5/6/58 p.2, c.4) On Tuesday, November 16, 1858, he was elected a vice president of a Republican Party meeting in Yonkers. (E-11/18/58 p.2, c.2) On Thursday, April 21, 1859, he married Anna Hopkins. They were married by Rev. V. M. Hulbert. (E-4/28/59 p.2, c.4) On the 1860 census he is listed as a 28-year-old merchant. His wife Anna was 27 years old, and they both apparently lived with her 73-year-old mother.

Peek, Peter F. During 1857 he was a mechanic and owned a successful manufacturing business. He had a mill, cooperage, and made barrels and casks. (E-2/19/57 p.2, c.1) During 1858 he built a brick house on the south side of Ashburton Avenue almost directly opposite his former residence. Apparently he was his own architect and builder. The house was estimated to cost $6,000. (E-1/20/59 p.2, c.4) During 1856 he was a member of the village Board of Trustees.

Peene, Joseph During 1857 he was the Captain of the sloop *Elias Hicks*. (E-5/14/57 p.2, c.7) During the latter part of 1858 he signed a petition to have a meeting of the taxpayers in School District #2 meet to reconsider the location of two new schools; one on the corner of Wood Place and Warburton Avenue, and the other on St. Mary's Street near the Catholic Church and school. (E-12/23/58 p.2, c.3) During 1859 he was the Yonkers agent for the Ben Franklin Line of Sloops. (E-12/22/59 p.2, c.7) On the 1860 census he is listed as a 30-year-old sloop captain with a personal estate of $1,500. His wife Sarah was 31 years old, and they had two children; Edward who was 4, and Stephen who was 2.

Peene, Joseph Sr. On March 3, 1858 he died at 67 years of age. He was waked at his son's house on Warburton Avenue. (E-3/4/58 p.3, c.3)

Peene, S. During 1857 he was the Captain of the sloop *Martin Hynes*. (E-5/14/57 p.2, c.7)

Pendergrast, Watt On Wednesday afternoon, November 28, 1860 he was working with Charles Wooster repairing a gasometer at a Mr. Mott's place in Riverdale when gas escaped and ignited. He inhaled the flames and died a couple of hours later. He was married and had children. (E-12/6/60 p.2, c.4)

Perrin, John G. On March 6, 1858 the house he was renting from John G. Horton on Centre Avenue in the village caught fire and was destroyed. Most of Mrs. Perrin's furniture was saved and the rest was insured. The estimated loss was $4,000. (E-3/11/58 p.2, c.5)

Perry, George W. During 1857 he was a dentist who graduated from the Baltimore College of Dental Surgery. He practiced with Dr. White and they had an office opposite the Getty House. (E-3/19/57 p.2, c.4) Apparently by December, 1857 White was no longer his associate. (E-12/10/57 p.3, c.4) During March, 1858 his house on Broadway was for rent. (E-3/11/58 p.3, c.3) On the 1860 census he is listed as a 30-year-old dentist with a personal estate of $1,000. His wife Adelia was 24 years old, and they had one child, Clara, who was 5 years old. They also had a servant.

Pettit, Catharine On Monday, August 1, 1859 she died at the age of 65. Her husband was William Pettit. (E-8/459 p.3, c.1)

Pierce, (Mr.) During 1859 at Glenwood he used a Grover and Baker noiseless sewing machine. (E-8/11/59 p.3, c.2)

Pilson, Conway He was a member of the Committee of Arrangements for the first annual Fire Department Fund Ball held to raise funds to help widows and orphans of deceased Yonkers firemen. The ball was held on Thursday evening, March 4, 1858. (E-2/18/58 p.3, c.5) On Thursday evening, March 25, 1858 at the Presbyterian Church he was married by Reverend Seward to Mrs. Jenny Hawkes. (E-4/1/58 p.3, c.2) On Tuesday, November 16, 1858, he was elected a vice president of a Republican Party meeting in Yonkers. (E-11/18/58 p.2, c.2) During 1859 he was a house and sign painter with a store on Main Street. On May 10, 1859 his partnership with William Shaw was dissolved. (E-5/12/59 p.3, c.1) He temporarily located his new business on Main Street next to Hoyt's feed store. (E-5/19/59 p.2, c.7) He moved his business to Main Street just below the office of the *Yonkers Examiner*. (E-7/14/59 p.2, c.3) On Thursday evening, September 1, 1859, at a fire department meeting he was appointed to a committee that was authorized to buy a new fire engine. (E-12/29/59 p.2, c.2) During 1859 he was assistant foreman of Hope Hook and Ladder Company Number 1. (E-12/29/59 p.2, c.3) On Thursday evening, September 6, 1860 he was again elected assistant foreman of Hope Hook and Ladder Company Number 1. During the renovations of Hope Hook and Ladder Company Number 1's fire house he and John McLain were painters. (E-9/13/60 p.2, c.2)

Pilson, James During 1859 he was Chairman pro tem of the Yonkers Light Guard. (E-10/27/59 p.3, c.5)

Platt, George On Monday night, December 17, 1860 he was installed as an officer into the Rising Star Lodge of Free and Accepted Masons as organist. (E-12/20/60 p.2, c.3)

Platt, Helen (Mrs.) On Wednesday, April 6, 1859, she died. She was 92 years old. (E-4/14/59 p.3, c.1)

Platt, Howard Jones On Tuesday night, March 23, 1858 he died from an overdose of strychnine which he used as a stimulant. He took deep sea soundings with lieutenant Berriman, and for the last half year he was an assistant editor of the *New York Evening Post*. He was the only son of Judge Zephaniah Platt. He was about 21 years old when he died. (E-3/25/58 p.2, c.3,4 and p.3, c.1)

Platt, Mary On probably May 20, 1859 she was married at the Presbyterian Church to Samuel J. Agnew. Zephaniah Platt of Yonkers was her father. (E-6/2/59 p.2, c.5)

Pollock, William On Wednesday, November 2, 1859, he won two boxes of cigars in a drawing at a target shooting contest at Weehawkan, New Jersey. He was a member of the Yonkers Hatters Guard. (E-11/3/59 p.2, c.6)

Polker, William On Wednesday, November 2, 1859, he won a gold pencil in a drawing at a target shooting contest at Weehawkan, New Jersey. He was a member of the Yonkers Hatters Guard. (E-11/3/59 p.2, c.6)

Post, David During 1853 he was a Commissioner of the Highways. (TRB)

Post, David A. During 1853 he was elected a Commissioner of the Highways. In 1854 and 1855 he was an Inspector of Elections for Election District Number One. In 1857 he was a Pound Master. (TRB)

Post, Harvey On Sunday evening August 9, 1857 he and ____ Bills had a harness stolen from their outbuilding. They lived just south of the village. (E-8/13/57 p.2, c,6) On Friday night, December 9, 1859 a valuable horse of his was stolen. (E-12/15/59 p.2, c.5) During 1853 he was a Pound Master. (TRB)

Post, Isaac In 1853 he was a Pound Master. (TRB) During 1860 he owned land on Kingsbridge Road south of Mill Road. (E-2/9/60 p.3, c.3) On the 1860 census he was a 45-year-old machinist with a personal estate of $2,000. His wife Nancy was a 35-year-old dressmaker. They had two sons and two daughters. John was 13 and Franklin was 7. Emily was 10 and Cora was 3. Also living in his household was Charles Reynolds who was a 50-year-old cabinetmaker from England and Lavinia Cook who was 75 years old and was from Massachusetts.

Post, J. A. During 1859 he had a furniture store on Dock Street. He sold Brother Jonathan's Patented Furniture Polish as well as Davis and Kidder's Electric Machines. (E-12/15/59 p.3, c.2) During the renovations of Hope Hook and Ladder Company Number One's fire house he supplied upholstery. (E-9/13/60 p.2, c.2)

Post, Lawrence On July 22, 1858 he signed a petition calling for a meeting of eligible voters in School District #2 to decide if the school district should become a Union Free School District. (E-8/5/58 p.4, c.3) On the 1860 census he was a 50-year-old master blacksmith with real estate property worth $5,000 and a personal estate of $1,500. His wife Marian was also 50 years old. Their daughter Sarah was 18 years old, and a Sarah Woods who was 83 years old also lived in their household. During 1857 he was the village Fire Warden. (AVD)

Post, Lawrence He owned a house in Mosholu, South Yonkers, near the store of Matthias Warner. On Tuesday, October 30, 1860 he auctioned off all the belongings in the house. (E-10/25/60 p.2, c.7)

Post, Lawrence Jr. During 1857 he was an auctioneer and lived on Mechanic Street. (E-2/19/57 p.5, c.3)

Post, Lawrence R. During March, 1859 he was selected to serve as a petit juror during the court session beginning Tuesday, March 18, 1859. (E-3/3/59 p.3, c.1)

Post, Mary Ann On Saturday, June 13, 1859, she died in South Yonkers from consumption at the age 18 years, 4 months, and 6 days. She was the youngest daughter of the late David Post. (E-6/30/59 p.3, c.1)

Post, Mary Matilda On Wednesday, September 16, 1857 she married Henry B. Archer. (E-9/17/57 p.2, c.7)

Post, William H. During 1857 and 1858 he was the Town Clerk. He served as village clerk from 1855 to 1860. (TRB and AVD) He owned the Broadway Book Store at #5 Wheeler Building. He advertised that his prices were competitive with those in NYC and implored people to "keep money in Yonkers." (E-1/29/57 p. 4, c.4) He later moved to a new building owned by A. B. Hoyt which was over the Nepperhan River between the Broadway House and Wheeler's building. (E-6/25/57 p.2, c.6) On October 15, 1857 his business was one of 33 businesses in Yonkers to announce they were closing their stores at 8 p.m. beginning on October 12, 1857 until March 27, 1858. (E-10/15/57 p.3, c.1) During 1857 he was District Clerk for School District Number 2. (E-11/26/57 p.2, c.7) On July 22, 1858 he signed a petition calling for a meeting of eligible voters in School District #2 to decide if the school district should become a Union Free School District. (E-8/5/58 p.4, c.3) He was nominated as Clerk for the first Village Charter election because people wanted to help him. Sometime before the nomination he had an accident which deprived him of the use of one of his hands. Consequently, he was not able to work at his trade. (E-3/3/59 p.2, c.2) During 1859 he expanded his business at 9 North Broadway to include fishing tackle. (E-6/9/59 p.3, c.3) On Friday evening, August 10, 1860, he was elected treasurer of the Yonkers Republican Wide Awakes. (E-8/16/60 p.2, c.6) On the 1860 census he is listed as a 27-year-old bookstore owner with $5,000 in real estate, and a personal estate of $300. His wife Sarah was 24 years old, and they had one child, Herbert, who was one year old.

Potter, John B. On November 19, 1860 at meeting of the village Board of Trustees he was appointed an assistant pound master. (E-12/6/60 p.2, c.4,7)

Powers, J. During 1860 he won a barrel of potatoes at a Yonkers Hatters Guard target shooting contest. (E-11/1/60 p.3, c.1)

Powers, Patrick On Wednesday, November 2, 1859, he won a cake basket in a target shooting contest at Weehawkan, New Jersey. He was a member of the Yonkers Hatters Guard. (E-11/3/59 p.2, c.6) During 1860 he won a cup at a Yonkers Hatters Guard target shooting contest. (E-11/1/60 p.3, c.1)

Proseus, E. Mrs. During 1857 she was a dressmaker with a shop in a new building one door north of the Baptist Church on North Broadway. (E-2/19/57 p.5, c.3)

Proseus, Joseph L. On Saturday, September 5, 1857 he was elected at a Republican primary meeting to be a delegate to the Republican First Assembly District convention. (E-9/10/57 p.2, c.6) On October 15, 1857 his business was one of 33 businesses in Yonkers to announce they were closing their stores at 8 p.m. beginning on October 12, 1857 until March 27, 1858. (E-10/15/57 p.3, c.1) On Monday, August 23, 1858 he was a delegate to the Westchester County Republican Party Convention at Durell's Hotel in Morrisania. (E-8/26/58 p.2, c.2) On Friday evening, September 17, 1858 he was elected temporary secretary of the Yonkers Republican Association. At the same meeting he was elected to the executive committee of the Yonkers Republican Association. (E-9/23/58 p.2, c.1) On Tuesday, November 16, 1858, he was elected a vice president of a Republican Party meeting in Yonkers. (E-11/18/58 p.2, c.2) On Thursday, August 13, 1859 he was elected to the executive committee of the newly formed Republican Association at a Republican Town meeting. He was also chosen at the same meeting to be a delegate to the Assembly District Convention. He was also chosen at the same meeting to be a delegate to the Republican County Convention. (E-10/20/59 p.3, c.1) On Tuesday evening, September 11, 1860 he was elected to the executive committee of the Yonkers Republican Association for a five-month term. (E-9/13/60 p.2, c.2) On Saturday, September 29, 1860 he was a delegate to the Republican First Assembly District Convention that was held in Morrisania Hall, Morrisania. (E-10/4/60 p.2, c.2) On October 29, 1860 he lost a pocketbook containing a large number of legal papers. His name was on the outside in felt letters, and he offered a $5 reward for its return. (E-11/1/60 p.3, c.2) On Monday night, December 17, 1860 he was installed as an officer into the Rising Star Lodge of Free and Accepted Masons as Steward. (E-12/20/60 p.2, c.3)

Pulver, John On December 28, 1853 a white and yellow spotted heifer entered his property. (TRB)

Pulver, William On Monday evening, May 23, 1859, he had a horse and a harness set stolen from his stable which was just north of the village. (E-5/26/59 p.2, c.4)

Purdy, Cornelius L. During 1855 he was a constable. In 1857 and again in 1860 he was an Inspector of Elections for Election District Number Two. (TRB)

Purdy, John M. On Wednesday morning, October 31, 1860, he died at 38 years, 9 months, and 13 days old. His funeral was held at St. Paul's Church in Eastchester on Friday, November 2, at 10 o'clock. (E-11/1/60 p.3, c.1)

Putnam, George Palmer During 1857 he was a member of the Lecture Committee of the Yonkers Lyceum. (E-2/5/57) In the early days of the Yonkers Library Association he received a life membership. (E-/3/12/57) Sometime during February of 1857 he donated 75 volumes to the library and supplied the library with the *Daily Times*. On March 2, 1857 he was elected President of the Yonkers Library Association. (E-3/5/57 p.2, c.6) He along with Jonathan W. Lester operated G. P. Putnam and Company in NYC. (E-3/5/57 p.3, c.4) Sometime during April of 1857 he donated an additional 40 volumes to the Library. (E-4/16/57 p.2, c.5) On Thursday, March 18, 1858 he read an essay written by a Yonkers schoolgirl before the Debating Society. He also retired on this date as the president of the Yonkers Library Association. (E-3/25/58 p.2, c.1) On Tuesday, April 13, 1858 he was formally thanked by the Yonkers Library Association for his valuable donation of engravings. (E-4/22/58 p.2, c.2) He was given an oak cane by F. J. Dreer. (E-6/23/59 p.3, c.1) See Who Was Who in America.

Quick, Stephen Francis During November, 1858 he was a member of the arrangement committee for the Second Annual Ball to benefit the widows and orphans of deceased Yonkers firemen. (E-11/25/58 p.2, c.7) During 1859 he and Nelson Ackert were practical builders and joiners at 3, 5, and 7 Atherton Street near Dock Street. (E-5/26/59 p.3, c.2) On Thursday evening, September 1, 1859 he was elected to the Finance Committee of Hope Hook and Ladder Company. (E-9/8/59 p.3, c.1) On Thursday evening, September 1, 1859, at a fire department meeting he was appointed by the committee that was authorized to buy a new fire engine to be a member of that committee. (E-12/29/59 p.2, c.2) On Monday evening March 26, 1860 he was elected one of thirty-two vice presidents of a Republican election rally meeting at the Getty House. (E-3/29/60 p.2, c.3)

Quinn, Hugh He lived at Glen Park and on Wednesday August 25, 1858 thieves took a wagon with a standing top. They were tracked to Mount Vernon at the railroad depot and then down 4th Avenue toward NYC. (E-9/2/58 p.2, c.6)

Radcliff, Julia E. On the morning of Thursday, June 3, 1858 she married Romeyn Bogardus who was from NYC. She was married in her father's house by Rev. V. M. Hulbert. (E-6/10/58 p.2, c.6)

Radcliff, P. E. During 1857 he owned the Peoples' Market which was a meat, fish, and produce market at #3 Wheeler Block. In the same year he brought James Schryver into business with him. (E-3/19/57 p.3, c.7 and E-7/9/57)

Radford, James On Monday evening, March 21, 1859, he read an essay before 400 members of the Yonkers Debating Society entitled "Benedict Arnold." (E-3/24/59 p.2, c.2) On the 1860 census he was listed as a 20-year-old [co]mmission dealer. His father was William Radford.

Radford, Thomas During 1858 he enlarged and renovated his house on the Post Road south of the village. The estimated cost was $5,000. (E-1/20/59 p.2, c.4) He is listed on the 1860 census as a 39-year-old gentleman with $10,000 in real estate, and a personal estate of $3,500. His wife Adelia was 37 years old, and they had nine children; Fanny who was 17, H[ilder] who was 16, A[dalane] who was 14, Thomas who was 12, Antoinette who was 10, Emma who was 8, Lizzie who was 5, Lewis who was 2, and William who was 1 month old. During 1860 he was a town Assessor. (TRB)

Radford, William During 1857 he ran a steamboat company that sailed between Yonkers and NYC. (E-2/19/57 p.2, c.7) Also during 1857 he was building two new buildings near the Broadway bridge. One of the buildings was to be occupied by William H. Sleight and Company. (E-7/2/57 p.2, c.5) On Tuesday, September 1, 1857 he was elected as a James Buchanan delegate to the County Democratic Convention to be held at West Farms on September 2, 1857. (E-9/3/57 p.2, c.7) The buildings he erected were built on a lot he bought from Thomas O. Farrington for about $5,000. The lot he purchased was directly alongside a lot he already owned. The buildings were brick and four stories high with a Philadelphia brick front. The second building was occupied by the dry goods store of Vail and Elting. The two buildings cost about $14,000. George Gilroy did the painting and Thomas C. Cornell was the architect. (E-12/31/57 p.2, c.2) During the early part of 1858 he owned land between Locust Street and Ashburton Avenue along a line that eventually became Woodworth Avenue. (E-1/7/58 p. 2, c.5) On Wednesday, June 30, 1857 he bought a lot on Washington Street for $870. He bought another lot on the same day on St. Mary's Street for $1,140. (E-7/1/58 p.2, c.2) On July 22, 1858 he signed a petition calling for a meeting of eligible voters in School District #2 to decide if the school district should become a Union Free School District. (E-8/5/58 p.4, c.3) During October, 1857 he began work on a new building over the Nepperhan Creek. The building was 52 feet by 50 feet and was three stories high. (E-11/4/58 p.2, c.1) The estimated cost was $6,000. (E-1/20/59 p.2, c.4) His steamboat line had at least two boats; the *Broadway* and the *Metamora*. He was also building a new steamer the *Daniel Drew*. (E-2/2/60 p.2, c.4) He was a member of the Wood wing of the Democratic Party, and on Monday, January 30, 1860 he was chosen by a convention at Tarrytown to be a delegate to a convention in Charleston. (E-2/2/60 p.2, c.5) On Monday morning, April 16, 1860, at about a quarter past three, a fire in the basement filled his entire house with smoke. The fire was put out and the house was saved, but damaged. The family escaped the smoke by means of ladders from the second story windows. (E-4/19/60 p.2, c.4) On Tuesday, October 9, 1860 he chaired a school board meeting. (E-10/11/60 p.2, c.3) On the 1860 census he is listed as a 47-year-old gentleman with $50,000 worth of real estate and a personal estate of $10,000. On page 101 of the 1860 census he is listed again as a 47-year-old gentleman. However, this time his real estate holdings were worth $75,000. His children were James R. who was a 20-year-old merchant, Edward who was 16, George who was a 17-year-old clerk, Alfred who was 9, and Ann who was 19. A Mrs. Sherman who was 71 years old also lived in his household. He was the first village president and he served in that capacity from 1855 through 1856 and into 1857.

Raillie, William During 1857 he was a gardener and had a new brick house on Spring Street. (E-4/23/57 p.2, c.7)

Raisbeck, Samuel M. On Tuesday, December 4, 1860, he was married by Rev. Carter to Ann D. Odell in her father's house. (E-12/6/60 p.2, c.6)

Read, Benjamin During 1856 he was a Pound Master for the town. (TRB)

Read, Jacob During 1857 he was a Trustee for the school in the village school district. (E-4/23/57 p.2, c.6) On March 2, 1857 he was an Inspector for the Village Election. In 1858 he was a Trustee for School District Number 2. (E-2/4/58 p.3, c.1) During November, 1858 he was a member of the arrangement committee for the Second Annual Ball to benefit the widows and orphans of deceased Yonkers firemen. (E-11/25/58 p.2, c.7) During 1858 he enlarged and improved his residence on Guion Street. The project cost him about $1,800. (E-1/20/59 p.2, c.3) On February 15, 1859 he, John Nairn, and Alonzo P. Speedling bought the lumber and coal business of Henry W. Bashford. (E-4/7/59 p.2, c.3) On the 1860 census he is listed as a 42-year-old owner of a lumber yard with $6,500 in real estate and a personal estate of $2,000. His wife Catherine was 36 years old, and they had six children; Amanda who was 13, George who was 11, Leonard who was 9, Sarah who was 7, David who was 5, and Elizabeth who was 9 months old. Their servant was Mary

Kelley who was 22 years old and was from Ireland. In 1853, 1856, and 1857 he was Commissioner of the Highways. During 1855 he was a member of the village Board of Trustees. (TRB) During this period of time he was also a road construction contractor.

Read, Oliver On Wednesday, June 22, 1859, he died of palsy. He was 77 years old. (E-6/30/59 p.3, c.1 also see Vol. 1 for Oliver Rhead.)

Reevs, G. P. (M.D.) During the latter part of 1857 he bought the drug store owned by J. T. Huestis on the corner of Dock Street and Warburton Avenue. (E-12/31/57 p.4, c.7) During 1860 he advertised as J. P. Reevs at the same location. (E-1/19/60 p.3, c.1) On the 1860 census his name was spelled Reeves. On the census he is listed as a 40-year-old druggist with $4,000 in real estate, and a personal estate of $2,000. His wife Mary was 38 years old, and they had three children; Robert who was 10, Mary who was 4, and Bertram who was 2. They had a 28-year-old Irish female servant, and a William Steph[sin] also lived in their household.

Reinfelder, Maximillian J. (MD) During 1860 he lived at Madam Migy's seminary opposite the Baptist Church. (E-12/20/60 p.2, c.7 also Vol. 1 p.67) On the 1860 census he is listed as a 40-year-old surgeon. His wife, R., was 35 years old, and they had one child, Susan, who was 3 years old. They also had a 17-year-old servant by the name of Jane. All four people were born in Germany.

Reynolds, George J. During December, 1860 he was a member of a committee that was organized to run the second annual ball of Neptune Engine Company Number 3 that was to be held at the Getty Lyceum on January 24, 1861. (E-12/13/60 p.2, c.7)

Reynolds, Nathaniel On Friday evening, September 17, 1858 he was elected one of six vice presidents of the Yonkers Republican Association. (E-9/23/58 p.2, c.1) During 1857 and 1858 he was an Inspector of Elections for Election District Number Three. (TRB)

Rhodes, Joseph During 1857 he owned a cleaning store on Mechanic Street next to Bashford's carriage factory. He cleaned, dyed, steam pressed, and repaired clothing. (E-6/18/57 p.3, c.3)

Rich, Caroline, M. (Miss) She was the daughter of Josiah Rich. On Monday, December 27, 1858 she married Herbert Wight who was from Milwaukee, Wisconsin. (E-12/30/58 p.2 c.5)

Rich, Josiah During 1857 he was a member of the Lecture Committee of the Yonkers Lyceum. (E-2/5/57) On March 2, 1857 he was elected a manager of the Yonkers Library Association. (E-3/5/57 p.2, c.6) During the early days of the library he received a life membership. (E-3/12/57 p.2, c.6) During 1857 he was a real estate broker. (E-6/18/57 p.3, c.7) During July and August of 1857, he wrote a series of interesting letters to the editor of the *Examiner* arguing with John Copcutt over Main Street. In one letter he noted that he came to Yonkers in 1847 to buy land. (E-7/2/57 p.2, c.4) On July 16, 1857 he advertised that he had about 150 lots to sell on

Wells Avenue, Warburton Avenue, Woodbine Street, River Street, Main Street, Depot Street, Hudson Street, Nepperhan Street, Market Place, Buena Vista Avenue, Prospect Street, Broadway, Jefferson Street, Adams Street, Clinton Street, Washington Street, and Grinnell Street. (E-7/16/57 p.4, c.3) He was a Director of the Yonkers Gas Light Company. (E-8/13/57 p.3, c.3) He was a past NYC Alderman and President of the first railroad company to build a railroad between NYC and Albany. (E-8/20/57 p.2, c.6) On Wednesday, July 29, 1857 he was again elected a director of the gas company. (E-8/27/57 p.3, c.5) On June 30, 1858 he sold 14 lots at auction. He made about $14,140 from the auction. (E-7/1/58 p.2, c.2) On Wednesday evening, August 18, 1858 he was elected a trustee for School District #2. (E-8/26/58 p.2, c.4) On Friday evening, September 17, 1858 he was elected to the executive committee of the Yonkers Republican Association. (E-9/23/58 p.2, c.1) His son Josiah, Jr. married Effie Tallman, the oldest daughter of John F. Tallman, on Thursday, July 7, 1859. They were married in the Church of St. John the Evangelist in NYC and they were from NYC. (E-7/14/59 p.2, c.6) During 1859 he was the Lecture Committee chairman for lectures given at Westminster Church on Warburton Avenue. (E-12/22/59 p.2, c.6) During 1860 he was again a trustee for school district #2. (E-8/9/60 p.3, c.1)

Rich, Robert F. On Tuesday, August 16, 1859, his son Robert O. Rich died at the age of 7 months and 11 days. (E-9/1/59 p.3, c.1) On Wednesday evening, December 21, 1859, he was elected Assistant Foreman of Hope Hook and Ladder Company. (E-12/22/59 p.2, c.6) Also, during 1859 he was assistant chief engineer of the Yonkers Fire Department. (E-12/29/59 p.2, c.2) On Monday night, December 17, 1860 he was installed as an officer into the Rising Star Lodge of Free and Accepted Masons as S.D. (E-12/20/60 p.2, c.3)

Richmond, Daniel During 1857 he and William White owned a grocery store. (E-5/28/57 p.2, c.2)

Riker, Anthony During 1857 he was a Trustee of the African Methodist Episcopal Zion Church. He was one of the owners of Rikers' Express which was a stage line that ran between Yonkers and NYC. (E-2/5/57) Sometime before April 23, 1857 they moved their office to 1 Manor Place. During the summer the stage left 1 Manor Place at 8 a.m. and drove to the paper warehouse of Sands, Paradise and Company at 15 Spruce Street, NYC. It left NYC at 3 p.m.. (E-4/23/57 p.2, c.2)

Riker, C. A. During 1860, and for sometime prior to that, he and N. S. Riker operated the Yonkers Express. On November 21, 1860 the partnership was dissolved, and he continued in the business with a new partner Oscar Riker. (E-12/6/60 p.3, c.1)

Riker, Joseph During 1857 he was a Trustee of the African Methodist Episcopal Zion Church. (E-2/5/57)

Riker, N. E. During 1857 he/she ran a confectionery and toy store at 1 Manor Place. (E-4/23/57 p.2, c.7)

Riker, Noah S. He occupied a tenement building next to the very old snuff mill, but evidently did not live there. On Tuesday morning, March 29, 1859, the mill caught fire and burned to the ground. The only thing left was the large water wheel. His tenement building also caught fire, but the fire department was able to put it out with some damage to the building. Both buildings were owned by John Copcutt. Both buildings were very old and were going to be pulled down anyhow to be replaced by other buildings. Arson was suspected since both buildings were not occupied by people. (E-3/31/59 p.2, c.2) During 1860, and for sometime prior to that, he and C. A. Riker operated the Yonkers Express. On November 21, 1860 the partnership was dissolved, and he left the business. (E-12/6/60 p.3, c.1) On the 1860 census he is listed as a 54-year-old in the express business with a personal estate of $375. His wife Martha was 51 years old, and they had four children; Oscar who was 20, Mary who was 17, Edgar who was 15, and Anna who was 10 years old.

Riker, Oscar On November 21, 1860 he became a partner with C. A. Riker in the Yonkers Express. (E-12/6/60 p.3, c.1)

Riley, E. During 1860 he won a vest at a Yonkers Hatters Guard target shooting contest. (E-11/1/60 p.3, c.1)

Riley, John On Wednesday, November 2, 1859, he won a gold ring in a drawing at a target shooting contest at Weehawkan, New Jersey. He was a member of the Yonkers Hatters Guard. (E-11/3/59 p.2, c.6) During 1860 he won $25 at a Yonkers Hatters Guard target shooting contest. (E-11/1/60 p.3, c.1)

Ritter, Lewis During 1860 he was a gardener selling grape vines and asparagus roots on the corner of Ashburton Avenue and Vineyard Avenue. (E-3/29/60 p.3, c.6)

Robbins, E. He owned a shoe store and its goods were auctioned off March 8, 1860. (E-3/8/60 p.2, c.7)

Robbins, J. During 1857 he donated $25 to the Yonkers Library Association and became a life member. (E-3/12/57 p.2, c.5) During 1859 he built a brick house west of his residence on Broadway that cost about $12,000. (E-1/12/60 p.2, c.1)

Robinson, A. (Dr.) During the latter part of 1858 he signed a petition to have a meeting of the taxpayers in School District #2 meet to reconsider the location of two new schools; one on the corner of Wood Place and Warburton Avenue, and the other on St. Mary's Street near the Catholic Church and school. (E-12/23/58 p.2, c.3) On Thursday morning, March 24, 1859 a building of his worth about $1,000 burned to the ground. (E-3/31/59 p.2, c.2)

Robinson, Ellen On Sunday, December 27, 1857 she married William Griffin. The marriage ceremony was performed by Rev. Tripp. (E-1/7/58 p.2, c.6)

Robinson, Solon During 1859 he moved to Yonkers just west of Hunt's Bridge. He was with the *New York Tribune*. (E-4/14/59 p.2, c.6)

Rockwell, Edgar During 1859 he was the sales agent in Yonkers for the book *Pillar of Fire, or Israel in Bondage*, by Rev. J. H. Ingraham. (E-4/28/59 p.2, c.6)

Rockwell, George On Monday, September 3, 1860 his daughter Francena died at the age of 24 years, 1 month and 14 days. (E-9/6/60 p.2, c.7) He is listed on the 1860 census as a 50-year-old lumber dealer with $7,000 in real estate, and a personal estate of $1,000. His wife Sarah was 52 years old, and they had four children; Frances who was 23, Maria who was 19, Hannah who was 16, and William who was 13. The Francena above is probably the Frances on the census. Her name was misspelled on one of them most likely on the census.

Rockwell, J. W. On Monday, October 12, 1857 he was a delegate to the Republican First Assembly District Convention. (E-10/15/57 p.2, c.2)

Rockwell, Samuel D. During 1857 he owned the Yonkers Jewelry Store opposite the Getty House. At one time he had a store at 110 Cherry Street, NYC. However, business was good enough in Yonkers to move. (E-1/29/57 p.4, c.4) During 1857 he was the Secretary of the Yonkers Savings Bank. (E-4/9/57 p.2, c.7) He was also an Inspector for an election of the Yonkers Gas Light Company. (E-8/13/57 p.3 c.3) On Monday, October 12, 1857 he was a delegate to the Republican First Assembly District Convention. (E-10/15/57 p.2, c.3) On October 15, 1857 his business was one of 33 businesses in Yonkers to announce they were closing their stores at 8 p.m. beginning on October 12, 1857 until March 27, 1858. (E-10/15/57 p.3, c.1) During April, 1858 he moved his store to the new building on the corner of Broadway and Main Street. (E-4/22/58 p.2, c.4) Also during April, 1858 he was an insurance agent for the Niagara Fire Insurance Company. (E-4/22/58 p.3, c.3) It seems that he had a hard time holding onto things. On Monday, June 14, 1858 he lost a leather case containing a gold bracelet and other jewelry either in the village or along Saw Mill River Road. Then on Sunday, June 20, 1858 he lost, somewhere on Broadway between the Presbyterian Church and Mr. Morgan's house, a black leather double seat cushion, a blue kersey horse blanket, and a driving whip. Early in 1857 and during 1858 he lost some other personal articles. (E-6/24/58 p.3, c.3) During 1858 he was a member of the Finance Committee and secretary of the Yonkers Savings Bank. (E-7/1/58 p.3, c.6) On Monday, August 23, 1858 he was a delegate to the Westchester County Republican Party Convention at Durell's Hotel in Morrisania. (E-8/26/58 p.2, c.2) On March 22, 1859 he was elected an Inspector of Election for next year's board of directors election for the Bank of Yonkers. (E-4/7/59 p.2, c.5) During 1859 he sold his jewelry store to Charles W. Starr who had been his assistant. (E-5/5/59 p.2, c.7) On June 28, 1859 he signed a letter addressed to Frederick A. Coe asking legal advice concerning a written promise of the Hudson River Railroad Company to construct a carriageway across the Nepperhan River near the draw bridge. (E-7/7/59 p.2, c.4) On Thursday morning, January 19, 1860, he was foreman of a coroner's jury to look into the death of Mrs. Field who died in a railroad accident at Tarrytown. He was listed as a bank clerk. (E-1/26/60 p.2, c.5 see Foster Jenkins for more details) On Thursday evening, October 25, 1860, he was one of twenty-two vice presidents at a Republican campaign meeting. (E-11/1/60 p.2, c.2) On the 1860 census he is listed as a 50-year-old clerk with $14,000 in real estate and a personal estate of $2,000. His wife O. J. was also 50 years old. Apparently John Rockwell was his father and he was 72 years old, and living in his son's home. They had two children; F. E. who was a 17-year-old female, and J. F. who was a 14-year-old male. Kate Wise who was 24 years old and from Ireland was their servant. During 1857 he was appointed by the village Board of Trustees an Inspector of Elections for Election District Number One to replace Ethan Flagg who had resigned. On May 5, 1859 he was appointed Village Assessor. (AVD)

Rogers, Albert On June 6, 1857 he married Rosetta Fisher at the Presbyterian Church. (E-6/18/57 p.3, c.1) On Tuesday, May 3, 1860 he died at the age of 27 years, 11 months, and 10 days. (E-5/10/60 p.2, c.6)

Rollins, Gustavus A. In the early days of the Yonkers Library Association he received a life membership. (E-3/12/57 p.2, c.5) He owned land that adjoined land of John Crisfield. (E-3/458 p.3, c.5) He is listed on the 1860 census as a 45-year-old broker with $1,000 in real estate, and a personal estate of $2,500. His wife was 43 years old, and they had three children; Helen who was 20, Edward who was 15, Isabella who was 11. Also, an Ellen Condon was in their household. She was 12 years old. He was born in Maine, and everyone else was born in New York. He had a servant and a gardener who were both from Ireland.

Roome, Samuel During 1857 he was a Second Sergeant at the Yonkers Collegiate Institute. (E-8/13/57 p.2, c.3)

Roonan, Patrick (Also spelled Rohan) During 1857 he applied for a grocery store license and probably was not granted one. (E-5/28/57 p.2, c.2 and E-6/4/57 p.2, c.3,4)

Roonan, William During 1858 he worked on the docks. On Thursday, September 2, 1858 after lunch he lay down underneath a railroad car in the shade to take a nap. A locomotive arrived from the city, hooked the car up, and drove over him. His left leg was broken near the thigh and again below the knee. The toes of his right foot were severed and his right hand completely crushed. He was taken into the baggage car and was attended to by Dr. Arnold, and he was given last rites by Father Lynch of St. Mary's Church. On the afternoon train he was taken to NYC and was put in the city hospital. He died Tuesday morning September 7, 1857. (E-9/9/58 pp.2,3 c.7,1)

Rooney, M. W. On October 15, 1857 his business was one of 33 businesses in Yonkers to announce they were closing their stores at 8 p.m. beginning on October 12, 1857 until March 27, 1858. (E-10/15/57 p.3, c.1) During April, 1858 he moved his millinery and dressmaking store to the store once occupied by Samuel D. Rockwell. (E-4/29/58 p.2, c.6)

Rooney, Mrs. During 1857 she owned a Fancy store. On Tuesday August 18, 1857 her store was broken into. An estimate made by her suggested that more $4,000 in goods were stolen. (E-8/20/57 p.2, c.7)

Ropes, William B. During 1860 he opened a medical practice at his house on Broadway opposite the Getty House. He was a surgeon and homeopathic physician. (E-10/11/60 p.2, c.7)

Rose, Levi P. During 1853 he owned a barley and flour mill on Mill Street. During June of the same year it burned down and this incident prompted the development of the fire department. (E-12/29/59 p., c.2) During 1857 he was summoned to be a juror at the Court of General Session at White Plains. (E-5/25/57 p.2, c.6) On February 3, 1858 his 18-day-old daughter Fanny M. died. His wife was Annie. (E-2/4/58 p.3, c.1) On the 1860 census he is listed as a 34-year-old merchant with $20,000 in real estate, and a personal estate of $3,500. His wife Ann was 23 years old, and they had two children; Park who was 8, and Hamilton who was 1. They had a 17-year-old coachman by the name of John Coffee.

Rost, Nicholas During 1857 he was a tavern owner. He applied for a hotel license and was evidently turned down. (E-5/28/57 p.2, c.2) However, on July 6, 1857 he was granted the license. (E-7/23/57 p.2, c.4) He applied for a hotel license in 1858. (E-6/3/58 p.2, c.5) During 1859 he was granted another hotel license. (E-8/11/59 p.2, c.7) During 1860 he received another hotel license. (E-7/26/60 p.2, c.6) During December, 1860 he was a member of a committee that was organized to run the second annual ball of Neptune Engine Company Number 3 that was to be held at the Getty Lyceum on January 24, 1861. (E-12/13/60 p.2, c.7)

Rowe, Matthew F. He was the publisher of the *Yonkers Examiner*. During 1857 he was secretary of the Yonkers Republican Association. (E-9/3/57 p.2, c.6) On Tuesday, September 8, 1857 he was appointed secretary of the First Assembly District Republican Convention. (E-9/10/57 p.2, c.5) On July 22, 1858 he signed a petition calling for a meeting of eligible voters in School District #2 to decide if the school district should become a Union Free School District. (E-8/5/58 p.4, c.3) On Monday, August 23, 1858 he was a delegate to the Westchester County Republican Party Convention at Durell's Hotel in Morrisania. (E-8/26/58 p.2, c.2) On Tuesday, November 16, 1858, he was elected a secretary of a Republican Party meeting in Yonkers. (E-11/18/58 p.2, c.2) On Monday evening March 26, 1860 he was elected one of several secretaries of a Republican election rally meeting at the Getty House. (E-3/29/60 p.2, c.3) On Saturday, August 11, 1860 he was elected secretary of a Republican First Assembly District convention. (E-8/16/60 p.2, c.3) During the Republican First Assembly District Convention held on Saturday, September 29, 1860 in Morrisania Hall, Morrisania he was a delegate and he was appointed one of two secretaries. (E-10/4/60 p.2, c.2) On Thursday evening, October 25, 1860, he was one of eight secretaries at a Republican campaign meeting. (E-11/1/60 p.2, c.2) On the 1860 census he is listed as a 30-year-old editor who lived in the household of William Montgomery. He was born in Pennsylvania.

Russell, George During 1857 he owned a factory. (AVD #19) During 1860 he and his wife Lydia owned property on Broadway near Guion Street. George Gaylor sued them for the property. (E-3/29/60 p.2, c.6) On Thursday evening, October 25, 1860, he was one of twenty-two vice presidents at a Republican campaign meeting. (E-11/1/60 p.2, c.2)

Ruttman, Ferdinand During the latter part of 1858 he signed a petition to have a meeting of the taxpayers in School District #2 meet to reconsider the location of two new schools; one on the corner of Wood Place and Warburton Avenue, and the other on St. Mary's Street near the Catholic Church and school. (E-12/23/58 p.2, c.3)

Ryan, Dennis On Wednesday, November 2, 1859, he won a goblet in a target shooting contest at Weehawkan, New Jersey. He was a member of the Yonkers Hatters Guard. (E-11/3/59 p.2, c.6) During 1860 he won a picture at a Yonkers Hatters Guard target shooting contest. (E-11/1/60 p.3, c.1)

Ryan, Edward During 1859 he was an Orderly Sergeant in the Yonkers Hatters Guard. On Wednesday, November 2, 1859 he went with the guard to Weehawken, New Jersey where the guard was involved in a shooting contest amongst themselves. At the target shooting contest he won a $5 gold piece. (E-11/3/59 p.3, c.6) During 1860 he was again elected Orderly Sergeant of the Yonkers Hatters Guard. (E-10/18/60 p.2, c.5) During 1860 he won a clock at a Yonkers Hatters Guard target shooting contest. (E-11/1/60 p.3, c.1)

Ryan, John During 1860 he won a cup at a Yonkers Hatters Guard target shooting contest. (E-11/1/60 p.3, c.1)

Ryan, Patrick During 1859 he built a wood-frame house and store on Jefferson Street that cost about $800. (E-1/12/60 p.2, c.1)

Ryan, Philip On Wednesday, November 2, 1859, he won in a drawing a hat at a target shooting contest at Weehawkan, New Jersey. He was a member of the Yonkers Hatters Guard. (E-11/3/59 p.2, c.6) During 1860 he won a thermometer at a Yonkers Hatters Guard target shooting contest. (E-11/1/60 p.3, c.1)

Ryan, Thomas During 1857 he lived on the flats probably on Main Street above and south of the Nepperhan River. On Friday, December 4, 1857 four warrants were issued against him, and given to officer Smith. When the officer went to his residence Ryan said he would shoot anyone who entered. Smith broke down the door and discovered that Ryan went out a back window and was running down Riverdale Avenue. On Monday, December 7, 1857 Ryan's family left for New York City and they were followed by Smith. When Mrs. Ryan went into a residence the officer went into a porterhouse opposite the residence and sat on a barrel and waited about four hours for Ryan to come. When Ryan did show up Smith went to the residence and was told by Mrs. Ryan that Thomas was not in. Smith didn't believe her and entered the house. He found Ryan sitting on a couch and a struggle, which was won by Smith, ensued. Ryan was taken to Yonkers where he apparently paid his back rent. The newspaper said that Ryan had spent time in the state prison for mail robbery. (E-12/10/57 p.2, c.7)

Ryer, Edwin B. During May, 1860 he was called on to serve on the petit jury. (E-5/31/60 p.3, c.3)

Ryer, W. C. On Wednesday, November 2, 1859, he won a barrel of flour in a target shooting contest at Weehawkan, New Jersey. He was a member of the Yonkers Hatters Guard. (E-11/3/59 p.2, c.6) During 1860 he won a hat at a Yonkers Hatters Guard target shooting contest. (E-11/1/60 p.3, c.1)

Sanders, James P. During April, 1860 he moved from the town of Westchester to Yonkers where he opened a law office in the Farrington Building. Before he went to Westchester he lived in Peekskill. (E-4/19/60 p.2, c.4) He lived in the Getty House. (E-5/10/60 p.4, c.3)

Sandford, Thomas During December, 1859, his wife was on the arrangement committee to give a benefit for their pastor John Taylor. The guest speaker was the Rev. Henry Highland Garnett, pastor of the Shiloh Presbyterian Church in NYC. Admission was 50 cents and the proceeds went to Rev. Taylor. He was also on the committee. (E-12/8/59 p.3, c.2)

Sarony, During 1858 he built a wood-frame house on the upper part of Palisade Avenue for about $3,000. (E-4/22/58 p.2, c.3)

Sawyer, Rollin A. (Rev.) He preached every Sunday at 10:30 a.m. and again at 7:30 p.m. at the Getty Lyceum. (E-10/15/57 p.3, c.1 and 1/28/58 p.2, c.6) He became the pastor of the Westminster Church on Warburton Avenue. (E-9/1/59 p.3, c.1) On the 1860 census he is listed as a 30-year-old clergyman. His wife Martha was also 30 years old, and they had two children; [Jessa] who was 2, and Lucy who was 2 months old. He also had a servant.

Saxton, Marcus, L. During 1857 he was a First Sergeant at the Yonkers Collegiate Institute. (E-8/13/57 p.2, c.3)

Schaeffer, John On Wednesday, November 2, 1859, he won a coffee pot in a target shooting contest at Weehawkan, New Jersey.

He was a member of the Yonkers Hatters Guard. At the same target shooting contest he also won $3. (E-11/3/59 p.2, c.6) During 1860 he won $2.50 at a Yonkers Hatters Guard target shooting contest. (E-11/1/60 p.3, c.1)

Schemerhorn, Abram During the 1850s he owned land on Riverdale Avenue. Apparently he died sometime during 1859 or January, 1860. (E-1/19/60 p.3, c.2)

Schenck, Abram During 1857 he was a Third Sergeant at the Yonkers Collegiate Institute. (E-8/13/57 p.2, c.3)

Schmozart, Frances She advertised during 1859 as a monthly nurse who was trained at the New York Infirmary. She gave Dr. Arnold as a reference. (E-2/10/59 p.3, c.3)

Schott, George Peter On Thursday afternoon, April 28, 1859, his friends met at the Getty House to honor him. (E-4/28/59 p.2, c.6)

Schryver, James During 1857 he may have been part-owner of the People's Market. (E-2/19/57 p.4, c.4)

Schultz, Howard T. On Tuesday, April 26, 1859 he was married by Rev. D. M. Seward to Caroline A. E. Woolcocks. (E-6/2/59 p.2, c.5)

Scoberk, A. J. During 1857 he added to his residence and improved his grounds all of which cost at least $8,000. (E-12/31/57 p.2, c.3)

Scott, J. R. (Rev.) During July, 1858 he became the pastor of the Baptist Church. Prior to this he was the pastor of the First Baptist Church in Rochester. (E-7/29/58 p.2, c.5) During September, 1860 he resigned as pastor because of illness. (E-9/13/60 p.2, c.5) On the 1860 census he is listed as a 44-year-old Baptist Minister who had $8,000 in real estate, and a personal estate of $1,000. He and his wife Catherine, who was 34 years old, were born in Massachusetts. They had four children, three of which were born in Massachusetts, while the infant was born in Yonkers. The children were Schuyler who was 12, Charles who was 4, George who was 2, and Ann who was 10 months old. Mary Turner who was 23 years old was their servant. Another J. R. Scott is also listed on the census with some differences. He had no real estate, but he had a personal estate of $1,000. All the names are initials, but his wife was 35 years old, and they had four children. The ages of the children were; 11, 5, 3, and 1. Two of the children were born in Massachusetts, and the youngest two were born in New York. They also had a cook and a nurse.

Scribner, G. Hilton During or just prior to 1859, he owned land along Woodbine Street which ran northerly from Wells Avenue to Locust Street, and it was the first street west of Warburton Avenue. Later the street became a section of Woodworth Avenue. (E-4/14/59 p.3, c.6)

Scrugham, William, W. (General) In 1857 he was a Democrat. (E-4/16/57 p.2, c.1) During 1857 he was Secretary, Treasurer, and a Director of the Yonkers Gas Light Company. (E-4/16/57 p.2, c.1)

On Wednesday, July 29, 1857 he was again elected a director of the gas company, and at a later meeting he was once again elected secretary of the company. At the same meeting he was also elected an Inspector of Elections for the next year. (E-8/27/57 p.3, c.5) On Tuesday, October 6, 1857 he was appointed a delegate to attend the Democratic County Convention. (E-10/8/57 p.2, c.) During 1858 he was a member of the Finance Committee of the Yonkers Savings Bank. (E-7/1/58 p.3, c.6) During August, 1858 he was very sick with a high fever and for a while was in critical condition. (E-8/12/58 p.2, c.3) Also during 1858 he was a candidate for the Democratic nomination for Congress. At the Democratic convention held in Nyack on Friday, October 8, 1858 on the first ballot he received 20 of forty votes cast for the nomination. William Radford, also from Yonkers received 2 votes and Gouverneur Kemble of Phillipstown received 18 votes. A clear majority was needed and on a subsequent ballot Kemble received the nomination. (E-10/14/58 p.2, c.2) During 1858 he was building a brick house on the Hudson River in the lower part of the village. The house was estimated to cost $12,000. (E-1/20/59 p.2, c.4) On Wednesday, February 23, 1859 he married (Mary) Kellinger. (E-2/24/59 p.2, c.1) On October 12, 1859 he was nominated to run for the Second Judicial District New York State Supreme Court by a Democratic Convention held in the Supreme Court Chambers in Brooklyn. The district comprised the counties of Kings, Queens, Suffolk, Richmond, Westchester, Putnam, Orange, Dutchess, and Rockland. He informed the convention that if elected he would move to Brooklyn because the pressure of the Court demanded it. (E-10/13/59 p.2, c.3) During November, 1859 he was elected to the New York State Supreme Court by a vote of 18,320 to 16,233. He won Westchester County by 6,608 to 4,807. (E-11/24/59 p.2, c.3) On Friday, May 4, 1860, he was elected one of ten members of the executive committee of the newly formed Yonkers Horticultural Society. (E-5/17/60 p.3, c.3) He is listed on the 1860 census as a 40-year-old judge with $15,000 in real estate, and a personal estate of $5,000. His wife Mary was 24 years old. He had a 4-month-old son, William, and three Irish servants. During 1856 and 1857 he was the Town Supervisor. (TRB)

Scrymser, James Prior to 1859 he lived on Buena Vista Avenue. (E-3/3/59 p.2, c.2)

Seeley, Lyman On Wednesday, August 26, 1857 he found a grey horse attached to a vegetable wagon in the village. He owned a livery stable on Mechanic Street. (E-8/27/57 p.3, c.1) On the 1860 census he is listed as a 64-year-old livery stable owner with a personal estate of $3,000. His wife Emaline was 54 years old and they had eight children; Julia who was 26, Anna who was 23, Matilda who was 21, Emaline who was 16, Jane who was 14, Henry who was 25, Charles who was 22, and James who was 20 years old.

Seeley, Aaron M. During 1857 he was notified to serve on the petit jury at White Plains. (E-8/27/57 p.2, c.4) During 1860 he was selected to serve as a grand juror in the Court of Sessions that sat Monday, March 12, 1860. (E-3/8/60 p.2, c.5)

Serister, L. During 1860 he won a cup at a Yonkers Hatters Guard target shooting contest. (E-11/1/60 p.3, c.1)

Serymser, James During the early days of the Yonkers Library Association he received a lifetime membership. (E-3/12/57 p.2, c.5)

Seward, Dwight M. (Rev.) During 1857 he was pastor of the Presbyterian Church. (E-4/9/57 p.2, c.4) On Tuesday, August 17, 1858 he and sixteen other men wrote C. Jerome Hopkins a letter requesting him to give another piano concert at the Getty House. (E-8/19/58 p.2, c.4)

Seward, Frederick D. On Sunday, May 8, 1859, he died at the age of 22. (E-5/12/59 p.2, c.6) He was born Monday, May 29, 1837, in Middletown, Connecticut. His maternal grandfather lived there and was the pastor of the First Congregational Church. His father, Rev. Dwight M. Seward, was pastor of the Congregational Church in New Britain, and in 1845 the family moved to West Hartford. They then moved to Yonkers in 1851. In September, 1853, at the age of 16, he was admitted to Hamilton College. After his freshman year he accepted a position as an assistant teacher at the College Grammar School of Brooklyn. As a seventeen-year-old teacher some of his students were older than he was. During 1855 he went back to college as a sophomore. As a sophomore he wrote *Slave Life as Described by Homer*, as a junior he wrote a *Comparison of Aeschylus and Shelley*, and as a senior he wrote the *Effect of Mechanical Inventions on Intellectual Culture*. Also as a senior he won a writing award for his *Unconscious Influence*. During July, 1858 he became a member of the Presbyterian Church in Yonkers, and on July 22, 1858, after he graduated from college, he returned as a teacher at the College Grammar School in Brooklyn. In March of 1859 he left the college due to severe pain assumed to be caused by rheumatism, and returned to Yonkers. He was only supposed to be away from the college for a few days, but apparently he developed pneumonia and died. (E-8/11/59 p.2, c.3,4)

Sewell, Robert During the latter part of 1858 he signed a petition to have a meeting of the taxpayers in School District #2 meet to reconsider the location of two new schools; one on the corner of Wood Place and Warburton Avenue, and the other on St. Mary's Street near the Catholic Church and school. (E-12/23/58 p.2, c.3)

Seymour, Silas (Hon.) On Wednesday, July 6, 1859, while on his way to the Piermont boat he was knocked down and severely injured by a horse as he was crossing Washington Street. The horse was harnessed to a light wagon which broke its shaft. The shaft hit him in the eye. He lost quite a bit of blood and was in pain, but he made it to the boat and arrived safely at his residence in Piermont. (E-7/14/59 p.2, c.6)

Seymour, William N. During the early days of the Yonkers Library Association he received a lifetime membership. (E-3/12/57 p.2, c.5). His father, Lewis Seymour, died on Tuesday morning November 10, 1857 at 84 years of age. Funeral services were held for his father in his house at Archdale on Thursday, November 19, 1857. (E-11/12/57 p.2, c.6) William may have been a real estate broker because he advertised to sell a school house on Palisade Avenue north of Ashburton Avenue. (E-3/4/58 p.4, c.2) A W. L. Seymour who lived in Yonkers was a real estate and insurance broker in business with S. J. Agnew at 19 Nassau Street, NYC, in room No. 5. (E-3/11/58 p.3, c.7) On Sunday night June 13, 1858 his horses ran away at the Presbyterian Church. They raced towards Kingsbridge, and they only stopped when one of the horses fell and received serious injuries. The carriage was also seriously damaged. (E-6/17/58 p.2, c.2) On Wednesday evening, August 18, 1858 he was elected a trustee for School District #2. (E-8/26/58 p.2, c.4) During 1859 he was president of the Yonkers Bible Society. (E-2/10/59 p.2, c.2) On April 9, 1860 he was elected a Vestryman at St. Paul's Free Church. (E-4/12/60 p.2, c.6) On Friday, May 4, 1860, he was elected one of three members of the music committee for the June exhibition of the newly formed Yonkers Horticultural Society. (E-5/17/60 p.3, c.3)

Seymour, Sarah H. On Wednesday, April 27, 1859 she was married to Jacob Odell at St. John's Church by Rev. Darius Brewer, rector of St. Paul's Church. She was the youngest daughter of William N. Seymour. (E-4/28/59 p.3, c.4)

Shannon, Daniel He applied for a store license in 1858. (E-6/3/58 p.2, c.5) On Wednesday, November 2, 1859, he won an order for $50 of clothes in a target shooting contest at Weehawkan, New Jersey. He was a member of the Yonkers Hatters Guard. (E-11/3/59 p.2, c.6) During 1859 he built a house almost directly opposite John Copcutt's that cost about $3,000. (E-1/12/60 p.2, c.1) During 1860 he won a tea set at a Yonkers Hatters Guard target shooting contest. (E-11/1/60 p.3, c.1)

Shannon, Dennis During 1858 he owned land in Yonkers near Laurel Street which was south of Guion Street. (E-1/28/58 p.3, c.1) On Wednesday, November 2, 1859, he won a cake basket in a target shooting contest at Weehawkan, New Jersey. He was a member of the Yonkers Hatters Guard. (E-11/3/59 p.2, c.6) During 1860 he was elected Treasurer of the Yonkers Hatters Guard. (E-10/18/60 p.2, c.5)

Shannon, John On Wednesday, November 2, 1859, he won $10 in a target shooting contest at Weehawkan, New Jersey. He was a member of the Yonkers Hatters Guard. (E-11/3/59 p.2, c.6)

Shannon, Peter On Wednesday, November 2, 1859, he won a tea pot in a target shooting contest at Weehawkan, New Jersey. He was a member of the Yonkers Hatters Guard. (E-11/3/59 p.2, c.6) During 1860 he won a half dozen forks at a Yonkers Hatters Guard target shooting contest. (E-11/1/60 p.3, c.1)

Shannon, William During 1858 he bought a 50 foot by 100 foot lot on the corner of Broadway and Ashburton Avenue for $1,600. He built two three-story brick buildings at a total cost of about $10,000. (E-4/22/58 p.2, c.3) During 1858 he also made improvements to several outbuildings at his residence which cost him about $1,000. (E-1/20/59 p.2, c.3)

Shaw, E. S. (Mrs.) During 1859 she was principal of the Prescott Seminary which was a boarding and day school for girls on Buena Vista Avenue. (E-11/10/59 p.3, c.4) On the 1860 census she is listed as a 40-year-old teacher with a personal estate of $5,000. In her household there were three teachers, two waiters, a cook, and a laundress. Also in her household was a D. Jenkins who was a 34-year-old surgeon with $5,000 in real estate, and a personal estate of $1,000. Also in her household was Elizabeth Jenkins who was 35, and Ellen Jenkins who was 25. There were 13 female students boarding with her.

Shaw, William On May 10, 1859 his partnership in the painting business with Conway Pilson was dissolved. (E-5/12/59 p.3. c.1) His store was on Palisade Avenue next door to Flagg's Hall. (E-5/19/59 p.2, c.7)

Shepherd, S. On April 9, 1860 he was elected a Vestryman at St. Paul's Free Church. (E-4/12/60 p.2, c.6)

Shepherd, Solomon He lived on the property formerly owned by Dr. J. R. Chilton on Buena Vista Avenue. On Sunday morning, June 12, 1859 his barn burned down. (E-6/16/59 p.2, c.3)

Sherwood, Isaac He is listed on the 1860 census as a 49-year-old farmer with a personal estate of $1,500. His wife Elizabeth was 42 years old, and they had two children; Caroline who was 16, and Martha who was 11. (See vol.1, p.71.) During 1857 he was a Pound Master. (TRB)

Sherwood, Jacob He is listed on the 1860 census as a 79-year-old farmer with $12,000 in real estate, and a personal estate of $3,000. His wife Ellen was 75 years old. They had a farm laborer, and a servant. (See vol.1, p.71.) During 1853 and again in 1855 he was a Pound Master. He was noted as living in Kingsbridge on September 9, 1855. (TRB)

Sherwood, John During February, 1858 he bought a 33 foot by 100 foot lot on Palisade Avenue near Ashburton Avenue for $600. He then built a wood-frame house on the lot for about $2,000. (E-4/22/58 p.2, c.3) On July 22, 1858 he signed a petition calling for a meeting of eligible voters in School District #2 to decide if the school district should become a Union Free School District. (E-8/5/58 p.4, c.3) He was in business with an Akerly, but the partnership was dissolved on November 24, 1860. He continued to run the business. (E-11/29/60 p.2, c.7) He is listed on the 1860 census as a 31-year-old carpenter with $4,000 in real estate, and a personal estate of $700. His wife Margaret was also 31 years old, and they had three children; John who was 5, Eugene who was 3, and Lila who was 2 months old. He and his wife were born in Ireland, and the children were born in New York.

Sherwood, Osborn He is listed on the 1860 census as a 52-year-old farmer with $8,000 in real estate, and a personal estate of $1,000. Jane Langly lived in his household. She was a 26-year-old tailoress. Priscilla, probably her sister, was a 22-year-old tailoress, and there were also two children living in his household. (See vol.1, p.72.)

Shipman, Ralph On Wednesday morning, June 8, 1859, two men came to his door and asked for food from his servant girl. She was the only one home and she gave them some food. They left, but the servant girl heard a noise in the house and one of them had returned to steal what he could. She screamed and threatened to shoot him. The Underhill family came to her rescue as the thief took off with a pair of boots which he threw away while on the run. Levi Flagg who was nearby went and got Benjamin A. Starr, and both men went looking for the thief. They found him hiding in the grass on Locust Hill Avenue. He was locked up, and apparently he had been apprehended several times previous to this incident. (E-6/9/59 p.2, c.4) On the 1860 census he is listed as a 56-year-old carpenter with $10,000 in real estate, and a personal estate of $2,000. His wife, Mrs. Shipman, was 54 years old, and they had two children; Anna who was 18, and Charles who was 15. Ann Neely, who was 18 years old and from Ireland, was their servant. This Ralph Shipman seems to be a different person than the one listed on the 1850 census who was a hat box manufacturer from Connecticut. This Ralph Shipman is listed as being born in New York. The anecdote above is probably about the Ralph Shipman in Volume 1 on page 72. During 1856 he occupied a brick building on the corner of Palisade and Locust Hill Avenues. (TRB)

Shonnard, Edward F. On March 10, 1857 he was elected an Inspector for the next election of the Bank of Yonkers. (E-3/12/57 p.2, c.7) During 1857 he was summoned to serve as a juror for the Court of General Sessions at White Plains. (E-6/25/57 p.2, c.7) On Saturday, September 5, 1857 he chaired a Republican primary meeting and was elected a delegate to the district convention. On Tuesday, September 8, 1857 he was called on motion of S. D. Gifford to chair the First Assembly District Republican Party Convention. At the same convention he was also appointed to the Judicial Convention, and a delegate to the First Assembly District Convention. Also at the same convention he was elected as a Senatorial delegate. (E-

9/10/57 p.2, c.6 and E-10/15/57 p.2, c.3) During 1857 he sold six or seven acres of land to William T. Coleman. The property was on the Post Road at the top of the hill north of the village. There were several buildings on the land that were built in 1811. He retained ownership of the buildings and moved them about a mile east to the brow of the hill overlooking the Saw Mill River Valley. (E-12/31/57 p.2, c.3) On Monday, August 23, 1858 he was a delegate to the Westchester County Republican Party Convention at Durell's Hotel in Morrisania. During the convention he was elected a delegate to the Congressional Convention. (E-8/26/58 p.2, c.2) On Friday evening, September 17, 1858 he was elected to the executive committee of the Yonkers Republican Association. (E-9/23/58 p.2, c.1) On Tuesday, November 16, 1858, he was elected a vice president of a Republican Party meeting in Yonkers. (E-11/18/58 p.2, c.2) During 1858 he built a farm house, barn and several outbuildings on his farm north of the village. The cost was estimated at $4,000. (E-1/20/59 p.2, c.4) On Saturday, August 20, 1859, he was appointed an alternate delegate to the Judicial Republican Convention. (E-8/25/58 p.2, c.3) On Thursday, August 13, 1859 he was elected to the executive committee of the newly formed Republican Association at a Republican Town meeting. He was also chosen at the same meeting to be a delegate to the Assembly District Convention. (E-10/20/59 p.3, c.1) On Monday evening March 26, 1860 he was elected one of thirty-two vice presidents of a Republican election rally meeting at the Getty House. (E-3/29/60 p.2, c.3) During March, 1860 he was elected a delegate to the Republican State Convention. (E-4/5/60 p.2, c.3) On Saturday, September 29, 1860 he was a delegate to the Republican First Assembly District Convention that was held in Morrisania Hall, Morrisania. (E-10/4/60 p.2, c.2) On the 1860 census he is listed as a 50-year-old gentleman with $80,000 in real estate, and a personal estate of $5,000. His wife, S. Shonnard, was 48 years old, and they had one son, Frederick who was a 19-year-old student. They also had a coachman, a servant, and a cook. During 1855 he was appointed to a town committee to find out the expense of a permanent lockup. (TRB)

Shonnard, E. F. (Mrs.) She helped take up a collection to help the Ladies of the Mount Vernon Association make the grave of president George Washington a public shrine. No donation larger than a dollar was accepted. However, for those who wanted to donate more, they could donate a dollar for each member of their family. (E-8/19/58 p.2, c.4) Later any amount could be donated. (E-9/9/58 p.2, c.4)

Simmonds, G. On Wednesday, November 2, 1859, he won two tons of coal in a target shooting contest at Weehawkan, New Jersey. He was a member of the Yonkers Hatters Guard. (E-11/3/59 p.2, c.6)

Simmonds, J. On Wednesday, November 2, 1859, he won a barrel of flour in a target shooting contest at Weehawkan, New Jersey. He was a member of the Yonkers Hatters Guard. (E-11/3/59 p.2, c.6) During 1860 he won a dish at a Yonkers Hatters Guard target shooting contest. (E-11/1/60 p.3, c.1)

Simmons, Charles W. During 1857 he was summoned to serve as a juror for the Court of General Sessions at White Plains. (E-6/25/57 p.2, c.7)

Simmons, E. During 1860 he won an opera cloak at a Yonkers Hatters Guard target shooting contest. (E-11/1/60 p.3, c.1)

Simmons. George Jr. During 1860 he won one barrel of flour at a Yonkers Hatters Guard target shooting contest. (E-11/1/60 p.3, c.1) On the 1860 census he is listed as a 43-year-old hatter with a personal estate of $400. His wife Mimi was 41 years old, and they had one child, Mary, who was 14 years old. Another George Simmons is also listed on the census as a 34-year-old hatter with a personal estate of $100. His wife Elizabeth was 34 years old, and they had six children; William who was 14, Reuben who was 12, Martha who was 11, Mary who was 8, George who was 2, and Lucy who was two months old.

Simmons, Jonathan During the latter part of 1859 he was a member of the arrangement committee for the fourth annual ball of Protection Fire Engine Company Number 1. (E-12/22/59 p.2, c.6) On Monday evening March 26, 1860 he was elected one of thirty-two vice presidents of a Republican election rally meeting at the Getty House. (E-3/29/60 p.2, c.3) On Tuesday evening, September 11, 1860 he was elected to the executive committee of the Yonkers Republican Association for a five-month term. (E-9/13/60 p.2, c.2) On Thursday evening, October 25, 1860, he was one of twenty-two vice presidents at a Republican campaign meeting. (E-11/1/60 p.2, c.2)

Simpson, Samson On Saturday, April 24, 1858 his foreclosed farm was to be auctioned. The farm was between the Albany Post Road and the Hudson River. It was bounded on the south by Railroad Avenue (Glenwood Avenue), and was almost two acres in size. (E-3/11/58 p.3, c.3 also Vol. 1, p.72)

Skinner, C. A. During 1859 he operated a stationery and book store on Dock Street near Broadway. (E-10/27/59 p.3, c.5)

Skinner, Edward During 1860 he was selected to serve as a petit juror in the Court of Sessions that sat Monday, March 12, 1860. (E-3/8/60 p.2, c.5)

Skinner, George B. On Saturday night, July 31, 1858 his wife died during childbirth. (E-8/5/58 p.3, 2)

Skinner, I. He invented the American Gas Cooking Stove. (E-11/3/59 p.3, c.6)

Skinner, Salmon (Dr.) During 1857 he was a Trustee of the school in the village school district. (E-4/23/57 p.2, c.7) In the same year he was a member of the Masons. (E-8/20/57 p.3, c.1) During 1857 he called the nominating meeting for village President to order. (E-2/26/57 p.2, c.1) On Tuesday, September 1, 1857 he was elected as a James Buchanan delegate to the County Democratic Convention to be held at West Farms on September 2, 1857. (E-9/3/57 p.2, c.7) He was a member of the Wood wing of the Democratic Party, and on Monday, January 30, 1860 he was chosen by a convention at Tarrytown to be an alternate delegate to a convention in Charleston. (E-2/2/60 p.2, c.5) On December 1, 1857 he resigned as a Trustee for School District Number Two.

Sleight, Caleb On the 1860 census he was a 35-year-old seaman with a personal estate of $200. His wife was Mary who was 25 years old.

Sleight, C. T. During 1857 he was a manufacturer and seller of ladies shoes with a store on Broadway opposite the Episcopal Church. He also manufactured and sold shoes for young ladies and children. Early in 1857 he was in partnership with J. K. Miller and at that time they had their store at 7 Wheeler Building. (E-6/4/57 p.2, c.7)

Sleight, William H. During 1857 he owned a company and he was to occupy one of the new buildings being built by Radford near the Broadway bridge. (E-7/2/57 p.2, c.5) During November or early December, 1857, he moved into the new building. His business was a hardware store. (E-12/3/57 p.3, c.3) On Thursday, August 19, 1858 he died in Poughkeepsie from typhus. (E-8/26/58 p.3, c.1)

Smelt, William He was a member of the Committee of Arrangements for the first annual Fire Department Fund Ball held to raise funds to help widows and orphans of deceased Yonkers firemen. The ball was held on Thursday evening, March 4, 1858. (E-2/18/58 p.3, c.5) During November, 1858 he was a member of the arrangement committee for the Second Annual Ball to benefit the widows and orphans of deceased Yonkers firemen. (E-11/25/58 p.2, c.7) He is listed on the 1860 census as a 35-year-old carpenter with a personal estate of $100. His wife Temperance was 27 years old, and they had two children; George who was 9, and Jane who was 7. During 1859 he was a Constable. (TRB)

Smith, Alfred On August 7, 1858 he died at the age of 29. He was a member of the American Protestant Association Yonkers Lodge No. 31. He left a wife and children. (E-8/12/58 p.3, c.1)

Smith, Benjamin B. During the latter part of 1858 he signed a petition to have a meeting of the taxpayers in School District #2 meet to reconsider the location of two new schools; one on the corner of Wood Place and Warburton Avenue, and the other on St. Mary's Street near the Catholic Church and school. (E-12/23/58 p.2, c.3) During 1859 he built a brick store on the corner of North Broadway and Baldwin Place that cost about $2,500. (E-1/12/60 p.2, c.2) During 1854 he was an Overseer of the Poor. (TRB)

Smith, Caleb On Saturday, January 2, 1858 he died at the age of 85. (E-1/7/58 p.2, c.7 See Vol. 1)

Smith, Caleb He is listed on the 1860 census as a 50-year-old farmer with $3,000 in real estate, and a personal estate of $100. His wife Sarah was 35 years old, and they had two children; Sarah who was 11 and Melissa who was 13.

Smith, Charles H. During the meeting to nominate a village President in 1857 he made a motion to elect a chairman. (E-2/26/57 p.2, c.1) Sometime between May 5, 1856 and March 5, 1857 he received $65.50 from the village Treasurer. (E-3/5/57 p.3. c.1) During 1859 he lived across the street from John Copcutt. On Friday night, August 12, 1859 thieves entered his house and stole a small amount of money. (E-8/18/59 p.2, c.5) During 1859 he was Captain of the Yonkers Hatters Guard. On Wednesday, November 2, 1859 he went, as Commander, with the guard to Weehawken, New Jersey where the guard was involved in a shooting contest amongst themselves. At the target shooting contest he won a barrel of flour. (E-11/3/59 p.3, c.6) During 1860 he was again elected Captain of the Yonkers Hatters Guard. (E-10/18/60 p.2, c.5) During 1860 he won a coffee urn at a Yonkers Hatters Guard target shooting contest. (E-11/1/60 p.3, c.1) During December, 1860 he was a member of a committee that was organized to run the second annual ball of Neptune Engine Company Number 3 that was to be held at the Getty Lyceum on January 24, 1861. (E-12/13/60 p.2, c.7) During 1855 and 1857 he was an Overseer of the Poor and a Constable. In 1857 he was also a Commissioner of the Highways. (TRB)

Smith, Isaiah N. During 1858 he received a store license. (E-6/17/58 p.2, c.6)

Smith, James Bryant During 1857 he owned the yacht *Hornet*. He kept it docked on the Palisade side of the Hudson River, and during the winter he kept it in the Harlem River. He lived on Warburton Avenue. (E-5/25/57 p.2, c.7) On July 22, 1858 he signed a petition calling for a meeting of eligible voters in School District #2 to decide if the school district should become a Union Free School District. (E-8/5/58 p.4, c.3) On Monday, April 25, 1859 his infant son Fitch James Schonborg Smith died at the age of 3 months and 24 days. The baby was buried in Greenwood. The mother was Margaret M. Smith. (E-5/5/59 p.3, c.1)

Smith, Joshua On Wednesday, November 2, 1859, he won $50 in a target shooting contest at Weehawkan, New Jersey. He was a member of the Yonkers Hatters Guard. (E-11/3/59 p.2, c.6) During 1860 he won a ton of coal at a Yonkers Hatters Guard target shooting contest. (E-11/1/60 p.3, c.1)

Smith, Lavinia On Wednesday, September 29, 1858 she married Col. J. R. Wicker who was from Chicago. (E-9/30/58 p.3, c.1)

Smith, Samuel L. On Wednesday evening, December 14, 1859, at their annual meeting in Yonkers he was elected Junior Deacon of

Rising Star Lodge, No. 450, of F. & A.M. (E-12/15/59 p.2, c.5) During 1860 he was a carpenter who was in business with C. D. Archer on Bashford Street. (E-6/21/60 p.3, c.2) On Monday night, December 17, 1860 he was installed as an officer into the Rising Star Lodge of Free and Accepted Masons as J.D. (E-12/20/60 p.2, c.3)

Smith, Thomas In 1857 he was elected Secretary of the village President nominating committee, and also was a teller during the nomination procedure. (E-2/26/57 p.2) On Tuesday, September 1, 1857 he was elected as a James Buchanan delegate to the County Democratic Convention to be held at West Farms on September 2, 1857. (E-9/3/57 p.2, c.7) During 1857 he was a Poor Master and during the depression of 1857-1858 he took $50 from the poor fund for services rendered. The *Yonkers Examiner* admonished him for doing so by stating "We doubt the propriety of placing such a charge among monies expended. If it be deserved compensation, and this we do not dispute, it should be passed upon by the Board of Town Auditors and paid like all other officers' accounts. It can not be taken before it is audited from the Poor Fund of the Town." He was a member of the Committee of Arrangements for the first annual Fire Department Fund Ball held to raise funds to help widows and orphans of deceased Yonkers firemen. The ball was held on Thursday evening, March 4, 1858. He was also secretary of the committee. (E-2/18/58 p.3, c.5) During 1857 and 1858 he was a Justice of the Peace. On March 30, 1858 he was defeated by James L. Valentine 515 votes to 320 votes for Justice of the Peace. His major support came from Spuyten Duyvil and the voters who came to Yonkers to vote for him stayed the day, got drunk, and interrupted the voting several times. He was also the publisher of the *Yonkers Herald*. (E-4/1/58 p.2 c.1,2) On July 22, 1858 he signed a petition calling for a meeting of eligible voters in School District #2 to decide if the school district should become a Union Free School District. (E-8/5/58 p.4, c.3) On Wednesday evening, August 18, 1858 he was elected trustee for School District #2. (E-8/26/58 p.2, c.4) On September 23, 1858 the *Yonkers Examiner* noted that he lost a bid to be Postmaster, but was rewarded by the Democratic Party by receiving a $1,100 a year position apparently in the Custom House. The paper also noted that before switching to the Democratic Party he had backed the Know Nothings. (p.2, c.6) During November, 1858 he was president of the committee for the Second Annual Ball to benefit the widows and orphans of deceased Yonkers firemen. (E-11/25/58 p.2, c.7) During the latter part of 1859 he was a member of the reception committee for the fourth annual ball of Protection Fire Engine Company Number 1. (E-12/22/59 p.2, c.6) On Tuesday, September 4, 1860, his son George C. died at the age of 1 year, 9 months and 27 days. (E-9/6/60 p.2, c.7) On Monday evening, September 17, 1860, he was elected a Trustee to fill a vacancy on the Fire Department Fund

Association. (E-9/20/60 p.2, c.7) In 1854 he was elected to a full term as a Justice of the Peace. In 1855 he was appointed to a town committee to secure a permanent lockup. (TRB)

Smith, William On Wednesday, November 2, 1859, he won a pair of pants in a target shooting contest at Weehawken, New Jersey. He was a member of the Yonkers Hatters Guard. (E-11/3/59 p.2, c.6) On the 1860 census he is listed as a 33-year-old hatter with a personal estate of $100. His wife Mary was also 33 years old, and they had three children; Anna who was 11, Albert who was 8, and Elizabeth who was 4 months old.

Smullin, William During 1860 he won $5 at a Yonkers Hatters Guard target shooting contest. (E-11/1/60 p.3, c.1)

Soame, C. During 1860 he bought the locksmith, bell hanger and gas fitting business from John Benson. (E-6/14/60 p.2, c.7)

Spaulding, Henry F. On Friday, May 4, 1860, he was elected one of ten members of the executive committee of the newly formed Yonkers Horticultural Society. (E-5/17/60 p.3, c.3)

Speedling, Albert H. On Monday evening, November 16, 1857 as he was leaving the post office he noticed a man dragging a large plank from the direction of Bashford's lumber yard. He questioned the man who said he was just borrowing it. The man carrying the plank then went to A. W. Myers to tell his story. Myers told him if he repeated such borrowing he would get free room and board at White Plains (county prison). (E-11/19/57 p.2, c.3) On Thursday, November 18, 1858 he married Miss Jane M. Archibald. (E-11/25/58 p.2, c.7)

Speedling, Alonzo P. On February 15, 1859 he, Jacob Read and John Nairn bought the lumber and coal business of Henry W. Bashford. (E-4/7/59 p.2, c.3) On Monday night, December 17, 1860 he was installed as an officer into the Rising Star Lodge of Free and Accepted Masons as J.M. Ceremonies. (E-12/20/60 p.2, c.3)

Speyer, M. During 1860 he won a barrel of potatoes at a Yonkers Hatters Guard target shooting contest. (E-11/1/60 p.3, c.1)

Splotsworth, J. During 1860 he won a cup at a Yonkers Hatters Guard target shooting contest. (E-11/1/60 p.3, c.1)

Spotswood, S. During the early part of 1860 his sister died in an apparent collapse of a building in Lawrence, Massachusetts. Two hundred people were known dead and an additional three hundred injured. (E-1/19/60 p.2, c.5) This seems to be an inordinate amount of people to be in one building even if it was a factory or a tenement.

Squire, John Jr. During 1858 he, Thomas O. Farrington, and Charles S. Archer owned a grocery store at 202 West Street, NYC. (E-9/9/58 p.3, c.7)

Stansfield, J. On Wednesday, November 2, 1859, he won a barrel of flour in a target shooting contest at Weehawken, New Jersey. He was a member of the Yonkers Hatters Guard. (E-11/3/59 p.2, c.6)

During 1860 he won one ton of coal and a $5 hat at a Yonkers Hatters Guard target shooting contest. (E-11/1/60 p.3, c.1)

Staples, George On Wednesday, November 2, 1859, he won a cake basket in a target shooting contest at Weehawkan, New Jersey. He was a member of the Yonkers Hatters Guard. (E-11/3/59 p.2, c.6)

Stapleton, W. During 1860 he won $10.00 at a Yonkers Hatters Guard target shooting contest. (E-11/1/60 p.3, c.1)

Starkweather, Mrs. During 1857 she and her family lived in a house next to the Mansion House. On Monday, November 9, 1857 a burglar attempted to enter her house through an upstairs window. The attempt woke her up and she lit a light. This frightened the burglar away, but he tore down the grape vine he had climbed up in his attempt to enter the house. (E-11/12/57 p.2, c.3)

Starr, Benjamin A. He was one of seven members of Hope Hook and Ladder Company No. 1 when it was first formed on August 15, 1853. The first meeting to form the fire department was held in his store. (E-12/29/59 p.2, c.2) During 1857 he was the village Collector of Taxes. His office was on Mechanic Street. (E-12/10/57 p.3, c.3) He was a member of the Committee of Arrangements for the first annual Fire Department Fund Ball held to raise funds to help widows and orphans of deceased Yonkers firemen. The ball was held on Thursday evening, March 4, 1858. (E-2/18/58 p.3, c.5) During 1859 he had a man's clothing store at 15 South Broadway. (E-2/7/59 p.3, c.5) At the same location he was a real estate agent. (E-2/17/59 p.3, c.2) During 1859 he sold his clothing store to Thomas S. Finin. After selling the store he was going to devote himself entirely to his real estate and insurance business. (E-4/28/59 p.2, c.5) On Wednesday, November 2, 1859, he was chosen as a judge of a target shooting match at Weehawkan, New Jersey, between the men of the Yonkers Hatters Guard. (E-11/3/59 p.3, c.6) In 1857 he was elected Village Collector. During 1859 he was appointed village Fire Warden. On October 15, 1857 his business was one of 33 businesses in Yonkers to announce they were closing their stores at 8 p.m. beginning on October 12, 1857 until March 27, 1858. (E-10/15/57 p.3, c.1) By April 22, 1858 he moved his clothing business on Mechanic Street to Getty's new building on the corner of Broadway and Main Street, and Hoyt and Brother moved their dry goods store into his old store. (E-4/22/58 p.2, c.2,3) He was also a real estate broker. (E-4/22/58 p.2, c.2) On July 22, 1858 he signed a petition calling for a meeting of eligible voters in School District #2 to decide if the school district should become a Union Free School District. (E-8/5/58 p.4, c.3) On Tuesday, November 16, 1858, he was elected a vice president of a Republican Party meeting in Yonkers. (E-11/18/58 p.2, c.2)

Starr, Charles W. During 1857 he was Secretary of the Hope Hook and Ladder Company Number 1. (E-8/13/57 p.2, c.7) During November, 1858 he was a the secretary for the Second Annual Ball to benefit the widows and orphans of deceased Yonkers firemen. (E-11/25/58 p.2, c.7) On Thursday evening, September 1, 1859, at a fire department meeting he was appointed to a committee that was authorized to buy a new fire engine. (E-12/29/59 p.2, c.2) He was the first secretary/treasurer of Hope Hook and Ladder Company No. 1 when it was first formed on August 15, 1853. (E-12/29/59 p.2, c.2) During 1859, and for some time prior to that, he was an assistant to Samuel D. Rockwell in Rockwell's jewelry business. Also, during 1859, he bought the business. He was also a watchmaker. (E-5/5/59 p.2, c.7 and p.3, c.2) On Thursday evening, September 1, 1859 he was elected Secretary of Hope Hook and Ladder Company. (E-9/8/59 p.3, c.1) He was a member of the Republican Young Men of Yonkers and at a meeting on Tuesday evening, July 31, 1860, which he chaired, resolutions were adopted to form the Republican Wide Awakes of Yonkers club. (E-8/2/60 p.2, c.3) On Friday evening, August 10, 1860, he was elected secretary of the Yonkers Republican Wide Awakes. (E-8/16/60 p.2, c.6) On Thursday evening, September 6, 1860 he was again elected secretary of Hope Hook and Ladder Company Number 1. (E-9/13/60 p.2, c.2) On Monday night, December 17, 1860 he was installed as an officer into the Rising Star Lodge of Free and Accepted Masons as S.M. Ceremonies. (E-12/20/60 p.2, c.3)

Starr, Nathaniel W. He was to be a juror for the petit court White Plains on June 21, 1858. (E-6/17/58 p.2, c.2) On Monday evening, November 15, 1858 he lived on North Broadway and he had a buffalo robe stolen with his name printed on the inside. He offered a $5 reward for the return of the robe, and an additional $10 reward for the conviction of the thief. (E-11/18/58 p.3, c.1) He was principal of the Yonkers Commercial and Collegiate Institute. In 1859 it celebrated its tenth annual "exhibition." (E-3/31/59 p.2, c.4) During November, 1859 he was called on to serve as a petit juror for the Court of Sessions in White Plains that was held on December 6, 1859. (E-12/1/59 p.2, c.7) On the 1860 census an N. A. Starr is listed as a 49-year-old teacher with $20,000 in real estate, and a personal estate of $2,500. He was born in Connecticut, and his 46-year-old wife, Mary, was born in Rhode Island. They probably had two daughters H. M. who was 18, and Ellen who was 17. William, who was a 20-year-old clerk, may have been their son. Besides Nathaniel there were three other teachers. Also, listed in his household were a seamstress, a cook, a laundress, two servants, a gardener, and 27 male students. The students ranged in age from 11 to 17, and they were born in several different states. One of the teachers was born in Spain, and another was born in France.

Starr, Oliver Winthrop On Monday, December 27, 1858, he married Miss Mary E. Lawrence who was from Hyde Park. They were married at the Zion Church in New York City. (E-12/30/58 p.2, c.5)

Starr, William During March, 1859 he was selected to serve as a 1859. (E-3/3/59 p.3, c.1)

Stearns, Jonathan, N. During 1860 he was chairman of the lecture committee of the Pastoral Aid Society lectures sponsored by St. John's Church. The price for attending six lectures was $1 and for attending one lecture $.25. Profits were for the relief of the poor. (E-12/6/60 p.2, c.7) He was a member of the Masons. (E-12/13/60 p.2, c.6)

Stedwell, J. H. During 1857 he was an agent for the Manhattan Life Insurance Company with an office at 9 Manor Place. (E-2/5/57 p.3, c.3) Sometime in February or March 1857 he donated 6 volumes to the Yonkers Library Association. On March 2, 1857 he was elected a manager of the library. (E-3/5/57 p.2, c.6) During 1857 he was a lawyer with an office in Getty Square. He was also a real estate broker. (E-4/9/57 p.3, c.6) On Saturday, September 5, 1857 he was elected at a Republican primary meeting to be a delegate to the Republican district convention. (E-9/10/57 p.2, c.6) During 1857 he was a member of the executive committee of the Republican party. (E-10/1/57 p.2, c.7) On Tuesday, October 6, 1857 he was a delegate to the Republican County Convention. (E-10/8/57 p.2, c.3) At the Republican Convention he was appointed Secretary. At the convention he moved that Ethan Flagg be nominated as the Republican candidate from the 1st Assembly District. (E-10/15/57 p.2, c.3) On Monday evening, March 1, 1858 he was again elected a manager of the Yonkers Library Association. (E-3/4/58 p.2, c.3) On Monday, August 23, 1858 he was a delegate to the Westchester County Republican Party Convention at Durell's Hotel in Morrisania. At that meeting he was elected a delegate to the State Convention. (E-8/26/58 p.2, c.2) On Friday evening, September 17, 1858 he was elected to the executive committee of the Yonkers Republican Association. (E-9/23/58 p.2, c.1) On Tuesday, November 16, 1858, he was elected a vice president of a Republican Party meeting in Yonkers. (E-11/18/58 p.2, c.2) On Monday evening March 7, 1859 he was elected a manager of the Yonkers Library Association. (E-3/10/59 p.2, c.7) During 1859 he was a member of the Republican Party's First Assembly District of Westchester County Committee. (E-8/4/59 p.2, c.1) Around August, 1859 the Library Association was incorporated and he became a member of the Board of Trustees. (E-8/14/59 p.2, c.4) On Saturday, August 20, 1859, he was appointed a delegate to the Senatorial Republican Convention, and also to the District Committee. (E-8/25/58 p.2, c.3) On Monday, October 17, 1859 he was appointed secretary for the Republican First Assembly District Convention held at Durell's Hotel in Morrisania. (E-10/20/59 p.2, c.4) On Thursday, August 13, 1859 he was elected secretary of the newly formed Republican Association at a Republican Town meeting. He was also chosen at the same meeting to be a delegate to the Assembly District Convention. He was also chosen at the same meeting to be a delegate to the Assembly District Convention. (E-10/20/59 p.3, c.1) During 1859 he was a member of the Yonkers Circulating Library Association lecture committee. (E-12/22/59 p.2, c.6) On Monday, January 23, 1860, at White Plains, he was appointed to a committee to draw up a constitution for the newly formed Westchester County Republican Campaign Club. At the same meeting he was elected one of the officers of the club. (E-1/26/60 p.2, c.7) He was apparently a member of the New York delegation to the national Republican convention held in Chicago during May, 1860. He wrote a very interesting, and historically valuable, letter to the *Yonkers Examiner* on May 19, 1860 describing how Abraham Lincoln was nominated for the presidency. (E-5/24/60 p.2, c.2,3,4) During August, 1860 he was elected to represent the First Assembly District at the Republican State Convention which was held in Syracuse. (E-8/16/60 p.2, c.2) On Friday evening, August 10, 1860, he was elected president of the Yonkers Republican Wide Awakes. (E-8/16/60 p.2, c.6) On Tuesday evening, September 11, 1860 he was elected secretary of the Yonkers Republican Association for a five-month term. (E-9/13/60 p.2, c.2) On Saturday, September 29, 1860 he was a delegate to the Republican First Assembly District Convention that was held in Morrisania Hall, Morrisania. (E-10/4/60 p.2, c.2) He was a member of the Masons. (E-12/13/60 p.2, c.6) On the 1860 census he was listed as a 25-year-old lawyer staying at the Getty House.

Steen, Jacob Sometime during October, 1859 his partnership with David Bate in their lumber and coal business at 6 Dock Street was dissolved and he continued on with the business. (E-10/13/59 p.3, c.2)

Stelwagon, John D. His wife was Anna M. Stelwagon. On Tuesday, February 28, 1860, their daughter Alice Seymour Stelwagon died at the age of 1 year and 4 months. (E-3/1/60 p.2, c.6)

Stelwagon, (Mrs.) During 1858 she built a house on South Broadway costing about $1,600. (E-1/20/59 p.2, c.4)

Stephens, Peter During 1858 he owned the Broadway Livery Stables on North Broadway above Wells Avenue. He ran a taxi service in the village especially for picking up passengers and bringing them to and from the railroad or the steamboat dock. (E-7/1/58 p.3, c.3) During 1859 he retired from his livery stable and sold his inventory at auction on Wednesday, June 15, 1859. (E-6/9/59 p.2, c.4) He lived on the corner of Warburton and Ashburton Avenues. On Thursday evening August 25, 1859 his home was broken into by thieves, but nothing was taken. (E-9/1/59 p.2, c.4) Late in 1859 he advertised to sell his business. (E-12/15/59 p.3, c.1)

Stephens, William On Tuesday, August 7, 1860, he died. He was from a well-to-do family, but left all his relatives behind when he left to live in Yonkers. He was not well known in Yonkers since he was somewhat of a recluse. He was foreman of the *Yonkers Herald* and was living in Yonkers about seven years. He was considered an eccentric. He was 35 years old. (E-8/9/60 p.2, c.2,7)

Stephenson, Odell Apparently during the early part of 1858 he resigned his office as Assessor for the eastern district of Yonkers. (E-3/11/58 p.2, c.2)

Stetson, James P. M. During 1857 he built a square brick house on the Hudson River next to and just south of Thomas W. Ludlow's residence. The house cost about $10,000. (E-12/31/57 p.2, c.1)

Stevens, John During 1857 he owned the Yonkers Paint Store on Dock Street. He sold paint, wall paper, and kerosene lamps. (E-2/5/57 p.3, c.2) On March 2, 1857 he was elected vice president of the Yonkers Library Association. (E-3/5/57 p.2, c.6) During 1857 he also sold Breckenridge coal. (E-3/12/57 p.2, c.5) Also during 1857 he was a Trustee of the school in the village school district. (E-4/23/57 p.2, c.7) Again during 1857 he was the Town Sealer of Weights and Measures. (E-12/31/57 p.4, c.2) The school district he was a trustee for was School District Number 2. (E-2/4/58 p.3, c.1) On Monday evening, March 1, 1858 he was elected president of the Yonkers Library Association. (E-3/4/58 p., c.2) On July 22, 1858 he signed a petition calling for a meeting of eligible voters in School District #2 to decide if the school district should become a Union Free School District. (E-8/5/58 p.4, c.3) His residence was on Irving Place near Warburton Avenue. (E-4/5/60 p.3, c.2) On Wednesday, August 15, 1860 he lost an election as trustee for school district number 2. He received 2 votes. (E-8/16/60 p.2, c.6) During 1858 he was again the town Sealer of Weights and Measures. On December 1, 1857 he was elected chairmen of the annual School District Two meeting. In 1858 he was an Inspector of Elections for Election District Number One. (TRB)

Stevenson, Odell During 1853 and 1856 he was an Assessor. He resigned that position during 1857. In 1853 he was also a Fence Viewer. (TRB) He is listed on the 1860 census as a 56-year-old farmer with $6,000 in real estate, and a personal estate of $1,000. His wife Elizabeth was 49 years old. Three other people were also listed in their household. (See vol.1, p.73.)

Stewart, David During 1858 he and J. Stewart built a brick house on Ashburton Avenue near Broadway which cost about $4,000. They built the house themselves. (E-4/22/58 p.2, c.3) He was a mason. (E-1/20/59 p.2, c.3) On Thursday evening, September 1, 1859, at a fire department meeting he was appointed to a committee that was authorized to buy a new fire engine. (E-12/29/59 p.2, c.2) On the 1860 census he is listed as a 35-year-old mason with a personal estate of $1,500. His wife Olive was 28 years old, and they had three children; David who was 5, George who was 3, and Olive who was one year old. They had two servants who were both from Ireland; Grace Hanlin who was 20 years old, and Maud Kenan who was 18 years old.

Stewart, George On May 14, 1857 he married Harriet Weeks in NYC. She lived in NYC. (E-5/21/57 p.2, c.6) On the 1860 census he is listed as a 25-year-old mason with a personal estate of $350. His wife Harriet was 25 years old, and they had one child, Ida, who was 2 years old. Mrs. Weeks, who was 62 years old, lived with them.

Stewart, James During 1858 he and D. Stewart built a brick house on Ashburton Avenue near Broadway which cost about $4,000. They built the house themselves. (E-4/22/58 p.2, c.3) He was a mason. (E-1/20/59 p.2, c.3) On Thursday evening, October 25, 1860, he was one of twenty-two vice presidents at a Republican campaign meeting. (E-11/1/60 p.2, c.2) On the 1860 census he is listed as a 40-year-old master builder with $7,000 in real estate, and a personal estate of $500. His wife Mary was 30 years old, and they had four children; W. H. Stewart who was 7, Marion who was 5, James who was 3, and Grace who was one year old. Their servant was Ann Boyce who was 14 years old. Another J. Stewart is also listed on the 1860 census, and there are striking similarities between the two. The second is listed as a 33-year-old builder with $4,000 in real estate, and a personal estate of $1,500. His wife Mary was 30 years old, and they had four children; William who was 8, Marion who was 6, Grace who was 2, and James Stewart who was 2. Ann Bell, who was 14 years old, is also listed in their household.

Stillings, Charles During 1858 he was a plumber who did about $3,500 worth of work on the Yonkers Collegiate Institute's buildings which were owned by Dr. Levi Flagg. (E-1/20/59 p.2, c.3)

Stilwell, Caroline M. On Tuesday, October 20, 1857 she married William G. Ackerman. She was the daughter of John Stilwell. (E-10/20/57 p.2, c.7)

Stilwell, John Until May 12, 1856 he was Treasurer of the village. (E-3/5/57 p.3, c.1) He is listed on the 1860 census as a gentleman with $125,000 in real estate, and a personal estate of $4,000. His wife was 35 years old, and they had three children; Cornelia who was 12, Fanny who was 10, and Benjamin who was 2. They also had two female servants from Ireland.

Stilwell, Martha Jane On Wednesday, May 4, 1859, she was married to Anson B. Hoyt by Rev. V. M. Hulbert in her residence. She was the daughter of John Stilwell. (E-5/5/59 p.3, c.1)

Stone, George L. (Rev.) During 1857 he was the minister of the Baptist Church. They had services on Sundays at 10:30 a.m. and again at 7:30 p.m.. (E-12/31/57 p.2, c.1)

Stone, Henry L. During November, 1859 he was asked to serve as a juror for the petit jury of Westchester County. (E-11/24/59 p.3, c.1)

Stone, Lyman On Wednesday, November 2, 1859, he won a barrel of flour in a target shooting contest at Weehawkan, New Jersey. He was a member of the Yonkers Hatters Guard. (E-11/3/59 p.2, c.6)

Stone, S. During 1860 he won $5 worth of bread at a Yonkers Hatters Guard target shooting contest. (E-11/1/60 p.3, c.1)

Stoney, William A. During 1860 he received a grocer's license. (E-7/26/60 p.2, c.6)

Strang, Nelson During 1853, 1855, and 1857 he was a Pound Master. In 1858 he was elected a Justice of the Peace. During May, 1860 he was appointed a Pound Master. (TRB)

Suau, Henry A. During 1857 he was a commission merchant and importer at 71 Broad Street, NYC. (E-3/12/57 p.3, c.2) On Friday, May 4, 1860, he was elected one of ten members of the executive committee of the newly formed Yonkers Horticultural Society. (E-5/17/60 p.3, c.3) On Friday, May 4, 1860, he was elected one of five members of the committee on Premiums for Fruits for the June exhibition of the newly formed Yonkers Horticultural Society. (E-5/17/60 p.3, c.3) He lived on the corner of North Broadway and Lamartine Avenue. (E-10/11/60 p.2, c.6)

Sullivan, William S. On Thursday, September 29, 1859, while he and his brother were herding cows on Nodine Hill they decided to throw some rocks. William threw one and immediately collapsed and died of an apparent heart attack. He was about 9 years old. (E-10/6/59 p.2, c.6)

Sution, Ralph On Wednesday, November 2, 1859, he won a vest in a target shooting contest at Weehawkan, New Jersey. He was a member of the Yonkers Hatters Guard. (E-11/3/59 p.2, c.6)

Suydam, Abraham On Monday night, September 10, 1860, his wood-frame carpenter's shop on Warburton Avenue between Wells Avenue and Dock Street was set on fire by an arsonist. He lost all his tools and inventory for buildings he was working on. (E-9/13/60 p.2, c.2)

Suydam, Mrs. During 1857 she was a ladies' nurse. Her residence was the first house above the Methodist Church on Broadway. (E-6/4/57 p.2, c.7)

Swann, Stephen During 1859 he opened the New York Saddlery and Harness Store on the corner of Palisade Avenue a few doors north of the Getty House. He also sold trunks, valises, and carpet bags. (E-6/16/59 p.3, c.2)

Taylor, DeWitt C. On Monday evening March 26, 1860 he was elected one of thirty-two vice presidents of a Republican election rally meeting at the Getty House. (E-3/29/60 p.2, c.3)

Taylor, Gilbert On Tuesday, September 1, 1857 he was elected a James Buchanan delegate to the County Democratic Convention to be held at West Farms on September 2, 1857. (E-9/3/57 p.2, c.7) On Tuesday, October 6, 1857 he was appointed one of two secretaries at the Democratic electors of the Town of Yonkers meeting. (E-10/8/57 p.2, c.2) His wife Maria Ann died on Wednesday, June 22, 1859, of consumption at the age of 53. (E-6/30/59 p.3, c.1) On the

1860 census he is listed as a 51-year-old farmer with $20,000 in real estate, and a personal estate of $2,000. Apparently he had four of his children living in his household. They were: William who was a 28-year-old carpenter, Nancy who was 26, Charles who was a 23-year-old carpenter, and Francis who was 16. Also in his household were two farm laborers and one servant. During 1853, 1856, 1857, and 1858 he was a Commissioner of Highways. During 1853 he was also a Fence Viewer, and in 1857 he was also a Pound Master. (TRB also Vol.1, p.74)

Taylor, John (Rev.) During 1859 he was sent from Norwalk, Connecticut to Yonkers in order to try and reform the African Methodist Episcopal Church. (E-8/25/59 p.2, c.4.) On Sunday morning and afternoon, September 3, 1859, he preached to a congregation at Fairy Grove. (E-9/8/59 p.3, c.1)

Tealk, W. During 1860 he won a barrel of potatoes at a Yonkers Hatters Guard target shooting contest. (E-11/1/60 p.3, c.1)

Terry, Daniel M. During the latter part of 1858 he and Walter H. Paddock bought the grocery store on Broadway and Ashburton Avenue from White & Richmond. (E-12/16/58 p.3, c.1) During 1860 the partnership was dissolved by mutual consent. (E-4/5/60 p.3, c.3)

Terry, James During 1859 he was a laborer working on Farrington's new building. On Tuesday, June 28, 1859, he lost his footing and fell three stories into the basement. He received some internal injuries that were not considered serious. (E-6/30/59 p.2, c.6)

Terry, Jeannette On Saturday, April 7, 1860, she was married by Rev. Waters to Stephen Bell at his residence. (E-4/19/60 p.2, c.7)

Thomas, Augustus N. During 1857 he donated $25 to the Yonkers Library Association and became a life member. (E-3/12/57 p.2, c.5) On October 15, 1857 his business was one of 33 businesses in Yonkers to announce they were closing their stores at 8 p.m. beginning on October 12, 1857 until March 27, 1858. (E-10/15/57 p.3, c.1) During 1858 he owned land near Locust Street. (E-5/20/58 p.2, c.1) On Friday, September 10, 1858 his mother, Isabella Thomas, fell down a flight of stairs at his residence on Warburton Avenue. The fall broke her neck and killed her. During September, 1858 there were three attempts to break into his house. (E-9/16/58 p.2, c.4) During the latter part of 1858 he signed a petition to have a meeting of the taxpayers in School District #2 meet to reconsider the location of two new schools; one on the corner of Wood Place and Warburton Avenue, and the other on St. Mary's Street near the Catholic Church and school. (E-12/23/58 p.2, c.3)

Thomas, George On Saturday, May 30, 1857, his son who was considered "a bright boy" drowned in the Mill Pond opposite Warburton Avenue. He was playing on the bank with another boy and accidentally fell in the water. (E-6/4/57 p.2, c.2)

Thomas, J. B. (Mrs.) During 1858 she ran the dressmaking department of the Millinery and Dressmaking Establishment of Miss Livingston's. (E-6/3/58 p.2, c.7)

Tier, Jeremiah Sometime in June or July, 1860 he died. (E-8/2/60 p.3, c.1 see also Vol. 1, p.75)

Tompkins, Gilbert H. On Thursday, December 9, 1858 he married Miss Mary M. Duff. (E-12/16/58 p.2, c.6)

Tompkins, Nathaniel W. During 1857 he was a hotel and tavern owner. (E-5/28/57 p.2, c.2) He applied for a hotel license in 1858. (E-6/3/58 p.2, c.5) He is listed on the 1860 census as a 43-year-old hotel owner. His wife Caroline was 36, and they had six children; William who was 14, Bertrand who was 12, Sarah who was 10, James who was 8, Ida who was 4, and May who was 2.

Tompkins, W. S. At about 2 a.m. Tuesday, September 21, 1858 his house was broken into. The thieves stole a watch, a small amount of money, and some silver. (E-9/23/58 p.2, c.4)

Thompson During 1857 he and Henry F. Brevoort bought a grocery store on the corner of Broadway and Getty Square from Thomas O. Farrington. (E-4/9/57 p.3, c.2) During 1859 they moved to the Radford Building on the bridge. (E-3/1059 p.3, 4)

Thompson, John On July 22, 1858 he signed a petition calling for a meeting of eligible voters in School District #2 to decide if it should become a Union Free School District. (E-8/5/58 p.4, c.3)

Thompson, Matilda On Sunday, July 24, 1859 she was married by Rev. King to James F. Duff. (E-7/28/59 p.2, c.7)

Thompson, R. L. On Thursday evening, September 1, 1859, at a fire department meeting he was appointed to a committee that was authorized to buy a new fire engine. (E-12/29/59 p.2, c.2)

Thompson, Sarah A. On May 23, 1860 she was married by Rev. Hulbert to Henry F. Brevoort in the home of her mother. (E-5/24/60 p.3, c.3)

Tobin, J. During 1860 he won a cup at a Yonkers Hatters Guard target shooting contest. (E-11/1/60 p.3, c.1)

Toburn, Joseph On Wednesday, November 2, 1859, he won a half dozen silver forks in a target shooting contest at Weehawkan, New Jersey. He was a member of the Yonkers Hatters Guard. (E-11/3/59 p.2, c.6)

Toplis, Robert J. During 1857 he sold Ayer's cathartic pills. (E-2/5/57 p.3, c.4) He also owned the drugstore in the Getty House which he sold to S. B. Hoffman probably during the early part of December, 1857 and retired. (E-12/31/57 p.3, c.2) However during 1858 he advertised his business as the Getty House Drug Store established in 1852. He also stated in the advertisement that he had over sixteen years experience as a druggist. (E-12/16/58 p.3, c.2) He sold genuine patent medicines and fresh Swedish leeches. (E-5/12/59 p.3, c.4) During Christmas time 1859 he decorated St. John's Episcopal Church for Christmas services. (E-12/22/59 p.2, c.5) He also had a soda fountain at his drugstore. He outfitted a tin piping system because carbonic acid water when it comes in contact with even a very small amount of lead creates a deadly poison. Lead was widely used in piping. (E-6/14/60 p.2, c.1,7)

Totten, Joseph On Wednesday, June 22, 1859, while working at Clark's Sash and Blind factory, he cut off portions of the second and third fingers of his left hand. He was adjusting a planing machine and was doing it too fast. (E-6/23/59 p.2, c.3)

Townsend, Benjamin During 1858 he and Thomas Oliver owned land on or near Laurel Street which was south of Guion Street. The land was to be put up for auction at the County Court House in White Plains, March 13, 1858. Both men probably lived in NYC. (E-1/28/58 p.3, c.1) During 1859 he built a wood-frame house near Daniel Shannon's for about $3,500. (E-1/12/60 p.2, c.1) He also owned land on Prescott Street between Oliver and Webster Avenues. He also owned land on the northwesterly corner of Oliver Avenue and a street that may now be Walnut Street or Victor Street then known as Brook Street. Each parcel was to be sold at auction on September 22, 1860 at the Getty House. (E-8/9/60 p.3, c.2)

Trancomb, Michael During 1858 he owned a lot on Mechanic Street near Dr. Amos W. Gates. (E-6/3/58 p.3, c.1)

Treadwell, Devoe During 1853 he was a Constable. (TRB)

Trenchard, Henry On the 1860 census he is listed as a 76-year-old farmer with $3,000 in real estate, and a personal estate of $2,000. In his household were Peter who was a 28-year-old laborer, and Jane who was 17. (See Vol. 1, p.76. On the 1850 census he was listed as being born in Nova Scotia. On the 1860 census he was listed as being born in New York.)

Tripp, Robert A. (Rev.) During 1857 he was the Pastor of the African Methodist Episcopal Church. He was accused of mishandling church funds. However, Thomas O. Farrington and Moses Patterson examined his books and found them to be in order. On May 16, 1857 he was again examined by Rev. Levin Smith and was reconfirmed as Pastor. (E-7/23/57 p.2, c.7)

Turniss, [This may be Alfred Turnip or Turniss.] During 1857 he and English owned a grocery store. (E-5/28/57 p.2, c.2)

Tunstall, John He was a former resident of Yonkers whose 11 or 12-year-old son was killed instantly when he was caught between a northbound express and a southbound train. He became confused and was hit by the express. It was originally reported in the *Peekskill Eagle*. (E-4/30/57 p.2, c.5)

Tuthill, Ira H. During 1858 he was a lawyer living in Yonkers with a practice at 10 Wall Street, NYC. (E-10/14/58 p.3, c.7)

Underhill Benjamin F. During 1853 he was an Inspector of Elections for Election District Number Three. (TRB)

Underhill, Caleb F. During May, 1860 he was called to serve on the petit jury. The newspaper had him as Caleb E. (E-5/31/60 p.3, c.3) During 1857 he was a Pound Master and an Inspector of Elections for Election District Number Three. In 1858 he was an Assessor and again an Inspector of Elections in the same district, and he was once again an Inspector of Elections in 1859 for the same district. (TRB)

Underhill, Charles P. During 1858 he received a store license. (E-6/17/58 p.2, c.6)

Underhill, David During 1856 he was a member of the Masons. (E-8/20/57 p.3, c.1)

Underhill, Edward (Captain) During 1857 he made a few additions to his buildings on Chicken Island. He was fitting them up for a foundry and machine shop. The project cost about $5,000. On Tuesday, April 27, 1858 all of his machinery was to be sold at auction to satisfy a defaulted mortgage. (E-4/22/58 p.3, c.1) Sometime in late April or early May, 1858 he began the Yonkers Ale Brewery Company on Chicken Island. He brewed pale and brown amber ales. He delivered free within seven miles of the brewery, and he supplied families with small casks of half and quarter barrels. (E-5/6/58 p.3, c.2) He converted the Eagle Factory into the brewery. (E-5/27/58 p.2, c.4) On Wednesday, November 2, 1859, he was chosen as a judge of a target shooting match at Weehawkan, New Jersey, between the men of the Yonkers Hatters Guard. (E-11/3/59 p.3, c.6) On Wednesday evening, December 14, 1859, at their annual meeting in Yonkers he was elected Treasurer of Rising Star Lodge, No. 450, of F. & a.m. (E-12/15/59 p.2, c.5) During 1859 he was apparently enlarging, or tearing down and building a new brewery, on Chicken Island that cost $10,000. He did his own carpentry work. (E-1/12/60 p.2, c.3) On Monday night, December 17, 1860 he was installed as an officer into the Rising Star Lodge of Free and Accepted Masons as Treasurer. (E-12/20/60 p.2, c.3) On the 1860 census he is listed as a 44-year-old brewer with $12,000 in real estate, and a personal estate of $4,000. His wife Ann was 42 years old, and they had nine children; Alice who was 17, Eleanor who was 15, Edward who was 13, Henry who was 11, S[elica] who was 9, Kate who was 7, Amy who was 5, Lora who was 3, and Arthur who was 4 months old. He, his wife, and the first four of their children were born in England. The remaining five children were born in New York. An Emily Bowlin also lived with them and she was 13 years old. They had one servant. During 1858 he was a member of the village Board of Trustees.

Underhill, Isaac N. During 1860 he was selected to serve on the petit jury November 19, 1960 in the Circuit Court. (E-11/15/60 p.3, c.2)

Underhill, L. (Mrs.) On Monday, October 11, 1858 she was driving her carriage with one of her children and a Miss Vogell from Rome, New York through the gates of the Sisters of Mercy when a heavy cart owned by Mr. Conlan and driven by a drunken Irishman crashed into them. The three passengers were thrown from the carriage, but they received only minor bruises. (E-10/14/58 p.2, c.3)

Underhill, Peter (Col.) During 1853 he owned property in the northeast section of the town. (TRB)

Underhill, Richard A. On Monday, June 6, 1859, he married Phoebe Elizabeth Harris at Buttermilk Falls, Orange County, New York. He lived on Kingsbridge Road about a half mile south of the village. He was a member of the Excelsior Club, and its president, which was exclusively for bachelors. On Tuesday, June 7, 1859 the club members gave him a large party and drummed him out of the club. George H. Bussing was the bride's uncle where they went to continue the party. The party went well into the next day. The club's secretary and Underhill had an agreement that whoever married first the other would get gloriously drunk, and the "Secretary was borne off the field vanquished." (E-6/16/59 p.2, c.4,5)

Underhill, Z. B. During 1855 he was a Pound Master. (TRB)

Underwood, H. A. During the early days of the Yonkers Library Association he received a life membership. (E-3/12/57 p.2, c.5) On July 22, 1858 he signed a petition calling for a meeting of eligible voters in School District #2 to decide if the school district should become a Union Free School District. (E-8/5/58 p.4, c.3) On the 1860 census he is listed as a 37-year-old broker with $45,000 in real estate, and a personal estate of $3,000. His wife Emma was 33 years old and they had four children; Walter who was 7, Allen who was 5, Louisa who was 2, and Edmund who was 1 year old. Mary Kinder, who was 24 years old and from Ireland, was their nurse. Emma Kinder, who was 15 years old and also from Ireland, was their cook, and Susan Snooks, who was 14 years old and also from Ireland, was their waitress. Ann Greeley, who was 25 years old and from Ireland, was another cook, and John Patrick, who was 24 years old and also from Ireland, was their coachman. Underwood was listed again on the same census. There are some differences though. This time he is 35 years old, and his wife is 30 years old. The children are exactly the same, but there are differences with the servants, and the cook.

Underwood, John A. On Monday evening March 26, 1860 he was elected one of thirty-two vice presidents of a Republican election rally meeting at the Getty House. (E-3/29/60 p.2, c.3) On Monday evening, September 10, 1860, he was married by Rev. Rollin A. Sawyer to Rose Alba Peale, daughter of Rembrandt Peale of Philadelphia. (E-9/13/60 p.2, c.7) On Thursday evening, October 25, 1860, he was one of twenty-two vice presidents at a Republican campaign meeting. (E-11/1/60 p.2, c.2)

Upham, George B. (Dr.) During 1857 he donated $25 to the Yonkers Library Association, and he lived on Warburton Avenue. (E-3/12/57 p.2, c.5 and E-8/27/57 p.2, c.7) During the latter part of 1858 he signed a petition to have a meeting of the taxpayers in School District #2 meet to reconsider the location of two new schools; one on the corner of Wood Place and Warburton Avenue, and the other on St. Mary's Street near the Catholic Church and school. (E-12/23/58 p.2, c.3) During August, 1859 he was elected a Trustee of the school district in the village. (E-8/18/59 p.2, c.6) On Thursday, August 13, 1859 he was chosen as a delegate to the Republican Assembly District Convention by the newly formed Republican Association at a Republican Town meeting. (E-10/20/59 p.3, c.1) He was a member of the Masons. (E-12/13/60 p.2, c.6) On Monday night, December 17, 1860 he was installed as an officer into the Rising Star Lodge of Free and Accepted Masons as a member of the standing committee. (E-12/20/60 p.2, c.3) On the 1860 census he is listed as a 35-year-old surgeon with $1,000 in real estate and a $2,000 personal estate. His wife Sarah was 33 years old, and she was from Maine. There were six other people in their household, some of whom may have been their children. They are Catherine who was 30 years old and was from Ireland, Mary who was 16 and was from New York, William who was 8 years old and was from Maine, George who was 6 years old and was from New York, Helen who was 4 years old and was from New York, and Frances who was 2 years old and was also from New York.

Vail, J. During October, 1857 he opened a dry goods store with Elting. The store was in the Radford Building. (E-10/1/57 p.3, c.1) On the 1860 census he is listed as a 35-year-old merchant who had a personal estate of $3,500. His wife Catherine was 34 years old, and they had at least one child, Emma, who was one year old. Also, in their household was Jonathan Warner who was a 22-year-old clerk, C. or O. Griffin was a 17-year-old female seamstress, and N. G[inn] was a 22-year-old male.

Vail, Jane On Saturday July 11, 1857 she married David Dougan at the Presbyterian Church. (E-7/16/57 p.2, c.7)

Valentine, Abraham He lived on the road from South Yonkers to Hunt's Bridge, which was probably Webster Avenue or Bronx River Road, where he had a large farm that was in the family for almost 200 years. His father had a small country store and he learned business from his father. At some point he left Yonkers and moved to New York City where he had a small business. His small store grew into one of the largest wholesale groceries in the city. He retired from business around 1828 with a large fortune, and bought the old farm in Yonkers. For 25 years he was the Warden at St. John's Church and for about 12 years its Senior Warden. He died on Monday, June 7, 1858. His wife Hannah survived him. They had three children, two of whom were daughters who died quite some time before he died. His son, Dr. Samuel Valentine, survived him and took over his father's business. Samuel was between 20 and 30 years old at the time of his father's death. (E-6/10/58 p.2, c.2. See also Vol. 1)

Valentine, Elijah During 1859 he owned land south of Mill Road near Hunt's Bridge running south along Kingsbridge Road near lands of Isaac Post, David Oakley, and David Horton, and then westerly to Tibbet's Brook. The land was to be sold by the sheriff at auction on October 6, 1859. (E-8/18/59 p.3, c.6 also see Vol.1 p.78) During 1860 he was selected to serve on the petit jury November 19, 1860 in the Circuit Court. (E-11/15/60 p.3, c.2) He is listed on the 1860 census as a 52-year-old farmer. His wife Mary was 50 years old. They had two servants.

Valentine, James L. On Tuesday, March 10, 1857 he was elected a Director of the Bank of Yonkers. (E-3/12/57 p.2, c.7) On Tuesday, September 1, 1857 he was elected a James Buchanan delegate to the County Democratic Convention to be held at West Farms on September 2, 1857. (E-9/3/57 p.2, c.7) On Tuesday, October, 6, 1857 he was appointed a delegate to the Democratic County Convention. (E-10/8/57 p.2, c.2) On March 22, 1859 he was again elected a Director of the Bank of Yonkers. (E-4/7/59 p.2, c.5) On Friday, May 4, 1860, he was elected one of six members of the committee on Premiums for Vegetables for the June exhibition of the newly formed Yonkers Horticultural Society. (E-5/17/60 p.3, c.3) During 1853 he was the town Supervisor. In 1854, 1856, 1857, and 1860 he was a Commissioner of the Highways. In 1856 and 1859 he was an Inspector of Elections for Election District Number One. In 1857 he was appointed to that position to fill a vacancy. In 1858 he was elected a Justice of the Peace. (TRB)

Valentine, John During 1855 he was a Pound Master. (TRB)

Valentine, Nathaniel B. On Monday, September 17, 1860 he was to serve on the petit jury of the Court of Sessions in Bedford. (E-8/30/60 p.3, c.1)

Valentine, Peter Sometime during 1859 he died. The executors of his will were Benjamin W. Valentine and Peter J. Valentine. (E-6/30/59 p.3, c.5)

Valentine, Staats On the 1860 census he is listed as a 60-year-old farmer with $100,000 in real estate, and a personal estate of $2,000. His wife Abigail was 57 years old. Two children were listed in their household; James who was a 30-year-old farmer, and Emily who was 18. (See Vol. 1, p. 79.)

Van Cortlandt, Augustus In 1857 he was nominated for the State Assembly on the Democratic ticket. However, he lost the nomination in 1857 by four votes because the Yonkers delegation split their votes. (E-10/22/57 p.2, c.2) On Tuesday, September 1, 1857 he was elected as a James Buchanan delegate to the County Democratic Convention to be held at West Farms on September 2, 1857. (E-9/3/57 p.2, c.7) In 1858 he was chosen by the Democratic party to run for the Assembly. (E-10/7/58 p.2, c.7) On Tuesday, November 9, 1858, he was appointed by the County Board of Supervisors to the Committee on Equalization of Assessments. (E-

11/18/58 p.2, c.6) During 1859 he was appointed to a Clerkship in the New York Customs House with a $1,200 salary. This meant he could not run for re-election to the Assembly. (E-7/21/59 p.2, c.3) On October 5, 1859 he was again nominated by the Democratic Party to run for office in the First Assembly District. The *Yonkers Examiner* said of his nomination and past two years in office that he had conducted himself "with such discretion that his constituents never heard of him, except in one unpleasant incident." (E-10/13/59 p.2, c.4) He lost the Assembly election to William T. B. Milliken 1,565 to 1,477 even though he won Yonkers 478 to 465. He lost the first election district of Yonkers 372 to 315. However he won Election District Two 121 to 73, and Election District Three 42 to 20. (E-11/10/59 p.2, c.1,3) During 1855 he was a town assessor. In 1857 he was an Inspector of Elections for Election District Number Two. In 1858 and 1859 he was elected Town Supervisor. (TRB)

Van Houten, Abraham R. He was the one of seven members of Hope Hook and Ladder Company No. 1 when it was first formed on August 15, 1853. (E-12/29/59 p.2, c.2) On Tuesday, October, 6, 1857 he was appointed a delegate to the Democratic County Convention. (E-10/8/57 p.2, c.2) On July 22, 1858 he signed a petition calling for a meeting of eligible voters in School District #2 to decide if the school district should become a Union Free School District. (E-8/5/58 p.4, c.3) On Sunday morning, November 14, 1858, between two and three o'clock, his carpet shop on Palisade Avenue, north of the fire station, was completely destroyed by fire. His loss was about $400, and another $350 worth of tools was also destroyed. (E-11/18/58 p.2, c.2) On the 1860 census he is listed as a 36-year-old master builder with real estate worth $5,000, and a personal estate of $1,000. His wife Margaret was 29 years old, and a William, who was 19 years old was a carpenter, lived with them. They had four children; Charles who was 11, De Witt who was 6, Albert who was 3, and Amanda who was 1 year old. Ellen, who was 40 years old, was their servant and was from Ireland. She had a 9-year-old daughter, Carmelia who apparently was born in New York. During 1859 and 1860 Van Houten was an Inspector of Elections for Election District Number One. (TRB)

Vanliew, Augustus He was the son-in-law of Henry Durell who was an early proprietor of the Getty House. Probably during July of 1857 he was either murdered or had a seizure. He was found dead at the corner of Canal and Mercer Streets, NYC and some personal belongings were missing. He was a bookkeeper at C. R. Woodworth and Company. He left a widow and 3 young children. He lived at 12 Hubert Street, NYC. (E-7/30/57 p.2, c.5)

Vann, William During the latter part of 1858 he signed a petition to have a meeting of the taxpayers in School District #2 meet to reconsider the location of two new schools; one on the corner of

Wood Place and Warburton Avenue, and the other on St. Mary's Street near the Catholic Church and school. (E-12/23/58 p.2, c.3)

Van Orden, Alfred He was a member of the Committee of Arrangements for the first annual Fire Department Fund Ball held to raise funds to help widows and orphans of deceased Yonkers firemen. The ball was held on Thursday evening, March 4, 1858. (E-2/18/58 p.3, c.5) During November, 1858 he was a member of the arrangement committee for the Second Annual Ball to benefit the widows and orphans of deceased Yonkers firemen. (E-11/25/58 p.2, c.7) He was the foreman of Lady Washington Engine Company. He left that post and on Thursday evening, July 7, 1859 he was presented with a gold watch and chain by Peter Stephens who represented the Company. The new foreman, Alexander B. Lawrence also made some complimentary remarks. (E-7/14/59 p.2, c.3) On the 1860 census he is listed as a 33-year-old mason with a personal estate of $200. His wife Susan was 28 years old, and they had five children; Clara who was 11, Emma who was 8, Julia who was 6, Lizzy who was 3, and Alfred who was 1 year old.

Van Pelt, Reuben W. In 1856 he ran for town supervisor and was defeated by William Scrugham. (E-4/1/58 p.2, c.1) At about 2 a.m. Tuesday, September 21, 1858 his house was broken into. The thieves ate a meal, and stole some provisions and some silver. (E-9/23/58 p.2, c.4) During the latter part of 1858 he signed a petition to have a meeting of the taxpayers in School District #2 meet to reconsider the location of two new schools; one on the corner of Wood Place and Warburton Avenue, and the other on St. Mary's Street near the Catholic Church and school. (E-12/23/58 p.2, c.3) During 1858 he improved his residence on North Broadway. The renovations cost about $2,000. (E-1/20/59 p.2, c.5) On July 28, 1859 he was mentioned as the probable Democratic candidate for County District Attorney. (E-7/28/59 p.2, c.1) During 1859 he did more renovations on his residence on North Broadway north of Baldwin Place that cost about $3,000. (E-1/12/60 p.2, c.2) On the 1860 census he is listed as a 34-year-old attorney with $7,500 in real estate, and a personal estate of $2,000. His wife Emily was 33 years old, and they had two children; Chandler who was 11, and El[len] who was 6 years old. Mary Avery, who was 27 and from New York, was their servant, and Martin McClay, who was 16 and was from Ireland, was their laborer. In 1855, 1856, and 1857 he was a member of the village Board of Trustees.

Van Tassell, Benjamin In 1855 a bay horse wandered onto his property. He lived in south Yonkers near a harness store. (TRB)

Van Tassell, Caleb During 1858 he was an Inspector of Elections for Election District Number Two. (TRB)

Van Wart, Stephen L. During 1858 he was secretary of the American Protestant Association Yonkers Lodge No. 31. (E-8/12/58 p. 3, c.1) On Monday, December 12, 1859 he was married by Rev.

Hulbert to Emma R. Friend. (E-12/22/59 p.2, c.6) On Tuesday, January 3, 1860 he was elected one of two representatives of Lady Washington Engine Company Number 2. (E-1/5/60 p.2, c.4) On Monday evening March 26, 1860 he was elected one of several secretaries of a Republican election rally meeting at the Getty House. (E-3/29/60 p.2, c.3) After a meeting of the Yonkers Republican Association held on Tuesday, September 11, 1860 was over, the Republican Wide Awakes held a meeting and elected him Orderly Sergeant of the club. (E-9/13/60 p.2, c.2) On Monday evening, September 17, 1860, he was elected vice president of the Fire Department Fund Association. (E-9/20/60 p.2, c.7) On the 1860 census he is listed as a 23-year-old butcher. His wife, Emma, was 22, and they had a David who was a 17-year-old blacksmith staying with them.

Varian, William A. (Dr.) On Saturday evening, October 20, 1860, he was elected President of the Spuyten Duyvil Republican Club at a meeting held at the Iron Foundry. (E-10/25/60 p.2, c.3) On Thursday evening, October 25, 1860, he was one of twenty-two vice presidents at a Republican campaign meeting. (E-11/1/60 p.2, c.2)

Vark, (Judge) During 1857 he owned land south of the creek, west of Broadway, and south of land owned by Dr. Ovid D. Wells and his brother Horace P. Wells. (E-7/2/57 p.2, c.4)

Vermilyea, Abraham F. On Saturday, September 5, 1857 he was elected at a Republican primary meeting to be a delegate to the Republican district convention. (E-9/10/57 p.2, c.6) During 1857 he was a member of the executive committee of the Republican party. (E-10/1/57 p.2, c.7) During November, 1859 he was asked to serve as a juror for the petit jury of Westchester County. (E-11/24/59 p.3, c.1) On Monday, September 3, 1860 he was to serve on the petit jury of the Court of Oyer and Terminer in White Plains. (E-8/30/60 p.3, c.1) On Thursday evening, October 25, 1860, he was one of twenty-two vice presidents at a Republican campaign meeting. (E-11/1/60 p.2, c.2) On the 1860 census he is listed as a 48-year-old farmer with $16,000 in real estate, and a personal estate of $2,000. His wife Louise was 38 years old, and they had four children; George who was 7, Benjamin who was 5, Clarence who was 3, and William who was 3 months old. They also had two farm laborers in their household. (See Vol. 1, p.81.) During 1855, 1856, and 1857 he was an Inspector of Elections for Election District Number Three. In 1856 he was also an Overseer of the Poor. (TRB)

Vermilyea, Dorothy She is listed on the 1860 census as a 60-year-old with $3,000 in real estate, and a personal estate of $3,000. Living in her household was Susan Vermilyea who was 55 years old with a personal estate of $2,500, and Maria Vermilyea who was 50 years old with a personal estate of $2,000.

Vernon, William On Wednesday, November 2, 1859, he won a card basket in a target shooting contest at Weehawkan, NJ. He was a member of the Yonkers Hatters Guard. (E-11/3/59 p.2, c.6)

Vollett, William A. During 1859 he was an orphan boy. He apparently inherited property near the top of Oliver Avenue. The property had a good view of the Hudson River and the area was called Vueville. The property was to be sold on Monday, November 14, 1859. Apparently it was to be auctioned off at the Getty House. (E-11/3/59 p.3, c.7) He owned two lots. One was 110 feet on Oliver Avenue and the asking price was $700. The other lot had a house on it and it was to be rented for $100 a year. (E-11/10/59 p.3, c.4)

Wackerly, Jacob During 1860 he was a Constable. (TRB)

Wadsworth, William On Monday, August 29, 1859, his wife, Mahal Wadsworth died at the age of 57 years, 3 months, and 1 day. (E-9/1/59 p.3, c.1)

Waggoner, George H. Sometime in late 1859 or early 1860 he died. He may have died in Syracuse, NY since his estate was being settled by Israel S. Spencer a lawyer in Syracuse. Catherine Waggoner was an executrix, and Peter Waggoner and Israel S. Spencer were executors. (E-3/15/60 p.3, c.1)

Wakeman, H. T. During 1857 he owned a hardware store on Broadway and he advertised for a gardener. (E-3/5/57 p.2, c.7) On October 15, 1857 his business was one of 33 businesses in Yonkers to announce they were closing their stores at 8 p.m. beginning on October 12, 1857 until March 27, 1858. (E-10/15/57 p.3, c.1) During the latter part of 1858 he signed a petition to have a meeting of the taxpayers in School District #2 meet to reconsider the location of two new schools; one on the corner of Wood Place and Warburton Avenue, and the other on St. Mary's Street near the Catholic Church and school. (E-12/23/58 p.2, c.3) He advertised a complete catalog of almost everything he sold, replete with pictures, and with tables describing sizes and shapes. For instance, a refrigerator chest 25" by 18" by 24" in height done in imitation granite cost $4.00, and a single upright ice box cost from $8.00 to $11.00. An old round or pot belly stove cost from $12.00 to as much as $52.00. His business was at 3 Broadway, at the sign of the Golden Tea Kettle. (E-4/7/57 p.4, c.3) On the 1860 census he is listed as a 31-year-old hardware store owner with $5,000 in real estate, and a personal estate of $5,000. His wife Elizabeth was 30 years old, and they had one son, Evert, who was 1 year old. All three of them were born in Connecticut. That means his son and wife came to Yonkers after he did. Three other people lived in his household; Hiram Wiggans who was a 17-year-old clerk was also born in Connecticut, Catherine Fr?? who was 13 years old and she was born in Ireland, and Jane Good who was a 20-year-old servant. She was also from Ireland.

Walchner, Anthony During 1860 he owned a small shoe store on Palisade Avenue next door to the Farrington Building. On Wednesday morning, August 15, 1860 he was attempting to board the 7:52 train to New York City when he slipped and fell onto the tracks. His arm was outstretched across the track, and the train ran over it and crushed the arm from the shoulder to the hand. He was brought to his house and was given medical attention, but he died. He was from Germany and left a wife. (E-8/16/60 p.2, c.5)

Waldeck, Mr. During early November, 1857, he lived on Mechanic Street and some ducks were stolen from him. (E-11/12/57 p.2, c.3)

Waldo, C. B. During the early days of the Yonkers Library Association he received a life membership. (E-3/12/57 p.2, c.5)

Walker, Robert A. During December, 1860 he was a member of a committee that was organized to run the second annual ball of Neptune Engine Company Number 3 that was to be held at the Getty Lyceum on January 24, 1861. (E-12/13/60 p.2, c.7)

Walsh, During the early part of 1857 he and David Bate sold lumber, coal, and more at 6 Dock Street. (E-3/5/57 p.3, c.5) Later in 1857 he was no longer in business with Bate. (E-7/2/57 p.3, c.4)

Walsh, (Judge) On Tuesday, September 1, 1857 he was elected a James Buchanan delegate to the County Democratic Convention to be held at West Farms on September 2, 1857. (E-9/3/57 p.2, c.7)

Walsh, Richard On Wednesday morning, July 18, 1860 his daughter Sarah Jane died. He was married to Agnes Walsh, and they lived in South Yonkers. (E-7/19/60 p.3, c.1)

Walsh, Richard J. On Tuesday, April 19, 1859, he married Eliza Lepper who was the youngest daughter of Paul Lepper. The Leppers lived in Quebec where the marriage took place. (E-4/28/59 p.2, c.4) An R. Walsh lived about a mile and a half from the village on the Post Road. (E-6/7/60 p.2, c.7)

Walsh, William H. On Tuesday, October 6, 1857 he was appointed chairman of the Democratic electors of the Town of Yonkers meeting. He was also appointed a delegate to the Democratic County Convention at White Plains. (E-10/8/57 p., c.2)

Ward, P. (Rev.) During 1858 he was the pastor of the Methodist Church. (E-1/28/58 p.2, c.6) During 1859 he left Yonkers to become a pastor of a church in the Yorkville section of NYC on 86th Street. (E-5/19/59 p.2, c.3)

Waring, Charles E. On Thursday evening, October 25, 1860, he was one of twenty-two vice presidents at a Republican campaign meeting. (E-11/1/60 p.2, c.2) He was a partner in J. T. Waring & Co. along with John T. Waring and David H. Ketchum. On December 1, 1860 Ketchum left the partnership. (E-12/13/60 p.3, c.1) During 1853 he was a licensed grocer. (TRB)

Waring, Chester C. In the early part of 1858 he was a partner in the manufacturing firm of Waring, Baldwin and Company. He and his father William C. Waring sold their shares in the business to their partners Anson Baldwin and Hall F. Baldwin on March 1, 1858. (E-3/4/58 p.3, c.5) On Sunday at 5 p.m. during a thunderstorm March 21, 1858 he died at the age of 21 years, 1 month, and 11 days. He was the eldest son of William C. Waring. He had a disease for several years; probably cancer. Before his death he spent at least some of the winter of 1856 in Havana, Cuba. When he returned he was not any better. During September, 1857 he took a voyage to Europe, and he planned to stay there for quite some time. While in Europe he visited England, France, and Italy, but he was forced to return home because of poor health. He arrived back in Yonkers Thanksgiving Day November 26, 1857. According to the *Yonkers Examiner* his last words reflected his concept of death as "going home." He entered his father's business when he was about 19 years old. (E-3/25/58 p.2, c.3 and p.3, c.1)

Waring, Edwin C. On Monday April 5, 1858 his house on the corner of Broadway and Prospect Street was broken into. He was asleep in his bedroom and the thief entered it and stole $36 in cash that was in his pantaloons (pants). The pants were found on the sidewalk. Several silver items and watches were also taken. The total loss was about $150. (E-4/8/58 p.2, c.2) The house was up for sale during September, 1860. His lot was 50 x 100 feet and the house was 23 x 32 feet. The house was two stories high with a finished attic and basement. He also had marble mantles in the front and back parlors. (E-9/27/60 p.2, c.7) On the 1860 census he is listed as a 33-year-old hat manufacturer with $20,000 in real estate, and a personal estate of $5,000. His wife Julia was 28 years old, and they had two children; Charles who was 9, and Hull who was 3. They had a cook, a gardener, and a nurse.

Waring, Jarvis A. During 1853 he was a licensed grocer. (Documents.) During 1857 he owned a grocery store. (E-5/28/57 p.2, c.2) On October 15, 1857 his business was one of 33 businesses in Yonkers to announce they were closing their stores at 8 p.m. beginning on October 12, 1857 until March 27, 1858. (E-10/15/57 p.3, c.1) He applied for a store license in 1858. (E-6/3/58 p.2, c.5) He received his license. (E-6/24/58 p.2, c.5) During 1859 he did some renovations to his store on Broadway and Main Street. Some of the renovations included tearing down the brick front on Main Street and replacing it with iron and glass. (E-4/14/59 p.2, c.2) On Saturday evening, May 21, 1859, while he was walking home in the dark after closing his store he fell into the basement of Farrington's new building which was under construction. He was unable to climb up the wall, so he yelled for help. James K. Miller came to assist him, but he also fell into the basement and received a sprained right arm. Others came to help and both men were rescued. Waring received no apparent injuries. (E-5/26/59 p.2, c.4) During 1859 he was granted another grocery license. (E-8/11/59 p.2, c.7) During 1860 he received a grocer's license. (E-7/26/60 p.2, c.6) On the 1860 census he is listed as a 45-year-old grocer with $11,000 in real estate, and a personal estate of $4,000. His wife, Mrs. Waring, was 40 years old, and they had five children; Oscar was a 20-year-old clerk, Phebe was 19, Rachel was 17, Emeline was 14, and Amelia was 12 years old.

Also in the household was W. H. Paddock who was 29 years old and he had a personal estate of $2,000. A. Paddock, apparently his wife, was 23 years old, and Mary Burns was a 27-year-old servant from Ireland.

Waring, John T. On March 10, 1857 he was elected a Director of the Bank of Yonkers. (E-3/12/57 p.2, c.7) During the spring of 1857 he made extensive improvements to his hat factory that cost about $15,000. (E-12/31/57 p.2, c.3) On March 22, 1859 he was again elected a Director of the Bank of Yonkers. (E-4/7/59 p.2, c.5) On Monday, August 1, 1859, his son John T. died at the age of 1 year and 11 months in South East, New York. His wife was Janet P. Waring. (E-8/4/59 p.3, c.1) During 1859 he enlarged and renovated his residence, moved an old carriage-house and other outbuildings further east, and renovated them. The cost of all the projects was about $9,300. (E-1/12/60 p.2, c.2) On Monday evening March 26, 1860 he was elected one of thirty-two vice presidents of a Republican election rally meeting at the Getty House. (E-3/29/60 p.2, c.3) On Friday, May 4, 1860, he was elected one of ten members of the executive committee of the newly formed Yonkers Horticultural Society. (E-5/17/60 p.3, c.3) On Friday, May 4, 1860, he was elected one of three members of the decoration committee for the June exhibition of the newly formed Yonkers Horticultural Society. (E-5/17/60 p.3, c.3) His company J. T. Waring & Co. was a partnership between him, Charles E. Waring, and David H. Ketchum. On December 1, 1860, Ketchum left the partnership. (E-12/13/60 p.3, c.1) On the 1860 census he is listed as a 35-year-old hat manufacturer with $20,000 in real estate, and a personal estate of $4,000. His wife Janetta was 30 years old, and they had three children; Arthur who was 7, Grace who was 5, and John who was 1. They also had a coachman, a nurse, and two cooks. Also, in their household was a Julia Paddock, who was 16 years old. She was born in New York.

Waring, John T. In the early part of 1858 he was a partner in the manufacturing firm of Waring, Baldwin and Company. He and his son Chester C. Waring sold their shares in the business to their partners Anson Baldwin and Hall F. Baldwin on March 1, 1858. (E-3/4/58 p.3, c.5) After that it was reported that he was erecting a large hat factory at Brewster's Station in Putnam County. (E-1/6/59 p.2, c.4) (E-3/4/58 p.3 c.5) On May 1, 1860 he, Anson Baldwin and Hall F. Baldwin formed the Union Hat Factory. They made wool hats. (E-5/3/60 p.2, c.6) On the 1860 census he is listed as a 52-year-old hat manufacturer with $25,000 in real estate, and a personal estate of $30,000. His wife Susan was 32 years old, and they had three children; Edna who was 15, William who was 10, and Ga[rrison] who was 1. They also had a cook, a servant, a seamstress, and a coachman. (See Vol. 1 for a different age for Susan Waring.) During 1854 he was elected a Justice of the Peace to fill a vacancy. (TRB) During

1855 he was elected to the village Board of Trustees. [This may be the father of the above John T. Waring, and some of the information above and here may be interchangeable.]

Warner, Adeline B. On Monday, February 20, 1860 in South Yonkers, she died at the age of 39. (E-3/1/60 p.2, c.6)

Warner, J. G. During 1859 he was a Lieutenant in the Yonkers Hatters Guard. On Wednesday, November 2, 1859 he went with the guard to Weehawken, New Jersey where the guard was involved in a shooting contest amongst themselves. At the target shooting contest he won a $10 gold piece. (E-11/3/59 p.3, c.6) During 1860 he won $25 at a Yonkers Hatters Guard target shooting contest. (E-11/1/60 p.3, c.1)

Warner, Matthias During 1857 he owned a grocery store. (E-5/28/57 p.2, c.2) During 1858 he received a store license. (E-6/17/58 p.2, c.6) At his store he sold Brandreth's Pills. The pills were good enough to cure almost anything from worms to pleurisy. (E-10/7/58 p.4, c.7) During 1859 he was granted another grocery license. (E-8/11/59 p.2, c.7) During 1860 he received a grocers license. (E-7/26/60 p.2, c.6) On the 1860 census there are two Matthias Warners. The first is listed as a 32-year-old merchant with a personal estate of $2,000. His wife Anna was 30 years old, and they had three children; Caroline was 7, Fanny was 5, and Matthias was 2. The second Warner is listed as a 66-year-old merchant with $20,000 in real estate, and a personal estate of $5,000. His wife Mary was also 66 years old, and apparently they had one son, John, who was living with them. He was 28 years old. They had two servants. George Kelly was 22, and Elizabeth Kelly was 20. They were both born in New York. (See Vol. 1, p. 83 for the older Warner.) During 1853 he was a Commissioner of the Highways, and also the Sealer of Weights and Measures. (TRB)

Waterbury, Frederick W. On Monday, August 23, 1858 he was a delegate to the Westchester County Republican Party Convention at Durell's Hotel in Morrisania. (E-8/26/58 p.2, c.2) On Friday, July 22, 1859 he died at about 40 years of age. He lived in Yonkers, but moved to New York City just before his death. At the time of his death he was Captain of the Metropolitan Police in the fourth precinct. In 1854 he was elected to the Assembly from the Second Westchester County Assembly District. He was buried Sunday, July 24, 1854. He left a wife and eight children. He died of consumption. (E-7/28/59 p.2, c.3)

Waterman, John S. On Monday, October 12, 1857 he was a delegate to the Republican First Assembly District Convention. (E-10/15/57 p.2, c.3) He was a member of the Committee of Arrangements for the first annual Fire Department Fund Ball held to raise funds to help widows and orphans of deceased Yonkers firemen. The ball was held on Thursday evening, March 4, 1858. (E-2/18/58 p.3, c.5) During November, 1858 he was a member of the arrangement committee for the Second Annual Ball to benefit the widows and orphans of deceased Yonkers firemen. (E-11/25/58 p.2, c.7) During December, 1860 he was a member of a committee that was organized to run the second annual ball of Neptune Engine Company Number 3 that was to be held at the Getty Lyceum on January 24, 1861. (E-12/13/60 p.2, c.7) On the 1860 census he is listed as a 30-year-old painter with a $200 personal estate. A Margaret lived with him. She was 64 years old. During 1857 and 1859 he was a constable. (TRB)

Waters, Michael W. On Sunday, May 4, 1860 he died at the age of 35. (E-5/17/60 p.3, c.1)

Waters, Olive S. On Monday, July 25, 1859 she died at the age of 31 years, 3 months, and 3 days. She was the wife of Michael Waters. (E-8/4/59 p.3, c.1)

Watts, Mrs. On Sunday night, September 27, 1857 while filling a lamp the kerosene caught fire and ignited her clothes and the clothes of her children. She lived near the Mansion House. Some of her neighbors helped her and she and her children received only minor burns. (E-10/1/57 p.2, c.2)

Weed, Frederick On Wednesday April 20, 1858 [Wednesday was actually the 21st] he died at the age of 73. (E-4/22/58 p.2, c.7)

Weed, H. O. On Tuesday, April 3, 1860 his only daughter, Lucinda, died at the age of 5 years, and 5 months. (E-4/5/60 p.3, c.2) On the 1860 census he is listed as a 35-year-old shipbuilder. His wife, whose name is not listed, was 33 years old, and they had a son, Willie, who was 9 years old.

Weeks, Harriet On Thursday, May 14, 1857 she married George Stuart in NYC. (E-5/21/57 p.2, c.6)

Welchman, F. On Wednesday, June 30, 1857 he bought a lot on Buena Vista Avenue for $4,050. (E-7/1/58 p.2, c.2)

Wells, Horace D. He and his brother Dr. Ovid P. Wells owned land south of the creek, west of Broadway, and north of Judge Vark's property. Their property was known as the Prospect Hill Tract. (E-7/2/57 p.2, c.4)

Wells, Lemuel W. On Tuesday, March 10, 1857 he was elected a Director of the Bank of Yonkers. (E-3/12/57 p.2, c.7) Later in 1857 he was an Inspector of Elections for the Yonkers Gas Light Company. (E-8/13/57 p.2, c.7) On Monday, October 12, 1857 he was a delegate at the Republican First Assembly District Convention. (E-10/15/57 p.2, c.3) On July 22, 1858 he signed a petition calling for a meeting of eligible voters in School District #2 to decide if the school district should become a Union Free School District. (E-8/5/58 p.4, c.3) At about 2 a.m. Tuesday, September 21, 1858 his house was broken into and a gold watch and chain, and some silver were stolen. (E-9/23/58 p.2, c.4) On March 22, 1859 he was again elected a Director of the Bank of Yonkers. (E-4/7/59 p.2, c.5) His estate was on South Broadway south of Prospect Street. It may have been the large section of land on the north corner of South Broadway and St. Mary's Street as shown on the 1858 map drawn by Thomas C. Cornell. (E-4/14/59 p.3, c.3) On June 28, 1859 he signed a letter addressed to Frederick A. Coe asking legal advice concerning a written promise of the Hudson River Railroad Company to construct a carriageway across the Nepperhan River near the drawbridge. (E-7/7/59 p.2, c.4) During 1855 and again in 1856 he was elected to the village Board of Trustees.

Wells, Ovid P. (Dr.) He and his brother Horace D. Wells owned land south of the creek, west of Broadway, and north of Judge Vark's property. Their property was known as the Prospect Hill Tract. (E-7/2/57 p.2, c.4)

Welsh, James On Monday, August 27, 1860, he fell into a tub of water on his father's premises and drowned. He was two years and four months old. (E-8/30/60 p.2, c.5)

Wemple, Henry Y. During 1857 he was a Captain at the Yonkers Collegiate Institute. He gave a "neat" speech in Patterson, New Jersey on Thursday, August 6, 1857. (E-8/13/57 p.2, c.3)

Westerfield, John G. On November 13, 1854 a red cow with white spots on her left eye wandered onto his property. (TRB) On Friday, January 23, 1857 the Hudson River was frozen solid and he drove a team of horses across the river and back again. (E-1/29/57 p.2, c.5) During 1857 he was a boatbuilder at 3 Dock Street. (E-2/19/57 p.3, c.3)

Westerfield, Peter On Sunday, August 19, 1860 he died at the age of 74. He lived in South Yonkers. (E-8/23/60 p.2, c.6)

Westlake, J. D. During 1859 he advertised for an "American or German" to work on his farm that was located on Saw Mill River Road. (E-4/14/59 p.3, c.2)

Weston, Edward During 1857 he made a $25 donation to the Yonkers Library Association and received a life membership. (E-3/12/57 p.2, c.5) During March, 1859 he was selected to serve as a grand juror during the court session beginning Tuesday, March 18, 1859. (E-3/3/59 p.3, c.1)

Wetmore, E. A. During 1857 he had a business, maybe real estate, on Warburton Avenue. (E-12/10/57 p.3, c.3) Also in 1857 he advertised that he wanted to buy for cash in or near Yonkers five to fifteen acres of land with comfortable buildings for around $5,000. (E-12/31/57 p.3, c.6)

Whallon, Patrick On Wednesday, November 25, 1857 he was knocked overboard by a foreboom on the sloop *Sylvester Gesner* opposite Haverstraw, and before help could get to him he drowned. He lived in Yonkers and he worked on the sloop. (E-12/3/57 p.2, c.6)

Wharmby, William On Wednesday, October 19, 1859 he was married by Rev. Seward to Ellen Charl. (E-11/10/59 p.3, c.2)

Wheeler, John During February, 1859 he had a cow and calf for sale. (E-2/24/59 p.2, c.2) During 1859 he was in general furnishing and was also an undertaker on North Broadway next to Post's book store. He also owned the Broadway Livery Stables. (E-5/26/59 p.3, c.2) He also sent a carriage to the railroad depot and docks to meet passengers and take them anywhere in the County. (E-6/23/59 p.3, c.1) During October, 1859 a man rented a horse and wagon from him and he did not return it. During the week of January 30 Andrew Archibald was in Kingsbridge and recognized the horse. He told Wheeler, who had the man arrested and his property returned. (E-2/9/60 p.2, c.5) On the 1860 census he is listed as a 38-year-old undertaker with $5,000 in real estate, and a personal estate of $4,000. His wife Elizabeth was 30 years old, and they had three children; John who was 10, Frank who was 3, and Charles who was one. They also had a servant. During 1860 he was elected to the village Board of Trustees.

White, William During 1857 he and Daniel Richmond owned a grocery store. (E-5/28/57 p.2, c.2)

White, (Dr.) During 1857 he was a dentist with an office opposite the Getty House. In the same year he brought Dr. G. W. Perry into the practice with him. (E-3/19/57 p.2, c.4)

Whitefield, Edwin His son, Harold who was about ten years old, jumped off a train at Riverdale and because of the motion of the train the boy fell onto the tracks. The train ran over one leg severing it above the knee and the other leg was broken in three places. It was doubtful that the boy would live. (E-10/15/57 p.2, c.7) However, two weeks later he was still alive. He had part of one leg below the knee amputated and the doctors thought he would recover use of the other leg. (E-10/29/57 p.2, c.2) The father did sketchings and then had them engraved. One of those sketchings was of Niagara Falls and the engravings were for sale. (E-2/18/58 p.2, c.7)

Whitett, Mary J. On Sunday, September 25, 1859 she was married by Rev. L. H. King at the Methodist Episcopal Church to Solomon W. Oakley. (E-10/20/59 p.3, c.1)

Whiting, J. R. Sometime early in 1857 he donated 9 volumes to the Yonkers Library Association. (E-3/5/57 p.2, c.6)

Whyte, John On Friday, October 23, 1857 he died of a gunshot wound to the abdomen. While he was hunting he rested his gun at his side to reach for some grapes. The gun slipped and discharged. He left a widow and five children. The accident occurred near the house of Edward Cromwell. He was taken there by Messrs. Mott, Bennett and McCabe but they were refused entry. They asked for a horse to convey him to a doctor and this was also denied. They asked for some brandy or other stimulant and again they were denied. A blanket was asked for and again another denial. The keepers of the house then locked all the doors. (E-10/29/57 p.2, c.1)

Wicke, George On Tuesday evening, August 17, 1858 he got into a fight with H. Osthaus. (See Osthaus for details.)

Wicker, James C. During the winter of 1856 and the spring of 1857 he built a two-story brick building with an attic and a basement. The building was located on the west side of Broadway near Underwood on the old farm of Sampson Simson. The building cost about $7,000. (E-12/31/57 p.2, c.2) On Tuesday, October, 25, 1859 his daughter Carrie Wicker died of congestion of the lungs at the age of 4 months and 14 days. His wife was Maria P. Wicker. (E-11/3/59 p.3, c.7)

Wiederhold, Charles During 1857 he bought out a business probably from Wickes. (E-4/9/57 p.4, c.5)

Wilkerson, Daniel During 1854 and 1856 he was a Constable. (TRB)

Wilkison, William During 1858 he was foreman of Lady Washington Fire Engine Company #2. (E-8/26/58 p.3, c.2)

Willard, A. J. On Tuesday, January 31, 1860 he and seven others sent a letter to R. J. DeCordova asking him to visit Yonkers and deliver his humorous lecture on "Wall Street." (E-2/16/60 p.2, c.5) On Monday evening March 26, 1860 he was elected one of several secretaries of a Republican election rally meeting at the Getty House. (E-3/29/60 p.2, c.3)

Williams, Benjamin On Thursday night, October 28, 1858 he broke into the school hall of Miss Hall on Broadway opposite the Episcopal Church. A family living above the hall was awakened and apparently began yelling. Police officers Waterman and Smelt were nearby and came to help. They found him lying in the hallway pretending to be drunk. He had entered the building by breaking a glass panel on the door. He was taken before a Justice and sentenced to ninety days in the county jail at White Plains. It was only a few weeks prior to this incident that he was let out of prison for stealing caps from S. S. Peck's store. (E-11/4/58 p.2, c.4)

Williams, John Henry On Wednesday evening, August 18, 1858 he was elected a trustee for School District #2. (E-8/26/58 p.2, c.4) He was one of the vice presidents of the Yonkers Savings Bank. (E-11/4/58 p.2, c.7) During March, 1859 he was selected to serve as a petit juror during the court session beginning Tuesday, March 18, 1859. (E-3/3/59 p.3, c.1) Around August, 1859 the Library Association was incorporated and he became a member of the Board of Trustees. (E-8/14/59 p.2, c.4) On Monday evening March 26, 1860 he was elected one of thirty-two vice presidents of a Republican election rally meeting at the Getty House. (E-3/29/60 p.2, c.3) During 1860 he was president of the Yonkers School Board. (E-10/11/60 p.2, c.3)

Williams, Maria E. On Wednesday, April 18, 1860 she was married by Rev. Seward to Marvin R. Oakley. (E-5/24/60 p.3, c.3)

Williams, Mary Sometime during 1859 she died. The executrix of her estate was Janet S. Sandford. (E-6/30/59 p.3, c.5)

Williams, Sarah Anna On Sunday evening, January 17, 1858 she married Isaac M. Briggs. She was from Yonkers and he was from Fordham. (E-1/28/58 p.2, c.6)

Williams, W. C. During 1859 and maybe earlier he donated several valuable works to the Yonkers Library Association. (E-4/14/59 p.2, c.4)

Willis, Valentine On Wednesday, June 30, 1857 he bought a lot on Depot Street for $710. He bought another lot on Washington Street for $610. (E-7/1/58 p.2, c.2)

Wisewell, M. N. During 1857 he was one of the principals of the Yonkers Collegiate Institute. (E-2/5/57 p.3, c.3) On Monday, March 2, 1857 he was elected a manager of the Yonkers Library Association. (E-3/5/57 p.2, c.6) Later in 1857 he sold a part interest in the Institute to George H. Fillmore. (E-10/29/57 p.3, c.1) However, later in the year he advertised that the partnership was not consummated and had been postponed. (E-12/31/57 p.2, c.7) On Monday evening, March 1, 1858 he was again elected a manager of the Yonkers Library Association. (E-3/4/58 p.2, c.3) Apparently he sold the Institute to Rev. George Cooke by April, 1858. He was staying on as a teacher though. (E-4/18/58 p.2, c.1) On Wednesday evening, December 14, 1859, at their annual meeting in Yonkers he was elected Senior Warden of Rising Star Lodge, No. 450, of F. & A.M. (E-12/15/59 p.2, c.5) On Thursday morning, January 19, 1860, he was on a coroner's jury to look into the death of Mrs. Field who died in a railroad accident at Tarrytown. He was listed as principal of the academy. (E-1/26/60 p.2, c.5 see Foster Jenkins for more details) On Saturday, April 28, 1860, a man using the name of A. J. Henderson approached him to enroll his brother in the Institute. He wanted to pay one quarter of the tuition in advance with a check that was about $30 over the amount of the tuition. Wisewell thought it might be a scam and refused to cash the check until he investigated. It turned out to be a scam. (E-5/10/60 p.2, c.4) On Monday night, December 17, 1860 he was installed as an officer into the Rising Star Lodge of Free and Accepted Masons as W.M. (E-12/20/ 60 p.2, c.3) On the 1860 census he is listed as a 33-year-old teacher with a personal estate of $2,000. His wife, E. A., was 26 years old, and they had two children; Ida who was 4, and Alice who was 6 months old. They had six servants, four teachers, a matron, a gardener, and 41 male students between the ages of 9 and 18.

Withington, Josiah Sometime during either late February or early March, 1859 he married Cornelia K. Cooper at the Chestnut Cottage in Yonkers. He was from Boston. (E-3/3/59 p.3, c.3)

Wood, Ralph On Wednesday, November 2, 1859, he won a full tea set in a target shooting contest at Weehawkan, New Jersey. He was a member of the Yonkers Hatters Guard. (E-11/3/59 p.2, c.6)

Wood, Sarah E. On Tuesday, January 31, 1860 she was married by Rev. King of the M. E. Church to Robert Embree. (E-2/23/60 p.2, c.7)

Wood, Thomas At about 2 A.M. Tuesday, September 21, 1858 his house was broken into. The thieves stole some money, and a small amount of silver. (E-9/23/58 p.2, c.4) During the latter part of 1858 he signed a petition to have a meeting of the taxpayers in School District #2 meet to reconsider the location of two new schools; one on the corner of Wood Place and Warburton Avenue, and the other on St. Mary's Street near the Catholic Church and school. (E-12/23/58 p.2, c.3) On Monday, September 3, 1860 he was to serve on the petit jury of the Court of Oyer and Terminer in White Plains. (E-8/30/60 p.3, c.1)

Woodbine, John T. During 1853 he was a partner in a liquor business with William W. Woodworth. (TRB) [This probably is the Woodbine after which Woodbine Street, now part of Woodworth Avenue, was named after.]

Woodfine, John J. During the early part of 1857 he acted as a teller during a meeting to nominate a village president. (E-2/26/57 p.2, c.1) Also in 1857 he was a hotel and tavern owner. (E-5/28/57 p.2, c.2)

Woodruff, F. During 1860 he won $10 at a Yonkers Hatters Guard target shooting contest. (E-11/1/60 p.3, c.1)

Woodruff, W. During 1860 he won a six-month subscription to a newspaper at a Yonkers Hatters Guard target shooting contest. (E-11/1/60 p.3, c.1)

Woodworth, Charles R. Probably in 1856 he started to build a house near the home of J. P. M. Stetson. The house was a large wooden structure that cost between $7,000 and $8,000 to build. It was probably finished sometime during 1857. (E-12/31/57 p.2, c.2) He owned a business at 74 Wall Street, NYC where he sold gas machines patented after the Maryland Portable Gas Company's machine. (E-12/31/57 p.3, 2) During March, 1859 he was selected to serve as a grand juror during the court session beginning Tuesday, March 18, 1859. (E-3/3/59 p.3, c.1) He is listed on the 1860 census as a 28-year-old worker or owner in a gas company with $10,000 in real estate, and a personal estate of $2,000. His wife Carrie was 25 years old, and they had one child, Jennie, who was 2 years old. They had two servants, a cook, and a coachman.

Woodworth, William W. During the early years of the Yonkers Library Association he received a life membership. (E-3/12/57 p.2, c.5) During 1857 he was a member of the Masons. (E-8/20/57 p.2, c.5) He was born on Monday, March 16, 1807 in New London Connecticut. In 1838, 1841, and 1843 he was Supervisor of Hyde Park, New York. [They were probably two-year terms.] In 1838 he was appointed a judge in Dutchess County and he resigned in 1843. He was a Democrat who served in Congress from 1845 to 1847. He had business interests in Cuba, and formed a stock company of the Hudson River State Company in Clinton, New York. He contracted to build a section of the Hudson River Railroad, and moved to Yonkers during 1849. He was involved in real estate and banking. He was president of the village of Yonkers during 1857 and 1858. In 1870 he was appointed Receiver of Taxes for the village. He died in Yonkers on Thursday, February 1873, and he is buried in Oakland Cemetery in Yonkers. (WWW, p.596) On Tuesday, September 1, 1857 he was elected as a James Buchanan delegate to the County Democratic Convention held at West Farms on September 2, 1857. (E-9/3/57 p.2, c.7) On Wednesday, June 30, 1857 he bought a lot on Warburton Avenue for $870. (E-7/1/58 p.2, c.2) During the latter part of 1858 he signed a petition to have a meeting of the taxpayers in School District #2 meet to reconsider the location of two new schools; one on the corner of Wood Place and Warburton Avenue, and the other on St. Mary's Street near the Catholic Church and school. (E-12/23/58 p.2, c.3) On Tuesday, May 8, 1860, he was elected one of two vice presidents of the newly formed Yonkers Horticultural Society. (E-5/17/60 p.3, c.3) During 1860 he broke ground for a new factory building on James Street, near Palisade Avenue, on the 3rd water power on the Nepperhan River. The building was five stories high, 44 x 104 feet, brick, and covered with iron. William MacFarlane was going to rent it and use it as a silk factory. (E-10/25/60 p.2, c.6) He is listed on the 1860 census as a 50-year-old gentleman with $50,000 in real estate, and a personal estate of $2,000. His children were; William who was 22, James who was 17, Kate who was 17, Gertrude who was 16, Atherton who was 7, Henrietta who was 4, and Washington who was 2. A Sophia Woodworth lived with him. She was 81. He had five Irish servants. Very little matches with the 1850 census. (See Vol. 1, p.86.) During 1853 he was a partner in a liquor business with John T. Woodbine. (TRB)

Woolcocks, Caroline A. E. On Tuesday, April 26, 1859 she was married by Rev. D. M. Seward to Howard T. Schultz. (E-6/2/59 p.2, c.5)

Woolcocks, Samuel T. On Tuesday, April 27, 1858 he died at 45 years of age. His funeral was on the 29th at the Presbyterian Church. (E-4/27/58 p.2, c.7)

Wooster, Charles During 1858 he owned the Yonkers Iron Foundry. E-4/1/58 p.3, c.3) On Monday evening March 26, 1860 he was elected one of thirty-two vice presidents of a Republican election rally meeting at the Getty House. (E-3/29/60 p.2, c.3) During 1860 he moved into a new building that was built and owned by John Copcutt on the south side of Nepperhan Street. Part of the building was to be used as a foundry and another part as a machine shop. (E-4/4/60 p.3, c.1) On Wednesday afternoon, November 28 he was repairing a gasometer with his employee Watt Pendergrast, when gas escaped and ignited. He was severely burned in the face and on the hands. It was presumed that a healthy beard and mustache saved him from breathing the flames into his lungs. Pendergrast was killed. (E-12/6/60 p.2, c.4)

Youmans, James During 1857 he lived on Warburton Avenue. (E-3/5/57 p.2, c.1) Also during 1857 he was building a two-story brick house with an attic and a basement. The house was on the west side of Warburton Avenue, above Point Street, in Glenwood. He was his own architect and builder, and the house cost him about $7,000. (E-12/31/57 p.2, c.4) During the latter part of 1858 he signed a petition to have a meeting of the taxpayers in School District #2 meet to reconsider the location of two new schools; one on the corner of Wood Place and Warburton Avenue, and the other on St. Mary's Street near the Catholic Church and school. (E-12/23/58 p.2, c.3) During 1858 he was a builder and helped renovate the house of Thomas Radford. (E-1/20/59 p.2, c.5) On the 1860 census he is listed as a 40-year-old builder with $25,000 in real estate, and a personal estate of $2,000. His wife Phebe Ann was also 40 years old, and they had four children; Mary who was 16, Charlotte who was 13, Ann who was 11, and Laura who was 5. A Mrs. Bazer who was 65, and a Mary who was 35 were also in his household.

Zariski, Louis On Wednesday, November 2, 1859, he won a writing desk in a drawing at a target shooting contest at Weehawkan, New Jersey. He was a member of the Yonkers Hatters Guard. (E-11/3/59 p.2, c.6)

Zeliff, Gilbert On Thursday evening, December 29, 1859 he was fishing through the ice on the Hudson River. As he was leaving to go home he was walking with his axe over his shoulder and pulling a sled full of fish behind him. As he was walking over the ice he fell into a hole in the ice that he couldn't see because it was dark and he drowned. (E-1/12/60 p.2 c.6)

Chapter 6

Yonkers 1853 - 1860

Yonkers During 1853

This chapter is the beginning of the transcriptions of the third and final Town Record Book. The Record Book covers the years 1853 to March 28, 1873. This chapter covers the years 1853 to 1860 because of space limitations and because 1861 starts the Civil War era which will be examined in Volume Three.

The record book is leather bound and is thirteen and a half inches in length, nine and three quarter inches in width, and it is three inches thick. The cover is three sixteenths of an inch thick. The inside of the cover has a marbled pattern, and pasted on the first and second pages are three election notices and a notice by the manufacturer who was also the seller. The advertisement reads; George H. Bell, 158 Nassau Street, opposite the Park, New York, General Dealer in Foreign and Domestic Stationery, Manufacturer of Envelopes, and Printer, Commercial and Law Blanks, Blank Account Books of every description, a large assortment of Writing, Letter and Note papers, plain and fancy with Envelopes to match, School Books, Copy Books and School Stationery, at low prices, Annual Publisher of the Lawyers Diary, Physicians Diary, Citizens Diary, Pocket and Miniature Diaries, Plain and Fancy Book Binding, executed to order, all kinds of printing at short notice.

The first election notice is dated August 31, 1857, the second is dated February 4, 1865, and the third is dated August 2, 1869. The first and third election notices are for regular state elections, while the second notice is for a special election to determine the outcome of an amendment to the State Constitution.

On the third page at the top right is written TT? $4.50, and centered in the middle of the page but to the left; Town of Yonkers. The first five pages are unruled while all the remaining pages are ruled. On page eight the following was written and centered on the page; Records of the Town of Yonkers by Samuel W. Chambers, Clerk, 1853. At the top of the page and starting in the center are three undecipherable lines. On pages ten through thirty-three there are notices from 1842 through 1852, which were transcribed in the first volume. On page thirty-four the actual records of the Town of Yonkers begin.

Yonkers During 1853

The Electors of the Town of Yonkers

County of Westchester and State of New York.

Assembled in an Annual Town Meeting held at the Getty House on the 5th day of April 1853 for the purpose of electing town officers for the ensuing year, and to transact such other business that may be brought before the meeting when it was resolved;

That the sum of twenty-five hundred dollars be raised for the support of the roads and bridges for the ensuing year.
resolved

That there be eight Pound Masters, whereupon David Horton, Benjamin Fowler, Harvey Post, John Golden, Benjamin Brown, Jonathan Hogeland, Jacob Sherwood, and Nelson Strang were nominated and appointed.
On motion

That the regulation regarding Hog Warden be rescinded. The motion was lost.
On motion

That O. C. Denslow be Hog Warden for the present year. Carried.
On motion

That the resolution be abolished in relation to delegates from school districts. Carried.

No further business they then proceeded to canvass the votes cast for town officers. The officers voted for were for a Supervisor, one Town Clerk, one Assessor, two Overseers of the Poor, one Commissioner of the Highways, one Collector, five Constables, one Sealer of Weights and Measures, one Justice of the Peace for a regular term, two Inspectors of Election for District number One, two Inspectors of Election for District number Two, and two Inspectors of Election for District number 3.

Whereupon the result of the canvass was that the following were elected;

James L. Valentine	Supervisor
Samuel W. Chambers	Town Clerk
Odell Stevenson	Assessor
William H. Lawrence	Overseer of the Poor
James Nodine	Overseer of the Poor
Jacob Read	Commissioner of the Highways
William H. Lawrence	Collector
James Nodine	Constable
William H. Lawrence	Constable
Lyman F. Bradley	Constable
Devoe Treadwell	Constable
Charles H. Cargill	Constable

Matthias Warner	Sealer of Weights and Measures
William F. Groshon	Justice of the Peace
John Crisfield	Inspector District No. 1
John H. Meyers	Inspector District No. 1
William J. Majory	Inspector District No. 2
William G. Ackerman	Inspector District No. 2
William R. Dederer	Inspector District No. 3
Benjamin F. Underhill	Inspector District No. 3

Were severally announced to have been elected and so declared. Whereupon the meeting adjourned.
Samuel W. Chambers
Town Clerk

Map and description of a new road in the northeast part of the town of Yonkers running through the lands of Peter Underhill.

Beginning at a point about six hundred feet from the road leading from the northeast part of the Town of Yonkers to the Town of Greenburgh by the way of Col. Peter Underhill and Wm. Dederer at a stake designated in the accompanying diagram or map as the place of beginning running thence by the stakes North forty degrees, and thirty minutes east seven hundred and twenty six feet: thence North twenty seven degrees and forty five minutes East two hundred sixty four feet: thence North sixteen degrees and forty five minutes East one hundred and thirty two feet: thence North thirty five degrees and forty five minutes East one hundred and ninety eight feet: thence North twenty nine degrees East two hundred and seventy three feet: thence North one degree and forty minutes West three hundred and forty five: then North fourteen degrees West one hundred and thirty two feet to the aforesaid road leading from the Northeast part of the Town of Yonkers to the Town of Greenburgh by the way of Col. Peter Underhill and William Dederer as aforesaid. Said road to be forty nine and a half feet wide in width, the whole length to be two thousand and seventy feet, the area of the said road is two acres one rood (rood varied between six and eight yards) and sixteen rods, more or less. Kingsbridge Oct. 12, 1852. Map filed April 12, 1853. L. J. Olmstead Surveyor. Recorded November 12, 1853. Samuel W. Chambers, Town Clerk.

Documents filed,

Oaths of office Wm. H. Lawrence, Lyman F. Bradley, James Nodine, Chas. H. Cargill as Constables, Wm. H. Lawrence, James Nodine as Overseers of the Poor, Jacob Read as Commissioner of the Highways, Odell Stevenson as Assessor, and Samuel W. Chambers as Town Clerk.

Acceptance of Isaac H. Post to the office of Pound Master.

Bonds and sureties of Charles H. Cargill as Constable, Lyman F. Bradley as Constable, James Nodine as Constable, and Wm. H. Lawrence as Constable.

Reports of Wm. H. Lawrence as Overseer of the Poor Nov. 4, 1852, Wm. H. Lawrence as Overseer of the Poor Nov. 10, 1853, and James Nodine as Overseer of the Poor Nov. 10, 1853.

Decision of Gilbert Taylor, and Odell Stevenson, Fence Viewers in the case of division line between William Underhill and James P. (Swain).

Minutes of the Commissioners of Excise May 2, 1853. Licenses granted to George L. Condit Tavern Keeper, William H. Hoyt Tavern Keeper, Oliver C. Denslow Tavern Keeper, Daniel L. Austin Tavern Keeper, Henry (Denell) Tavern Keeper, Dewitt C. Kellinger Tavern Keeper, Dennis McGrath Grocer, Charles W. (Crofrit) Grocer, and J. and E. Waring grocers.

Bond and surety of William W. Woodworth and John I. Woodbine to the Commissioners of Excise for license to sell strong spirituous liquors.

Poll list of election April 5, 1853.

Canvass of election April 5, 1853.

Stray

Came to the premises of John Pulver a (Pye'd) heifer spotted white and yellow about 3 years old coming spring on Wednesday De. 28, 1853. Jan. 2, 1854 John Pulver.

In the matter of laying out a highway in the Town of Yonkers through improved lands of Ethan Flagg, Lemuel W. Wells, and Wm. W. Scrugham

Documents filed in relation thereto. The application. Consent of owners. Order and survey. The following is the order of the Commissioners of the Highways. Westchester County S.S.

It is hereby ordered and determined by David A. Post, Matthias Warner, and Gilbert Taylor the Commissioners of Highways of said Town of Yonkers upon the application of Wm. W. Scrugham, and the consent of Ethan Flagg, Lemuel W. Wells and William W. Scrugham through whose improved lands all of the highway hereinafter described is to pass that a highway be laid out in the said Town of Yonkers to be bounded as follows; beginning at a point on the southeasterly side of Guion St. in the village of Yonkers nineteen feet distant measuring along the southeasterly side of said Guion St. from land of Jane Ann Hibbard, wife of Timothy R. Hibbard, and running thence north 50 degrees East 138 feet, thence north 32 degrees East 570 feet, thence North fifty eight degrees west 50 feet, then south 32 degrees west 570 feet, thence south 50 degrees west 70 feet, and thence South 7 degrees 30 minutes west 77 feet to the place of beginning.

Dated Yonkers December 3, 1852. David Post, Gilbert Taylor, Matthias Warner Commissioners of the Highways.

Canvass of election District No. 1 Nov. 8, 1853.
Poll list of election District No. 1 Nov. 8, 1853.
Oath of office of M. Warner Sealer of Weights and Measures.
Oath of office James L. Valentine Supervisor.
Tavern Keeper bonds of H. (Denell) and D. C. Kellinger.
Account of receipts and expenditures of school money by Geo. W. Francis.
Account of Jacob Read Commissioner of the Highways, Gilbert Taylor Commissioner of Highways, D. A. Post Commissioner of the Highways, John Garrison Commissioner of the Highways, and William Warner Commissioner of the Highways.
Survey of the road from Yonkers to Riverdale.
Application and certificate of free holders in the matter of laying out a highway and altering the road through the land of John Stilwell from the Post Road to the landing.
Appointment of the Commissioners to assess the damage.

[The following is on the next to the last page of the Town Record Book, and is transcribed here because it all pertains to the year 1853. No other entries were made on the page.]

Lien Docket

[The following are six headings that run lengthwise across the page near the binding; Claimants, Against Whom Claims, Owners, Buildings, Amount Claimed, and What proceedings have been had. [The last heading was subdivided into Date of Notice and Filed. [In order to fit everything across and keep the integrity of the document the author's headings are not used here and words are substituted below to make it clear. The categories Owners and Buildings contain no information. This is the only time this section was used.]

Claimant Bayles Sloat against J. Coleman Hart for $437.96 filed May 30, 1853.
Claimant Theodore P. Butler against James M. Dayton for $89.19 filed Sept. 6, 1853.
Claimant Peter [Therrio] against James M. Dayton for $68.93 Date of notice July 20, 1853 filed Sept. 6, 1853.
Claimant Henry W. Bashford against Robinson & Clough & Edward W. Candee for $275.50 Date of notice Oct 31, 1853 filed Sept. 6, 1853.
Claimant Henry W. Bashford against Robinson & Clough & John McDonald for $255.28 Date of notice Oct. 31, 1853 filed Nov. 12, 1853.
Claimant Evert Gale against Catherine Boyer & John Boyer for $500.00 Date of notice Oct. 31, 1853 filed Nov. 12, 1853.

Claimant Daniel Blauvelt against Catherine A. Pendelton & Robinson & Clough for $815.53 Date of notice Aug. 24, 1853 filed Nov. 12, 1853.

Claimant Daniel Blauvelt against Robinson & Clough & Edward Candee for $808.38 Date of notice Aug. 24, 1853 filed Nov. 12, 1853.

Claimant Daniel Blauvelt against Robinson & Clough & William W. Woodworth for $320.16 Date of notice Aug. 24, 1853 filed Nov. 12, 1853.

Yonkers During 1854

Annual Town Meeting held at the Getty House March 28, 1854 for the purpose of electing Town officers and to transact such other business that may be brought before the meeting when it was resolved

that the sum of ninety dollars be levied upon and collected in the Town of Yonkers to be paid to Robert Getty for the rent from the 28th August last to the 28th March 1855 of the lock up house belonging to him and used for the Town.

Resolved that the sum of two thousand and seven hundred dollars be levied and raised in the Town of Yonkers for the repair of the roads and bridges in said town for the coming year, and that the Commissioners of the Highways be authorized to borrow the sum of $200 immediately to be expended upon the bridge now being built over the Bronx River at Tuckahoe and the said sum of $200 so to be borrowed to be paid with the interest out of the sum of $2,700 above authorized as soon as the same shall be effected.

No further business they then proceeded to canvass the votes.

The offices voted for were for a Supervisor, one Town Clerk, one Assessor, two Overseers of the Poor, one Commissioner of Highways, one Collector, five Constables, one Justice of the Peace for a regular term, one Justice of the Peace to fill a vacancy, two Inspectors of Election for District No. 1, two Inspectors of Election for District No. 2, and two Inspectors of Election for District No. 3.

Town Officers for the Year 1854

William G. Ackerman	Supervisor
Anson B. Hoyt	Town Clerk
Oliver C. Denslow	Assessor
William H. Lawrence	Overseer of the Poor
Benjamin B. Smith	Overseer of the Poor
James L. Valentine	3 years Commissioner of the Highways
William H. Lawrence	Collector
John Archer	Constable

William H. Lawrence	Constable
Lyman F. Bradley	Constable
Daniel Wilkerson	Constable
Daniel Blauvelt	Constable
Thomas Smith	Full Term Justice of the Peace
William C. Waring	Vacancy Justice of the Peace
David A. Post	Inspector District No. 1
David Horton	Inspector District No. 1
William J. Majory	Inspector District No. 2
William G. Ackerman	Inspector District No. 2
William Dederer	Inspector District No. 3
James Dusenbury	Inspector District No. 3

were severally announced to have been elected and so declared, whereupon the meeting adjourned.
Anson B. Hoyt
Town Clerk
Documents filed

Oath of office of William G. Ackerman as Supervisor, Anson B. Hoyt as Town Clerk, O. C. Denslow as Assessor, William H. Lawrence as Overseer of the Poor, William H. Lawrence as Constable, John Archer as Constable, Lyman F. Bradley as Constable, Daniel Wilkerson as Constable, Henry M. Coffin as Sealer of Weights and Measure, and James L. Valentine as Commissioner of the Highways.

Appointment of Lyman F. Bradley as an Overseer of the Poor.

Oath of office of Lyman F. Bradley as an Overseer of the Poor.

Minutes of the Commissioners of Excise May 1, 1854. Licenses granted to George G. Condit Tavern License, G. G. Woodfine Tavern License, O. C. Denslow Tavern License, W. W. Hoyt Tavern License, Nick (Revh) Tavern License, Sarah Kellinger Tavern License, Ackerman and Deyo Grocery License, J. A. and C. E. Waring Grocery License, and Denny McGrath Grocery License.

(Written along the left edge of the paper with a ball point pen Warburton Avenue.)

In the matter of laying out a highway in the Town of Yonkers documents filed in relation thereto; the application order and survey. The following is the order;

State of New York County of Westchester Town of Yonkers SS

Whereas upon the application of Edward N. Cander resident in said town and a householder and a freeholder and taxpayer therein, and liable to be assessed to work the highways therein, and liable to be assessed to work on the highways herein after described and laid out, and on the certificate of twelve refutable freeholders of the said town duly canvassed and sworn after due public notice as required by law certifying that such highway was necessary and proper, and all the owners and occupants of the land through which said highway is to run if any such there were having dedicated the same to public use, or having abandoned the same to the public, or having released the town from all claims for damages by reason of the laying out of the said highway; We the undersigned Jacob Read, James L. Valentine, and Gilbert Taylor the Commissioners of Highways in said town of Yonkers, after hearing all the reasons for and against the said application, having meant this day to decide thereon do hereby order determine and certify that a public highway shall be, and the same is hereby laid out pursuant to said application whereof a survey has been made, and which highway is described as follows. Beginning at a point on the northerly side of Dock Street, or a street running from the Hudson River to the Post Road, or Broadway mainly parallel with the Saw Mill River and now called or commonly known as Dock Street in said town of Yonkers as the said Dock Street has been recently widened, said point being also distant one hundred and fifty feet six inches in a direction north seventy five degrees forty minutes west from the Post Road now called Broadway, and running from said point north fifteen degrees east five thousand six hundred and fifty three feet or thereabouts to the southerly land of E. F. Shonnard to a point on said southerly line which is distant a thousand and ninety feet in a direction about north sixty four degrees west from the intersection of the southerly line of said Shonnard's land with the westerly line of said Post Road running thence along the southerly line of said Shonnard's land about north sixty two degrees forty five minutes west fifty feet to a point in the southerly line of said Shonnard's land distant eleven hundred and seventeen feet in a direction south sixty two degrees forty five minutes east from the intersection of said southerly line with the easterly line of land belonging to the Hudson River Railroad Company, and thence running from said last point parallel with the first mentioned course, and fifty feet distant there from south fifteen degrees west five thousand six hundred and fifty three feet or thereabouts to the northerly line of Dock Street aforesaid, and to a point in the northerly line of said Dock Street as aforesaid two hundred feet six inches in a direction north seventy five degrees forty minutes west from the Post Road, or Broadway, and thence along the northerly side of Dock Street as aforesaid fifty feet to the point or place of beginning and the line of said survey to be the center of the said highway which is to be fifty feet in width.

Dated Yonkers July 27, 1854

Gilbert Taylor, Jacob Read, James L. Valentine Commissioners of the Highways.

[Warburton Avenue ran north from Dock Street to just south of Phillipse Place directly across from Trevor Park.]

Documents filed 1854

Stray   Came to the premise of the subscriber the 6th day of December 1854 a red and white cow about 7 years with a white spot on her forehead, dark teats, and gives milk. Samuel Keeler, a (???? ???? it might be Village of Yonkers), farmer.

Stray   Came to the premises of the subscriber on the 13th day of November 1854, a red cow with a white spot on the left eye about 12 years old and gives milk. John G. Westerfield, Yonkers.

Yonkers During 1855

Annual Town Meeting held at the Getty House March 27, 1855 for the purpose of electing town officers and to transact such other business that may be brought before the meeting when it was resolved that there will be eight Pound Masters appointed for the ensuing year and that the following named persons be and are hereby so appointed, that is, David Horton, Z. B. Underhill, Benjamin Fowler, Robert Embree, Benjamin Brown, John Valentine, Jacob Sherwood, and Nelson Strang.

Resolved, that the sum of twenty five hundred dollars be raised for the support of roads and bridges for the ensuing year.

Resolved, that no animals shall be commoners.

Resolved, that all partition fences be four and a half feet high made of good and sufficient material.

Resolved, that a committee of three be appointed to select a suitable temporary place for securing vagrants and prisoners, and report at the next Town Meeting the necessary amount to procure a permanent lockup. Thomas Smith, Edward Shonnard, and Fielding S. Grant were appointed to the said committee.

Resolved, that the sum of forty dollars be raised for payment of fitting up the room of Justice Groshon for the transaction of Town and Court business.

The officers voted for were for a Supervisor, Town Clerk, one Assessor, two Overseers of the Poor, a Commissioner of Highways, a Collector, five Constables, a Sealer of Weights and Measures, one Justice of the Peace, and six Inspectors of Election.

Town Officers for the Year 1855

William G. Ackerman	Supervisor
Anson B. Hoyt	Town Clerk
Augustus VanCortlandt	Assessor
William H. Lawrence	Overseer of the Poor
Charles Smith	Overseer of the Poor

Gilbert Taylor	Commissioner of the Highways
William H. Lawrence	Collector
Charles Smith	Constable
William H. Lawrence	Constable
William Little	Constable
Cornelius L. Purdy	Constable
Edward Garrison	Constable
Henry W. Bashford	Full Term Justice of the Peace
John Crisfield	Sealer of Weights and Measures
David A. Post	Inspector District No. 1
John H. Myers	Inspector District No. 1
Thomas J. Delancey	Inspector District No. 2
William G. Ackerman	Inspector District No. 2
William R. Dederer	Inspector District No. 3
Abraham Vermilyea	Inspector District No. 3

were severally announced to have been elected and so declared, whereupon the meeting adjourned.

Anson B. Hoyt
Town Clerk

Documents filed 1855

Oath of office of William G. Ackerman as Supervisor, Anson B. Hoyt as Town Clerk, Augustus VanCortlandt as Assessor, William H. Lawrence as Overseer of the Poor, William H. Lawrence as Constable, Charles Smith as Constable, and Gilbert Taylor as Overseer of the Highways. (The Town Clerk probably meant Commissioner instead of Overseer.)

Bonds and Sureties of Wm. H. Lawrence as Constable.
Poll list of election held March 27, 1855.
Canvass of election held March 27, 1855.
Appointment of Nelson Strang as Pound Master May 12, 1855.

Stray Came to the premises of Benjamin VanTassell January 7, 1855 a bay horse about 10 years old, long tail, and long main with a white spot on the forehead. Benjamin VanTassell Southern Yonkers near harness store.

Appointment of Lyman F. Bradly as Overseer of the Poor July 13, 1855.
Oath of office of Lyman F. Bradly as Overseer of the Poor July 13, 1855.
Bond and sureties of Lyman F. Bradly as Overseer of the Poor July 13, 1855.
Appointment of John R. McKenzie as Constable of the Town Yonkers July 17, 1855.
Oath of office of John R. McKenzie as Constable July 17, 1855.

Bonds and sureties of John R. McKenzie as Constable July 17, 1855.

Resignation of Lyman F. Bradly Overseer of the Poor July 19, 1855.

Documents filed in the matter of laying out a highway in the Town of Yonkers from Riverdale to Spuytendyvil (Spuyten Duyvil). Application and consent. Notice and proof of (?) voting and certificate of freeholders

Stray Came to the premises of Jacob Sherwood September 16, 1855 a brown horse about 14 hands high long tail, 12 or 14 years old. Jacob Sherwood, Kingsbridge.

In the matter of laying out a highway in Yonkers from Riverdale to Spuyten Duyvil order of Commissioners October 13, 1855.
Poll list of election November 6, 1855 District Number 1.
Canvass of election November 6, 1855 District Number 1.
Poll list of election November 6, 1855 District Number 2.
Canvass of election November 6, 1855 District Number 2.
Poll list of election November 6, 1855 District Number 3.
Canvass of election November 6, 1855 District Number 3.

Associated Village Document 1

Resolution to prohibit bathing. July 2, 1855. Adopted. Filed July 2/55 W. H. Post Clerk

Resolved, that bathing in any of the waters within the corporate bounds of this village or in the Hudson River adjacent thereto be and hereby is prohibited between the hours of 7 o'clock in the morning and 7 o'clock at night, unless in a suitable bathing dress or covering. Any person violating this ordinance shall be subject to a fine of not less than two dollars no matter each offense. Adopted July 2/55 R. W. VanPelt W. H. Post Clerk.

[R. W. VanPelt was a Trustee of the Village and he probably sponsored the ordinance.]

Associated Village Document 2

Ordinance on bathing passed July 2, 1855. Adopted. Filed July 2, 1855 9 o'clock AM W. H. Post Clerk

Resolved, that bathing in any of the waters within the corporate bounds of this village or in the Hudson River adjacent thereto be and hereby is prohibited between the hours of 7 o'clock in the morning and 7 o'clock at night, unless in a suitable bathing dress or covering. Any person violating this ordinance shall be subject to a fine of not less than two dollars no matter each offense. Wm. H. Post, Clerk. W. Radford.

Associated Village Document 3

Corporation Ordinances

[Each of the following resolutions has a pencil line drawn through them. They are on one document.]

Passed June 18, 1855.
Resolved, that no dog shall be allowed to run at large in any street or highway in this village without being properly muzzled, and if any dog shall be found so running at large the owner thereof as person harboring the same, shall be subject to a fine of five dollars.

Resolved, that all dogs found running at large not muzzled, be taken to the pound by the proper authorities, and detained twenty four hours. If not reclaimed within that time, such dogs may be disposed of by killing or otherwise as in the judgement of the pound keeper. The person so claiming any dog shall at the time pay to the pound keeper the sum of five dollars and his fees; and in the case of any dog being killed herein directed the owners thereof shall not be liable for the penalty. Takes effect July 7, 1855.

[The following is on the same document.]

Corporation Ordinances
Passed July 2, 1855
Resolved, that bathing in any of the waters within the corporate bounds of this village, or in the (waters is crossed out) Hudson River adjacent thereto, be and is hereby prohibited between the hours of seven o'clock in the morning, and seven o'clock at night, unless in a suitable bathing dress or covering.

Any person violating this ordinance shall be subject to a fine of not less than two nor more than five dollars for each offense. Takes effect July 2, 1855.

Sections 71 and 73 as amended July 2, 1855.
Resolved, the section 71 of the ordinances relating to the licensing of theatrical performances, shows, and company be amended by inserting the amount to be paid for such license, to be not less than five nor more than twenty dollars, instead of not less than twenty nor more than fifty dollars as before.

Resolved, that section 73 of the ordinances relating to the protection of officers be amended by inserting the fine to be paid for interfering with any person driving animals to the pound, to be not less than ten nor more than fifty dollars, instead of not less than twenty nor more than fifty dollars as before.

Associated Village Document 4

[This document has a hole in it, and except for the signatures at the bottom it was written in pencil.]

Resolution to prohibit Picnics from landing in the Village. Adopted July 24, 1855.

Resolved, that no steamboat, barge, or other vessel shall land within the corporate limits of this village of Yonkers any picnic or pleasure party of persons for the purpose of roaming about the grounds and streets of this village without the written consent of a majority of the Trustees.

Any captain, owner, or other person having charge of any steamboat or vessel violating this ordinance shall be subject to a penalty of $50 for each offense.

This prohibition shall not apply to any regularly plying steam boat. Adopted July 24, 1855. Wm. H. Post Clerk. Wm. Radford President Village of Yonkers.

Associated Village Document 5

[This document was written on ruled paper, and is essentially the same as the above document.]

Resolution to prohibit steamboats, barges from landing Picnics. July 24, 1855. Adopted. July 24, 1855 W. H. Post Clerk.

Resolved, that no steamboat, barge, or other vessel shall land within the corporate limits of this village of Yonkers any picnic or pleasure party of persons for the purpose of roaming about the grounds and streets of this village without the written consent of a majority of the Trustees.

Any captain, owner, or other person having charge of any steamboat or vessel violating this ordinance shall be subject to a penalty of $50 for each offense.

This prohibition shall not apply to any regularly plying steam boat. Adopted July 24, 1855. Wm. H. Post Clerk. Copy. Wm. Radford President Village of Yonkers.

Associated Village Document 6

[This document is on a small piece of ruled paper.]

Resolved that the President be directed to prosecute all captains or owners of steam Boats or other vessels bringing to this place large parties of persons contrary to Law.

Adopted August 16, 1855.

Associated Village Document 7

[This document is essentially the same as the above document, but the context was written with a pencil.]

Resolution to Prosecute Steam Boat Captains. August 16, 1855. Adopted. Filed August 16, 1855. W. H. Post Clerk.

Resolved that the President be directed to prosecute all captains or owners of steam Boats or other vessels bringing to this place large parties of persons contrary to Law. August 16, 1855. Adopted August 16, 1855. W. H. Post Clerk.

Adopted Aug. 16, 1855.

Associated Village Document 8

[This document is very hard to read.]

Resolution Meeting inhabitants gas September 10, 1855. Adopted. Filed September 10, 1855. Wm. H. Post Clerk.

Resolved, that a meeting of the taxable inhabitants of this village be held at the Hall of the (????) on 25th day of September inst. at 5 o'clock PM for the purpose of voting upon a proposal to light Broadway, Mechanic and a part of Dock Street with gas, or such portions of said streets, or any streets, as said meeting may direct, and that notice of such meeting be published in the Village Newspaper. Adopted September 10, 1855. Wm. H. Post Clerk.

Yonkers During 1856

The electors of the Town Yonkers, County of Westchester, State of New York, assembled in an Annual Town Meeting held at the Franklin House on the 25th day of March 1856 for the purpose of electing town officers for the ensuing year, and to transact other such business that may be brought before the meeting.

Resolved that the sum of three thousand dollars be raised for the support of roads and bridges of the town during the ensuing year, and that one half of this sum be expended upon the roads and bridges within the corporate limits of the Village of Yonkers.

The following persons were then appointed Pound Masters for the ensuing year; Charles Gilchrist, Benjamin Archer, Vermilyea Fowler, Benjamin Read, Zalmon S. Hynard, and Gilbert Fowler.

No further business before the meeting they then proceeded to canvass the votes cast for town officers.

The offices voted for were for a Supervisor, one Town Clerk, one Assessor, two Overseers of the Poor, one Commissioner of Highways, one Collector, five Constables, a Superintendent of Common

Schools, one Justice of the Peace for a regular term, one Justice of the Peace to fill a vacancy, two Inspectors of Election for District No. 1, two Inspectors of Election for District No. 2, and two Inspectors of Election for District No. 3.

Town Officers for the Year 1856

William W. Scrugham	Supervisor
Anson B. Hoyt	Town Clerk
Odell Stevenson	Assessor
William H. Lawrence	Overseer of the Poor
Abraham F. Vermilyea	Overseer of the Poor
Jacob Read	Commissioner of the Highways
William H. Lawrence	Collector
Benjamin C. Nodine	Constable
William H. Lawrence	Constable
Henry Crabb	Constable
Daniel Wilkinsen	Constable
John Golden	Constable
George W. Francis	Superintendent of Common Schools
John Crisfield	Full Term Justice of the Peace
Isaac G. Johnson	Justice of the Peace (Vacancy)
James L. Valentine	Inspector District No. 1
Ethan Flagg	Inspector District No. 1
J. M. Horton	Inspector District No. 2
John L. Berrian	Inspector District No. 2
William R. Dederer	Inspector District No. 3
Abraham F. Vermilyea	Inspector District No. 3

were severally announced to have been elected and so declared.
Anson B. Hoyt
Town Clerk

Documents filed 1856

Oath of office of William W. Scrugham as Supervisor, Anson Hoyt as Town Clerk, Odell Stevenson as Assessor, Jacob Read as Commissioner of the Highways, W. H. Lawrence as Constable, David Wilkersen as Constable, and Benjamin C. Nodine as Constable.

Bonds and sureties of W. H. Lawrence as Constable, Daniel Wilkersen as Constable, Benjamin C. Nodine as Constable, and W. H. Lawrence as Overseer of the Poor.

Poll list of election March 25, 1856.
Canvass of election March 25, 1856.
Report of Jacob Read Commissioner of the Highways.
Report of Gilbert Taylor Commissioner of the Highways.
Report of James L. Valentine Commissioner of the Highways.

In the matter of the discontinuing of a part of the old Albany Post Road in the Town of Yonkers. Application certificate, order, and map.
Poll list of election November 4, 1856 District Number 1.
Canvass of election November 4, 1856 District Number 1.
Poll list of election November 4, 1856 District Number 2.
Canvass of election November 4, 1856 District Number 2.
Poll list of election November 4, 1856 District Number 3.
Canvass of election November 4, 1856 District Number 3.
Memorandum of challenges at the State election held in the 1st election district in Town of Yonkers. November 4, 1856.
Memorandum of challenges at the State election held in the 3rd election district in Town of Yonkers. November 4, 1856.

[The next page is blank, and the next three pages were cut out of the book.]

Associated Village Document 9

Report of Committee on amending the Charter. March 31, 1856. Laid on the table.

The Special Committee appointed to propose amendments to the Charter respectfully reports that they have given the subject much consideration which its importance demands and propose the following amendments to the Charter, and recommend their adoption by this Board. Thomas O. Farrington, R. W. VanPelt, Lemuel W. Wells, Com. March 31st.

[There are no proposals on the document.]

Associated Village Document 10

Boundaries Locust Hill Avenue
Shelf 23 896
"A"

Lemuel W. Wells and others to the President and Trustees of the Village of Yonkers. Deed of Locust Hill Avenue. Description of Boundaries.

For the westerly boundary of said Avenue, beginning on the northerly side of Palisade Avenue at a point 75 feet distant easterly from the westerly side of a brick building belonging to or occupied by Ralph Shipman, measuring on said northerly line of Palisade Avenue, and running thence on the westerly line of a street formerly known as Academy Street as the same was surveyed and laid out for Lemuel W. Wells by Andrew Findlay in 1846, being along land occupied by said Shipman and along land of Edwin Underhill N.26'30"E.361 feet to the northeasterly corner of said Underhill's land. Thence, through lands of Jane E. Cornell, of William W. Woodworth and Thomas C. Cornell, of Robert Grant and of William C. Waring, in a direction parallel with the face of the stone wall on the front of the land of John T. Waring and 50 feet distant then from N 25'45" E 334 feet to a point in the westerly line of the above mentioned street formerly called Academy Street, as surveyed and laid out by said Findlay. Thence along the westerly line of said street as surveyed by said Findlay N.19'45" E. 1245 feet to Ashburton Avenue; the above described lines forming the westerly boundary line of the hereby described. Thence along said Ashburton Avenue easterly to a point 50 feet distant from a line continuous with the above described westerly line of the hereby described Avenue, measuring at right angles thenwith. Thence for the easterly of the hereby described Avenue running in a direction always parallel with the above described westerly line and always 50 feet distant therefrom southerly 1909 feet to Palisade Avenue aforesaid. Thence along said Palisade Avenue westerly to the place of beginning. Thomas C. Cornell Civ Eng. Yonkers 4th December 1856.

[The original name of Locust Hill Avenue was Academy Street. This makes sense since Wells built an academy on top of the hill. Academy Street was a private street, and in 1856, when it was renamed, it became a public street.]

Yonkers During 1857

Annual Town Meeting Town of Yonkers held March 31, 1857

At the annual Town Meeting of the Town of Yonkers held March 31, 1857 at the Franklin House in said Town for the purpose of electing Town officers for the ensuing year, and for the transaction of such other business as may come before the meeting
On Motion it was

Resolved, that the sum of three thousand five hundred dollars ($3500.00) be raised by tax the ensuing year for the support of Roads and Bridges in said Town.

Resolved, that the sum of four hundred dollars ($400.00) be levied and raised by tax for the support of the poor for the ensuing year.

Resolved, that Caleb F. Underhill, Isaac Sherwood, Nelson Strang, David Horton, Gilbert Taylor, Benjamin Brown, John Crisfield, and David A. Post be appointed Pound Masters of the Town for the ensuing year.

Resolved, that the next Town Meeting be held at the Franklin House in said Town. A. B. Hoyt, Town Clerk.

We the presiding officers of the annual Town Meeting held in the Town of Yonkers in the County of Westchester on the 31st day of March 1857 do hereby in pursuance of the directions given in Section 21, Title 3, Article 3 of the act entitled an act respecting elections other than for Town and Militia officers passed April 5, 1842 do hereby appoint

Leonard M. Clark District No. 1, Augustus VanCortlandt District No. 2, and Caleb F. Underhill District No. 3 to be associated respectively with the two who have this day been elected for each said district, and each to be an inspector of elections in and for his district in all elections held in said districts during the present year. The said Leonard M. Clark, Caleb F. Underhill, and Augustus VanCortlandt each being one of the two persons in their election districts respectively who had the highest number of votes next to the two inspectors who were elected.

Given under our hands this 31st day of March 1857. Thomas Smith, H. W. Bashford, Wm. F. Groshon Justices of the Peace. Anson B. Hoyt Town Clerk.

Town Officers 1857 & 8

William W. Scrugham	Supervisor
William H. Post	Town Clerk
Oliver C. Denslow	Assessor
William H. Lawrence	Overseer of the Poor
Charles H. Smith	Overseer of the Poor
James L. Valentine	Commissioner of the Highways
William H. Lawrence	Collector
Benjamin C. Nodine	Constable
William H. Lawrence	Constable
John S. Waterman	Constable
Wm. P. Littell	Constable
Charles H. Smith	Constable
Wm. F. Groshon	Justice of the Peace
John H. Myers	Inspector of Elections District No. 1
Ethan Flagg	Inspector of Elections District No. 1
Leonard M. Clark	Inspector of Elections District No. 1
Caleb H. Bosworth	Inspector of Elections District No. 2
Cornelius L. Purdy	Inspector of Elections District No. 2
A. VanCortlandt	Inspector of Elections District No. 2
Nathaniel Reynolds	Inspector of Elections District No. 3
Abraham F. Vermilyea	Inspector of Elections District No. 3
Caleb F. Underhill	Inspector of Elections District No. 3

[Apparently the above title that includes 1858 meant the time of election in 1857 to the time of re-election in 1858.]

1857 Documents filed by Wm. H. Post Town Clerk.
Poll list Town Meeting March 31, 1857.
Canvass list Town Meeting March 31, 1857.

Oath of Office

of Wm. W. Scrugham Supervisor
of Wm. H. Post Town Clerk
of Jas. L. Valentine Commissioner of Highways
of Wm. H. Lawrence Overseer of the Poor
of Chas. H. Smith Overseer of the Poor
of O. C. Denslow Assessor
of Chas. H. Smith as Constable
of Wm. H. Lawrence as Constable
of Benj. C. Nodine Constable
of Wm. P. Littell Constable
of John S. Waterman Constable
of John Stevens Sealer of Weights and Measures Bond
of Wm. H. Lawrence Overseer of the Poor
of Wm. H. Lawrence Constable
of B. C. Nodine Constable
of Wm. P. Littell Constable
of C. H. Smith Constable
Appointment of Nelson Strang and David Horton Pound Masters.
Acceptance of the office of Pound Master by David Horton and Nelson Strang.
Bond
of Matthias Warner Grocers License
of Alfred Turnip & Co. Grocers License [Turnip is quite clear, but it could also be Turniss.]
of Ackerman and Deyo Grocers License
of Dennis McGrath Grocers License
of Thompson and Brevoort Grocers License
of Jarvis A. Waring Grocers License
of Hallock and Page Grocers License
of Lawrence R. Condon Grocers License
of Wm. White and Richmond Grocers License
of Wm. B. Edgar Grocers License
of H. McElrone Innkeeper License
of R. L. Bucklin Innkeeper License
of J. J. Woodfine Innkeeper License
of O. C. Denslow Innkeeper License
of N. W. Tompkins Innkeeper License
of Geo. Holberton Innkeeper License
of N. Post Innkeeper License
Copy of the minutes of proceedings of the Board of Excise of the County of Westchester relating to the Town of Yonkers.

Resignation of Ethan Flagg Inspector of Elections in District Number 1 Town of Yonkers.

Appointment of James L. Valentine Inspector of Elections District Number 1 Town of Yonkers.

Appointment of John Stevens Sealer of Weights and Measures of the Town of Yonkers.

List of bills audited by the Board of Town Auditors of the Town of Yonkers (Jn) 5 and 6 1857.

Notice of two stray cows by Galmon Hynard.

List of persons qualified to serve as jurors in the Town of Yonkers.

In the matter of an encroachment on the easterly side of the old Albany Road in the Town of Yonkers. Complaint and map.

Poll list District No. 1 General Election November 3, 1857.

Canvass list District No. 1 General Election November 3, 1857.

List of challenged voters District No. 1 General Election November 3, 1857.

Poll list District No. 2 General Election November 3, 1857.

Canvass list District No. 2 General Election November 3, 1857.

Poll list District No. 3 General Election November 3, 1857.

Canvass list District No. 3 General Election November 3, 1857.

Report of Wm. H. Lawrence Overseer of the Poor.

Report of Overseers of the Poor to Town Auditors as to amount to be raised for ensuing year for the support of the poor.

In the matter of establishing an Union Free School in School District No. 1 in the Town of Yonkers.

Notice, Proceedings of Trustees and other papers relating thereto.

Resignation of Odell Stevenson Assessor of the Town of Yonkers.

In the matter on encroachment on the easterly and westerly sides of the old Albany Road in the Town of Yonkers. Complaints.

Report of Jacob Read Commissioner of the Highways.

Report of James L. Valentine Commissioner of the Highways.

Report of Gilbert Taylor Commissioner of the Highways.

Report of Wm. H. Lawrence Commissioner of the Highways.

Report of C. H. Smith Commissioner of the Highways.

Associated Village Document 11

List of persons taxed for personal property in the Village of Yonkers for Taxes 1857. Filed (Jan.) 16, 1857 Wm. H. Post Clerk.

[On the top left the pages are number 1, 2, and 3. The page number 1 is the total page. Consequently, the pages are arranged 2, 3, and 1 in the sequence noted in the subtotals.]

Mr. Melah	500
Cap't. J. Garrison	9000
Jacob Read	2000
Anthony Archer	4000
F. S. Cozzins	5000 [This name is crossed out.]
G. W. Mitchell	3000
John Stephens	500
Ralph Shipman	8000
G. B. Skinner	10000 [This name is crossed out.]
Mrs. P. W. Paddock	4500
H. Ireland	500
L. F. Wheeler	1000
T. W. Budsell	1000
J. B. Kinslow	300 [This name is crossed out.]
Mr. Schoburgh	3000
A. Frendenbergh	500 [This name is crossed out.]
A. Thomas	5000
R. J. Douglass	1000
J. C. Duly	1000
W. H. Varm	450
S. W. Jones	500
W. G. Anderson	1500 [This name is crossed out.]
Ester Bei???	2760
Bank of Yonkers	150000
David Bates received	500
Jas. C. Bet???	4000
Silas Crawford	800
	=======
	216060
Richard Archer	4000
John Hobbs	200
Ethan Flagg	10000
Estate of Wm. Lawrence	9000
Mrs. L. Flagg	6000
L. W. Wells	15250
S. S. Barry	7500
Miss Bells	2000
Ackerman and Deyo	2000
J. C. Bell	10000
Wm. C. Arthur	3000 [This name is crossed out.]
F. S. Gant	5000
P. W. Dyroat	2000 [This name is crossed out.]
F. A. Coe	3000
H. S. Anstice	5000
R. Shannon	5000
Charles Bl????	4000

Dr. A. W. Gates	1000
J. Deneress	500
J. D. Stealweyzer	4000
O. C. Denslow	500
E. Martin	1000
Wm. C. Waring	1000
John Stillwell	2000
	=======
	102950

David Collins	500	
Hannah Cers???	500	[This name is crossed out.]
J. G. Donaldsen	1500	[The number 1 is circled.]
G. Gea????	1000	
A. W. Greenleaf	2000	
Thomas Morris	250	
Mrs. A. Nesbit	1800	
John M. Purdy	8000	
W. H. Post	500	
S. S. Peck	500	
M. W. Roony	500	
Lyman Seely	1000	
W. H. Sleyh???	2000	
Oscar Schenck	400	
(Henry) Sayermen	4000	[This name is crossed out.]
Thompson and Brevoort	2000	
White and Richmond	1200	
Vail and Elting	2000	
S. N. Waller	800	
Hoyt and (Smith)	1000	
	=======	
	31450	

Gustav Kustis	200
	=======
	31650

216060
102950
=======
350660

Associated Village Document 12
Resolution. Pay of Pound Masters for killing Dogs. August 3, 1857. Adopted. February 3, 1857. W. H. Post Clerk, W. Woodworth President.

Resolved, that the Pound Masters be allowed 50 cents for each dog impounded and not reclaimed, which he may kill and properly dispose of in accordance with the ordinance regulating the running at large of dogs. Getty.

[Getty was a Trustee during 1857, and he may have proposed this change in the ordinance.]

Associated Village Document 13

Resolution to forward amended Charter to Albany. March 18, 1857. Adopted. Filed March 18, 1857. W. H. Post Clerk. Approved W. W. Woodworth President.

Resolved, that the Charter as amended be referred to a special committee of three to forward the same to Albany and request passage by the Legislature. Getty. Dated March 18, 1857. W. H. Post Clerk.

Associated Village Document 14

Petition of F. S. Gant and 40 others to prohibit the running at large of milk cows. March 18, 1857. Referred to a committee. Reported on April 6, 1857.

To the Hon. the President and Trustees of the Village of Yonkers.

The undersigned hereby petition your Hon. body for the passage of an ordinance preventing the running at large of milk cows, and all other animals not included in the present ordinance passed June 4, 1855.

Yonkers March 16, 1857.

F. S. Gant

Ebenezer Baldwin, George N. Hallock, Jas. H. Page, Lawrence Post, Wm. N Sleight, Robert Embree, Jarvis A. Waring, N. Y. (Wakeman), P. S. Deyo, G. Ackerman, Wm. White, Daniel (N.) Richmond, James (F.) Huestis, Francis S. Miles, V. Melah, ? D. Bate, S. M. Clark, H. W. Bashford, John (H.) Myers, A. W. (Gore???), John R. McKenzie, John Milne, John (Nairn), H. G. Jones, John Archer, W. B. Edgar, A. Robinson, R. Stewart, (D. C. Stennel), F. Helwick, Abm. Fradenburgh, Joseph Moore, G???? Gil???, J. C. (Nickey), Joseph C. G??????, John Davis Hatch, Wm. (C.) Oakley, Peter N. Hustin, Nathan N. (Tray), A. D. Duffy.

Associated Village Document 15

Resolution to amend Section 66 of the ordinances. Passed April 6, 1857. Filed April 6, 1857.

Resolved, that Section 66 of the ordinances be and the same is hereby amended by inserting the words, from the first of May to the first of November, after the word "(excepted)" in the first line of said ordinance. Passed April 6, 1857 Wm. H. Post Clerk. Approved W. W. Woodworth President.

Associated Village Document 16

An ordinance to regulate the landing of Picnics. Passed July 9, 1857. Filed July 9, 1857 Wm. H. Post Clerk.

Sect. 1 Resolved, that no steamboat or barge while making an excursion of pleasure from the city of New York or elsewhere shall land any passenger or passengers from the same within the corporate limits of the Village of Yonkers without having first obtained a permit in writing from the President or two of the Trustees of said Village.

Sect. 2 The captain, owner, or person in charge of any such steamboat or barge violating the above ordinance shall be subject to a fine not exceeding one hundred dollars.

Sect. 3 The President or any two Trustees of said Village are hereby authorized and empowered to grant such permit to the captain, owner, or person in charge of any steamboat or barge making an excursion of pleasure to said Village on such captain, owner, or person in charge thereof applying for the summer and paying the said President or Trustees a sum the first of them not less than five dollars nor more than fifty dollars, which sum of money shall be paid over to the treasurer to be applied to the support of the police of said Village.

Sect. 4 The ordinance passed July 24, 1855, in relation to such steamers or barges landing passengers in said Village, is repealed.

Approved W. W. Woodworth, President. Passed July 9, 1857 Wm. H. Post, Clerk.

Associated Village Document 17

Ordinance in relation to receiving and entertaining Picnics. Passed August 3, 1857. Filed August 3, 1857. Wm. H. Post, Clerk. Approved W. W. Woodworth, President.

Sect. 1 Resolved, that no person shall receive or entertain upon or within his grounds and premises in the Village of Yonkers any party of passengers, landing within the limits of said Village from any steamboat or barge while making an excursion of pleasure from the City of New York or elsewhere, unless such landing shall have been first permitted pursuant to the provisions of the ordinance passed July 10, 1857.

Sect. 2 Any person violating the above ordinance shall be subject to a fine not exceeding one hundred dollars.

Associated Village Document 18

Petition of J. C. Derby and others in relation to Bathing. August 3, 1857. Referred to Committee on Police and Prisons. Filed June 17, 1858. Wm. H. Post, Clerk.

Glenwood, Yonkers July 1857

To the President and Trustees of the Village of Yonkers,

Gentlemen:

The petition of the undersigned respectfully set forth, that Whereas by a recent resolution of your Board, bathing in the River is permitted at or after the hour of 8 PM. And whereas this permission to bathe at that hour is extensively availed of much to the inconvenience and annoyance of families residing opposite the Glenwood landing or station, restricting ladies from the walks along the cliffs and banks of the river just at the hour when they are most pleasant, namely when there is sufficient light to discern objects on the water, and when the heat of the day is past.

Therefore your petitioners pray that your Board will so amend the resolution above referred to as to prohibit persons from bathing before the hour of nine P.M. at which time darkness having succeeded to the twilight of 8 o'clock in these summer evenings, it will not be so much of a privation to the ladies residing in the neighborhood in question to have to remain indoors.

E. P. Hawthorne, J. C. Derby, Napoleon ??????, A. W. Greenleaf, Jas. R. Campbell, A. J. Willard, J. Smith (Homans), ?. S??erley, Jas. W. Murp?y, Stephen VanRansselar Cooper, N. V. Otis, ?. ?. Brown, ?. ???ord???, H. S. Bruckard Prin. of Fernale Class Serv., F. B. Crusson????, W. L. Crowell, James H. Pulver, Peter ???alemon, J. Burns.

[Allison has a Norton Prentiss Otis listed in the index. However, the middle initial of the above Otis is quite clearly not a P.)

Associated Village Document 19

Resolution in relation to smoke from George Russell's factory. September 10, 1857. Adopted. Filed September 10, 1857 Wm. H. Post, Clerk. Approved W. W. Woodworth, President.

Resolved, that Mr. George Russell the proprietor of the (Logwood) Factory on the Nepperhan River be requested to increase the height of the chimney of his works or adopt some effectual method of carrying off the smoke from the same so that it may not inconvenience the public by dispersing itself through the village. September 10, 1857. Adopted W. H. Post, Clerk.

Associated Village Document 20

Locust Hill Avenue. H. Curran $500 File 10. Hugh Curran. To E. Howland Esq. Treasurer of the Village of Yonkers,
Yonkers November 25, 1857. Sir: Please pay to the order of Hugh Curran the sum of five hundred dollars out of money to be collected for grading and (care) of Locust Hill Avenue. Approved W. W. Woodworth, President. Wm. H. Post, Clerk.

Associated Village Document 21

Resolution to procure handcuffs. December 8, 1857. Adopted. Approved W. W. Woodworth, President. Filed December 8, 1857. W. H. Post, Clerk.
Resolved, that the committee on Police Watch and Prisons be and they are hereby authorized to purchase three to six sets of handcuffs for the use of the police. Getty.

Associated Village Document 22

In the matter of grading Locust Hill Avenue.
The Treasurer of the Village of Yonkers will please pay to Hugh Curran on order the sum of five hundred dollars on account of the above matter. $500.00. W. W. Woodworth, President. Yonkers December 21, 1857. Wm. H. Post, Clerk.

[The document is folded and on the front fold is written the following.]

Locust Hill. H. Curran. $500. [Hugh Curran signed the document across the fold.]

Associated Village Document 23

[This document is folded in half as the above document and was signed by Hugh Curran across the fold near the middle of the page.]

In the matter of grading Locust Hill Avenue the Treasurer of the Village of Yonkers will please pay to Hugh Curran on order the sum of five hundred dollars on account of the above matter. $500.00. Yonkers December 21, 1857. Wm. H. Post, Clerk. W. W. Woodworth, President.

Yonkers During 1858

Annual Town Meeting of the Town of Yonkers held March 30, 1858.

At the annual Town Meeting of the Town of Yonkers held at the Franklin House in the Village of Yonkers on the 30th day of March 1858 for the election of Town officers, and for the transaction of the other necessary town business the following persons were declared elected by the presiding officers of said meeting.

Augustus VanCortlandt	Supervisor
William H. Post	Town Clerk
Wm. G. Ackerman	Assessor full term
Caleb F. Underhill	Assessor to fill vacancy
William H. Lawrence	Overseer of the Poor
Wm. McCabe	Overseer of the Poor
Gilbert Taylor	Commissioner of the Highways
William H. Lawrence	Collector
Wm. McCabe	Constable
William H. Lawrence	Constable
Benjamin C. Nodine	Constable
Thomas Cuddy	Constable
Edward Crisfield	Constable
James L. Valentine	Justice of the Peace
John Stevens	Inspector of Elections District No. 1
Leonard M. Clark	Inspector of Elections District No. 1
Wm. G. Ackerman	Inspector of Elections District No. 2
Caleb VanTassell	Inspector of Elections District No. 2
Wm. R. Dederer	Inspector of Elections District No. 3
Caleb F. Underhill	Inspector of Elections District No. 3

Wm. H. Post Town Clerk

At the annual Town Meeting of the Town of Yonkers held at the Franklin House in the Village of Yonkers on the 30th day of March 1858, on motion it was

Resolved that the sum of two thousand dollars be raised by tax for the support of Roads and Bridges outside of the Village of Yonkers for the ensuing year. Wm. H. Post Town Clerk.

We the presiding officers of the annual Town Meeting held in the Town of Yonkers on the 30th day of March 1858 do hereby appoint George P. Abbott in Election District No. 1, Charles Gilchrist in election district no. 2, and Nathaniel Reynolds in election district no. 3 in said Town Inspectors of Elections in said districts respectively to be associated with the two in each of said districts respectively who have this day been elected Inspectors of Elections for the ensuing year. The said George P. Abbott, Charles Gilchrist, and Nathaniel Reynolds each being one of the two persons who received at said Town Meeting the highest number of votes respectively for said office of Inspector next to the two Inspectors so elected.

Dated Yonkers this 30th day of March 1858. H. W. Bashford and Jno. Crisfield Justices of the Peace.

In the matter of laying out a highway in the Town of Yonkers through lands of Frederick Weed, Osborn Sherwood, and others

Documents filed relative thereto; application, map, certificate of freeholders, order &c. Filed duly July 14, 1858.

Order

At a meeting of the Commissioners of the Highways of the Town of Yonkers in the County of Westchester at the Franklin House in the Village of Yonkers in the said Town on the twenty fourth day of November one thousand eight hundred and fifty seven. All the said Commissioners having met and deliberated on the subject matter of this order upon the application of Charles Campbell, a resident in said Town, for the laying out of the highway hereafter described and on the certificate of twelve reputable freeholders of said Town convened and duly sworn after due public notices required by the statute certifying that such highway is necessary and proper, and notice on meeting of at least three days having been given in due form of law to Wm. D. Lynt, Frederick Weed, Osborn Sherwood, James Smith, Lewis Lyons, Christian Dederer, Patrick Mullon (could also be Mallon), Charles Campbell, Lancaster Underhill, and Nicholas Underhill occupants of the land through which the highway hereafter described is to run, that the undersigned Commissioners of Highways would meet at this time and place to decide on the application aforesaid, and the undersigned (next page at the top written with a red pencil Grassy Sprain Road) having heard all the reasons offered for and against laying such highway it is ORDERED determined and certified that a public highway shall be and the same is hereby laid out pursuant to said application whereof a survey hath been made and is as follows to wit the road is to be three rods in width and the center line thereof is described as follows viz: Beginning on the northerly side of the Tuckahoe Road at a stake set in the ground on land of Frederick Weed, and running thence through said land of Weed and crossing the Sprain Brook, and through lands of Osborne Sherwood S 40' E 558 feet to a stake. Thence still through said lands of Sherwood W 31' E 408 feet to a stake which is 24 feet 9 inches distant easterly from the easterly side of the stone fence on the westerly side of the lane of said Sherwood. Thence still through said lands of Sherwood and in a direction parallel with said lane fence and always 24 feet 9 inches distant easterly face thereof N 22' E 200 feet. Thence still through said land of Sherwood N 16' E 380 feet to a point 24 feet 9 inches distant westerly from the westerly face of a stone fence situated on the easterly side of said Sherwood's lane. Thence still through said lands of Sherwood N 14'30" E 450 feet to lands of James Smith at a point 24 feet 9 inches distant easterly from the easterly face of the stone fence situated on the westerly side of a lane through said land of Smith. Thence still through said land of Smith in a direction parallel with said fence on the westerly side of said Smith's lane and through lands of Lewis Lyons N 14'30" E 1550 feet to a stake in said lands of Lyons. Thence still through said lands of Lyons and crossing a brook and through lands of Dykeman Lynt, and through lands of Christian Dederer N 20' E 2475 feet to a marked hickory sapling standing on said Dederer's land near the top of the hill.

Thence still through said lands of Dederer N 31' E 75 feet to lands of Patrick Mallon at a point 24 feet 9 inches distant easterly from the middle of the stone fence dividing the said lands of Mallon on the west from lands of Dederer. Thence through said lands of Mallon in a direction parallel with said last mentioned stone fence and always 24 feet 9 inches distant easterly therefrom N 42'30" E 654 feet. Thence still through said lands of Mallon N 52' E 417 feet to lands of Charles Campbell at a point 24 feet 9 inches distant westerly from the westerly face of a stone fence on said Campbell's land. Thence through said lands of Campbell and parallel with said last mentioned stone fence W 38' E 671 feet. Thence still through said lands of Campbell and through lands of Lancaster Underhill N 31' 15' 2,166 feet to a stake in said lands of Lancaster Underhill.

Thence still through said lands of Lancaster Underhill N 25' E 843 feet to lands of Nicholas Underhill at a point 24 feet 9 inches distant easterly from lands of (Jesse) Devoe. Thence through the said lands of Nicholas Underhill in a direction parallel with the line dividing the same from land of said Devoe northerly 282 more or less to the southerly boundary line of the Town of Greenburgh.

In witness whereof we the said Commissioners of Highways of the said Town of Yonkers have hereunto subscribed our names this twenty fourth day of November eight hundred and fifty seven. James L. Valentine, Jacob Read, Gilbert Taylor Commissioners of Highways of the Town of Yonkers.

(Apparently the above description of Grassy Sprain Road was transcribed in 1858 into the Town Record Book from the original document created 11/24/1857. Why the documents were not filed until 7/14/1858 is not clear.)

Documents Filed
List of Special Constables March 30, 1858.
Appointment of 3rd Inspectors April 1, 1858.
Oath of office of Gilbert Taylor Commissioner April 2, 1858.
Oath of office of Wm. McCabe Overseer of the Poor April 3, 1858.
Oath of office of Wm. McCabe Constable April 3, 1858.
Oath of office of A. Van Cordtlandt Supervisor April 5, 1858.
Oath of office of Wm. H. Post Clerk April 5, 1858.
Oath of office of B. C. Nodine Constable April 6, 1858.
Oath of office of Wm. G. Ackerman Assessor April 6, 1858.
Oath of office of Wm. H. Lawrence Constable April 7, 1858.
Oath of office of Wm. H. Lawrence Overseer April 7, 1858.
Oath of office of Wm. H. Lawrence Collector April 7, 1858.
Oath of office of Edward Crisfield Constable April 7, 1858.
Oath of office of Wm. P. Littell Constable April 13, 1858.
Oath of office of Caleb Underhill Assessor April 22, 1858.

Oath of office of James Cuddy May 8, 1858.
Appointment of Wm. P. Littell Constable April 13, 1858.
Appointment of James Cuddy Constable April 27, 1858.
Appointment of Nelson Strang (W? P. Justice of the Peace? no date).
Appointments of Littell and Wm. H(????) Pound Masters May 4, 1858.
Bond of B. C. Nodine Constable April 6, 1858.
Bond of Wm. McCabe Constable April 6, 1858.
Bond of Ed Crisfield Constable April 7, 1858.
Bond of Wm. H. Lawrence Constable April 8, 1858.
Bond of Wm. P. Littell Constable April 14, 1858.
Bond of Gilbert Taylor Commissioner April 21, 1858.
Bond of Wm. McCabe Overseer April 26, 1858.
Bond of James Cuddy Constable May 3, 1858.
Poll list and canvass sheet annual Town Meeting March 30, 1858, March 31, 1858.
Receipt from Charles A. Smith for $17.00. Poor money. February 1, 1858.
Acceptance of Wm. P. Littell Pound Master May 24, 1858.
Proceedings of school meeting District No. 2 Town of Yonkers in the matter of establishing a union free school in said district. Filed August 25, 1858.
Notice of application for land under the water of the Hudson River by Thos. Lawrence September 7, 1858.
Names of persons licensed in the Town of Yonkers
Bond of Matthias Warner grocer September 23, 1858.
Bond of Wm. B. Edgar grocer September 23, 1858.
Bond of Geo. N. Hallock grocer September 23, 1858.
Bond of James H. Page grocer September 23, 1858.
Bond of Ackerman and Deyo grocers September 23, 1858.
Bond of White and Richmond grocers September 23, 1858.
Bond of Dennis McGrath grocer September 23, 1858.
Bond of Lawrence R. Condon grocer September 23, 1858.
Bond of Jarvis A. Waring grocer September 23, 1858.
Bond of Robt. W. Nesbit grocer September 23, 1858.
Bond of Oliver C. Denslow Innkeeper September 23, 1858.
Bond of R. L. Bucklin Innkeeper September 23, 1858.
Bond of Valentine Melah Innkeeper September 23, 1858.
Bond of H. McElrone Innkeeper September 23, 1858.
Bond of Alexander Logue Innkeeper September 23, 1858.
Poll list general election District No. 1 Nov. 3, 1858.
Poll list general election District No. 2 Nov. 3, 1858.
Poll list general election District No. 3 Nov. 3, 1858.
Statement of result general election District No. 1 Nov. 3, 1858.
Statement of result general election District No. 2 Nov. 3, 1858.
Statement of result general election District No. 3 Nov. 3, 1858.

Statement of the result of an election submitting the question of calling a convention to revise the constitution and amend the same Districts Nos. 1, 2, and 3 filed Nov. 3, 1858.
Canvass list District No. 1 filed Nov. 3, 1858.
List and memorandum of challenged voters District No. 1 Nov. 3, 1858.
Report of Wm. H. Lawrence Overseer of Poor Nov. 4, 1858.
Appropriation of $800 support of the poor Nov. 6, 1858.
Petition of Dennis McGrath Dec. 11, 1858.
Bond of Jarvis A. Waring grocer Dec. 11, 1858.
Bond of Hallock and Page grocers Dec. 11, 1858.
Bond of Ackerman and Deyo grocers Dec. 11, 1858.
Notice of stray Daniel Fitzpatrick Oct. 4, 1858.

Associated Village Document 24

Resolution to appoint special committee for relief of poor & c. January 13, 1858. Adopted. Rescinded February 4, 1858. Approved W. W. Woodworth, President. Filed January 13, 1858. Wm. H. Post, Clerk.

[When the document was unfolded it turned out to be two documents glued at the top left. The documents are folded in thirds, and the first transcribed document is on the bottom after the documents are opened. A large portion of the document near the middle is missing.]

Resolved, that a Special Committee of three trustees be appointed by the President to receive such funds as may be contributed for the relief of destitute families and individuals residing within this Village and to disburse the same amongst such destitute persons as they may think proper.
Resolved that ---- Seventy five dollars be and ----- contributing in equal ------ for the relief of such poor and destitute persons the same to be disbursed by the committee approved for that purpose.
(On the back of the second document) Approved W. W. Woodworth.
Resolved, that the special committee of this board for the relief of the poor be instructed to cooperate with any committee for a similar purpose that may be appointed by a meeting of citizens.

Associated Village Document 25

Locust Hill. Commissioners. $84. Plan 23. Thomas O. Farrington, John Olmsted, Wm. H. Arthur.
In the matter of grading &c Locust Hill Avenue. The Treasurer of the Village of Yonkers will please pay to the order of Thomas O. Farrington, John Olmsted, and Wm. H. Arthur the sum of eighty

four dollars for services rendered as Commissioners in the above matter.

$84.00. W. W. Woodworth, President. Yonkers January 21, 1858.
Wm. H. Post, Clerk.

Associated Village Document 26

Locust Hill. M. F. Rowe. File 10. $1.52. (Stan) 152.

In the matter of the grading &c of Locust Hill Avenue. The Treasurer of the Village of Yonkers will please pay to M. F. Rowe or bearer the sum of one 52/100 dollars on account of advertising in the above matter.

$1.52. W. W. Woodworth, President. Yonkers February 1, 1858.
Wm. H. Post, Clerk.

Associated Village Document 27

Grading Locust Hill. Thomas C. Cornell $30. Feb. 15th.

In the matter of grading &c Locust Hill Avenue. The Treasurer of the Village of Yonkers will please pay to the order of Thomas C. Cornell the sum of Thirty dollars for services rendered as Inspector in the above matter.

$30.00. W. W. Woodworth, President. Yonkers February 1, 1858.
Wm. H. Post, Clerk.

Associated Village Document 28

Locust Hill Avenue. Wm. H. Post.

In the matter of the grading &c of Locust Hill Avenue. The Treasurer of the Village of Yonkers will please pay to the order of Wm. H. Post the sum of Five dollars for services rendered in the above matter.

$5.00. W. W. Woodworth, President. Yonkers February 1, 1858.
Wm. H. Post, Clerk.

Associated Village Document 29

Locust Hill Avenue. F. A. Coe. $110. Feb. 8.

In the matter of the grading &c of Locust Hill Avenue. The Treasurer of the Village of Yonkers will please pay to the order of Frederick A. Coe the sum of one hundred and ten dollars for counsel fees in the above matter.

[The following is on the left hand side of the paper.]

692.97
110
―――
802.97

[Evidently he had already been paid $692.97.]

$110.00. W. W. Woodworth, President. Yonkers February 1, 1858. Wm. H. Post, Clerk.

Associated Village Document 30

Locust Hill. (Cornell $85.)

In the matter of the grading &c of Locust Hill Avenue. The Treasurer of the Village of Yonkers will please pay to the order of Thomas C. Cornell the sum of Eighty five dollars for services rendered as Civil Engineer in the above matter.

$85.00. W. W. Woodworth, President. Yonkers February 1, 1858. Wm. H. Post, Clerk.

Associated Village Document 31

Grading Locust Hill. M. F. Rowe. 8.35. Feb. 15.

In the matter of the grading &c of Locust Hill Avenue. The Treasurer of the Village of Yonkers will please pay to M. F. Rowe or bearer the sum of Eight 35/100 dollars on account of advertising in the above matter.

$8.35. W. W. Woodworth, President. Yonkers February 1, 1858. Wm. H. Post, Clerk.

Associated Village Document 32

Resolution in relation to annual and special Village Elections to be held March 2, 1858. February 4, 1858. Adopted. Approved W. W. Woodworth, President. Filed February 4, 1858. Wm. H. Post.

[This document is two pages glued together, and folded in thirds. The document also has several holes in it and is in very bad condition.]

Resolved, that the next charter Election for Village officers of the Village of Yonkers be held at the Village Hall on Palisade Avenue on Tuesday the second day of March 1858. And, that the polls of said Election open at sunrise and close at sunset of that day.

Resolved, that Jacob Read, Samuel D. Rockwell, and Lawrence Post be and the same are hereby appointed inspectors of the next charter Election of the Village of Yonkers to be held at the Village Hall on Palisade Avenue on Tuesday the second day of March 1858.

Resolved, that three weeks notice be given in both the Village papers by the inspectors duly appointed. That the next charter Election of the Village of Yonkers will be held at the Village Hall on Palisade Avenue on the second day of March 1858 at which election the following officers are to be chosen. Viz. A President in the place of Wm. W. Woodworth, a Clerk in place of Wm. H. Post, a Treasurer in place of Egbert Howland, a Collector in place of Benj. A. Starr, three Trustees in place of Charles C. Merchant, Reuben W. VanPelt, and Bailey Hobbs.

Adopted February 4, 1858. Wm. H. Post, Clerk.

[The following is crossed out. "Also a Trustee to fill the vacancy occasioned by the resignation of Henry F. Devoe." The following is on the second page.]

Resolved, that notice be given in the Village papers by the Inspectors of Election hereby appointed. That a Special Election will be held at the same time and place of the Annual Election for a Trustee to fill the vacancy in the Board of Trustees occasioned by the resignation of Henry F. Devoe. Adopted February 4, 1858. Wm. H. Post, Clerk.

Associated Village Document 33

In the matter of grading Locust Hill Avenue.

In the matter of grading Locust Hill Avenue. The Treasurer of the Village of Yonkers will please pay to Hugh Curran the sum of Five hundred dollars on account of his contract in the above matter.

$500.00 W. W. Woodworth, President. Yonkers February 16, 1858. Wm. H. Post, Clerk.

Associated Village Document 34

Resolution to refer the proposed amendments to the charter to a special committee. March 9, 1858. Adopted. Approved W. W. Woodworth, President. Filed March 9, 1858 W. H. Post, Clerk.

Resolved, that the resolution heretofore passed as recommending certain amendments of the Charter together with the proposed amendments to the Charter of this Village be referred to a committee to consider and adopt the propriety and feasibility of said amendments proposed the purport and effect of the same. [The following is crossed out. "And that the Legislature be respectfully requested to [part of the page is missing] the proposed amendments to the Charter now before them until otherwise requested by this board."]

Adopted March 9, 1858 W. H. Post, Clerk. J. Copcutt, E. Underhill, and B. Hobbs Committee.

Associated Village Document 35

Report of Committee on amendment to the Charter. Approved W. W. Woodworth, President, March 23, 1858. Filed March 23, 1858. Wm. H. Post, Clerk.

The Special Committee to whom was referred the resolution of John Copcutt Esq. respectfully report that they have examined the Amendment referred to and see nothing in them that they do not think just and proper. And, your Committee believes they imply all that the gentleman wishes to have them <u>read</u>, but your Committee does not think it could so be worded as it would be an acknowledgement that we had levied some Illegal assessments whither this Board do not nor <u>can</u> not acknowledge nor believe, but if it should be shown that we had levied Illegal assessments the Legislature have nothing to do with as that belongs to a <u>Court of Law</u> to decide after a full and fair hearing.

Your Committee has heard all the arguments of the gentlemen and they are unable to arrive at any other conclusion then the above, and they are compelled not only from a sense of duty but from a sense of consistency against the resolution.

As your Committee can not be convinced that the Legislature has or <u>can</u> have anything to do with the illegal acts of this Board for that most surely must be passed upon by a <u>Court of Law</u>.

And your Committee would recommend for adaption the following resolution.

Resolved, that in the opinion of this Board there is nothing in the Amendments now before the Legislature at Albany but what is just and proper, and nothing injurious to the rights of any individual, and nothing that will prevent any one from contesting in a <u>Court of Law</u> and illegal or legal acts of this Board.

[The following is crossed out. "Resolved, that Mr. Copcutt have leave to withdraw the resolution above referred to."]

Bailey Hobbs, Edward Underhill Special Committee. Dated March 23, 1858. Report received and Resolution adopted March 23, 1858. W. H. Post, Clerk.

Associated Village Document 36

Minority Report Committee on amending the Charter. March 23, 1858. Filed March 23, 1858. W. H. Post, Clerk.

Resolved, that the following section be inserted in the act to amend the charter of the Village of Yonkers now before the Legislature of the state.

7 & 8 Nothing in this act contained or contained in the act entitled an "act to amend an act entitled an" act to incorporate the village of Yonkers passed April 12, 1855, and to extend the powers of the corporation of said village passed April 17, 1857 shall in any manner affect extend or apply to any rights or remedies vested in or belonging to any person in respect to laying out opening or widening any street in said village prior to the said 17th day of April 1857, but all such rights and remedies shall be and remain as effectual in such person as if this act and the said act passed on the 17th day of April 1857 had not passed.

Yonkers March 23, 1858. John Copcutt. No action.

Associated Village Document 37

Resolution to sign the Preamble and Resolutions in relation to the amendments to the charter. April 5, 1858. Adopted. Filed April 5, 1858. Wm. H. Post, Clerk.

[This document has the village seal on it. The words on the seal are "CORPORATION OF YONKERS." In the middle of the seal there is an image of George Washington almost surrounded by thirteen stars. Under the bust of Washington there is a draped lance with the point of the lance facing right, and pointing to the period after YONKERS.]

Resolved, that each of the Trustees of the Village of Yonkers who are in favor of the passage of the amendments to the Charter now before the Legislature sign the Preamble and resolutions just adopted and ordered to be sent to our representative in Albany. Adopted April 5, 1858. W. W. Woodworth, President of this Village of Yonkers. W. H. Post, Clerk.

[Woodworth signed his name with very large letters and it is clear he did it for emphasis.]

Associated Village Document 38

Preamble and Resolutions in relation to the proposed amendments to the charter and the collection of assessments in arrears and unpaid. Adopted April 5, 1858. Filed April 5, 1858. Wm. H. Post, Clerk.

[This document is impressed with the corporate seal twice. One impression is at the lower right corner of the document, and is very clear. The second impression is at the top right corner of the document and is not very clear. Because of the folds on the document it is clear that it was stamped twice.]

Whereas it is represented that a remonstrance is being circulated against the amendments recently proposed to the Village Charter.

And, whereas it is necessary that the same pass in order to protect the credit of said Village, and to enforce its laws and ordinances.

And, whereas without the passage of said amendments it will be unsafe for the Village to proceed with any further improvements.

It is hereby Resolved, that the Legislature of the State of New York be earnestly requested to enact the said amendments and that this preamble, and resolution, be sent to our Representative and Senator, under the hands of the President and Clerk and the Corporate Seal of said Village.

And, it is hereby further resolved that the Counsel of said Village be, and he is hereby authorized and directed to take all lawful ways and means to enforce the payment of assessments in arrear and unpaid.

And, it is hereby further resolved that the Counsel of said Village be and he hereby is authorized and directed to take all lawful ways and means to procure the enactment of the said amendments, and to answer any and every remonstrance made against the same.

Adopted April 5, 1858. W. W. Woodworth, President Village of Yonkers. Wm. H. Post, Clerk. Rob't. P. Getty, L. M. Clark, Ethan Flagg, Edward Underhill, Bailey Hobbs Village Trustees.

Associated Village Document 39

Resolution to issue a warrant for the collection of all Taxes remaining unpaid. June 7, 1858. Adopted. Filed June 7, 1858. W. H. Post, Clerk.

Resolved, that the President of the Board be and he is hereby requested to issue immediately to the Collector such a warrant as is contemplated in Section 2 of title 4 of the Charter for the Collection of taxes now remaining unpaid. Adopted June 7, 1858. W. H. Post, Clerk. Approved Bailey Hobbs, President Protem.

Associated Village Document 40

Resolution appointment B. Hobbs President Protem. June 7, 1858. Adopted. Filed June 7, 1858 Wm. H. Post, Clerk.

Whereas, Hon W. W. Woodworth the President of the Village is absent, and whereas the Charter in Title 2, Sect. 8 confers upon the Trustees the power to elect from their own number a President to act during such absence. Therefore resolved that Bailey Hobbs is hereby appointed President Protem of the Village of Yonkers to act as such until the return of Hon. W. W. Woodworth.

Yonkers June 7, 1858. Adopted June 7, 1858. Wm. H. Post, Clerk. Approved Bailey Hobbs, President Protem.

Associated Village Document 41

Ordinance as to Bathing July 12, 1858. Lost. [The following is crossed out. "Approved W. W. Woodworth, President".]

[The document is folded in quarters and on the inside the following is written.]

Ordinance to prevent Bathing within the limits of the Village of Yonkers.
S.1.   Open bathing in any public water adjacent to or within the limits of the Village of Yonkers at any time of day or night is hereby prohibited.
S.2.   Any person violating this ordinance shall pay a fine of not less than $5.00, and not exceeding $25.00.
S.3.   Nothing in this ordinance shall prohibit bathing in said waters provided the same shall be in a bathing house, or provided the person of the bather shall at all times be sufficiently clothed to prevent any improper exposure of the person.
S.4.   On the first Mondays in the months of May, June, July, August, and September in each and every year it shall be the duty of the Clerk to cause printed copies of this ordinance to be posted in conspicuous places along the shores of said waters within the limits of said Village.

Associated Village Document 42

Resolutions to appoint a Committee to revise and amend the Charter. September 27, 1858. Adopted. Approved W. W. Woodworth, President. Filed September 27, 1858.

Resolved, that a Special Committee of three be appointed to revise the Village Charter and propose such amendments as they may think proper and necessary, and report to the board at an early day.

September 27, 1858. Getty. Adopted September 27, 1858. Wm. H. Post, Clerk. Getty, Flagg, Hobbs Committee.

Associated Village Document 43

[The following is a description of a May 20, 1858 map of the Village area drawn by Thomas C. Cornell, Civil Engineer and reproduced by Snyder, Black and Sturn who were located at 92 William St. in New York City. The map shows the west side of the village from Locust Street on the north south to Vark Av. The Hudson River is on the west and Locust Hill Av., James St, a part of Chicken Island, and part of Mechanic St. on the east. The map has a thick black border. The border enclosing the northern and southern section is not

continued and there is no border enclosing the eastern portion. This indicates that the map continued into the eastern section of the Village, but that portion is missing.

The streets depicted on the map starting from the north are Locust Street, Pond Street with the word Street missing, Locust Hill Avenue, Cromwell Place, Bell Place, Baldwin Place, North Broadway, Warburton Avenue, Woodbine Street, Atherton Street, River Street, Water Street, Front Street, Dock Street, Nepperhan Street, Mill Street, Market Place, Main Street, Mechanic Street, James Street, Engine Place with the letters En missing, South Broadway, Hudson Street, Depot Street on the north side of Hudson Street, Buena Vista Avenue continuing from Depot on the south side of Hudson Street, Grinnell Street east of Buena Vista, Clinton Street east of Grinnell, Riverdale Avenue east of Grinnell, Jefferson Street east of Riverdale running from Prospect Street south to Vark Avenue, and St. Mary Street north of Vark Avenue.

The map has elevations on it. Getty Square is 41.3 feet above sea level. Meanwhile the foot of Locust Hill Avenue is 50 feet, and at the top of the hill opposite Cromwell Place the elevation is 151.5 feet. In just a short distance of less than 800 feet Locust Hill rises 101.5 feet. That makes the incline about 13 degrees. The map shows Baldwin Place and Cromwell Place as running from Locust Hill Avenue west to North Broadway. However, the incline was too steep for more than foot paths. In some places there are cliffs, and stairs were eventually built down the hill connecting both Baldwin and Cromwell to North Broadway.

The map also notes two steamboat docks. The northerly dock is located along Front Street. The second dock is located about 500 feet south of the first dock and is located at the foot of Main Street. At the southerly dock there is a boat house. About 1,800 feet further to the south at the foot of Vark Street there is another structure that protrudes into the Hudson River. It may be a third dock, but there is no note that it is. On this protrusion there are three structures which may be warehouses.

The map also contains two meandering lines one drawn in with red ink and the other drawn with black ink. The red line begins at the northwest corner of South Broadway and Washington Street. It meanders northwesterly to the Nepperhan at Main Street about 150 feet north of Market Place. Near the middle of the line is written "new channel", "dam", and again "new channel". The black line begins just to the north of the red line and runs southwesterly for about 750 feet then it turns southerly and ends at the border of the map. Under the line is written "original outlet to the stream".

The map clearly shows that the village planners purposely used the grid plan for laying out streets. The only meandering street is Broadway which was originally called Highland Turnpike. This street was an ancient highway that ran through Yonkers from New York

City. It predated the extensive use of dynamite and therefore the road had to conform to the rugged topography of Yonkers.

The map also clearly shows that the original Lemuel Wells Estate was divided into plats. Most of the plats have numbers which are street numbers. Plats that do not have numbers do not interfere with the street numbering scheme. Also, some of the plats have structures on them, but most do not. This is a clear indication that the village section was divided up according to a plan.

The map also shows what probably is a bridge crossing the Nepperhan Creek to an unnamed street leading to Mechanic Street. There are two structures on this street.]

Yonkers During 1859

Notice of stray James M. Dayton March 18, 1859.
Report of Jacob Read Commissioner March 22, 1859.
Report of Jas. L. Valentine Commissioner March 22, 1859.
Report of Gilbert Taylor Commissioner March 22, 1859.
Report of Wm. H. Lawrence Overseer of the Poor March 22, 1859.
Report of Wm. McCabe Overseer of the Poor March 22, 1859.
[The above notice and reports were on the same page as the list that closed the previous Chapter because the political year went from the beginning of April through March of the next year.]

At the annual Town Meeting of the Town of Yonkers held at the Franklin House in the Village of Yonkers on Tuesday the 29th day of March 1859 for the election of Town officers, and for the transaction of the other necessary town business the following persons were declared elected by the presiding officers of said meeting.

Augustus VanCortlandt	Supervisor
Lyman Cobb Jr.	Town Clerk
Isaac V. Fowler	Assessor
William H. Lawrence	Overseer of the Poor
George W. Mold	Overseer of the Poor
David Horton	Commissioner of the Highways
William H. Lawrence	Collector
Wm. McCabe	Constable
William H. Lawrence	Constable
John Archer	Constable
William Smelt	Constable
John S. Waterman	Constable
George L. Andrews	Justice of the Peace
Abm. R. VanHouten	Inspector of Elections District No. 1
James L. Valentine	Inspector of Elections District No. 1
Richard Berrian	Inspector of Elections District No. 2
Joseph I. Bicknell	Inspector of Elections District No. 2

Caleb F. Underhill   Inspector of Elections District No. 3
Charles Campbell   Inspector of Elections District No. 3

It was also resolved that the sum of four thousand dollars be levied and collected by tax on the town of Yonkers for the support of roads and bridges.

Documents Filed

Poll list annual town meeting March 29, 1859.

Oath of office of Augustus VanCortlandt Supervisor April 2, 1859, Lyman Cobb Jr. Town Clerk April 2, 1859, David Horton Commissioner Highways April 2, 1859, Isaac V. Fowler Assessor March 31, 1859, William H. Lawrence Overseer of the Poor April 5, 1859, George W. Mold Overseer of the Poor April 7, 1859, William H. Lawrence Collector April 5, 1859, William McCabe Constable April 6, 1859, William Smelt Constable April 4, 1859, John S. Waterman Constable April 4, 1859, and John Archer Constable April 1, 1859.

Names of persons licensed in Town of Yonkers.

Nicholas Post Innkeeper Bond July 1, 1859
Ernest E. Hasse Innkeeper Bond July 1, 1859
Oliver C. Denslow Innkeeper Bond July 1, 1859
James Jackson Innkeeper Bond July 1, 1859
Robert L. Bucklin Innkeeper Bond July 1, 1859
Valentine Melah Innkeeper Bond July 1, 1859
Alexander Logue Innkeeper Bond July 1, 1859
George L. Condit Innkeeper Bond July 1, 1859
L. R. Condon Innkeeper Bond July 1, 1859
Ackerman and Deyo Storekeeper Bond July 1, 1859
Jarvis A. Waring Storekeeper Bond July 1, 1859
Robert W. Nesbitt Storekeeper Bond July 1, 1859
John Gaffney Storekeeper Bond July 1, 1859
Matthias Warner Storekeeper Bond July 1, 1859
Paddock and Terry Storekeeper Bond July 1, 1859
Dennis McGrath Storekeeper Bond July 1, 1859
Thompson and Brevoort Storekeeper Bond July 1, 1859
Frederick Helinck Storekeeper Bond July 1, 1859
William B. Edgar Storekeeper Bond July 1, 1859
Morris (?) Edwards Storekeeper Bond 1859

Appointment of third Inspectors of Election in Districts 1, 2, and 3 March 30, 1859.

Acceptance of Wm. P. Littel, Pound Master June 27, 1859.

Notice of establishment of Pound.

Proceedings of school meeting District No. 2 Town of Yonkers in matter of balloting for Trustees to fill vacancy August 19, 1859.

Papers in the matter of laying out a highway in Yonkers through land of Wm. H. Popham October 15, 1859.

Appointment of Wm. H. Post Inspector of Election to fill vacancy of Albert Keeler absent October 18, 1859.

Register of voters of District No. 2 April 19, 1859.

Register of voters of District No. 3 April 19, 1859.
Register of voters of District No. 1 April 21, 1859.
Affidavit of W. H. Post on delivering up his papers to successor April 4, 1859.
Bond of J. S. Waterman and Evert K. Baldwin and Benjamin A. Starr his sureties April 4, 1859.
William H. Lawrence and John B. Crisfield his surety April 6, 1859.
William McCabe and William H. Lawrence and Abraham R. Van Houten his sureties April 6, 1859.
John Archer and Thomas Smith his surety April 8, 1859.
Register of voters District No. 2, corrected November 3, 1859.
Register of voters of District No. 1 corrected November 11, 1859.
Poll list and checked register General Election District No. 1 November 10, 1859.
Poll list and checked register General Election District No. 2 November 10, 1859.
Poll list and checked register General Election District No. 3 November 10, 1859.
Statement of the result General Election District No. 1 November 9, 1859.
Statement of the result General Election District No. 2 November 9, 1859.
Statement of the result General Election District No. 3 November 9, 1859.
Sheet General Election November 9, 1859.
Affidavits of unregistered voters Annual election November 8, 1859, November 10, 1859.
Report of Wm. H. Lawrence Overseer of the Poor November 10, 1859.
Appropriation of $1000 for support of the poor November 10, 1859.
Bond of Wm. H. Lawrence Overseer of the Poor November 10, 1859.
Abstract of Town account November 12, 1859, November 14, 1859.
Notice of stray James Bennett December 9, 1859.
Proceedings of School Meeting District No. 3 Town of Yonkers in the matter of establishing Union Free Schools in said district. Filed December 20, 1859.

Resolved, that the sum of one thousand dollars be appropriated for the temporary relief of the Poor of the Town of Yonkers for the coming year. Being the amount adjudged necessary by Overseers of the Poor. Dated Yonkers November 10, 1859. A. VanCortlandt, Supervisor. Lyman Cobb Jr., Town Clerk. James L. Valentine, Wm. Groshon, John Crisfield Justices.

Associated Village Document 44

Resolution. Appointment B. Hobbs President Protem. January 11, 1859. Adopted. Filed January 11, 1859. W. H. Post, Clerk.

Whereas the Honorable W. W. Woodworth the President of the Village has stated to this Board that it is his intention to be absent from the Village most of the winter, therefore Resolved that Bailey Hobbs be and is hereby appointed President Protem of this Village as provided for by Section 8 title two of the Charter to act as such at all times during the absence of the President. Adopted January 11, 1859. W. H. Post, Clerk.

Associated Village Document 45

Resolution. Committee to engross the amendments to the Charter and have the same published. January 13, 1859. Adopted. Approved Bailey Hobbs, President Protem. Filed January 13, 1859. W. H. Post, Clerk.

Resolved, that the Charter as amended be assigned to a committee of three to engross the same and prepare the amendments for publication forthwith and that said Committee have power to have the same published in the *Yonkers Herald* and *Examiner* at an expense not to exceed $15 for each paper. R. P. Getty. January 13, 1859. Adopted January 13, 1859. W. H. Post, Clerk.

Associated Village Document 46

Resolution. Committee to forward Charter to Albany, and have it presented to the Legislature. January 25, 1859. Adopted. Approved Bailey Hobbs, President Protem. Filed January 25, 1859. W. H. Post, Clerk.

Resolved, that the Committee on amendments to the Charter be and they are hereby instructed to have drafted a proper memorial to the Legislature praying for the passage of the amendments to the charter which have been adopted by this board and signed by the President and all of the Trustees who are in favor of the same, and attested by the Charter.

Resolved, that the same committee are hereby authorized and directed to take immediate measures to have the Charter as amended forwarded to Albany and to have the same presented to the State Legislature at the earliest moment through our representative in the Assembly. (W.) VanCortlandt. Adopted January 25, 1859. Getty. W. H. Post, Clerk.

Associated Village Document 47

Resolution in relation to the annual Charter Election to be held March 1, 1859. February 7, 1859. Adopted. Approved Bailey Hobbs, President Protem. Filed February 7, 1859. W. H. Post, Clerk.

Resolved, that the annual Charter Election for Village officers of the Village of Yonkers be held at the "Village Hall" on Palisade

Avenue on Tuesday the first day of March, and that the polls of said Election be opened at sunrise and closed at sunset of that day.

Resolved, that L. W. Wells, A. R. VanHouten, and Jacob Read be and the same are hereby appointed the inspectors of the annual Charter Election of the Village of Yonkers to be held on the first day of March 1859 at a compensation of three dollars each.

Resolved, that three weeks notice be published in both of the Village papers, that the annual charter Election of the Village of Yonkers will be held at the "Village Hall" on Palisade Avenue on Tuesday the first day of March 1859 at which election the following officers are to be elected. Viz.

A President in place of Wm. W. Woodworth, a Clerk in place of Wm. H. Post, a Treasurer in place of Evart R. Baldwin, a Collector in place of Benjamin A. Starr, and three Trustees in place of Ethan Flagg, Robert P. Getty, and Edward Underhill.

Yonkers February 7, 1859. Adopted February 7, 1859. W. H. Post, Clerk.

Associated Village Document 48

Resolution appointing A. C. Mott Clerk Protem. February 28, 1859. Adopted. Approved Bailey Hobbs, President Protem. Filed March 2, 1859. W. H. Post, Clerk.

Whereas William H. Post Clerk of the Village has communicated to this Board his inability on account of sickness to attend to the duties of Clerk either this evening or at the Annual Charter election to be held on Monday March 1 Prox. Therefore resolved that Abraham C. Mott be and he is hereby appointed Clerk Protem to act as such this evening and also to act as such at the Annual election to be held March 1st Proximo. February 28, 1859. Adopted February 28, 1859. (Proximo means next or coming month.)

Associated Village Document 49

Resolution vote of thanks to W. W. Woodworth, President. March 7, 1859. Adopted. Approved Bailey Hobbs, President Protem. Filed March 7, 1859. W. H. Post, Clerk.

Resolved, that the thanks of this board are due and are hereby tendered to the Hon. W. W. Woodworth President for his uniform courtesy, firmness, and impartiality as presiding officer. Adopted March 7, 1859. W. H. Post, Clerk.

Associated Village Document 50

Resolution vote of thanks to Bailey Hobbs President Protem. March 7, 1859. Adopted. Approved W. W. Woodworth, President. Filed March 7, 1859. W. H. Post, Clerk.

Resolved, that our thanks are due and are hereby tendered to Bailey Hobbs Esq. for the efficient manner in which he has discharged his duties as President Protem. Adopted March 7, 1859. W. H. Post, Clerk.

Associated Village Document 51

John Copcutt's resolution in relation to the legality of the Charter Election held March 1, 1859. April 4, 1859. Lost.

Resolved, that a committee be appointed to confer with the counsel of the board, or if thought proper, to inquire of other counsel concerning the legality of the late election of the present board of Trustees. April 4, 1859. Lost.

Associated Village Document 52

Report of Special Committee on Charter. May 2, 1859. Received and adopted after striking out the resolution of a vote of thanks. Robert P. Getty, President. Filed May 2, 1859. W. H. Post, Clerk.

The Special Committee to whom was assigned the duty of forwarding to the Legislature at its last session the proposed amendments to our Village Charter respectfully report:

That immediately after the adoption of said amendments by the Board of Trustees they had a bill drawn in proper form by our counsel Mr. Coe embracing the alterations and amendments asked for and in accordance with your instructions. Said bill together with a petition from this Board signed by all the members but one and duly attested by the President and Clerk was forwarded to Mr. Augustus VanCortlandt the representative elect from this district.

After waiting some time for an acknowledgement of the receipt of the bill by Mr. VanCortlandt he was written to by one of your Committee and in reply stated that he had reviewed the papers and was only waiting a favorable opportunity to introduce the bill, and that no time had been lost yet so far as the passage of the bill was concerned.

Again a week or two elapsed without our hearing from Mr. VanCortlandt anything in regard to the bill or that it had been introduced.

About this time your Committee heard it stated that Mr. VanCortlandt was opposed to a section in the bill which made this incorporation a separate road district, and exempting it from tax for roads in the Town outside of the Village.

Upon hearing this one of your Committee visited Albany and had an interview with Mr. VanCortlandt and found that he objected to that Section. It was then stated to him that there was no doubt the Village would be satisfied to have that Section struck out provided it was done so as to place our citizens within the incorporation on the same footing with those of the Town outside, Viz our being permitted to vote at the Town Meeting on the question of raising money for the support of Roads and Bridges which privilege by our present Charter we are denied. This concession appeared to be satisfactory to him and he made no other objections, nor did he intimate that any other person had. The Bill was introduced and passed the House about ten days before the expiration of the session, and was sent to the Senate. Rumor however said that the bill had passed the House with the consent of our representative there only upon the assurance that it would be killed in the Senate. This may not be strictly true, yet we have it from reliable authority that Mr. VanCortlandt privately if not publicly spoke against the bill and also that he was present in the Senate Chamber sitting at the side of Senator Brandreth when he opposed its final passage.

After the bill had passed the House and gone to the Senate Mr. Coe was requested to go to Albany and see that the bill was right as passed by the House and urge its passage through the Senate. Mr. Coe states that he found from conversation with Senator Brandreth that he was opposed to the bill for two reasons. First, that he had received a remonstrance from seventeen highly respectable and very wealthy citizens against its passage, and secondly that its passage would be injurious to his party.

Mr. Coe on his return reported this to the Committee and a petition in favor of its passage was prepared and in a few hours seventy four signatures were obtained of respectable citizens without distinction of party.

As but two days of the session remained after the intelligence it was necessary that some one should proceed to Albany at once and the President consented to go and present this petition, which he reports he did to Senator Brandreth and had with him a conversation in which he stated he had never said he would oppose the amendments on personal or political grounds, but that as he had not yet read the bill and having a remonstrance against it he could not commit himself in its favor "but now" said he, "this petition is my guarantee or warrant and the bill shall pass." This conversation took place in the afternoon about half past five P.M. About two hours afterwards when he was spoken to on the subject he stated that he had been informed that it was a Republican measure and therefore he would oppose it and that all of his Democrat colleagues would have to vote against it. He was then assured that such a charge had no foundation. He was requested to ask the opponents of the bill to meet its friends before him and then decide.

He determined to do this and persisted in his determination to defeat the bill. And, when it came up on its final reading he made a speech against it in which (if he is correctly reported) he made statements which were not warranted by anything embraced in the bill when it went into the hands of the Senate Committee. The bill was lost by a vote of 12 to 11.

Your Committee deemed it proper to furnish the foregoing details as a part of their action in the matter, and in order that the responsibility may rest where it belongs, and that our Citizens may be informed of the course pursued towards them by those whom they elected as their representatives in the Legislature. Your Committee can not imagine how assumption, egotism, or tyranny can go further than in the case of a representative professedly Democratic refusing to respect the wishes of a people when fairly, unequivocally, and authoritatively expressed in regard to matters of purely local interest in which they alone are concerned as was the case in regard to those amendments.

They having been discussed and adopted by the Board of Trustees and then published in both Village papers, and invitation extended to all Citizens that thought proper to do so to meet with the Trustees at a time fixed to make suggestions or offer objections, and after a hearing accordingly to appointment the amendments were adopted unanimously except as to one article which was voted against by a single member.

And, the petition to the Legislature signed by all save one member, and while the bill was pending before the Legislature an Election was held for Trustees at which two Gentlemen were elected who were not members of the previous Board one of who was Elected unanimously, and again all the members of the new Board petitioned for the passage of the amendments (one member excepted). Such was the unanimity of the Trustees in regard to these amendments and it is believed that our Citizens were equally unanimous in favor of them, and yet they were defeated by those claiming to represent us.

Your Committee thinks that a proper acknowledgement is due to the following gentlemen and therefore offers for adaption the following resolution.

[The above parentheses are on the document. The following resolution is crossed out.]

Resolved, that our thanks are due and they are hereby tendered to Messrs. Hubbel and See representatives of the upper assembly district of this county, and to Senator Sloan from the second senatorial district for their attentions to our wishes and exertions in our behalf.

Ethan Flagg, Bailey Hobbs Special Committee on the Charter. Dated May 2, 1859. Received and adopted May 2, 1859 W.H. Post, Clerk.

Associated Village Document 53

Resolution appointing Dr. A. W. Gates President Protem May 23, 1859. Adopted. Filed May 22, 1859. W. H. Post, Clerk.

Whereas Robert P. Getty President of the Village is absent from the Village. Therefore resolved that Dr. Amos W. Gates be and hereby is chosen President protem and act during the absence of the President as provided in Section eight title two of the charter. Adopted May 23, 1859. W. H. Post, Clerk.

Yonkers During 1860

Bond of George W. Mold Overseer of the Poor January 17, 1860.
Vouchers for School Money 1858 March 20, 1860.
Vouchers for Sheep Money 1860 &c March 20, 1860.
Vouchers for School Money 1859 March 20, 1860.
Vouchers A. VanCortlandt Supervisor 1858 - 9 March 20, 1860.
Report Wm. H. Lawrence Overseer of the Poor March 20, 1860.
Report Geo. W. Mold Overseer of the Poor March 20, 1860.
Report of Gilbert Taylor Commissioner of the Highways filed March 26, 1860.
Report of James L. Valentine Commissioner of the Highways filed March 26, 1860.
Report of David Horton Commissioner of the Highways filed March 26, 1860.

At an annual Town Meeting of the Town of Yonkers held at the Franklin House in the Village of Yonkers on Tuesday the 27th day of March 1860 for the transaction of business, and electing of Town officers, and for the ensuing year the following named persons were declared elected at such meeting.

Ethan Flagg	Supervisor
Lyman Cobb Jr.	Town Clerk
Thomas Radford	Assessor
William H. Lawrence	Overseer of the Poor
William McCabe	Overseer of the Poor
James L. Valentine	Commissioner of the Highways
William H. Lawrence	Collector
William McCabe	Constable
William H. Lawrence	Constable
John Houston	Constable
Jacob Wackerly	Constable
John O'Meara	Constable
Abm. R. VanHouten	Inspector of Elections District No. 1
Charles W. Chamberlain	Inspector of Elections District No. 1
Cornelius L. Purdy	Inspector of Elections District No. 2
Pembroke Lawrence	Inspector of Elections District No. 2
Charles R. Dusenberry	Inspector of Elections District No. 3
William R. Dederer	Inspector of Elections District No. 3

It was also resolved that the sum of four thousand six hundred dollars be raised by tax in the Town of Yonkers for the support of Roads and Bridges of which six hundred dollars shall be applied in addition to four hundred dollars now in the Commissioners' hands to the improvement of the causeway leading from Kings Bridge to Spuyten Duyvil Bridge on the West and of said causeway, and Two thousand Dollars for the support of Roads and Bridges outside of the limits of the Village Corporation, and Two thousand dollars for the support of Roads and Bridges within the limits of said Village Corporation.

Also resolved, that the sum of one thousand dollars be raised by tax in the Town of Yonkers for the relief of the poor.

Also resolved, that the sum of Four hundred dollars be appropriated by the Town of Yonkers for the purpose of purchasing an iron safe for the safe keeping of the Town papers.

In the matter of altering a part of Riverdale Avenue. Document filed relative thereto, order, application, consent of owners, and map.

Order. Whereas in the year 1853, a highway now known as Riverdale Avenue was duly laid out in the Town of Yonkers by Gilbert Taylor, James L. Valentine, and Jacob Read at that time Commissioners of Highways of said Town, and which said highway passed through a certain tract of land known as Riverdale, then belonging to W. W. Woodworth, Henry L. Atherton, Samuel D. Babcock, and C. W. Foster in a straight line bearing S 24'30" W. from lands belonging to the estate of the late Abraham Schermerhorn to land belonging to William L. Morris as shown on the map and survey hereto annexed, and whereas in order to lessen the cost and improve the grade of said highway, and with the consent and approval of the Commissioners of Highways of the town for the time being, and with the consent and approval of the owners of said land known as Riverdale the said Highway was opened and fenced and worked, and has since been traveled, and kept in repair on a line that does not in all its parts conform to the lines as described in the original order laying out said road, but was and still is fenced and traveled upon and kept in repair according to the lines which we show on the map and survey hereto annexed as the lines of the present road: And, whereas the said Henry L. Atherton and Samuel D. Babcock who are now the owners of said lands through which the alterations in said Road have been made have applied to the Commissioners of Highways of said town to confirm said alterations, and have given consent in writing to such alterations which said writing is hereto annexed. Now therefore, we Gilbert Taylor, James L. Valentine, and David Horton, Commissioners of Highways of said town of Yonkers, do order and determine that the said Highway shall be thus altered, and shall be laid out through the said lands of Atherton and Babcock as now heretofore opened and fenced and used, and as shown on the survey and map heretofore annexed; the said Highway to be fifty feet in width and the Westerly line thereof described as follows, viz, Beginning on the Southerly side of the said land belonging to the estate of the late Abraham Schermerhorn at the point where it intersects the Westerly line of said Riverdale Avenue as originally laid out in 1853 and now fenced, and running thence along said fence and along the Westerly side of said Avenue as originally laid out S. 24'30" W. 550 feet, thence along the fence as it now stands , first S. 32' W 100 feet, then S 39' W 150 feet, then S 30' W 135 feet, then S 23' W 175 feet, then S 21'30" W 200 feet and then S 10'30" W 200 feet to a point in the aforesaid Westerly line of said Highway as originally laid out, and thence along said original line S 24'30" W 350 feet to land of William L. Morris.

And we also consent that so much of the said Road as originally laid out as is not included within the above boundaries shall be reclaimed and enclosed by the said Henry L. Atherton and Samuel D. Babcock and their assigns.

In witness whereof we have hereunto subscribed our names the 27th day of March in the year 1860. David Horton, Gilbert Taylor, and James L. Valentine Commissioners of Highways of Town of Yonkers.

Documents Filed

Poll list Annual Town Meeting held March 27, 1859 March 28, 1859.

List of Challenged Voters Annual Town Meeting held March 27, 1859 March 28, 1859.

Canvass List Annual Town Meeting held March 27, 1859 March 28, 1859.

Resolution appropriating money for Roads and Bridges March 27, 1859.

Resolution appropriating money for the Poor March 27, 1859.

Resolution appropriating money for an iron safe March 27, 1859.

Oath of office of Ethan Flagg, Supervisor March 31, 1859.

Oath of office of Lyman Cobb Jr., Town Clerk March 31, 1859.

Oath of office of James L. Valentine, Commissioner of Highways April 3, 1859.

Oath of office of Wm. H. Lawrence, Collector March 31, 1859.

Oath of office of Wm. H. Lawrence, Overseer of the Poor March 31, 1859.

Oath of office of William McCabe, Overseer of the Poor March 31, 1859.

Oath of office of William H. Lawrence, Constable March 31, 1859.

Oath of office of John Houston, Constable April 3, 1859.

Oath of office of John O'Meara, Constable April 4, 1859.

Oath of office of William McCabe, Constable March 31, 1859.

Oath of office of Jacob Wackerly, Constable April 3, 1859.

Bond of William H. Lawrence, Overseer of the Poor April 2, 1859.

Bond of William McCabe, Overseer of the Poor March 31, 1859.

Bond of William H. Lawrence, Constable March 31, 1859.

Bond of John O'Meara, Constable April 5, 1859.

Bond of Jacob Wackerly, Constable April 5, 1859.
Bond of John Houston, Constable April 6, 1859.
Appointment of O. C. Denslow, Assessor April 28, 1859.
Oath of office of O. C. Denslow, Assessor April 30, 1859.
Appointment of Zalmon S. Heznard, Pound Master May 8, 1859.
Appointment of Richard Farrington, Pound Master May 14, 1859.
Acceptance of James B. Strang, Pound Master May 14, 1859.
Bond James Valentine, Commissioner of Highways June 25, 1859.
[Written at the top of the page is 1859, and then dittos all the way down. All of the above 1859s should be 1860. Ethan Flagg is listed above as the Supervisor who was elected in 1860. He was not the Supervisor in 1859.]
Notice of stray W. Warner August 3, 1860.
List of persons qualified to serve as jurors July 3, 1860.
Vouchers A. VanCortlandt, Supervisor July 24, 1860.
Names of persons licensed in Town of Yonkers
Nicholas Post Innkeeper August 4, 1860
Hugh McElrone Innkeeper August 4, 1860
Geo. L. Condit Innkeeper August 4, 1860
Valentine Melah Innkeeper August 4, 1860
James Jackson Innkeeper August 4, 1860
Ernest E. Hasse Innkeeper August 4, 1860
Timothy Coleman Innkeeper August 4, 1860
Oliver N. Doty Innkeeper August 4, 1860
Jarvis A. Waring Storekeeper August 4, 1860
Ackerman and Deyo Storekeeper August 4, 1860
Wm. (A.) Stoney Storekeeper August 4, 1860
Meyers and Horner Storekeeper August 4, 1860
Edmund Y. Morris Storekeeper August 4, 1860
Wm. B. Edgar Storekeeper August 4, 1860
Joseph Logel Storekeeper August 4, 1860
Thompson and Brevoort Storekeeper August 4, 1860
Walter H. Paddock Storekeeper August 4, 1860
Lawrence R. Condin Storekeeper August 4, 1860
Matthias Warner Storekeeper August 4, 1860
Appointment of Daniel Blauvelt, Sealer of Weights and Measures August 25, 1860.
Notice of election October 1, 1860.
Appointment of three Inspectors of Election October 3, 1860.
Register of Voters District No. 3 October 16, 1860.
Register of Voters District No 2 October 17, 1860.
Register of Voters District No 1 October 18, 1860.
Corrected Register of District No. 3 November 2, 1860.

    At a meeting of the Board of Town Officers of the Town of Yonkers held at the Post office in the Village of Yonkers on Monday the 1st day of October 1860 the following resolutions were adopted.

    Resolved, that the place of election for Election District No. 1 be at the Franklin House, and that the place of election for Election District No. 2 be at the brick house north of Warner's store at Mosholu, and that the place of Election for Election District No. 3 be at the District School House at Tuckahoe.

Resolved, that the Clerk be authorized to advertise notice of Election in the Village newspapers for three weeks previous to Election, and that he cause notices to be printed and posted, eight in each district.

Also resolved, that we proceed to <u>redistrict</u> the <u>Town</u> of <u>Yonkers</u>.

Resolved, that the Town of Yonkers be divided into <u>four</u> election districts.

Resolved, that <u>District No. 1</u> include all the territory included within the following described boundaries, viz: Beginning at the mouth of the Saw Mill River and running thence Northerly along the Easterly shore of the Hudson River to the Southerly line of the Town of Greenburgh, thence Easterly along the Southerly line of Greenburgh aforesaid to the Sprain Road, then Southerly along the Easterly line of said Sprain Road to the road leading from Yonkers Village to Tuckahoe, thence along said Tuckahoe Road to Mile Square Road, thence still in a Southerly direction along the Easterly side of the Mile Square Road to the road passing Elijah Valentine's leading from the Village of Yonkers to Mount Vernon, thence Westerly along the Southerly side of said last mentioned road to the Saw Mill River near land of W. N. Seymour, thence along the Southerly line of said Saw Mill River in a Westerly direction to the place of beginning. All persons, the entrance to whose residence is situated on the Sprain Road, and Mile Square Road, as above described, and all on the Southerly side of the road leading to Mount Vernon Village from the Village of Yonkers as above described be included in District No. 1.

Resolved, that <u>District No. 2</u> include all the territory within the following described boundaries, viz: Beginning at the Southerly side of the mouth of the Saw Mill River, and running thence Southerly along the Easterly shore of the Hudson River to the Northerly line of land belonging to the Sisters of Charity known as "Mount St. Vincent" thence in an Easterly direction along the Northerly line of said land belonging to the Sisters of Charity to Riverdale Avenue, thence Southerly along the Westerly line of Riverdale Avenue to a point opposite the lane leading from Riverdale Avenue to the old Albany Post Road at George F. Coddington's thence Easterly along the Northerly line of said lane to the old Albany Post Road to a point opposite the road leading to Mile Square passing the residence of William H. Lawrence, thence along the Southerly side of said road leading to Mile Square to the Easterly side of said Mile Square Road to the Southerly boundary line of District No. 1, thence along the Southerly boundary line of District No. 1 in a Westerly direction to the place of beginning, and that all persons the entrance to whose residence is situated on Mile Square Road as above described belong to District No. 2.

Resolved, that <u>District No. 3</u> include all the territory within the following described boundaries, viz: Beginning on the Easterly bank of the Hudson River at a point where the Northerly boundary line of land belonging to the Sisters of Charity known as Mount St. Vincent intersects the Hudson River, thence in a Southerly direction along the Easterly shore of the Hudson River to the Southerly boundary line of the Town of Yonkers, then Easterly along said Southerly boundary line to the Easterly boundary line of the Town of Yonkers, then Northerly along the Easterly boundary line to the Bridge crossing the Bronx River known as "Hunt's Bridge" thence Westerly along the Southerly side of a road leading from Hunt's Bridge to the Village of Yonkers, to the Mile Square Road near Elijah Valentine's, thence along the Easterly boundary line of District No. 2 aforesaid in a Southerly direction to the Southerly line of the Road leading from the Mile Square Road to the old Albany Post Road passing the residence of William H. Lawrence, thence in a Westerly direction following the Southerly boundary line of District No. 2 aforesaid to the Hudson River and place of beginning.

Resolved, that <u>District No. 4</u> include all the remaining territory within the Town of Yonkers, not included in the foregoing districts, and which is bounded as follows, viz: Beginning on the Easterly boundary line of the Town of Yonkers at "Hunt's Bridge" so called, thence running in a Northerly direction along the Easterly boundary line of the Town of Yonkers to the Southerly boundary line of the Town of Greenburgh, thence Westerly along the Southerly boundary line of the Town of Greenburgh aforesaid to the Easterly line of District No. 1, thence Southerly along the Easterly line of District No. 1 to the Northerly boundary line of District No. 3 near Elijah Valentine's, thence Easterly along the Northerly boundary line of District No. 3 to Hunt's Bridge aforesaid, and the place of beginning. All persons residing on the North side of the road leading from Elijah Valentine's to Hunt's Bridge belong to District No. 4, and all residing on the South side of said road belong to District No. 3. Adopted October 1, 1860.

Ethan Flagg Supervisor, Lyman Cobb Jr. Town Clerk, O. C. Denslow Assessor, and Isaac V. Fowler Assessor.

List of Bills audited by Board of Auditors November 8, 1860.
Report of Wm. H. Lawrence Overseer of the Poor November 8, 1860.
Poll list and checked register District No. 1 General Election November 8, 1860.
Tally sheets General Election District No. 1 November 8, 1860.
Oaths of unregistered voters (100) District No. 1 November 8, 1860.
Certificate of Canvass State District No. 3 November 10, 1860.
Certificate of canvass Electors District No. 3 November 10, 1860.
Poll list General Election District No. 3 November 10, 1860.

Certificate of canvass State District No. 1 November 10, 1860.
Poll L (This looked as if was erased. Ditto marks are across the page so that State District No. 1 November 10, 1860 is repeated.)
Poll List General Election District No. 2 November 10, 1860.
Checked Register General Election District No. 2 November 10, 1860.
Certificate of Canvass State District No. 2 November 10, 1860.
Certificate of Canvass Electors District No. 2 November 30, 1860.
In the matter of laying out a road in Yonkers through the lands of David A. Post and others November 10, 1860.

Associated Village Document 54

Letter from Thomas C. Cornell, Esq., President Yonkers Gas Light Co. February 6, 1860. Filed February 6, 1860. W. H. Post, Clerk.

Office of the Yonkers Gas Light Co.
Yonkers 19th January, 1860

To Dr. A. W. Gates
John Copcutt
L. M. Clark, Esqs.

Gentlemen:

You inform me that application has been made to the Board of Trustees of the Village for permission to lay Mains from a new gas company which it is said may be formed, and which when formed, it is said will furnish gas at lower prices than we have obtained, and you ask whether our Company intends in (the) future to reduce its prices.

I do not believe that any men will be found, able and willing to invest money in constructing new gas works in this place, and it is hardly worth while therefore to treat the matter seriously, until, at least, responsible men have expressed their willingness to become legally bound to make and sell gas of a good quality on the terms proposed for a definite number of years. But, as we have always intended to reduce the price of gas as soon as we could do so with justice to our stockholders, I am willing, now that the matter has come up, to state briefly my views of the subject.

The Trustees of the Village have, of course, only to consult the interests of the public in the matter, and if they believe that those interests will be not prohibited by giving permission to a rival Company to use the streets of the Village they should grant such permission. But, you do not need to be retold what must be obvious to everyone, that two rival companies can not manufacture and sell gas through a long term of years at low prices as a single company can afford to do it when occupying the whole ground. When this Company had but half of its present consumers it could do no more than pay expenses, and for several years we have been able to pay no dividends. But now, having 300 consumers we have been able to declare a semi annual dividend of 3 1/2 percent, payable on the first of the present month, and we hope to be able to continue such dividends for the future. And, if we prosper as we have now every reason to hope to do during the present year, we shall be able with the beginning of next year, to reduce the price of gas to three and a half dollars per thousand feet. As soon thereafter as its growing business will justify, the Company will further reduce its price to three dollars per thousand feet, and before its consumers average one hundred to each mile of Street Main I do not doubt but that the price will be reduced to two dollars and a half per thousand.

In regard to Street lamps I can only say that we will furnish gas, and if required also lamps and posts, and keep them in repair and light and extinguish them on as low terms as any Company similarly situated can afford to do the same. What such terms will be must of course depend upon the number of hours the lamps are to be lighted, the size of the burners, and other considerations first to be agreed upon.

And finally, that this Company is able to manufacture gas of as good quality, and to sell it at as low prices as any company compelled to pay the same prices for coal and labor, is a fact which no one competent to form a judgment in the matter will dispute.

Thomas C. Cornell
President

Associated Village Document 55

Report of Special Committee on petition of Timothy C. Dwight February 6, 1860. Adopted. Robert P. Getty, President. Filed February 6, 1860. W. H. Post, Clerk.

To the President and Trustees of the Village of Yonkers.

The Special Committee to whom was referred the petition of Timothy C. Dwight asking permission to lay gas pipes in the streets of the Village respectfully report that they have had said petition under consideration, and have come to the conclusion that the time has not arrived when it would be proper to grant said petition, would therefore offer for adoption the following resolution.

Resolved, that for the present this Board declines granting said petition, and that the petitioner (has come) to withdraw the same. Yonkers 6th February, 1860. A. W. Gates, L. M. Clark, and John Copcutt Special Committee. Report received and resolution adopted February 6, 1860 W. H. Post, Clerk.

Associated Village Document 56

Resolution Committee on Streets to have nuisances abated by enforcing ordinances. Adopted May 7, 1860. Thomas F. Morris, President. Lyman Cobb Jr., Clerk.

Resolved, that the Committee on Streets be and they are hereby directed to have all nuisances abated in the public streets in reference to slops and waste water and that they are hereby directed to have all ordinances in reference to streets enforced.

Associated Village Document 57

Resolution requiring Committee on printing to procure handbills ordinances restraining running cattle &c. Adopted May 7, 1860. Thomas F. Morris. Lyman Cobb, Jr., Clerk.

Resolved, that the Committee on Printing cause one hundred handbills to be printed and posted in all parts of the Village of the ordinance in reference to the running at large of the various animals &c the ordinance passed this evening. Clerk. May 7, 1860.

Associated Village Document 58

[This document is folded in thirds and a smaller document is inside the larger document. The smaller document is folded in half. The outside of this document reads as follows.]

Resolutions fixing amount to be raised by tax upon the property in Village of Yonkers for 1860. Adopted July 2, 1860. Thomas F. Morris, President. Lyman Cobb, Jr., Clerk. Filed July 3, 1860. Lyman Cobb, Jr., Clerk.

[Inside the larger document is folded a smaller document. The larger document contains two resolutions, and the smaller document one resolution. The top of the larger document is ragged indicating the top part was neatly ripped off. The smaller document has similar indications on the bottom. However, the small ragged portions do not match. The larger document is transcribed first.]

Resolved, that the sum of twenty five hundred dollars be assessed upon the estate real and personal within the boundaries of the corporate limits of the Village for the purpose of the contingency fund for said Village and that the same be collected from the several owners and occupants thereof. John Copcutt and John Wheeler.

Resolved, that the sum of twenty five hundred dollars be assessed upon the estate real and personal within the boundaries of the corporate limits of the Village for the repairs of roads and bridges the ensuing year within the Village limits, and that the same be collected from the several owners and occupants thereof. John Copcutt and John Wheeler.

Resolved, that the sum of seven hundred and ninety seven dollars and fifty cents be assessed upon the estate real and personal within the corporate limits of the Village for the purpose of paying the bond and interest due and to be to be coming due the ensuing year in the matter of building the Village Hall and that the same be collected from the several owners and occupants thereof. John Copcutt and John Wheeler.

Associated Village Document 59

Regulations requiring police officers to arrest parties violating ordinances. Adopted September 17, 1860. Thomas F. Morris. Lyman Cobb, Jr., Clerk. Filed September 20, 1860

Resolved, that the police officers be and are hereby instructed to arrest all persons found breaking and violating the ordinance in relation to the firing of guns in the Village of Yonkers. Also, the violation of the State Law in reference to the preservation of game in the County of Westchester. (The following was crossed out. A reward of five dollars to be paid to such officer or others on the arrest and conviction of every such person.)

Associated Village Document 60

Petition of John Loud for remittance of fine. Granted in part conditionally. Filed October 4, 1860. Lyman Cobb Jr, Clerk.

[The above was written on a fold of a blue four page paper by Lyman Cobb Jr. The first page is the request of John Lowth. Glued to the top left of the blue paper is a smaller brown document written by Frederick A. Coe. The first transcription is that of Coe's letter.]

To the President and Trustees of the Village of Yonkers.
Gentlemen:

On the 24th inst. I recovered a judgment against John Lowth, called Loud, for the penalty of $50.00.

As I understand he intends to apply to your body for a remission of some portion of this judgment. I feel it is my duty to state the following facts.

This defendant was fined about fours years since for breaking into the pound and a judgment recovered against him for $20 and costs. This fine was remitted upon his paying the costs and promising future good behavior. Since that period his cows and pigs have been the general complaint of the citizens of the north part of the Village as violators of the Village ordinances and as nuisances that should be abated. He or some member of his family have been detected repeatedly in tearing down the fences and opening the gates of Citizens in order to furnish these nuisances of his with food at the expense of his neighbors. When remonstrated with for such and similar illegal proceedings his replies have been abusive. He uniformly drives his cows over the flagged sidewalks of the Village, rendering passage over the same offensive. On the 18th day of May last, one of his sons rescued 4 cows while being driven to the pound. On the 1st of September inst. his wife rescued one cow, and on the 15th inst. he in person rescued 4 hogs.

If the Village ordinances are to be observed and the integrity of the Village authorities to be maintained these offenses should not be condoned or overlooked by your body.
Yours Respectfully
Frederick A. Coe
N.Y. September 28, 1860.
[The following transcription is that of the larger document.]

Yonkers October 1, 1860
To the Honorable the Board of Trustees of the Village of Yonkers,

The under signed would most respectfully request to your Honorable body the fact on the eve of Saturday September 16th he went to care of property which consist of cattle and swine that in the act of doing so the swine got loose from their enclosure without his knowledge. That immediately on ascertaining the fact of their being loose and not wishing to break the ordinance of your honorable body he followed them for the purpose of recovering and to place them in their proper enclosure when he found them in the hands of the Pound Master of the Village of Yonkers.

The undersigned would respectfully state further that he was on the following Monday summoned before his Honor Justice Groshon by the said Pound Master on the charge of violating the law of the Village of Yonkers whereon he was fined in the sum of fifty two dollars from which penalty he the undersigned would most respectfully (request) your Honorable Body to release him.
John Louth

Associated Village Document 61

Thos. S. Morris Esq. President
Dear Sir,

I would respectfully call your attention to the fact that hogs are allowed to run at large in the Village south of the creek. I have requested the Pound Master to shut them up, and have gone so far as to offer 25 cents for everyone that he would put in the pound, but the nuisance still exists and a great deal of damage is done by them.

Very Respectfully &c
Cyrus Cleveland
November 17, 1860

Chapter 7

Epilogue

The period of time from 1853 to 1860 was important, not only for Yonkers, but also for the United States and the rest of the world. While the village of Yonkers was absorbing hundreds of immigrants, the Crimean War in Europe was raging towards a conclusion.

On March 28, 1854, the Crimean War broke out with England and France declaring war on Russia. Interestingly for us living today, part of the reason for the war was to secure Serbia. The war left an indelible mark on the literature of the world, and humanitarianism. On October 25, 1854 the famous Charge of the Light Brigade took place, and during the battle of Inkerman on November 5, 1854 Florence Nightingale was tending to wounded allied troops.

Slavery was the burning issue in the United States. For the opponents of slavery, the Dred Scott decision was especially unnerving. Five southern democrats on the United States Supreme Court voted against granting Dred Scott his freedom. On March 6, 1857, the majority opinion written by Supreme Court Justice Taney was released to the public. Although Dred Scott had lived on free soil with his owner for five years, Taney opined that he was a black slave and therefore had no right to sue in a Federal Court. Instead of dismissing the case, Taney took the issue further by noting that the Fifth Amendment forbade the taking of private property without due cause, and declared the Compromise of 1820 unconstitutional. He further declared that Congress had no power to declare any territory free, regardless of what the territory wanted. Taney stated, "But the power of Congress over the person or property of a citizen can never be a mere discretionary power under our Constitution and form of Government." (McLaughlin, p. 559)

The Dred Scott decision was illogical and pernicious. In Yonkers, the importance of the decision did not go unnoticed. The *Yonkers Examiner* responded to the decision by stating, "We do not propose to argue with this decision now; yet we conceive it to be by no means a giant's task to tear aside its thin veil of sophistries and show its utter groundlessness in fact and reason....Is it not sad and humiliating to see our country thus standing alone in the world, brazen-faced, and justifying this crime against humanity? Is it not sad and humiliating to see the repository of justice turned into the stronghold of old oppression and wrong? Against it, the spirit of our fathers protest; against it, the voice of Christianity protests; against it, the cry of an advancing humanity loudly protests. But let us not despair, for Justice still sits on her eternal throne." (E-3/12/57 p.2, c.1)

The Yonkers Examiner continued its assault on the decision and on the institution of slavery. (E-p.2,c.1) On 7/2/57 the same paper blasted slavery, and the southern influence in Kansas. The paper correctly predicted the outcome of the Lemmon Slave case by stating "The Dred Scott case will be logically followed by the Lemmon Slave case, and the rights of the slave owner to carry his slave whithersoever he will, still further corroborated." (E-7/2/57 p.2,c.1)

Nationally, as well as locally, the Dred Scott decision split the Democratic Party in two between Northern Democrats and Southern Democrats. This split assured the election of a minority president, Lincoln, in 1860, and assured the secession of South Carolina and civil war.

While slavery was the main issue between 1853 and 1860, it was not the only one. Another bone of contention, having its roots back to 1812 and earlier, was the practice of some foreign, and particularly English, ships of sending boarding parties onto American vessels, and in some cases impressing into British service any seamen they considered to be citizens of Great Britain. Though the major reason for the War of 1812 was the desire for western expansion and the conquest of Canada on the part of the United States, it was inextricably combined with the need to carry on commerce without foreign interference. Thus, the United States considered the boarding of her ships an illegal and provocative act. The War of 1812 ended with the signing of the Treaty of Ghent on December 24, 1814. The treaty was in reality an armistice, or agreement to end hostility, and it did not address the issue of boarding ships. Thus, the impressment problem was not settled, and in 1858 it raised its ugly head again.

As early as 1807, the United States and Great Britain had agreed to stop the slave trade. Later, in 1842, the Webster-Ashburton Treaty provided for the United States and Great Britain to jointly stop the slave trade and for each country to provide squadrons to enforce the treaty's provisions. However, the United States never actively participated in enforcing the provision. After the Crimean War ended in 1857, the British returned to the practice of boarding American ships and demanding of the captain the ship's manifesto, supposedly to determine if the ships, even though they were flying the American flag, were really American ships. This practice led to strained relations with Great Britain, and in late 1858 the United States agreed to use American squadrons, with identical orders as British squadrons, to patrol the Caribbean in an attempt to stop the slave trade. Even though patrol activity was increased, it had little effect on the continuation of the slave trade. (Bemis, pp. 330-3)

Residents of Yonkers were kept abreast of these happenings by papers in New York City and by the *Yonkers Examiner*. In an editorial on May 20, 1858, the paper lashed out at the British by stating that "In each case the vessel has been boarded and her papers demanded and examined, by the orders, all the aggressors state, of the British Government." The paper went on to note that three fourths of the slave trade was carried on by Americans, and it was "True," that "our government has been shamelessly recant in the performance of its plighted duties, but international comity required that England should explicitly make a demand for our help and state the position which she should be forced to take in the event of our refusal to render her the assistance sought. She has not taken this course, but has preferred to insult our flag by the rude exercise of doubtful powers, and without those preliminary warnings and consultations which might altogether have averted the difficulty." (E-5/20/58 p.2, c.1)

As noted above, an agreement was struck with England which had little effect on slave trading. The *Yonkers Examiner* was quick to point out on January 6, 1859 that even though the slave trade was against the law, it still flourished, and the paper noted that there was a "recent landing of African slaves in Georgia by the yacht *Wanderer*." (E-1/6/59 p.2, c.2)

While the United States and Great Britain were ironing out things on the high seas, another significant event was occurring under the waves of the Atlantic Ocean. During 1858 the first cable was laid on the floor of the Atlantic Ocean, and the first message was sent and delivered. The *Yonkers Examiner* rejoiced in this significant accomplishment by noting that "yesterday's celebration of the successful laying of the Atlantic Telegraph Cable commemorated an event of which the human mind can hardly grasp the full value and significance." Swept away with technological awe, the editor of the paper in a mood of futurism asked, "what is to be the next achievement....Shall it be the union of oceans across the continents, as continents have been now united over a wide ocean? Will it be the inauguration of new means of locomotion? A further annihilation of space and time, or some nameless improvement in some now known principle of art or science? Or will it be something as new, as startling, as undreamed of now as even the Ocean Telegraph a score of years ago? Time will show." If Matthew F. Rowe knew how profound his words were in reality, he probably could have been a contributor to the *American Scientific* that grew from an eight-page weekly to a 16-page weekly on July 1, 1859. (E-9/2/58 p.2, c.2 & 6/10/59 p.2, c.4) Of course after the first message was sent in 1858 the cable promptly broke, and communications were intermittent until 1866, when a heavier cable was laid and permanent communications were finally established.

Nationally, as noted before, the pervading issue was slavery. Associated with the issue was the infamous question of a Bleeding Kansas, and the equally notorious raid by John Brown at Harper's Ferry. Residents of Yonkers were well informed of these events, but closer to home, the emotional debate was raging in New York City and its environs over the reading of the King James version of the Bible in most schools. Most of America was primarily settled by English Protestants, however, during the 1840s and 1850s, large numbers of Irish Catholics immigrated to the United States and established themselves primarily in the northern cities of Boston and New York. Eventually, New York became the home of the largest Irish population of any city in the world. They brought with them a history of political and religious conflict with the British, and it was inevitable that trouble should break out in the United States. The Protestants adhered to the King James version of the Bible, while the Catholics considered that it was written by a heathen and the only true version was the Douay-Rheims version as revised by Bishop Challoner in 1750. Religious differences led native-born xenophobic British Americans to widely practice ethnic discrimination. In turn, the Irish discriminated against blacks, whom they saw as competitors for jobs on the docks and elsewhere. Hence, their sympathies were not with the abolitionists. Interestingly, the bitterness between natural-born American citzens and the Irish led to the development of the two major school systems we find today in the United States: one public and the other Catholic parochial.

During the 1850s, the battle of the two Bibles raged. Many Irish families could not afford to send their children to Catholic schools, and instead sent them to the public schools. In the public schools the King James version was read in most schools "at 8:45 a.m." The schools in Yonkers were no exception. Even though apparently most boys were outside playing, Irish residents of Yonkers were, like their counterparts in New York City, upset over the reading of the King James version. In an attempt to resolve the issue, the *Yonkers Examiner* suggested, "If there are prejudices against the received version, commonly called the King James translation, let those prejudices be met by an alternate reading of the Douay version, and of the Baptist Bible (if they have one,) but let there be Bible reading and the Lord's Prayer at the opening of all public schools, and that daily by selections from the former at the discretion of the head teachers of the schools."

Internal political/religious arguments also raged in the western part of the country. During 1857, the Governor of Utah was Brigham Young, who led the Mormons to the Utah territory in 1846 - 1847 because of persecution in Illinois. In Utah, Governor Young held such a tight hand over the government that President Buchanan felt Washington had no control over the territory. Consequently, he dispatched troops to the territory, where the settlers harrassed them, but no serious conflict occurred. Back in Yonkers, the people read a reprint from the *Evening Post* in the *Yonkers Examiner* which, perhaps in a facetious manner, noted that the Utah War was "purely a contrivance to bleed the Treasury for the benefit of a few contractors, that Lecompton votes in Congress might be multiplied." (E-9/23/58 p.4, c.1)

Meanwhile, Yonkers was a mecca for famous people. On December 6, 1858 Herman Melville, author of Moby Dick and several other books, visited Yonkers and gave a speech that was so funny that the audience in response to the "hilarity was too great to allow of other exertion. The facetious tone of Mr. Melville is beyond description." (E-12/9/58 p.2, c.2)

Since human luminaries visited Yonkers, why shouldn't heavenly luminaries also visit? On Sunday, August 28, 1859 residents of Yonkers were entertained by a grandiose display of the Aurora Borealis. It began at dusk on the northern horizon and then spread across the entire sky. Light green was interspersed with scarlet and purple. A little after 9:00 p.m., "long nebulous transcendent flakes of scarlet, green and purple light" along with all the colors of the "rainbow" lit the night sky. At about 9:30 the sky turned completely purple. The event must have been magnificent, but to many uneducated people, fright prevailed, and the thought of a mystical end of the world may have crossed the mind of a few of them. (E-9/1/59 p.2, c.4)

Yonkers by 1860 was a capricious mixture of hard-working, hard-drinking, pugnacious, religious Irish; local businessmen starved for the elegance of the arts and humanities; prosperous businessmen who knew how to attain the best in entertainment, arts, humanities and politics; and farmers, although fewer in number, but wealthier - many of whom kept the party of Jefferson and Jackson for the most part intact in the town. Sympathies almost always were in favor of freedom over arbitrary despotism, as evidenced by the creation of a Garibaldi Fund, whose only reason for existence was to help Garibaldi attain a perceived freedom for the Italian people. (E-10/18/60 p.2, c.5 and earlier papers.)

Though political, social, and educational dichotomies existed in Yonkers, one theme was constant to all groups: progress. Residents of Yonkers believed in progress for the town, the village, business, and of course, in their personal lives. Road building and repairs, and travel by water and railway were correctly seen as vehicles of progress in the aforementioned categories. By the late 1850s, the railroad on the east shores of the Hudson River had become an important economic asset competing commercially with river traffic, but the infrequency of trains, the inconveniently placed location of the New York City terminal, and the fact that it did not run at night were negative aspects to commuter travel. As early as 1853, an inland railroad from New York City to Yonkers was proposed, and a franchise to use certain New York City streets for the railroad passed the New York City Board of Aldermen in 1859, but it was vetoed by the Mayor, who wanted to receive one million dollars for the franchise, or in lieu of that, an annual income of $70,000 for the city. (E-12/22/59 p.2, c.3) Despite the veto, Yonkers' interested parties continued to agitate for the inland railroad route.

During the years 1853 to 1860, the workers in Yonkers worked, the shakers shook, and the thinkers planned for the prosperity of the future. Each went about doing their business, with little thought to the consequences of the 1860 presidential election. Nor could they have imagined that the neat era of almost unbroken and unprecedented growth and prosperity was going to be turned on its head by a very destructive civil war.

REFERENCES

Allison, Charles Elmer. *The History of Yonkers.* New York: Wilber B. Ketcham, 1896.

Appleby, Joyce O. *Materialism and Morality in the American Past: Themes and Sources, 1600 - 1860.* Reading, Massachusetts: Addison-Wesley Publishing Company, 1974.

Atkins, Thomas Astley. *History of Yonkers.* Unpublished. Typed by Kate Atkins 1930, c. 1895.

Bemis, Samuel Flagg. *A Diplomatic History of the United States*: 4th ed., New York: Henry Holt and Company, 1955.

Bolton, Robert Jr. *History of Westchester County.* New York: Alexander S. Gould, 1848.

Brown, Henry Collins. *1646 - 1922 Old Yonkers.* New York: Henry Collins Brown, 1922.

French, Alvah P. *History of Westchester County.* Vol. II. New York: Lewis Historical Publishing Co., Inc., 1925.

French, Alvah P. Editor and Manager. *Westchester County Magazine.* White Plains, NY: Westchester Magazine Publishing and Printing Company, 1909.

Getty, Robert P., alleged author. *Chronicles of Yonkers.* Yonkers, NY: Privately printed for the benefit of the United States Sanitary Commission, 1864.

Griffen, Ernest Freeland. *Westchester County and Its People.* New York: Lewis Historical Publishing Co., Inc., 1946.

Hutchinson, Thomas. *Westchester County Directory 1860-61.* New York: Thomas Hutchinson, 1860.

Jenkins, Stephen. *The Story of the Bronx.* New York: G. P. Putnam's Sons, 1912.

Kane, Joseph Nathan. *Famous First Facts: A Record of First Happenings, Discoveries and Inventions in the United States.* New York: The H. W. Wilson Company, 1964.

Langer, William L. *An Encyclopedia of World History.* Boston: Houghton Mifflin Company, 1952.

Lyman, Susan Elizabeth. *The Story of New York.* New York: Crown Publisher's, Inc., 1964.

Martindell, Jackson, Publisher. *Who Was Who in America: Historical Volume 1607 - 1896.* Chicago: Marquis-Who's Who, Inc. 1963.

New York Times

Shonnard, Frederick, & Spooner, W. W. *The History of Westchester County to the Year 1900.* New York: The New York History Company, 1900.

Sobel, Robert. *Panic on Wall Street.* New York: Truman Talley Books, 1988.

The Gazette

The Yonkers Herald

Walton, Frank L. (1951) *Pillars of Yonkers.* Kingsport, TN: Kingsport Press, Inc.

Yonkers Illustrated

50th Anniversary Celebration Committee, *Souvenir History of Yonkers,* (1922) Fernhead & Bleakley; Yonkers.

INDEX

ABBOTT, 69 78 80 288
ACHERT, 80
ACKERLY, 79 104
ACKERMAN, 13 19 68 69 79
 102 110 122 125 159 237
 264 267 268 270 280 282
 284 288 290 292 303 313
ACKERT, 11 209
ADAMS, 78 80 82
AGATE, 12 13
AGNEW, 81 148 206 223
AIKEN, 81
AINSWORTH, 81
AKERLY, 225
AKERT, 166
ALCORN, 81
ALLEN, 81
ALLISON, 34 77 286
AMBLER, 81
AMES, 81
ANDERSON, 13 60 82 83 104
 123 282
ANDREWS, 68 70 83 165 302
ANSTICE, 84 203 282
APPLETON, 84
ARCHER, 69 84 85 132 179
 187 207 230 231 267 268
 275 282 284 302-304
ARCHIBALD, 85 231 256
ARNOLD, 85 86 179 180 216
 220
ARTHUR, 19 86 97 282 292
ASHBURTON, 322
ATHERTON, 13 34 86 311 312
ATKINS, 59 61

ATWATER, 86
ATWOOD, 87
AUSTICE, 87
AUSTIN, 87 265
BABCOCK, 13 34 311 312
BACK, 87
BADDE, 87
BAILEY, 68 69 87
BAIRD, 13 14 87-89 104
BAKER, 88
BALDWIN, 6 10 11 14 19 68-
 70 72 88 89 134 143 250
 252 284 304 306
BALL, 90
BANCROFT, 145
BANGS, 90
BARCLAY, 90
BARD, 90
BARKER, 90
BARNES, 90 93
BARRETT, 90
BARRY, 90 282
BARTHOLOMEW, 90
BARTLETT, 91
BASHFORD, 10 11 13 14 20
 60 91 192 211 231 266 271
 279 284 288
BATE, 92 235 250 284
BATES, 94 282
BATTEN, 93
BATTIN, 197
BAUM, 93
BAUR, 93
BAXTER, 10 12 13 81 90 93
BAZER, 261

329

BEAL, 93
BEAN, 94
BEASLEY, 94
BECK, 13
BEERS, 94
BEI, 282
BELKNAP, 94
BELL, 13 14 33 63 65 69 70 72 94-96 130 148 192 237 239 262 282
BELLS, 282
BENEDICT, 96
BENNETT, 96 97 185 256
BENSON, 97 153 231
BENZIGER, 97
BERGMAN, 97
BERRIAN, 97 276 302
BERRIMAN, 206
BERTINE, 97
BERWICK, 97
BET, 282
BETTNER, 98
BETTS, 170
BIBBY, 11
BICKER, 98
BICKNELL, 68 72 73 98 302
BILLS, 72 98
BIRDSALL, 14 98
BISHOP, 99 120
BLACK, 191 299
BLACKNELL, 99
BLACKWELL, 99 127 175
BLAIR, 97
BLAUVELT, 69 99 118 267 268 313
BLEAKLEY, 93
BLEEKER, 100
BLIVEN, 100 108
BLOOM, 118
BLOOMER, 100 101
BLUTE, 101
BODINE, 162
BOGARDUS, 101 210
BOGLE, 101
BOLAND, 101
BOLMER, 101

BOLTON, 98
BOSWORTH, 101 279
BOWERS, 101 102
BOWLER, 102
BOWLES, 102
BOWLIN, 242
BOYD, 72 102 110
BOYER, 266
BRACE, 195
BRADLEY, 62 102 263-265 268
BRADLY, 271 272
BRAGDON, 102
BRANDRETH, 308
BRECKINRIDGE, 63 65
BRENNAN, 103
BREVOORT, 11 35 103 240 280 283 303 313
BREWER, 103 114 134 161 194 223
BRIGGS, 103 258
BRINK, 103
BROMMLEY, 103
BROTHER, 13
BROWN, 7 72 78 79 82 83 86 88 92 99 102-104 172 175 200 201 263 270 278 286 323
BRUCE, 104
BRUCKARD, 286
BRYANT, 104 105
BUCHANAN, 63 150 180 183 210 228 230 238 245 250 260 324
BUCKHOUT, 105 132
BUCKLIN, 10 11 105 127 280 291 303
BUDSELL, 282
BUNKER, 105
BURCHARD, 106
BURNS, 27 106 125 183 252 286
BUSSARD, 107
BUSSING, 107 243
BUTLER, 157 266
CABLE, 107

CALDWELL, 107
CALUM, 107
CAMPBELL, 107 286 289 290 303
CANDEE, 107 266 267
CANDELL, 107
CANDER, 268
CARBAY, 108
CARGILL, 108 263 264 265
CARLSON, 13
CARPENTER, 108 195
CARR, 108 160
CARRY, 108
CARTER, 88 89 91 108 129 134 196
CARY, 83
CATLOW, 108
CAULDWELL, 149
CENTER, 130
CERS???, 283
CHADEAYNE, 36 100 108 109
CHALLONER, 324
CHAMBERLAIN, 67 70 73 109 310
CHAMBERS, 109 262-264
CHARL, 109 255
CHASE, 109
CHATTERTON, 109 161 165
CHILTON, 87 109 224
CHOATE, 109
CLAPP, 14 102 107 110
CLARK, 25 68 69 103 110 111 192 195 241 279 284 288 298 316 317
CLARKE, 18 111
CLAUS, 111
CLEVELAND, 10 111 126 137 320
CLINTOCK, 111
CLOUGH, 266 267
COATES, 15 112
COATS, 112
COBB, 69 70 72 112 302-304 310 312 315 317-319
CODDINGTON, 314

COE, 27 33 84 86 90 106 112 113 138 152 168 175 189 191 216 255 282 293 307 308 319 320
COEY, 164
COFFEE, 113 217
COFFEY, 113
COFFIN, 113 268
COGAN, 113 114
COGER, 114
COLEMAN, 11 14 114 115 152 226 313
COLES, 114 183
COLGATE, 115
COLLINS, 283
COLWELL, 134
CONDIN, 313
CONDIT, 115 265 268 303 313
CONDON, 13 116 216 280 291 303
CONKLIN, 116
CONLAN, 242
CONNELL, 116
COOK, 206
COOKE, 116 145 258
COON, 91
COONS, 116
COOPER, 102 117 258 286
COPCUTT, 14 25-33 35 68 69 117 154 202 212 214 223 229 296 297 307 316-319
CORNELL, 10 11 32 42 60 117 120 135 143 161 210 255 278 293 294 299 316 317
CORSA, 197
CORSOR, 118
COSTELLO, 118
COSTIGAN, 118
COTTON, 118 141
COWDREY, 10 11 118
COX, 119
COYNE, 119
COZZENS, 10 13 119
COZZINS, 282
CRABB, 119 276

CRAFT, 119
CRAMBERT, 119
CRANE, 120
CRASSOUS, 120
CRAWFORD, 86 120 282
CRISFIELD, 68 120 137 216 264 271 276 278 288 290 291 304
CROFRIT, 265
CROMWELL, 13 256
CROWELL, 121 286
CROWLEY, 121
CRUSSON, 286
CUDDY, 68 121 288 291
CUMMINGS, 121
CUNNINGHAM, 121 189 202
CURLEY, 121
CURRAN, 121 122 193 287 295
CURSER, 194
CURTICE, 122
CUTHBERT, 122
DALEY, 122
DANK, 202
DANKS, 122
DARBY, 122
DARK, 122
DARKE, 122
DAVIDSON, 122
DAVIS, 137
DAYTON, 266 302
DEAL, 112
DEAN, 91 197
DECORDOVA, 15 90 114 144 153 185 190 257
DEDERER, 69 73 123 264 268 271 276 288-290 310
DELAFIELD, 123
DELANCEY, 123 271
DELONG, 123
DEMAREST, 123 176
DEMEREST, 82
DENELL, 265 266
DENERESS, 283
DENSLOW, 28 123 263 265 267 268 279 280 283 291

DENSLOW (Continued) 303 313 315
DERBY, 124 286
DESMOND, 124
DEVINES, 21 23
DEVOE, 6 19 29 37 39 68 106 124 125 290 295
DEYO, 13 79 102 110 125 268 280 282 284 291 292 303 313
DIAMOND, 125
DIBBLE, 125
DICKERSON, 123
DICKINSON, 126
DIDSON, 126
DIETZEL, 126
DIGMAN, 126
DISBROW, 126
DOBSON, 126
DOLSON, 126
DON, 112
DONAHUE, 141
DONALDSEN, 283
DONALDSON, 127
DONNELLY, 127 183
DONOHUE, 127
DONOVAN, 127
DOOLEY, 127
DOREMUS, 127
DOREN, 67 68 127 192
DORSON, 95
DORTIC, 127 188
DOTY, 127 190 313
DOUBRING, 159
DOUGAN, 128 244
DOUGHTY, 128
DOUGLAS, 63 65 128
DOUGLASS, 128 282
DOWNES, 128
DOYLE, 128 129
DRAKE, 10 12 13 129
DREER, 209
DUESENBERRY, 72
DUFF, 129 131 240
DUFFEY, 129
DUFFY, 284

DUKE, 14
DULY, 282
DUNN, 112
DURELL, 129 246
DURKEE, 129
DUSENBERRY, 73 129 130 310
DUSENBURY, 268
DWIGHT, 130 317
DYCKMAN, 130
DYROAT, 282
EAGAN, 130
EAST, 130
EATON, 130
EBERSPECKERS, 164
EDGAR, 130 280 284 291 303 313
EDWARDS, 131 189 303
EHART, 142
EICKMEYER, 131
ELLER, 131
ELLIOT, 33
ELTING, 13 36 131 210 244 283
ELWELL, 131
EMBREE, 131 259 270 284
EMOTT, 27
ENGLISH, 131
ERNEST, 125
ERWIN, 163
EVERETT, 129 131
FALON, 132
FARLEY, 132
FARLING, 73 132
FARRELL, 132
FARRINGTON, 6 10 11 28 60 62 67 84 103 105 132 149 203 210 231 240 241 277 292 313
FARROU, 133
FERDON, 118
FERGUSON, 133
FERRIS, 6 133
FIELD, 82 101 139 156 159 161 163 216 258
FILLMORE, 133 258

FINDLAY, 277 278
FININ, 88 133 232
FISHER, 134 216
FITCH, 134
FITZGERALD, 134
FITZPATRICK, 135 292
FLAGG, 19 29-31 37 39 41 60 66-72 74 113 135 136 195 202 216 225 234 237 265 276 279 281 282 298 299 306 309 310 312 313 315
FLANAGAN, 169
FLETCHER, 137
FLEWELLING, 137
FLOOD, 111 137 159
FLYNN, 159
FOLEY, 123
FOOT, 137
FOOTE, 137
FORREST, 137
FOSTER, 137 155 311
FOUNNEY, 86
FOWLER, 137 169 263 270 275 302 303 315
FOX, 137
FRADENBURGH, 138 284
FRANCIS, 120 137 169 266 276
FRANKLIN, 138
FRAZIER, 138
FREDENBURGH, 138
FREELAND, 139
FREMONT, 63
FRENDENBERGH, 282
FRIEND, 139 248
FULLER, 139 140
FURNISS, 139
GAFFNEY, 139 303
GALE, 140 266
GALLAUDET, 140
GALLENA, 140
GALVIN, 140
GANT, 40 60 62 140 282 284
GARDENER, 140 141
GARDINEER, 68
GARDINER, 69

GARIBALDI, 325
GARNETT, 109 141 148 149
  154 167 219
GARRISON, 11 123 141 142
  266 271 282
GATES, 14 19 69 70 141 164
  194 241 283 309 310 316
  317
GAUL, 118 141
GAULT, 141 142
GAYLOR, 141 142 218
GEA????, 283
GERALD, 86
GESNER, 142
GETLER, 142
GETTY, 6 10 13 19 26-32 37
  39 40 42 60 62 67-72 142
  144 145 190 267 284 287
  298 299 305-307 309 317
GIFFORD, 225
GIL, 284
GILCHREST, 69
GILCHRIST, 144 275 288
GILDAY, 144
GILES, 144
GILROY, 13 116 145
GIROUD, 145
GLASSER, 14
GLEESON, 145
GODWIN, 145
GOETSCHIUS, 145
GOLDEN, 145 263 276
GOOD, 249
GOODMAN, 145 146
GORE, 79 284
GORMAN, 146
GOUCH, 146
GOURLIE, 10 11 14 69 146
GOVAERT, 158
GRAFTON, 146
GRAHAM, 146
GRANGER, 146 197
GRANT, 19 60 146 270 278
GRANTHAM, 147
GRANY, 177
GREELEY, 71 147 243

GREEN, 18
GREENLEAF, 13 147 283 286
GREENWOOD, 147
GREVERT, 148 166
GRIDLEY, 148
GRIFFIN, 81 148 214 244
GRIFFING, 148
GRIMES, 148
GRIMSHAW, 149
GROOT, 149
GROSHON, 120 135 149 264
  270 279 304 320
GROW, 149
GUION, 149
GUMMERSON, 149
G[INN], 244
HABERN, 149
HAGANY, 149
HAGGERTY, 176
HALEY, 150
HALL, 150 193 257
HALLER, 150
HALLET, 87 150
HALLEY, 153
HALLIOHAN, 150
HALLOCK, 78 80 150 202 280
  284 291 292
HALLORAN, 150
HALORN, 150
HALSEY, 120
HAMLIN, 150
HAMPSON, 151 152
HANLIN, 236
HANNIGAN, 152
HARBOR, 152
HARDY, 152
HARNEY, 152
HARRIS, 86 243
HART, 266
HARVEY, 79 91
HASBROUCK, 152
HASKIN, 149
HASSE, 152 303 313
HASSEE, 112 114
HATCH, 152 284
HATFIELD, 153

HAWES, 153
HAWKES, 153 205
HAWKINS, 13
HAWKS, 153
HAWTHORNE, 286
HAYES, 24 198
HAYNES, 154
HAZELTON, 154
HELINCK, 303
HELWICK, 154 284
HENDERSON, 154 258
HENNEBERGHER, 154
HENRY, 108 154
HERMAN, 151
HERRICK, 23
HERRIOT, 154
HETZELBURG, 90
HEZNARD, 313
HIBBARD, 10 12 154 265
HILL, 154 179
HILLIARD, 155
HINDLEY, 155
HIRST, 155
HITCHCOCK, 155
HOBBS, 10 14 25 28 29 37 39
 68 155 156 282 295 296
 298 299 304-307 309
HODGES, 156 197
HOFFMAN, 156 240
HOGAN, 86 156
HOGELAND, 157 263
HOLBERTON, 157 159 280
HOLBROOK, 120
HOLLAND, 157
HOLLOCK, 117
HOLLOWAY, 24
HOLT, 108
HOMANS, 157 286
HOMMANS, 157
HOOD, 157
HOPKINS, 85 91 94 98 108
 110 111 116 136 146 149
 157 160 163 190 204 222
HOPP, 157
HORNER, 313
HORTON, 66 157 245 263 268

HORTON (Continued)
 270 276 278 280 302 303
 310-312
HOUGHTALING, 148
HOUSTON, 72 74 158 310 312
 313
HOWARTH, 158
HOWE, 15 158
HOWELL, 158
HOWLAND, 68 158 287 295
HOYT, 13 69 158 159 165 178
 207 237 265 267 268 270
 276 278 279 283
HUBBARD, 41 159 186
HUBBEL, 309
HUESTIS, 108 160 212 284
HUGHES, 160
HULBERT, 103 108 113 121
 139 157 158 160 202 204
 210 237 240 248
HUNTINGTON, 120 161
HURD, 109 159 161 165
HUSTIN, 284
HUTH, 161
HYATT, 161
HYDE, 161
HYNARD, 161 275 281
ILES, 162
IMHOF, 162
IMHOFF, 150
INGRAHAM, 215
INLAY, 162
IRELAND, 162 282
ISAAC, 162
ISAACS, 162
JACKSON, 80 162 163 303
 313 325
JEFFERSON, 325
JENKINS, 13 82 101 156 159
 163 164 216 224 258
JENNINGS, 67 97 164
JOHNSON, 86 164 165 203
 276
JOHNSTON, 165
JONES, 109 155 159 161 165
 166 282 284

JORDAN, 166
JORDON, 148
JOYCE, 166
KEEFE, 102
KEELER, 166 174 270 303
KELLAM, 166
KELLEY, 167 212
KELLINGER, 34 167 265 266 268
KELLOGG, 167
KELLY, 167 253
KEMBLE, 221
KEMP, 167
KENAN, 236
KENT, 167
KERRIGAN, 167
KETCHUM, 167 250 252
KEY, 168
KIFFEN, 168
KINDER, 243
KING, 95 100 108 129 131 156 168 196 197 240 256 259
KINSLEY, 168
KINSLOW, 13 67 70 115 168 282
KNAPP, 169
KNIFFIN, 169
KNIGHT, 169
KNOWLES, 169
KNOWLTON, 169
KNOX, 14 69 138 153 169 170
KUSTA, 171
KUSTIS, 283
LABVINCIER, 191
LACHAUME, 171
LAGES, 171 199
LALLEY, 171
LANGLY, 225
LAWRENCE, 10 13 66 68 72 73 133 149 172-174 233 247 263-265 267 268 270 271 276 279 280-282 288 290 291 292 302-304 310 312 314 315
LECOMPTON, 73 97
LEEDS, 174

LEMMON, 322
LENT, 174
LEONARD, 175
LEPPER, 161 250
LESTER, 209
LETTREE, 175
LILIENTHAL, 99 175
LILLIENTHAL, 175
LINCOLN, 63-65 67 235 322
LITTEL, 68 69 175 303
LITTELL, 279 280 290 291
LITTLE, 161 170 172 175 271
LIVERMORE, 176
LIVINGSTON, 152 176 240
LOGEL, 313
LOGUE, 176 291 303
LONG, 168 169
LORD, 177
LOUD, 319
LOUTH, 320
LOWTH, 319
LOYD, 176
LUCE, 13 177
LUDLOW, 14 42 177 236
LUND, 188
LUX, 128
LYELL, 197
LYMAN, 130
LYNCH, 13 177 179 180 216
LYNT, 289 290
LYON, 13 154 178
LYONS, 178 289
MACADAM, 178
MACFARLANE, 6 10-12 31 95 159 178 179 260
MACHIN, 179
MACKAY, 109
MAHR, 179
MAIDEN, 179
MAJOR, 179
MAJORY, 179 264 268
MALDEN, 179
MALLON, 290
MALLOY, 179 180
MALONE, 180
MALONY, 180

MALTHIE, 180
MANGIN, 180
MANKIN, 11 180
MANN, 174 180
MANNING, 180
MANY, 118
MAPES, 181
MARTIN, 181 283
MASON, 10 73 181
MATHER, 181
MATTHEWS, 182
MAYO, 14 182
MCCABE, 68 72 182 256 288 290 291 302-304 310 312
MCCALL, 182
MCCARTY, 183
MCCLANLY, 189
MCCLAY, 247
MCCLEINE, 106 183
MCCLOSKEY, 168
MCDERMOTT, 136
MCDONALD, 266
MCELRONE, 183 280 291 313
MCFARLANE, 183
MCGRATH, 183 265 268 280 291 292 303
MCKENLY, 173
MCKENZIE, 183 271 272 284
MCLAIN, 183 206
MCRONALD, 114 183
MCRONE, 183
MCSWEENEY, 184
MEAD, 184
MEAKIN, 184
MEEKER, 184
MELAH, 184 282 284 291 303 313
MELVILLE, 325
MERCER, 185
MERCHANT, 28 29 39 60 185 295
MERRILL, 97 185
MESSENGER, 185
MEYERS, 119 185 264 313
MIGY, 185
MILES, 185 186 284
MILLER, 109 186 228 251
MILLIKEN, 246
MILNE, 187 284
MINOR, 146
MINTURN, 187
MITCHELL, 19 187 282
MOFFAT, 187
MOLD, 69 72 73 188 302 303 310
MOLINAOR, 188
MONCKTON, 68 72 188
MONLUN, 188
MONTGOMERY, 12 14 188 218
MOORE, 121 189 284
MOREHOUSE, 189
MORGAN, 65 189
MORRIS, 71 131 189-191 283 311-313 317-320
MORRISEY, 95
MOTRAM, 191
MOTT, 73 191 256 306
MOTTRAM, 191
MULHOLLAND, 191
MULLER, 191
MULLON, 289
MURP?Y, 286
MURPHY, 191
MYERS, 60 118 192 231 271 279 284
NAIRN, 92 192 211 231 284
NARBURST, 192
NEELY, 225
NELSON, 65 66
NESBIT, 110 192 283 291
NESBITT, 303
NEUBAUER, 192
NEVILLE, 192
NEVINS, 192
NEWCOMB, 193
NEWELL, 193
NEWMAN, 193
NICKEY, 284
NIGHTINGALE, 321
NISBETT, 36 193

NODD, 193
NODINE, 68 69 193-195 263-265 276 279 280 288 290 291
NORTH, 195
NORTON, 195
NUGENT, 112
O'BRIEN, 196
O'CONNELL, 196
O'CONNOR, 196
O'DONNELL, 80 128
O'HANLIN, 197
O'MARRA, 198
O'MEARA, 69 72 198 199 310 312
OAKLEY, 81 196 245 256 257 284
ODELL, 11 14 118 146 156 166 196 197 211 223
OLIVER, 197 241
OLMSTEAD, 197 264
OLMSTED, 20 93 197 198 292
ORME, 194 199
ORMES, 199
OSTHAUS, 199 257
OTIS, 6 14 78 199-201 286
PACKER, 202
PADDOCK, 202 239 252 282 303 313
PAGAN, 121 202
PAGE, 117 150 202 280 284 291 292
PALMER, 202 203
PARKS, 203
PARNELL, 203
PARTRIDGE, 203
PATRICK, 243
PATTERSON, 132 203 241
PEAKE, 203
PEALE, 243
PEARCE, 203
PEASE, 204
PECK, 157 204 257 283
PEEK, 180 204
PEENE, 141 204 205
PENDELTON, 267

PENDERGRAST, 205 260 261
PERKINS, 84
PERRIN, 205
PERRY, 187 205 256
PETTIT, 205
PIERCE, 63 205
PIERSON, 111
PILSON, 153 183 195 205 206 224
PLATT, 81 189 206
POLIOCK, 206
POLKER, 206
POLLOCK, 175 179 180
POPHAM, 303
POST, 10 12 13 60 68-72 84 131 158 206 207 245 256 263-266 268 271 272 274 275 278-281 283-288 290 292-299 303-307 309 310 313 316 317
POTTER, 208
POWERS, 208
PROCE, 140
PROSEUS, 208
PULVER, 209 265 286
PURDY, 13 69 73 209 271 279 283 310
PUTNAM, 209
QUICK, 14 80 166 209
QUINN, 134 210
RADCLIFF, 101 210
RADFORD, 6 10 14 28 62 69 70 72 210 221 228 261 272 274 310
RAILLIE, 211
RAISBECK, 196 211
RALSTON, 12
RAND, 14
READ, 29 60 62 92 192 211 212 231 263 264 266 269 275 276 281 282 290 295 302 306 311
REDFIELD, 145
REEVES, 212
REEVS, 160 212
REINFELDER, 212

REVH, 268
REYNOLDS, 68 69 73 206 212
 279 288
RHODES, 92 212
RICE, 145
RICH, 10 14 15 25 31 60 169
 203 213
RICHMOND, 213 239 256 280
 283 284 291
RICK, 212
RIKER, 213 214
RILEY, 136 189 214
RITTER, 214
ROBBINS, 11 214
ROBINS, 14
ROBINSON, 148 214 215 266
 267 284
ROCK, 91
ROCKWELL, 10 11 14 28 31
 60 67 215-217 233 295
ROGERS, 134 216
ROLLINS, 216
ROOME, 216
ROONAN, 216
ROONEY, 136 217
ROONY, 283
ROPES, 217
ROPLIS, 240
ROSE, 217
ROST, 165 217
ROWE, 189 217 293 294 323
RUSSELL, 38 117 218 286
RUTTMAN, 218
RYAN, 178 218 219
RYER, 219
S??ERLEY, 286
SANDERS, 219
SANDFORD, 219 258
SARONY, 168 219
SAWYER, 219 243
SAXTON, 219
SAYERMEN, 283
SCHAEFFER, 219
SCHEMERHORN, 220
SCHENCK, 220 283
SCHERMERHORN, 311 312

SCHMOZART, 220
SCHOBURGH, 282
SCHOTT, 220
SCHRYVER, 210 220
SCHULTZ, 220 260
SCOBERK, 220
SCOTT, 220 321 322
SCRIBNER, 220
SCRUGHAM, 13 41 120 198
 220 247 265 276 279 280
SCRYMSER, 31 203 221
SEARING, 22
SEE, 141 309
SEELEY, 186 221 222
SEELY, 283
SERISTER, 222
SERYMSER, 222
SEWARD, 64 81 106 109 111
 121 129-131 148 153 183
 189 196 205 220 222 255
 257 260
SEWELL, 15 222
SEYMOUR, 81 197 222 223
 314
SHANNON, 223 224 282
SHAW, 205 224
SHEPHERD, 224
SHERMAN, 211
SHERWOOD, 224 225 263 270
 272 278 288 289
SHIPMAN, 14 60 225 277 282
SHONNARD, 11 41 101 114
 164 225 226 269 270
SHORT, 144 183
SILLIMAN, 24
SIMMONDS, 226 227
SIMMONS, 227
SIMPSON, 164 227
SIMSON, 257
SINDEREN, 202
SKINNER, 14 67 127 227 282
SLEIGHT, 186 228 284
SLEYH???, 283
SLOAN, 309
SLOAT, 266
SMART, 128

SMELT, 72 73 228 257 302 303
SMITH, 6 10 14 18 67-71 84 146 219 228-231 241 267 268 270 271 279-281 283 286 289 291 304
SMULLIN, 231
SNOOKS, 243
SNYDER, 299
SOAME, 97 231
SPAULDING, 13 231
SPEEDLING, 85 92 192 211 231
SPENCER, 249
SPEYER, 231
SPLOTSWORTH, 231
SQUIRE, 84 132 231
STANSFIELD, 231
STAPLES, 232
STAPLETON, 232
STARKWEATHER, 232
STARR, 68-71 134 158 216 225 232 233 295 304 306
STEALWEYZER, 283
STEARNS, 234
STEDWELL, 10 102 234
STEEN, 93 235
STELWAGON, 235
STENNEL, 284
STEPHENS, 83 235 282
STEPHENSON, 236
STEPH[SIN], 212
STETSON, 236 259
STEVENS, 35 69 126 236 280 281 288
STEVENSON, 73 236 263-265 276 281
STEWART, 12 13 187 236 237 284
STILLINGS, 237
STILLWATER, 62
STILLWELL, 20 283
STILWELL, 69 70 79 158 237 266
STONE, 237 238
STONEY, 238 313

STRANG, 238 263 270 271 278 280 291 313
STUART, 120 254
STURN, 299
SUAU, 13 238
SULLIVAN, 238
SUTION, 238
SUYDAM, 238
SWAIN, 265
SWANN, 238
SWEET, 23
TALLMAN, 136 213
TANEY, 159 321
TANSEY, 74
TAPPAN, 135
TAYLOR, 26 27 68 109 141 148 149 154 167 219 238 239 265 266 269 271 276 278 281 288 290 291 302 310-312
TEALK, 239
TERRY, 95 202 239 303
THOMAS, 176 239 240 282
THOMPSON, 11 35 103 240 280 283 303 313
TIEMAN, 20
TIER, 240
TILLEY, 163
TITUS, 115
TOBIN, 240
TOBURN, 240
TOMPKINS, 129 240 280
TOPOLIS, 156
TOTTEN, 241
TOWNSEND, 197 241
TRANCOMB, 241
TRAY, 284
TREADWELL, 241 263
TRENCHARD, 241
TRIPP, 132 140 148 149 162 203 214 241
TUCKER, 15
TUNSTALL, 241
TURNER, 220
TURNIP, 241 280
TURNISS, 241 280

TUTHILL, 241
UNDERHILL, 10 13-15 68 69
    180 225 241-243 264 265
    270 277-279 288-290 296
    298 303 306
UNDERWOOD, 10 11 243
UNION, 188
UPHAM, 165 243
VAIL, 13 36 128 210 244 283
VALENTINE, 19 20 68 72 134
    230 244 245 263 266-269
    276 279-281 288 290 302
    304 310-315
VANBUREN, 202
VANCORDTLANDT, 290
VANCORTLANDT, 18 68 245
    270 279 288 302-305 307
    308 310 313
VANHOUTEN, 19 73 246 302
    304 306 310
VANLIEW, 129 246
VANN, 246
VANORDEN, 247
VANPELT, 13 27 28 29 33 37
    39 60 62 69-71 159 172
    247 272 277 295
VANRAN, 191
VANTASSELL, 69 247 272 288
VANWART, 139 247
VARIAN, 248
VARK, 126 248 254
VARM, 282
VERMILYEA, 68 69 248 271
    276 279
VERNON, 248
VOGELL, 242
VOLLETT, 249
WACKERLY, 72 249 310 312
    313
WADSWORTH, 249
WAGGONER, 249
WAKEMAN, 114 249 284
WALCHNER, 249
WALDECK, 250
WALDO, 250
WALKER, 250
WALLER, 283
WALLIS, 33
WALSH, 161 250
WALTON, 7
WARD, 250
WARING, 11 14 19 60 62 88 89
    106 167 250-252 265 268
    278 280 283 284 291 292
    303 313
WARNER, 207 244 253 264-
    266 280 291 303 313
WASHINGTON, 111 297
WATERBURY, 253
WATERMAN, 69 172 199 257
    279 280 302-304
WATERS, 95 195 239 254
WATTS, 254
WEAVER, 195
WEBSTER, 322
WEED, 12 15 79 254 288 289
WEEKS, 237 254
WELCHMAN, 254
WELLES, 11
WELLING, 82 160
WELLS, 19 41 60 62 70 248
    254 255 265 277 282 302
    306
WELSH, 255
WEMPLE, 255
WEST, 144
WESTERFIELD, 255 270
WESTLAKE, 255
WESTON, 11 255
WETHERED, 95
WETMORE, 255
WHALLON, 255
WHARMBY, 109 255
WHEELER, 6 74 85 256 282
    318 319
WHITE, 205 213 239 256 280
    283 284 291
WHITEFIELD, 256
WHITETT, 196 256
WHITING, 256
WHYTE, 256
WICKE, 199 257

WICKER, 229 257
WICKES, 257
WIEDERHOLD, 257
WIGGANS, 249
WIGHT, 212
WILKERSEN, 276
WILKERSON, 159 257 268
WILKINSEN, 276
WILKISON, 257
WILLARD, 257 286
WILLETTE, 65
WILLIAMS, 14 42 103 196 257 258
WILLIS, 258
WILSON, 27 122
WISE, 216
WISEWELL, 133 258
WITHINGTON, 117 258

WOLFE, 8
WOOD, 131 258 259
WOODBINE, 259 260 265
WOODFINE, 67 259 268 280
WOODRUFF, 259
WOODS, 207
WOODWORTH, 10 15 26 27 29 31 34 42 60 68 83 120 203 246 259 260 265 267 278 283-287 292-299 305 306 311
WOOLCOCKS, 220 260
WOOLCOX, 139
WOOSTER, 205 260
YOUMANS, 261
YOUNG, 324
ZARISKI, 261
ZELIFF, 261

www.ingramcontent.com/pod-product-compliance
Lightning Source LLC
Chambersburg PA
CBHW050332230426
43663CB00010B/1826